Contents

Practical Leadership and Management in Nursing

Eleanor J. Sullivan and Gayle Garland

Harlow, England • London • New York • Boston • San Francisco • Toronto • Sydney • Singapore • Hong Kong
Tokyo • Seoul • Taipei • New Delhi • Cape Town • Madrid • Mexico City • Amsterdam • Munich • Paris • Milan

Pearson Education Limited
Edinburgh Gate
Harlow
Essex CM20 2JE
England

and Associated Companies throughout the world

Visit us on the World Wide Web at:
www.pearsoned.co.uk

First published 2010

ISBN: 978-0-13-232027-6

British Library Cataloguing-in-Publication Data
A catalogue record for this book is available from the British Library

Library of Congress Cataloging-in-Publication Data
Sullivan, Eleanor J., 1938-
   Practical leadership and management in nursing / Eleanor J. Sullivan and Gayle Garland.
      p. ; cm.
   U.K. adaptation of: Effective leadership and management in nursing / Eleanor J. Sullivan, Phillip J. Decker.
   Includes bibliographical references and index.
   ISBN 978-0-13-232027-6 (pbk.)
   1. Nursing services–Administration. 2. Leadership. 3. Nursing–Great Britain. I. Garland, Gayle.
II. Sullivan, Eleanor J., 1938–Effective leadership and management in nursing.   III. Title.
      [DNLM: 1.   Nursing, Supervisory–Great Britain. 2.   Leadership–Great Britain.
   3.   Nurse Administrators–Great Britain. 4.   Nursing Care–organization & administration–
Great Britain.   WY 105 S949p2010]
   RT89.S85 2010
   362.17'3068–dc22

                                                                                                2009041072

10 9 8 7 6 5 4 3 2 1
13 12 11 10 09

Typeset in 9 Interstate-Light by 73
Printed and bound in Great Britain by Henry Ling Ltd., at the Dorset Press, Dorchester, Dorset

The publisher's policy is to use paper manufactured from sustainable forests.

Practical Leadership and Management in Nursing

Visit the *Practical Leadership and Management in Nursing* Companion Website at www.pearsoned.co.uk/garland to find valuable learning material including:

- Resources to support learners in academic settings as well as people who want to be better leaders and managers in practice. Leadership and management challenges from practice are described with approaches that lead to success.

Supporting resources

Visit www.pearsoned.co.uk/garland to find valuable online resources

Companion Website for Learners

- Resources to support learners in academic settings as well as people who want to be better leaders and managers in practice. Leadership and management challenges from practice are described with approaches that lead to success.

For Educators

- In order to help you reach your goal of helping students to see themselves as leaders and managers no matter what their role, group and individual activities are suggested to support each section of the book.

For more information please contact your local Pearson Education sales representative or visit www.pearsoned.co.uk/garland

About the authors

Eleanor J. Sullivan, PhD, RN, FAAN, is the former dean of the University of Kansas School of Nursing, past president of Sigma Theta Tau International, and editor of the *Journal of Professional Nursing*. She has served on the board of directors of the American Association of Colleges of Nursing, testified before the U. S. Senate, served on a National Institutes of Health council, presented papers to international audiences, been quoted in *Chicago Tribune*, *St. Louis Post-Dispatch*, and *Rolling Stone Magazine*, and named 'Who's Who in Health Care' by *Kansas City Business Journal*. She earned nursing degrees from St. Louis Community College, St. Louis University, and Southern Illinois University and holds a PhD from St. Louis University.

Dr Sullivan is known for her publications in nursing, including the award-winning textbook, *Effective Leadership & Management in Nursing*, and *Becoming Influential: A Guide for Nurses* from Prentice Hall. Other publications include *Creating Nursing's Future: Issues, Opportunities and Challenges* and *Nursing Care for Clients with Substance Abuse*.

Today Dr Sullivan is a professional speaker and mystery author. Her mystery series (*Twice Dead*, *Deadly Diversion*, *Assumed Dead*) features nurse sleuth Monika Everhardt. By showing nursing realistically, she hopes that readers will understand the complexity of nursing care and the skills and knowledge involved in being a nurse.

Learn more at www.EleanorSullivan.com

Gayle Garland, MSN, RGN, RN is the Head of the Academic Unit for Management and Leadership within the Institute for Innovation in Professional Practice at the School of Healthcare, University of Leeds. She is a former Director in the Centre for the Development of Healthcare Policy and Practice prior to its integration into the Institute, and has been instrumental in providing practical leadership development to thousands of front-line and mid-level leaders in the National Health Service and wider public services. She is a master trainer for the Leading an Empowered Organisation (LEO) programme and has been involved in leading the National LEO programme commissioned by the NHS National Leadership Centre.

Gayle earned her nursing degree at the University of Calgary, Canada and her Master's of Science in Nursing at the California State University, Dominguez Hills. She immigrated to the UK in 1997 and has dedicated her career to supporting effective leadership and management for health and social care professionals. She was inspired to adapt this classic text on leadership and management for the UK to support front-line leaders to lead and manage their teams in a way that enhances professional practice and quality care.

Preface

Practical leadership and management in nursing is a UK adaptation of the classic American text *Effective leadership and management for nurses*, written by Sullivan and Decker and used over many years to guide nurses in the development of their skills to lead and manage within their roles.

Leading and managing are part of every nurse's job from staff nurse through to executive roles. Planning, organising, delivering and evaluating care are management responsibilities that occur every day while a nurse is at work. Discovering better ways to care for patients, anticipating future needs, influencing others to make improvements in care and acting in an ethical and responsible way are all examples of leading with integrity.

Leadership by nurses at all levels in the organisation and all stages of their careers is more important now than ever. The UK faces unprecedented changes in society and in the expectations of the public that will challenge nurses to respond and shape services for the future. The fundamental relationship between patients and health professionals is changing from one of 'doctor knows best' to 'patients as equal partners', and this change, whilst welcome, will need leading.

Nurses are challenged to manage effectively with fewer resources and to meet exacting care standards, service targets and patient expectations. Clinical teams are increasingly diverse and health care organisations are changing to meet the increasingly complex health service needs of the public: these changes will need managing.

Organisation of the book

The text is organised into three sections that provide the essential information needed to develop leadership and management skills that nurses must learn to succeed in today's world of health care.

Part 1 Putting Leadership and Management in Perspective

Part 1 provides a framework of important information from which to build your skills in leading and managing.

Chapter 1 describes the importance of leadership and management for the future and some of the changes that nurses face.

Chapter 2 looks at the evolution of management theories from the early days of the Industrial Revolution to modern times. It also explores you as a leader and manager, your responsibilities for managing yourself and the patient care you provide and the leadership skills needed in a variety of nursing roles.

Chapter 3 looks at the nature of organisations, and how they affect the way in which people lead and manage. The new and emerging organisational forms within the National Health Service are included.

Chapter 4 explores the nature of power, politics and policy that affect health care on a large scale. Power and politics, the constant companions of publicly funded health care, are explored, as an understanding of both is necessary for nurses to succeed and prosper.

Part 2 Practical Skills for Leading and Managing

Part 2 describes the concepts and skills associated with effective leadership and management.

Chapter 5 looks at the nature of teams and the dynamics of influencing and organising groups of people to deliver the complex services needed.

Chapter 6 explores communication, one of the most important tools for managing and leading.

In Chapter 7 we discuss effective delegation: the allocation of responsibility to others in a way that assures safe and effective care.

Chapter 8 explores motivation and the skill needed to help you and others to stay focused, interested and enthusiastic about the work you are doing.

Chapter 9 provides tools for dealing with the conflict that arises from differences in how people approach their work.

Chapter 10 describes the skills of creative and critical thinking, problem-solving and decision-making. These skills are needed to analyse and design services to meet needs that arise.

Chapter 11 looks into the skills for leading and managing change.

Chapter 12 focuses on personal skills of self-care, and how you can manage stress and time to stay healthy and effective in your role.

Part 3 Practical First-Level Management

Part 3 provides a guide to undertaking the responsibilities associated with first-level management roles such as ward management or team leadership in hospitals and communities.

Chapter 13 provides information on finance and budget management, and the ward manager/team leader's responsibility for staffing within the available funds.

Chapter 14 describes the process of recruiting and hiring staff.

Chapter 15 explores the responsibilities for clinical supervision, managing capability and performance, all of which form a vital part of each ward sister's and team leader's roles.

Chapter 16 provides an overview of quality management.

Chapter 17 looks at the emerging responsibilities for information management at the clinical team level.

Acknowledgements

Author's acknowledgements

The successful adaptation of this first UK edition of the classic US text *Effective leadership and management in nursing* has been due to the contribution of many front-line leaders including team leaders and ward sisters, nursing colleagues in leadership roles such as directors of nursing, modern matrons and colleagues within the School of Healthcare. In particular, I am enormously grateful to the facilitators and participants of the Leading an Empowered Organisation programme through which I have been able to learn of the challenges of leadership you face, and what works on a practical level. It is this experience that has driven this adaptation from the start, and I rely on you to help me to further refine this text to continue to meet the needs of leaders in the editions to come.

I would like in particular to thank my colleagues from the Centre for the Development of Healthcare Policy and Practice at the University of Leeds who have enabled my passion for front-line leadership to remain the focus of my work. Helen Chin, Susan Smith, Susan Hamer, Elaine McNichol, Gill Collinson, Beverley Haynes, Angela Bradshaw, Jan Mitcheson, Fiona O'Neill and Ben Totterdell, thank you, I have learned from you all.

I would like to thank the editorial team at Pearson for bringing this opportunity to me, and sticking by me through the initial halting attempts at writing to the final manuscript, understanding that I had a day job to do as well.

I am especially grateful to the reviewers, formal and informal, who have given me feedback along the way, and on whom I will rely for an even better second edition.

Gayle Garland, MSN, RGN, RN

Publisher's acknowledgements

We are grateful to the following for permission to reproduce copyright material:

Figures

Figure 2.1 from The Leadership Grid® figure, Paternalism Figure and Opportunism from *Leadership Dilemmas - Grid Solutions,* by Robert R. Blake and Anne Adams McCanse (Formerly the Managerial Grid by Robert R. Blake and Jane S. Mouton). Houston: Gulf Publishing Company, Grid Figure: p. 29, Paternalism Figure: p. 30, Opportunism Figure: p. 31. Copyright 1991 by Scientific Methods, Inc. Reproduced by permission of the owners; Figure 2.2 Reprinted by permission of *Harvard Business Review*. From 'How to choose a leadership pattern', by Tannenbaum, R. and Schmidt, W.H., 51, 164, 1973. Copyright © 1973 by the Harvard Business School Publishing Corporation; all rights reserved; Figure 2.3 from *Management of Organizational Behavior*, 8th ed.

(Hersey, P., Blanchard, K. H. and Johnson, D. E. 2001) 189 and 196 © Copyright 2006. Reprinted with permission of the Center for Leadership Studies. Escondido, CA 92025. www .situational.com. All Rights Reserved; Figure 3.2 from Longest, B. B., Rakich, J. S., and Darr, K. 2000 *Managing Health Services Organizations and Systems,* p. 124, Baltimore: Health Professions Press, Inc., Reprinted by permission; Figure 8.2 from *Organizational Behavior,* 8 ed., Wiley (Schermerhorn, J. R., Hunt, J. G. and Osborn, R. N. 2003) p. 107; Figure 10.3 from *A Competency-based Approach,* 9 ed., South Western Publishers, USA, part of Cengage Learning, Inc. Reproduced by permission. (Hellriegel, D., Jackson, S. E. and Slocum, J. W. Jr 2002) p. 221; Figure 10.4 from *Management: A Competency-based Approach,* 9 ed., South-Western Publishers USA, part of Cengage Learning, Inc. Reproduced by permission. (Hellriegel, D., Jackson, S. E. and Slocum, J. W. 2002) p. 229; Figure 14.2 from NHS Employers, www.nhsemployers.org; Figure 15.1 from The NHS Knowledge and Skills Framework (NHS KSF) and the Development Review Process 2004, © Crown copyright; Figure 16.2 adapted from *Incident Reporting and Investigating Policy,* p. 17. Reproduced with kind permission from Leeds Teaching Hospitals NHS Trust, Leeds.

Tables

Table 4.1 adapted from and Table 4.3 from *Becoming Influential: A Guide for Nurses,* 1 ed., Prentice Hall (Sullivan, E.J. 2004) p. 35, with permission of Pearson Education Inc., Upper Saddle River, NJ.; Table 5.1 from *Developing Team Working in Health Care: A Guide for Managers,* 1 ed., Aston University (Borrill, C. and West, M. 2001) p9; Table 5.2 from Belbin team roles and descriptions. Reproduced by kind permission of Belbin Associates (www.belbin.com); Table 7.1 adapted from 'Delegation': How to Deliver Care Through Others, *American Journal of Nursing,* 92 (3), pp. 87–88 (Hansten, R. and Washburn, M. 1992); Table 8.1 from *The Adult Learner,* 5th edn., Butterfield: Heinemann (Knowles, M.S., Holton III, E.F. and Swanson, R.A. 1998) pp. 64–69, Reed Elsevier; Table 12.1 from The social readjustment rating scale, *Journal of Psychosomatic Research,* 11 (2) (Holmes, T.H. and Rahe, R.H. 1967); Table 15.1 from The Knowledge and Skills Framework (NHS KSF) and the Development Review Process 2004, © Crown Copyright.

Text

Box 4.1 adapted from *Leadership in Organizations,* 5 ed., Prentice Hall (Yukl, G. 2002) 146–152, with permission of Pearson Education, Inc., Upper Saddle River, NJ.; Extract on page 81 from *Developing Team Working in Health Care: A Guide for Managers,* 1 ed., Aston University (Borrill, C. and West, M. 2001) p. 9; Extract on page 118 from *Advice on delegation for registered nurses and midwives,* The Nursing and Midwifery Council (Nursing and Midwifery Council 2008b); Extract on page 118 from *The Code: Standards of Conduct, Performance and Ethics for Nurses and Midwives,* The Nursing and Midwifery Council (Nursing and Midwifery Council 2008a); Box 10.1 from Critical Thinking Skills for at-the-bedside success, *Nursing Management,* vol. 32 (1), pp. 37–39 (Ignatavicius, D. D. 2001); Box 10.4 adapted from The four phases of the model, Introduction to Appreciative Inquiry (Seel, R. 2008), www.new-paradigm.co.uk / introduction to ai.htm; Text on pp. 207–8 from www.nhsdirect.nhs.uk/articles/article.aspx?-articleId=350, nhs direct, © Crown Copyright; Text on pp. 238–41 from NHS Employers, www.nhsemployers.org; Text on pp. 286–88 from Supporting Transformation: A Practical Guide to NHS Connection for Health, © Crown copyright.

In some instances we have been unable to trace the owners of copyright material, and we would appreciate any information that would enable us to do so.

Part 1

Putting Leadership and Management in Perspective

Chapter 1
The Importance of Leadership and Management by Nurses

Key terms

National Health Service
NHS Trust
Health service reform
Patient involvement
Patient choice
Payment by results (PBR)
Block contract

Quality care
Gross domestic product
Care Quality Commission
Long-term condition
NHS Direct
Social enterprises

Introduction

This chapter will help you to understand the events and decisions that have led to health system reform and help you think about the challenges in the future for nurses who manage and lead. The health care services reforms undertaken in the past decade have been driven by a fundamental change in the relationship between those who use health care services and those who provide them. The public are increasingly knowledgeable, and have high expectations not only for safe and compassionate care, but also for choice in when and where their care is provided.

The importance of effective leadership and management by nurses cannot be underestimated in the success so far, and in the continued success of health care reform. Nursing is still the largest single discipline in health care, and has remained close to the patient's experience. It is from this place that nursing has the opportunity to continue to lead.

This chapter explores the trends that are affecting the focus and direction of health services, the role of nurses in patient care and public health, and the challenges for managers and leaders into the future.

Imagine

You have been invited to a 'futures event' to help your trust to plan for the changes that are likely to come about in the next ten years. As a nurse you are not only knowledgeable about nursing, but also close to the patient experience and you understand their needs. What trends do you see that will have an impact on nursing and patient care in the future?

The National Health Service

The **National Health Service** (NHS) is the organisation established by the British government, and funded through taxation, to provide coordinated and integrated health services to the general public. It was formed in 1948 to meet the growing health needs of the population. The founders of the NHS believed that a civilised society should ensure that everyone has access to health care, not just those who can afford it. Different models of national provision were proposed, but eventually the model suggested by Aneurin Bevan, which had the following features, was adopted:

- The NHS is financed virtually 100 per cent from central taxation. This model was seen as the fairest way to fund the service because the rich pay more in taxes and therefore pay more proportionately than the poor for comparable benefits.
- Everyone is eligible for care - even people temporarily residing in or visiting the country. Anybody could be referred to any hospital, local or more distant.
- Health care was free at the point of need.

The main accomplishment of the early days of the NHS was to bring hospital services, family practice and community services into one organisation for the first time. Holding everything together and keeping everyone on board was a big challenge made more difficult by financial shortages in the first two decades of the NHS. It was impossible to predict the use of services by people who had previously had no access, and public expectations rose quickly (Rivett, 2008a).

Many of the tensions that emerged in the early days have continued to challenge the government ever since. The fundamental questions of how to organise and manage the service, how to fund it adequately without crippling taxation, and how to balance the often conflicting demands of patients, staff and taxpayers remain today. Bevan, the principal architect of the NHS, foresaw this fundamental tension:

We shall never have all we need. Expectations will always exceed capacity. The service must always be changing, growing and improving - it must always appear inadequate.

Aneurin Bevan quoted in Rivett (2008a)

The role of the patient in the early days of the health service was 'to be patient', that is, to wait their turn for services struggling to cope with demand and to be grateful for services that were largely unavailable prior to the creation of the NHS. Services were designed and run by government officials and medical professionals, and whilst services were managed for the greater good of the public as a whole, the individual patients had little voice in their care (Rivett, 2008a).

Health services reform

During the 1970s and 1980s a growing catalogue of failures to provide safe and compassion-ate care came to light, and became the driving forces for fundamental change. The term **health service reform** refers to a series of structural and functional changes to the NHS in-tended to bring the service in line with the current and future expectations of the people who work in and who are served by the NHS. The first of many stages of reform happened in the 1980s, when trusts were formed.

An **NHS trust** is a public sector corporation run by a board of executive and non-executive di-rectors, funded by the Department of Health and responsible for providing health services to their community. There are five types of trust: acute trusts, which consist of hospital services and may contain more than one hospital; primary care trusts, which provide community ser-vices and commission care; mental health trusts; ambulance trusts; and care trusts (DoH, 2008a). Care trusts are the newest form of trust set up to provide health and social care. Trusts have financial and corporate accountability as well as responsibility for the quality and safety of care.

More reforms followed the initial reforms of the 1980s. The white paper 'The new NHS: modern, dependable' published in 1997 (DoH, 1997) outlined a reform programme intended to put patients at the centre of the service, and to shift the focus from providing services that do things 'to and for' patients, to one that works with patients. Each trust is expected to have frameworks for **patient involvement**, which is a process of seeking the views and opinions of their patients and the public that they serve. Members of the public serve on the board of directors of each trust, and there is a requirement to have public forums, meetings and patient groups to inform strategy and policy for each organisation.

Another cornerstone of health service reforms has been the provision of **patient choice** in services. Prior to the recent reforms, general practitioners (GPs) referred patients to an indi-vidual consultant: depending on the demand for that consultant, patients could be waiting many months. Referrals are now handled very differently. GPs refer to a service (for example orthopaedics or ophthalmology), which then contacts the patient to offer a choice of where and when they can be seen (DoH, 2008c).

Health services reforms included significant changes in the way health care provider or-ganisations are funded. Previously, health care provider organisations were given a **block contract**, that is, a set amount of money to fund all services, typically based on previous spending, and not necessarily linked to the services provided. This system led to cost overruns when demand for services rose, and an inability to plan for and invest in the future.

Now trusts, and in particular foundation trusts (see Chapter 3), have two sources of fund-ing. Each receives a block contract to pay for unscheduled care such as emergency surgery, general medical care and care of the elderly. Funding for planned and scheduled care comes through a scheme called **payment by results** (PBR), where funding is linked to the choice patients make. Each patient needing surgery, for example, is given the choice of several local hospitals that offer that service. Only the hospital that is chosen will receive payment for the service. That means that if a hospital has a good reputation in the community it will likely have more patients choosing to go there, and therefore will get more money from PBR. If a hospital has a poor reputation, patients will not choose to go there, and their funding will fall. This provides an incentive for trusts to ensure that they provide excellent care and patient satisfaction so that patients will choose the hospital again. In 2008, over 60 per cent of the average hospital's income is through this system, making it a very important source of contin-ued success (DoH, 2008b).

'High quality care for all' (DoH, 2008b) sets out the priorities for the next 10 years of health service reform. Based on the success of having achieved significant improvements in waiting times and access to care, the emphasis in the report is on quality. **Quality care** is described in this document as safe and effective care, available locally and encompassing a satisfying and pleasant experience. The element of care has come more strongly to the fore, and will remain a key focus for the future.

Rising costs – soaring demand

According to the World Health Organization (2007), the UK spends US $2,560 per person per year on health, which represents 8.3 per cent of **gross domestic product** (GDP), a measure of the total value of goods and services produced by a nation. For that expenditure, Britain enjoys one of the highest life expectancy figures internationally and is comparable to many countries that spend more on health. For example, France spends 10.5 per cent GDP on health (US $3,050 per person) and has life expectancy figures virtually identical to those of the UK. Germany spends even more than France and has no significant difference in health outcomes for the added cost. The United States spends 15.4 per cent GDP on health (over US $6,000 per person) to achieve lower life expectancy than the UK.

Spending on health in the UK has risen steadily year on year. In 1997 when the reform plan was put into place, the UK was spending £53,142 million on health, which represented 6.6 per cent GDP for that year. The latest figures available for 2005 indicate that total spending has virtually doubled to £101,509 million, representing 8.3 per cent GDP (Office of National Statistics, 2007). Much of the additional funding has been contingent on significant improvements in the factors that are most important to the public; principally, how long they have to wait for treatment. Waiting times for inpatient treatment and outpatient appointments are now the lowest they have ever been, and are closely monitored and published by the **Care Quality Commission**, the inspection and assessment body for health and social care.

The recent economic pressures caused by the 'credit crunch' of 2008-9 will put pressure on the health services to continue to improve the responsiveness and quality of service within budget. Owing to the NHS being funded principally from general taxation, economic downturns mean less money in the treasury; therefore even if the NHS continues to be funded at the same percentage of GDP, the actual amount of money available will be less.

The changing face of the UK

According to the Office of National Statistics (2009), the UK population is changing in a number of important ways. The population as a whole is increasing. Prior to the mid-1990s the population grew mainly through births within the country after which the trend shifted to one where the main source of population increase was from migration into the country. That trend reversed again in 2008, as birth rates rose within the country and the economic downturn made the UK a less attractive destination for immigration. It is difficult to know the exact number of migrants from the European Union because they are free to live and work in the UK without seeking permission. Migrants from Asia, Africa and elsewhere are tracked, and since 1998 their numbers have risen from 69,000 annually to 179,000, predominantly from Pakistan, India, Afghanistan and the Philippines. Migration from Africa has also risen sharply.

The number of people seeking asylum in the UK varies from year to year, though 30,000 asylum applications were received in 2005 alone. These statistics paint a picture of increasing diversity in culture as well as economic status, a trend that is expected to continue.

In 2005, 16 per cent of the population were aged 65 or over, a rise of 13 per cent since 1971. Over the same period, the proportion of people aged under 16 fell from 25 per cent to 19 per cent. Though the birth rate is rising slowly, the population is clearly ageing, and this has implications for the provision of health services, in that older people tend to use health services more than the young (Office of National Statistics, 2007).

Cultural diversity is increasing in the UK, varying in different geographical areas. For example, London has been identified as one of the most ethnically diverse cities in the world, while cities in the north of the country tend to be less diverse, although Birmingham, Bradford and Leicester amongst others have relatively large Asian communities (Office of National Statistics, 2007).

The influx of immigrants means that the complexity of health care provision is increased. Those who decide health care policies and those who offer health services must consider the values, beliefs and lifestyles of a number of diverse cultures. This is no small challenge. Becoming aware of the differences and similarities among cultures, being sensitive to different perspectives, and providing care within the cultural belief system of the patient requires commitment, respect and persistence. Leininger (2001) suggests that culturally congruent care is provided by (a) accepting and complying with an individual's beliefs; (b) planning, negotiating and accommodating culturally specific practices; and (c) restructuring care based on knowledge about the culture.

The standard of living in the UK is at its highest ever. A strong economy for the past two decades with high employment rates has led to unprecedented levels of home ownership, travel and spending on consumer goods. This relative affluence has been accompanied by rising expectations of public services, including the health service (DoH, 2008b).

Mass media, particularly television, is now practically universal in UK homes. Computer ownership is widespread but, for those who do not own one, computers are also available in schools, libraries and the workplace. This gives the public unprecedented access to a wide range of information on health and illness. People are in a position to investigate treatment options and are often vocal in lobbying for access to new drugs and treatments that have the potential to increase costs in the NHS significantly. This poses a dilemma for health professionals and organisations who want to provide the best care for individuals whilst insuring that there are sufficient resources to meet the needs of the many (DoH, 2008b).

Health needs of the future

Factors that put health at risk are very different today than in the past. People are living longer: since the 1970s the increase in life expectancy among older people has risen sharply. Unfortunately, the number of years in poor health is also rising. Older people can now expect to spend 10 years with a **long-term condition** (such as diabetes, heart disease or asthma) that cannot be cured, and therefore must be managed to prevent the condition worsening or causing further complications such as poor circulation. Heart disease remains the most common cause of death in the UK even though the rates of heart disease have reduced by more than half. Cancers are the second most common cause of death, but survival rates are improving and incidents of lung cancer have dropped dramatically due to a decrease in smoking (Office of National Statistics, 2007).

Child health is improving overall, but there are some worrying trends. The good news is that the number of women breastfeeding has gone up. Nearly all children in the UK are immunised, though with the recent controversy over the measles, mumps and rubella (MMR) vaccine, the uptake of vaccination for children born between 2003 and 2006 has dropped below the desirable level of 90 per cent. This is expected to cause a rise in measles, mumps and rubella as a consequence and early figures do show a rise in mumps in teenagers and adults (Office of National Statistics, 2007). Public awareness campaigns to increase the amounts of fruit and vegetables eaten by children in the home have improved eating habits, but childhood obesity continues to rise: between 1995 and 2005 the levels of obesity in children under 15 years of age rose to 18 per cent (Office of National Statistics, 2007).

Lifestyle linked to health risk is also a growing problem for adults. Obesity is on the rise, as is the incidence of heavy drinking. Smoking varies by social group, with people in manual occupations more likely to smoke. There is an increase in the number of sexually transmitted diseases being reported. Mental illness is on the rise, particularly for people in the most deprived social settings: it can be linked to drug taking and is certainly a risk for suicide (Office of National Statistics, 2007).

These trends have important implications for health care in the future. Whilst hospital treatment for acute conditions will continue, people with long-term conditions will be managed in the community. Hospital treatment for people with long-term conditions will be more complex and therefore hospital stays may increase in length. Hospitals will become sites for only the most intensive care needs, and community care will become more complex. With long-term conditions such as diabetes and heart disease likely to increase, the nurses of the future will need to be skilled in managing people with more complex social and health needs as health advice and lifestyle guidance become increasingly important in health care provision (DoH, 2008b).

Nursing evolves

It was through the efforts of women such as Florence Nightingale that nursing became a respected discipline. Born into a privileged family and privately educated, Nightingale dedicated her life to a number of social causes including hospitals, public health and nursing. Nightingale argued that taking care of sick people in hospital was a skilled and important role. She and other like-minded women were instrumental in founding schools of nursing where 'respectable' women were recruited to become trained nurses (Florence Nightingale Museum Trust, 2008).

Nursing has come a long way since then. Nursing education moved out of the hospitals and into higher education in the 1990s, though nursing education continues to be paid for through the NHS. Nursing education at university is therefore not subject to the fees paid by other students, and diploma students are paid a bursary whilst studying. The education programme is organised so that specialisation occurs prior to registration. All nursing students share a common foundation year and then specialise into educational programmes resulting in registration as a mental health nurse, adult nurse, children's nurse or learning disability nurse. This system has had some merit in being able to plan for future work force needs, but it can limit a nurse's choices of career. There was also a growing consensus that nursing as it is currently structured is not well suited to the future needs of health care provision (DoH, 2008d).

In 2007–8, the Office of the Chief Nursing Officer undertook a consultation on the future of nursing careers with a view to increasing career options and progression opportunities for nurses. The results suggest that it is time for nursing to become an all-graduate profession, with a first degree being the entry level to nursing (DoH, 2008e).

According to the Office of National Statistics (2007), there are nearly 400,000 nurses and midwives working in England and Wales and 1.5 million people working in the health care sector as a whole. The cultural diversity seen in the general population is also reflected in nursing. Based on the national census from 2001, 89 per cent of nurses are white and the remaining 11 per cent identified as non-white, which is consistent with the population diversity as a whole.

Approximately one in six nurses was born outside the UK. Nurses from Asia and Africa were actively targeted for recruitment between 1997 and 2003 to address the shortage of nurses needed to meet the needs of the rapid expansion of health services linked to health service reforms. London has the highest proportion of non-white nurses – 33 per cent.

Challenges for nursing managers and leaders

Nursing and all other disciplines involved in health care will be challenged to respond to the changing needs of the public, and the changing nature of society. 'High quality care for all' (DoH, 2008b) identifies six areas of challenge for the NHS and British society in the twenty-first century: rising expectations; demand driven by demographics (the population is unevenly distributed across the UK, making it difficult to provide local access to all types of treatment); the continuing development of the information society; advances in treatment; the changing nature of disease; and the changing expectations of the health workplace. Meeting these larger challenges will require that the system for delivering health care will continue to change.

Here are a few specific challenges for nurse managers and leaders.

Emerging roles

Nurses are now leading and coordinating care as well as providing it. They are also often working more independently, especially in managing long-term conditions and keeping people healthy. This requires nurses in management roles to examine the needs of these nurses for continuing professional development, supervision and support (DoH, 2008b). Some traditional roles, especially those in the community, are expected to evolve so that they are better aligned to the emerging nature of disease. For example, health visiting and school nursing are well placed to take the lead in emerging health and social concerns such as the prevention of childhood obesity.

Modernised careers

The consultation on modernising nursing careers (DoH, 2008e) suggests that reform of the career structure will make it easier in the future for nurses to move between fields of practice. The new structure would make it possible for a nurse who is general trained and has worked in hospital to change focus to pursue a career in the community working with older people. The challenge for nurse managers and leaders will be to create flexible roles and career pathways that keep nurses engaged and therefore inspire them to remain within the profession.

Educational reform

The expectation that nursing education will change is described in 'Nursing: towards 2015' (Nursing and Midwifery Council, 2007) and includes the move to an all-graduate profession. When that transition is made, nurses in management and leadership roles will need to support the nurses graduating from the new programmes and continue to support nurses prepared by previous methods. Working closely with schools of nursing will be very important in enabling newly qualified staff and experienced staff to work well together. The formal development of preceptor programmes for new staff is expected as well as an expectation of continuing development (DoH, 2008d).

Staff involvement

There is an expectation that staff from all backgrounds will be involved in decision-making at both the clinical and organisational level (DoH, 2002). This will challenge nurse managers and leaders to keep staff informed and to develop forums for joint decision-making. The proposed NHS constitution will commit to the involvement and development of staff, and secure a place for staff at the decision table (DoH, 2008a).

Cultural diversity

As the population of the UK is changing, so will the profile of nurses and health workers as a whole. Nursing has an important role in leading the development of new ways of bringing care to non-traditional communities, especially in the cities, through the development of community clinics and walk-in centres. Cultural awareness will be an important skill for nurses of the future.

Nurses in leadership or management roles must develop sensitivity to cultural differences among their staff as well as their patients and be responsive to these differences within the work environment. Induction and training programmes need to take into consideration the differences in nursing practice in the country of origin so as to support effective integration of new staff. Though nurses from abroad are generally proficient in English, differences in accent and word use can make communication difficult.

Technology

Nurses are already in the forefront of technology-based care such as **NHS Direct**, the telephone- and Internet-based patient and public advice service. Technology-based care is expected to continue to develop so that nurses managing long-term conditions may, for example, keep track of blood glucose results via text messaging and give advice over the phone. Nurses may be working from home more, and challenges for clinical supervision and audit will be significant. Nurse leaders will need to consider quality and professional practice issues in these new configurations.

Cost-effectiveness and financial constraints

As Bevan said many years ago, there will never be enough money to satisfy all needs. NHS trusts will remain accountable not only for the quality of care but also for their management of resources. Nurses in management and leadership roles will continue to feel the pressure of delivering high-quality services within a budget. This will require constant review of the system of care delivery to ensure that the best use is being made of all the talents of the nursing staff.

New organisations

The NHS has recently encouraged nurses and others to consider starting up a social enterprise (DoH, 2008b). **Social enterprises** are small businesses that can bid for funds to deliver services, but instead of being driven by profit, they are driven by social benefit. Any excess within the business is reinvested in new services. For example, a group of district nurses might decide to set up a social enterprise for the management of isolated older people with long-term conditions in their homes. The emergence of these opportunities challenges nurses to develop their business understanding as well as their clinical and management skills.

Managing change and ambiguity

Changes in the way nurses deliver care and the health care system as a whole will continue. Everyone in health care must learn to live with ambiguity and be flexible enough to adapt to the changes it brings.

Management and leadership skills are essential to the future of patient care. Preparation for leading and managing must be an integral part of nursing education, and specific training in management skills should accompany promotion into ward leadership, senior clinical or management roles. It is essential that nurses are enabled to apply their newly acquired skills to the job itself. This means that all nurses in leadership or management roles also need skills in coaching and facilitating in order to create an environment in which effective leadership can thrive.

What you know now

- The nature of illness, the expectations of the public and the health care system itself are all changing, and will continue to change in the foreseeable future.
- Patients of the future will be equal partners with health care staff and managers to design and deliver health care.
- Providing health care successfully will require a balance between patient needs and wants, community support, staff commitment and efficiency.
- The tension between providing care and paying for that care will continue.
- Cultural diversity will continue to demand nurses' attention and to shape the nursing workforce.
- The nurse leader is an active participant and plays a key role in the success of health care organisations.

Questions to challenge you

1. How is your community changing, and what will you need to prepare for as a nurse?
2. What will be the advantages of a more flexible career path for nurses in the future?
3. What roles that are currently being done are well suited to nursing taking a stronger lead?
4. What should be the focus of nurses who lead and manage in the future?

References

Department of Health (DoH) (1997) *The New NHS: Modern, dependable*. London: Department of Health.

Department of Health (DoH) (2002) *Working Together: Staff involvement*. London: Department of Health.

Department of Health (DoH) (2008a) *NHS Fact Sheet: Primary care trusts*. London: Department of Health.

Department of Health (DoH) (2008b) *High Quality Care for All: NHS next stage review final report*. London: Department of Health.

Department of Health (DoH) (2008c) *Choice at Referral: Guidance and supporting information for 2008/9*. London: Department of Health.

Department of Health (DoH) (2008d) *A High Quality Workforce: NHS next stage review*. London: Department of Health.

Department of Health (DoH) (2008e) *Towards a Framework for Post-registration Nursing Careers: Consultation response report*. London: Department of Health.

Florence Nightingale Museum Trust (2008) *Florence Nightingale*. Available at http://www.florence-nightingale.co.uk.

Leininger, M. M. (2001) *Culture Care Diversity and Universality: A theory of nursing*. Sudbury, MA: Jones and Bartlett.

Nursing and Midwifery Council (2007) *Nursing: Towards 2015: Alternative scenarios for healthcare, nursing and nurse education in the UK in 2015*. London: Nursing and Midwifery Council.

Office of National Statistics (2007) *Social Trends No. 37, 2007 Edition*. Basingstoke: Palgrave Macmillan.

Office of National Statistics (2009) *Population Change*. Available at http://www.statistics.gov.uk/cci/nugget.asp?ID=950.

Rivett, G. (2008a) *National Health Service History*. Available at http://www.nhshistory.net.

Rivett, G. (2008b) *The Start of the NHS*. Available at http://nhshistory.net/shorthistory.htm#_ednref7.

World Health Organization (2007) *World Health Statistics 2007*. Geneva: WHO Press.

Chapter 2
Understanding Management and Leadership

Key Terms

Charismatic leadership
Autocratic leadership
Democratic leadership
Laissez-faire leadership
Bureaucratic leadership
Situational leadership
Transactional leadership
Transformational leadership
Quantum leadership
Shared leadership
Servant leadership
Management
Manager

Leadership
Leader
Planning
Contingency planning
Strategic planning
Organising
Directing
Controlling
Formal leadership
Informal leadership
First-level manager
Middle-level manager
Upper-level management

Introduction

Today, all nurses are managers, not always in the formal organisational sense but in practice. They plan, organise and deliver care to patients on a daily basis, and often direct the work of support staff and others. Care needs are becoming more complex and many nursing roles now also require the coordination of care between disciplines. As such, all nurses need to learn management skills to be more efficient and effective.

Today, all nurses are also leaders, because leadership is about influencing the nature of patient care, and being willing to change. As we saw in Chapter 1, much is changing. Health reform and improving care for patients will continue. Influencing that change through setting direction, motivation, communication and team working is increasingly important.

In this chapter, we will explore the nature of management and leadership and look at some of the roles nurses take. The specific skills for leadership and management such as effective delegation, communication, motivation, managing conflict, decision-making and problem-solving are the subject of Part 2 of this book.

Imagine

You have been asked to take on the responsibility for managing a service user support group in your trust. What would you understand your responsibilities to be? Now imagine you have been asked to lead the service user support group. Would you be doing the same things as the manager or would your role be different?

Management and leadership theories

Heroic leadership is the seed of many a good story through the ages, of kings and queens, politicians and ordinary people rising to greatness and inspiring loyal following from others. Though nursing has its share of heroic and inspirational leaders, it is not that form of leadership on which this book will dwell. Instead, we will introduce the idea of everyday leadership, that is, the inspiration and influence that emerges from competent and motivated individuals intent on delivering the best possible patient care. Every competent and committed nurse can and does demonstrate everyday leadership. Though this type of leadership has a recognised value (DoH, 2008a), there has been little research in nursing on the nature and development of everyday leadership from the front line of care.

Management and leadership theories have emerged primarily from the study of people in formal management roles within organisations. As the thinking about organisations has evolved, so has the search for the best way to manage and lead in organisations. Each phase and focus of research has contributed to insights and understandings about management and leadership and their development. Management theories developed alongside organisational theories in that as the nature of the organisation changed, so did the approach to management and leadership. Chapter 3 describes the development of organisations and the changes of leadership that have been needed.

Here are a few of the important landmarks in the development of management and leadership theory.

Scientific management

Prior to the Industrial Revolution, little was written about management. Factories and mills needed large numbers of people working together to produce the goods for market, and that work needed to be coordinated and overseen by people who were knowledgeable and could direct the unskilled workforce. These people were the first managers to be studied, and how they did their work formed the basis for the earliest management theories.

Scientific management, developed by Taylor (1911), evolved to align with the classical theory of organisation developed during the Industrial Revolution. Classical organisational theory suggests that standard methods should be used for each job, and that variation should be eliminated. People are seen as operating most productively within a rational and well-defined organisational structure that spells out each person's tasks and defines the relationship between employees.

Fayol (1916) was one of the first people to describe the primary functions of management: planning, organising, commanding, coordinating and controlling. We still use Fayol's categories of management today and recognise the value of structuring work in an organised way.

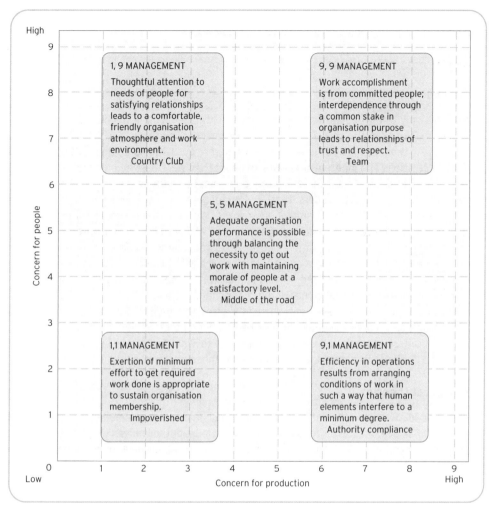

Figure 2.1 The managerial grid.

From The Leadership Grid ® figure, Paternalism Figure and Opportunism from *Leadership Dilemmas - Grid Solutions*, by Robert R. Blake and Anne Adams McCanse (Formerly the *Managerial Grid* by Robert R. Blake and Jane S. Mouton). Houston: Gulf Publishing Company, Grid Figure: p. 29, Paternalism Figure: p. 30, Opportunism Figure: p. 31. Copyright 1991 by Scientific Methods, Inc. Reproduced by permission of the owners.

Scientific management was also the beginning of some of the quality improvement tools we now use, such as process re-engineering and lean thinking, in that scientific management advocated that work should be timed and measured to produce the greatest efficiency. Workers who were expected to dig holes were given shovels with handles proportional to their height to enable them to work faster and produce more.

The problem with scientific management is that it did not take into consideration the human aspects of work, the need for people to feel noticed and valued, and to feel a contribution to the work. The idea emerged that in order for organisations to be effective, managers also had to be able to lead: that is, to provide workers with a sense of purpose and motivation to do the job well. Figure 2.1 illustrates managerial styles that result from differing emphasis that managers can place on production or people. Ideally, high concern for production is combined with high concern for people to create effective teamworking.

Early theories of leadership

Trait theory

Historically, only a few people were seen as leaders: those born into royalty, or who rose to prominent positions in the church, the military or politics. There was one school of thought, the 'Great Man theory', which believed that leaders were born; that is, that people who rose to leadership positions had inherent traits which meant they were destined for that role.

In an effort to understand the nature of leadership, the early writers began to study the characteristics of successful leaders; that is, what leaders are. Early attempts to identify the definitive set of traits produced ambiguous results. Whereas some successful leaders (e.g. religious leaders) showed traits such as charisma, the ability to inspire, purposefulness, commitment and principled working, others (e.g. political and military leaders) showed traits such as ruthlessness, single-mindedness and aggression. The list of leadership traits evolved along with society and later writers added other qualities, for example being a good communicator, self-awareness, emotional intelligence, integrity and intelligence.

In practice, trait theories have limited use in explaining effective leadership: not everyone with the traits of a leader becomes an effective leader, and effective leaders do not always have those traits. Nonetheless, people continue to be fascinated with the personal qualities of leaders, and continue to benchmark people against those qualities.

Behavioural theories

Research on leadership in the early 1930s, when the human relations models of organisation were developed (see Chapter 3), focused on the behaviours of the leaders, that is, what leaders do. In the behavioural view of leadership, personal traits only provide a foundation for leadership; effective leaders acquire a pattern of learned behaviours. Weber (1905) described two types of leader, the bureaucratic and the **charismatic leader**. Bureaucratic leaders have a highly structured approach and follow procedure, moving step by step to ensure that things are done thoroughly and correctly. Weber suggested that this style of leadership was suited to organisations such as hospitals, universities and banks that needed to ensure quality, security and safety. The charismatic leader leads by infusing energy and enthusiasm into others, and ensuring success by commitment and hard work. This type of leadership was seen as suited to business, where innovation and drive were needed to succeed.

Lewin, Lippitt and White (1939) studied leadership styles amongst groups of teenage boys and identified three different styles of leadership: autocratic, democratic and laissez-faire. The **autocratic leadership** style assumes that individuals are motivated by external forces, such as power, authority and the need for approval; the leader makes all the decisions and uses coercion, punishment and direction to change followers' behaviour and achieve results.

The **democratic leadership** style assumes that individuals are motivated by internal drives and impulses, want active participation in decisions and want to get the task done. The leader uses participation and the group get the chance to inform the leader's decisions about setting goals and how the work is accomplished. The **laissez-faire leadership** style also assumes that individuals are motivated by internal drives and impulses and that they need to be left alone to make decisions about how to complete the work; the leader provides little direction or facilitation.

Crail (2001) and some other modern writers suggest that the three leadership styles of autocratic, democratic and laissez-faire exist on a continuum. He suggests, for example, that the autocratic leadership style can range from bullying to a benign dictatorship, a much more acceptable form of leadership to followers. Crail goes on to suggest that democratic leadership is most effective when the leader is trying to instil a sense of personal growth and job satisfaction. Democratic leadership is not the best choice, however, when difficult decisions need to be taken, the team is inexperienced or important standards are not being met. Laissez-faire leadership can be criticised for being too loosely controlling; and yet with a highly experienced, committed and self-directed team, it may be the best choice.

Jenkins and Henderson (1984) added a fourth style, that of **bureaucratic leadership**, first proposed by Weber. The bureaucrat assumes that employees are motivated by external forces. This leader trusts neither followers nor self to make decisions and therefore relies on organisational policies and rules to identify goals and direct work processes. Table 2.1 compares the four leadership styles.

The next step in the understanding of leadership came when researchers started noticing that one individual can use different leadership styles depending on the situation. This led to the development of contingency theories of leadership.

Contingency theories

Contingency approaches suggest that leaders adapt their styles in relation to changing situations. According to contingency theory, behaviours range from authoritarian to permissive (which is much like autocratic to laissez-faire) and vary in relation to current needs and future probabilities. Figure 2.2, on page 19, illustrates a range of leadership behaviours that could be chosen, depending on the situation. A nurse may use an authoritarian style when responding to an emergency situation such as a cardiac arrest but use a participative style to encourage the team to take on a self-rostering project. The manager might delegate the responsibility for developing a new system of handover to a highly experienced and eager group. Conversely, the leader might keep personal control of a task that is highly controversial and likely to need careful handling.

Contingency theorists suggest that the most effective leadership style is the one that best complements the organisational environment, the tasks to be accomplished, and the personal characteristics of the people involved in each situation. Numerous contingency models have been developed. One of the best known examples of contingency theory is **situational leadership** developed by Hersey, Blanchard and Johnson (2001). Expanding the earlier work of Fiedler (1967), who suggested that leadership style should be based on the relationship between the manager and the employee, the power in the role and the nature of the task, the theory of situational leadership added the idea that the follower's competence and willingness to perform the role should also be considered. Situational leadership therefore matched leadership style to the developmental level of the follower.

Leaders use a telling style (S1 – high task, low relationship) with followers who are unable and unwilling or insecure about performing the task (R1). Leaders use a selling style (S2 – high task, high relationship) with followers who are unable but are willing or confident in performing the task (R2). Leaders use a participating style (S3 – low task, high relationship) with followers who are able but unwilling or lacking in confidence in performing the task (R3). Finally, leaders use a delegating style (S4 – low task, low relationship) with followers who are both able and willing and have confidence in performing the task (R4). Figure 2.3, on page 20, illustrates the situational leadership model.

Table 2.1 Comparison of leadership styles

Leadership style	Assumed employee motivators	Leader characteristics	Impact on the team
Authoritarian (autocratic)	External forces, e.g. power and authority, needs for approval	Concerned with task accomplishment rather than relationships Uses directive behaviour Makes decisions alone Expects respect and obedience of staff Lacks group support generated by participation Exercises power with coercion Proves useful (even necessary) in crisis situations	Gives the team certainty and clarity Can be appropriate in emergency situations Highly directive style can be good when the team is inexperienced The negative variant of this style (cold authoritarianism) can create high levels of staff sickness, absenteeism, low initiative, lack of commitment and high staff turnover
Democratic (participative)	Internal drives and impulses	Is primarily concerned with human relations and teamwork Fosters communication that is open and usually two-way Creates a spirit of collaboration and joint effort that results in staff satisfaction	Team members feel involved Can encourage accountability and shared responsibility When overused, can result in delays to decisions, a lack of confidence in the leader's ability and uncertainty
Permissive (laissez-faire)	Internal drives and impulses	Tends to have few established policies; abstains from leading Is not generally useful in highly structured organisations (e.g. health care institutions)	Can be appropriate in highly developed teams with high levels of commitment When used inappropriately, can result in a lack of consistency in work, staff feeling unsupported and poor teamworking
Bureaucratic	External forces	Lacks a sense of security and depends on established policies and rules Exercises power by applying fixed, relatively inflexible rules Tends to relate impersonally to staff Avoids decision-making without standards or norms for guidance	Can be necessary in highly regulated situations such as health and safety, narcotic control and use of dangerous substances and procedures When used inappropriately, can cause the team to become frustrated Can result in lack of initiative, low innovation, low staff satisfaction, high turnover and high rates of sickness.

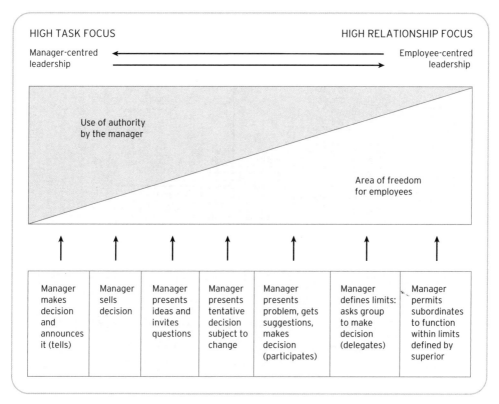

Figure 2.2 Continuum of leadership behaviour.

Reprinted by permission of *Harvard Business Review*. From 'How to choose a leadership pattern' by Tannenbaum, R. and Schmidt. W.H., 51, p. 164, 1973. Copyright © 1973 by the Harvard Business School Publishing Corporation; all rights reserved.

Contemporary theories

Trait, behavioural and contingency theories represent conventional approaches to leadership and have provided important foundations for practical leadership within organisations and groups. Current views of leadership are neither complete reformulations nor simple refinements of conventional perspectives.

The earlier theories of leadership were developed from studying management and leadership within hierarchical organisations. Leaders in today's health care environment place increasing value on collaboration and teamwork across different services within an organisation or between organisations. It is recognised that as partnerships develop between different organisations, or teams are formed from across organisations, the usual manager–employee relationship changes. A nurse may be responsible for a project that needs health visiting and community midwives to work together, yet both groups may formally report to different people. Where partnerships are developing outside the formal reporting relationships, it is still important that leadership occurs. Leaders must use additional skills, especially group and political leadership skills, to create collegial work environments.

Contemporary approaches to leadership are underpinned by the belief that information power that was previously restricted to the professionals or managers that provided the service is now available to all. Patients and staff alike can access untold amounts of information.

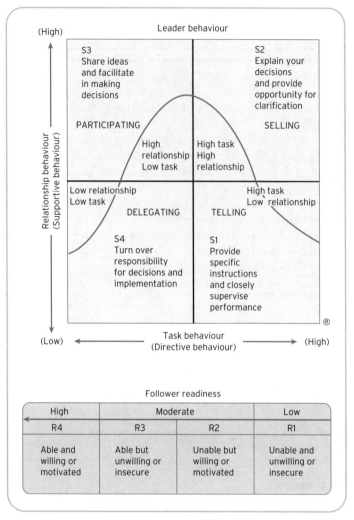

Figure 2.3 Situational Leadership® model.

Source: From *Management of Organizational Behavior*, 8th ed. (Hersey, P., Blanchard, K. H. and Johnson, D. E. 2001) 189 and 196 © Copyright 2006 Reprinted with permission of the Center for Leadership Studies. Escondido, CA 92025. www. situational.com. All Rights Reserved.

The challenge, however, is to assist patients to evaluate and use the information they have. Because staff have access to information only the manager had in the past, leadership and management become shared activities, requiring everyone involved to develop excellent interpersonal skills and a willingness to work collaboratively.

Transactional leadership is aimed at maintaining equilibrium, or the status quo, by performing work according to policy and procedures, and stabilising both the process and outcome of care. Leaders are successful to the extent that they understand and meet the needs of followers and use reward and punishment to enhance employee loyalty and performance. A leader may take a transactional approach to leadership when consistency and reliability are of great importance. For example, the director of a clinical laboratory may use a transactional approach to ensuring that the laboratory tests are done to the expected standards, within time frames and using the correct procedure. Staff are rewarded for ensuring that the equipment they use is calibrated correctly and that quality assurance procedures are undertaken.

Transformational leadership emphasises the importance of interpersonal relationships (Ward, 2002). The transformational leader inspires followers and uses power to instil a belief that followers also have the ability to do exceptional things. Transformational leaders also encourage others to exercise leadership. The goal of the transformational leader is to generate employees' commitment to the vision or ideal rather than to themselves.

Transformational leaders may seem a natural model for health care leaders, because professionals, including nurses, have traditionally been driven by the ethic of human service. Alimo-Metcalfe et al. (2007), in their study of crisis resolution teams, found that transformational leadership had many advantages. They found that the leaders who engaged with staff and demonstrated vision, capability and competence were more likely to have staff with positive attitudes towards work and well-being at work. They also found that engaging leadership resulted in a greater achievement of goals and objectives. Engaging leaders consistently did the following things to achieve these results:

- Involve stakeholders (including staff) from the outset when change occurs
- Focus on the quality of service
- Use non-hierarchical teams with devolved leadership
- Create a supportive and informal culture
- Implement successful change leadership

However, in order to be effective in complex modern health care organisations it is important to develop skills in transformational and transactional forms of leadership. Nurses are responsible for ensuring that policy and procedures are followed, and that safe and satisfying care is provided, whilst also inspiring others to develop ideas, make changes that improve care and build trust and loyalty. Patients want to know that there is someone in charge, coordinating services and managing people to ensure their immediate needs are met (DoH, 2008a). This can sometimes require giving direction to others, setting boundaries, monitoring performance and giving feedback. Those actions will be better received if there is a relationship of trust and respect between the leader and the follower.

Quantum leadership

Quantum leadership is based on the concepts of chaos theory (see Chapter 3). Reality is constantly shifting, and levels of complexity are constantly changing. Movement in one part of the system reverberates throughout the system. Roles are fluid and outcome-oriented. It matters little what you did; it only matters what outcome you produced. Within this framework, employees become directly involved in decision-making as equitable and accountable partners, and managers assume more of an influential facilitative role, rather than one of control (Porter-O'Grady and Malloch, 2002).

Shared leadership

Reorganisation, decentralisation and the increasing complexity in health care have led some to recognise the value of **shared leadership**, which is based on the empowerment principles of participative and transformational leadership. The application of shared leadership assumes that a well-educated, highly professional, dedicated workforce is comprised of many leaders.

Different issues call for different leaders, or experts, to guide the problem-solving process. A single leader is not expected always to have knowledge and ability beyond that of other members of the work group. Examples of shared leadership in nursing include:

- Self-directed work teams. Work groups manage their own planning, organising, duty roster and day-to-day work activities.

- Shared governance. The staff are formally organised to make key decisions about clinical practice standards, quality assurance and improvement, staff development, professional development and some policies and procedures. Decision-making is conducted by representatives of the staff who have been authorised to make those decisions. Shared governance is different from committee work in that committees are normally advisory bodies only and seldom have the authority to actually make decisions.

- Co-leadership. Two or more people work together to execute a leadership role. This kind of leadership has become more common in directorate structures, where the skills of the nurse leader, general manager and consultant are all needed to lead the service. The development of co-leadership roles depends on the flexibility and maturity of all individuals, and such arrangements usually require coaching for continued success.

Servant leadership

Servant leadership is based on the premise that leadership originates from a desire to serve; and that in the course of serving, one may be called to lead. According to Greenleaf (1991), servant leadership occurs when other people's needs take priority, when those being served 'become healthier, wiser, freer, more autonomous, and more likely themselves to become servants' (1991: 7). The servant leader must address the question of whether the least advantaged in society benefit from the leader's service.

The concept of servant leadership may have some substantive appeal for health care leaders because health professions are founded on the principles of caring, service and the growth and health of others. Nurse leaders serve many constituencies, often quite selflessly, and consequently bring about change in individuals, systems and organisations. Alimo-Metcalfe suggests that the model of engaging leadership described above resembles the servant leadership concept, and it may be that transformational leadership, used in complex health care organisations, is evolving to more closely match this model (Alimo-Metcalfe, 2008).

Leadership and management

A number of modern writers, e.g. Drucker and Stone (1998), believe that it is of little value to confront the difference between managers and leaders; the terms and roles have become largely interchangeable. Effective managers and leaders are skilled at balancing the needs of patients, the health care organisation, the staff and themselves. Good managers are often good leaders, having the traits and behaviours that create vision, inspiration and commitment among followers as well as skills to set goals, organise services and deliver results.

Whilst the terms manager and leader are often used interchangeably, there is some benefit in looking at the systems of action called leadership and management. **Management** is about coping with complexity, and providing order and consistency to quality of care and work roles (Kotter, 1990). A **manager** is an individual employed by an organisation who is responsible and accountable for efficiently accomplishing the goals of the organisation. Managers focus on coordinating and integrating resources, using the functions of planning, organising, supervising, staffing, evaluating, negotiating and representing. Interpersonal skill is important, but a manager also has authority, responsibility, accountability and power defined by the organisation. The manager's job is to create stability and predictability; to maintain a set of operating principles that will provide consistent results (Kotter, 1990).

Leadership is about coping with change. Part of the reason that leadership has been much talked about since the 1970s is that the rate of change and the need to meet the rising expectations of the public are ever-growing (Kotter, 1990). A **leader** is anyone who uses interpersonal skills to influence others to accomplish a specific goal. The leader exerts influence by using a flexible repertoire of personal behaviours and strategies. The leader is important in forging links – creating connections – among an organisation's members to promote high levels of performance and quality outcomes. Antrobus and Kitson (1999) found that leaders are skilled in empowering others, creating meaning and facilitating learning, developing knowledge, thinking reflectively, communicating, solving problems, making decisions and working with others. Leaders generate excitement; they clearly define their purpose and mission. Leaders understand people and their needs; they recognise and appreciate differences in people, individualising their approach as needed.

The nature of management

The core functions of management identified by Fayol remain largely unchanged in modern texts on management; they are planning, organising, directing and controlling.

Planning is a four-stage process designed to:

1. Establish objectives (goals)
2. Evaluate the present situation and predict future trends and events
3. Formulate a planning statement (means)
4. Convert the plan into an action statement.

Planning is important on both an organisational and personal level and may be an individual or group process that addresses the questions of what, why, where, when, how and by whom. Decision-making and problem-solving are inherent in planning. Organisation-level plans, such as determining organisational structure and staffing or operational budgets, evolve from the mission and goals of the organisation. Service planning is more likely to involve ward managers and team leaders in developing specific goals and objectives for their area of responsibility.

Planning can be contingent or strategic. **Contingency planning** refers to the identification and management of the many problems that interfere with getting work done. Contingency planning may be reactive, in response to a crisis, or proactive, in anticipation of problems or in response to opportunities. How would you manage if two nurses called in sick for night shift? What if you were a manager for a specialty unit and received a call for an admission, but had no more beds? Or what if you were in charge of an elderly ward and found that one of the patients had developed a suspected *Clostridium difficile* infection? Planning for crises such as these are examples of contingency planning.

Strategic planning is the process of planning the future direction and goals of the organisation and the methods for attaining those goals. Strategic planning occurs at many levels in organisations. The executive team of the trust or organisation puts together detailed plans

Case Study 2.1   Planning

Phil, the leader of a community mental health team, plans to establish a stress-reduction programme for schoolchildren experiencing exam stress. He knows that part of the trust's mission is early identification and treatment of stress before it leads to depression, drug or
alcohol use or antisocial behaviour. To implement this programme effectively, he would need
to address:

- How the programme supports the organisation's mission
- Why the service would benefit the community and the organisation
- Who would be candidates for the programme
- Who would provide the service
- How staffing would be accomplished
- How costs would be covered or directed from other programmes.

for attaining goals including financial plans that typically span a number of years. At divisional or department level, the managers also plan for their areas, for example the surgical division planning for meeting the targets for reducing waiting times for planned surgeries. At
ward or team level, the ward sister or team leader is involved in planning staffing levels to
meet future changes to the service. Strategic planning at team level covers at least the next
year, and sometimes runs several years into the future.

Organising is the process of coordinating the work to be done. Formally, it involves identifying the work of the organisation, dividing the labour, developing the chain of command and
assigning authority. It is an ongoing process that reviews systematically the use of human and
material resources. In health care, the mission, formal organisational structure, delivery systems, job descriptions, skill mix and staffing patterns form the basis for the organisation. In
organising the school-based stress-reduction programme in Case Study 2.1, Phil develops job
descriptions, determines how many positions are required and writes a training plan, policies
and procedures for the staff delivering the service.

Directing involves giving instruction, coordinating activities and guiding the process of
getting the organisation's work done. Power, authority and leadership style are intimately related to a manager's ability to direct. Communication abilities, motivational techniques and
delegation skills are also important. In today's health care organisation, professional staff are
autonomous, requiring guidance rather than direction. The manager is more likely to sell the
idea, proposal or new project to staff rather than tell them what to do. The manager coaches
and counsels to achieve the organisation's objectives. In fact, it may be the nurse who assumes the traditional directing role when working with support staff. In directing the school
stress-reduction project, Phil assembles the team of nurses to provide the service, explains
the purpose and constraints of the programme, and allows the team to decide how they will
staff the project, giving guidance and direction when needed.

Controlling functions involve establishing standards of performance, determining the
means to be used in measuring performance, evaluating performance and providing feedback.
The efficient manager strives constantly to improve productivity by incorporating techniques

of quality management, evaluating outcomes and performance and instituting change as necessary.

Today, managers share many of the control functions with the staff. Clinical supervision is often undertaken by peers and audit is delegated to team members. When Phil introduces the new service, the team of nurses involved in the programme identify professional standards for identifying suicide risk and referral, and discuss the supervision needs of the team. A subgroup of the team conducts routine audits and identifies ways to improve the programme.

Planning, organising, directing and controlling reflect a systematic, proactive approach to management. This approach is used widely in all types of organisations, health care included. Timmereck (2000) found that health care managers used these classic functions extensively.

The nature of leadership

Kotter (1990) identified the main functions of leadership as setting the direction, aligning people and motivating people. The intention is to inspire and persuade, to move people on in their thinking and to harness energy for change.

Setting the direction is about developing a clear vision of the future. It involves identifying trends and anticipating what may occur in the future. In Chapter 1 we explored the trends in population change, health and illness, and economic, social and technical advances. This activity could be described as setting the direction in that it encourages people to think about what might need to be in place in order to meet demand in ten years' time.

The Department of Health and other bodies publish documents to set the direction for health services. A recent example of this is 'High quality care for all' (DoH, 2008a), which sets out the reasons for continued reform of health services and important standards about the value of care and compassion. This could be described as connecting vision to values, encouraging nurses and others to 'buy in' to the values underlying the vision.

Aligning people represents the idea that if we are to be successful, everyone has to be pointed in the same direction. It is not uncommon in health care for different disciplines to have different priorities. For example, doctors are most concerned about curing illness whilst nurses are often more concerned about the impact of that illness on the patient and their family. These areas of concern are complementary but can result in a lack of consistency: a doctor may want to discharge an elderly woman to home as soon as her x-ray shows that her pneumonia is resolving, but the nurse may want her to stay a couple more days to increase her strength. Both the nurse and the doctor have the best interests of the patient at heart, but have differences of opinion about the patient's readiness for home. Aligning these two disciplines would be a leadership role: if agreement can be reached about the best point at which to send the person home, taking into account the clinical disease, functional strength and social support of the patient, a common vision and practice will emerge.

Creating motivation is about building interest and energy for the task at hand. This is very different to simply assigning work, which is a management responsibility. This is about inspiring people to want to do what is asked. Sometimes motivation is created by providing incentives to people and this can work well if it is used infrequently. For example, a ward manager may offer to bring in cakes for the team as a reward for clearing a backlog of audit reports. Used too much, incentives can lose their motivating influence.

Case Study 2.2   **Motivation**

A ward manager would like to introduce a different handover system because the current handover is taking too long, and the patients often have to wait for care at busy shift-change times. The ward manager knows that the nurses like their current system, which they see as thorough and as promoting good relationships between shifts. How would you go about suggesting this change in handover? What examples would you collect? What specific values would you tap into (patient safety, satisfaction, confidence)?

Motivation is often better accomplished by linking the change to the values of the individual. Most nurses truly want what is best for the patient, and want to give compassionate, safe and effective care. Therefore, linking changes to these values is more likely to be successful. Case Study 2.2 gives you an opportunity to think about how you would take to motivating people to adopt a new way of working. For further help, see Chapter 8.

Nurses as managers and leaders

Leadership may be formal or informal. **Formal leadership** exists where responsibilities for bringing about change and ensuring that patient care is of a high standard are described in a job title (e.g. Director of Nursing, Nurse Consultant, Modern Matron). The conferring of a formal leadership responsibility is of course not sufficient to ensure effectiveness; the leader must learn and apply leadership skill. Insightful formal leaders recognise the importance of their own informal leadership activities and the informal leadership of others who affect the work in their areas of responsibility.

Informal leadership is influence exercised by a staff member who does not have a specified leadership or management role. A nurse whose thoughtful and convincing ideas substantially influence the quality of care is exercising leadership skills. Informal leadership depends primarily on one's knowledge, experience, credibility and personal skills in persuading and guiding others.

All nurses have the potential to be managers and leaders whether or not they have a formal management role. Most nurses recognise that they are managers of care, if not people. Effective management is part of the everyday experience of the nurse, who plans, organises and evaluates the care that they give. Once a nurse has been qualified a short time they also manage teams, taking on the responsibility for planning, organising and evaluating the care for a group of patients. Done well, this role requires skills in managing people and tasks, even if the duration of the management role is a few hours.

It is important to remember that if you are in a management role, even as a team leader for a shift, you are also looked to for leadership. Those working with you will look to you for advice, direction and motivation: in short, for leadership. Leadership often can and does arise from people with no formal responsibilities for management or indeed leadership. Another nurse, a student, a support worker, a doctor or another health professional can influence the way care is delivered, and can inspire and motivate others by their approach. Some of the best leaders are those who lead from within teams, inspiring others with their knowledge, compassion and integrity.

The necessity of all staff to take a leadership role in improving services has been recognised in a number of recent policy documents published by the Department of Health (DoH, 2008a). Huge investments in leadership development for front-line staff were made though the NHS Leadership Centre during the first wave of service reform. Staff nurses, ward sisters, team leaders, matrons and others contribute to leadership in the following ways:

- Sharing their expertise and experience in caring for patients with others
- Bringing the patient and carer experience to the forefront of service changes
- Interacting with and listening to patients and carers, their needs, wants and expectations, and then embedding these into the way care is delivered
- Developing good professional relationships with colleagues so that ideas are shared, respected and acted on
- Influencing those at other levels of the organisation in order to ensure understanding
- Ensuring that the values on which care is based – safety, patient and carer involvement, compassion – are clear when planning changes
- Being open to different ways of working.

Formal leadership and management roles for nurses

There are many different roles in nursing with formal leadership and management responsibilities: each role is different, having a different emphasis. One of the factors that determine the nature of the role is where it fits in relation to the work of patient care. Figure 2.4 illustrates typical roles within different levels of management.

Staff nurse

Although not formally a manager, the staff nurse working with other professionals and support staff has to be able to manage a variety of situations as well as lead change in patient care. Management responsibilities involve supervising others to ensure safe, quality patient care and as such require skills in communication, delegation and motivation. Leadership is also part of every nurse's job in that keeping patient care safe and effective entails constant change and gaining the cooperation and support of the team to accomplish this. The impact of leadership among front-line staff is now being recognised in health care. Improvements in clinical care and patient experience originate at the bedside and support for the development of leadership skills at all levels is needed.

First-level management

The **first-level manager**, also known as a front-line manager, is responsible for supervising the work of front-line staff and coordinating the day-to-day activities of a ward or team. Though the specific responsibilities of ward managers and team leaders may vary from place to place, typically he or she is responsible for assigning staff to patients, supervising patient care, supervising and developing staff, ensuring that health and safety and other regulations are followed, providing advice and direction, coordinating care with other services and interfacing with the public. Whilst a team leader or ward manager may not have control over the staffing establishment, he or she is responsible for ensuring that staffing levels are adequate for care demands and the efficient use of supplies and equipment.

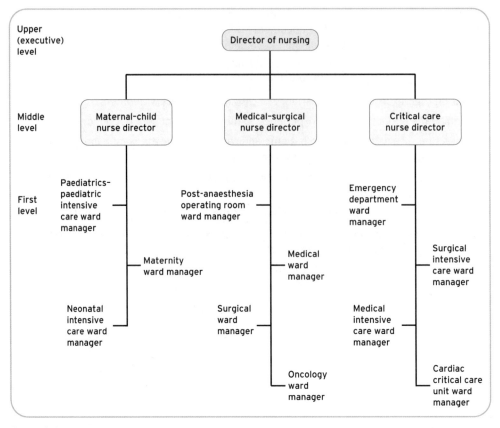

Figure 2.4 Levels of management for a hospital setting.

With primary responsibility for motivating the staff to achieve the organisation's goals, the first-level manager represents staff to other levels of management, and vice versa. This means that first-level managers are often involved in meetings or creating reports that are used to inform others within the organisation about the patient care and staff needs of their area.

Where services are provided over 24 hours, the ward managers will usually have 24-hour accountability for the management of a ward or team. In the hospital setting, the first-level manager is usually the ward sister or charge nurse, ward manager or shift leader. In other settings, such as a community team, a first-level manager may be referred to as a team leader. Box 2.1 describes a first-level manager's day.

Middle-level management

The **middle-level manager** supervises a number of first-level managers, usually within a directorate or service team. Middle-level managers are responsible for the people and activities within the directorates they supervise, and they too have 24-hour responsibility for their defined area. Typically, middle-level managers act as a liaison between upper management and first-level managers. A middle manager may be referred to as a modern matron, director, or assistant or director of nursing.

Box 2.1   **A Day in the Life of a First-Level Manager**

As the ward manager for a paediatric intensive care unit (PICU), Barbara Johnson is routinely responsible for supervising patient care, troubleshooting, maintaining compliance with standards, and giving guidance and direction as needed. In addition, she has responsibilities for service planning, staff review and clinical supervision. The following exemplifies a typical day.

As Barbara came on duty, she learned that there had been a car accident and that two of the victims were children aged 2 and 5 currently in surgery and destined for the unit. The nursing office had called in an additional bank nurse with experience in PICU but her experience was not recent. It was decided that the bank nurse would not be the primary nurse for either new admission; she would facilitate the transfers and help out the other nurses. Barbara had to arrange for the transfer of two children out of PICU to make room for the new admissions. She got in touch with the bed management team who would be in contact with the consultant and facilitate the transfers.

Other staffing problems were at hand: the unit was scheduled to have students on the day, a factor that would probably make things more difficult in view of how preoccupied the qualified staff would be. The annual health and safety update was scheduled though it was now doubtful that anyone from the unit could be freed up to attend. Fortunately, Barbara had only one meeting and would be available to help on the unit for the entire shift except for one hour. Barbara received a call from the modern matron. Unfortunately the ward that was to receive the transfers had an outbreak of MRSA and was closed to admissions. Barbara referred the issue to bed management and waited to see what could be arranged.

As the first patient returned from surgery, Barbara went to help admit the patient and receive handover from recovery. As the patient was stable, she passed the care on to another nurse and went back to sort out the staffing situation for the evening shift. She reviewed staffing for the next 24 hours and noted that an extra nurse was needed for both the evening and night shifts because of the increased workload. After finding staff, she was able to help out on the ward so that a couple of people could attend the health and safety update.

A typical day in the life of a middle-level manager is described in Box 2.2.

Many changes are continuing to occur in first- and middle-level management in hospitals and other health care organisations today. In some, middle management positions are being consolidated and/or eliminated. Rather than just being responsible for a clinical directorate, the middle manager may hold a portfolio of responsibilities for such things as patient and public involvement, clinical audit, practice development or pathway coordination. In addition, departments previously under separate management, such as allied health professionals, may now be under the Director of Nursing. Conversely, nursing within directorate structures is often under the supervision of general managers.

Upper-level management

Upper-level management, or executive-level management, refers to board-level executives such as the Director of Nursing, to whom middle managers report. This role is primarily responsible for establishing organisational goals and strategic plans for the organisation

> **Box 2.2** **A Day in the Life of a Middle-Level Manager**
>
> Bridget Connolly is a middle-level manager. She is the assistant director of nursing for women's and children's services at a large trust. Within her division are the paediatric unit, PICU, newborn intensive care unit (NICU), midwifery and gynaecology wards. Four ward managers report to her. Bridget routinely meets with her managers to identify patient or employee issues. A typical day might look like this.
>
> Bridget usually starts her day by checking her diary for meetings and appointments and looking to visit wards and meet with ward managers in between times. From the bed management reports she notes that both the paediatric and PICU are full, whilst midwifery and the NICU have room.
>
> Today, the first thing on Barbara's agenda is a meeting to discuss clinical placements for students. She makes a note to meet with the midwifery ward manager to see if they can take additional students next term.
>
> Bridget next meets with the manager of NICU, who has reported that two transport teams have been called out to bring sick babies into the ward from outlying areas, and that there is a potential for a third. Bridget helps the ward manager to sort out additional staff and alerts the bed management team to the pressure on the ward. A meeting with the paediatric ward manager is brief because she is busy helping the staff.
>
> Bridget returns to her office, where one of the consultants, Mr Santos, is waiting to discuss the possibility of implementing a new procedure, and the director of the laboratory wants an urgent meeting to discuss a problem with maintaining hazard precautions with placentas.
>
> After a quick lunch, Bridget heads to the patient involvement meeting, which she chairs. She returns the phone calls she received earlier before heading home for the day.

and directing the nursing contribution to the whole. It is also becoming more important for executive managers to work outside the organisation, informing policy, managing political situations locally and nationally and interpreting the wider perspective for nurses and others. Box 2.3 describes a typical day for a nurse in an upper-level role.

Modern matrons

In nursing today there are a number of roles that do not fit the traditional levels of management; the modern matron is one of these. Modern matrons are usually regarded as mid-level managers and typically have advisory authority rather than line authority over ward managers. Although the job description varies from organisation to organisation, the modern matron role is principally responsible for ensuring that ward teams or clinical teams in the community are meeting standards that affect patient care and experience. In an acute setting, the modern matron is responsible for safety and cleanliness, quality of food and ensuring that ward areas have the supplies and equipment needed. Modern matrons take on responsibilities for supporting clinical teams, allowing ward sisters and charge nurses to take on a more clinical role. The role has a coordinating function ensuring that care standards are consistent between clinical areas and that audit and other quality measures are in place. Skills in facilitation, communication, coordination and development are necessary for effectiveness in the role.

> ### Box 2.3   A Day in the Life of a Senior Nurse
>
> Noreen Walker is a Director of Nursing and Quality in a large mental health trust. As such, she is intimately involved with setting policy and direction for the trust and has ultimate accountability for patient care. On any given day she may meet with other executives and directors and often meets with community or professional leaders, representatives of the Department of Health or the directors of other commissioning and provider organisations. Noreen spends much of her time gathering and sharing information.
>
> Noreen has ultimate responsibility for the quality and appropriateness of the nursing care provided in the organisation. As director of nursing, she is mutually responsible for establishing and maintaining a safe, caring environment for nursing practice and patient care. This involves an assessment of the internal and external environment. Internal factors include patient type and care needs, nursing staffing, skills and knowledge, research and education activities, available resources and care outcomes. External factors include legislation and regulations, public and health policy, community needs and expectations, economic climate and technology.
>
> Noreen also needs to be able to forecast trends, participate in strategic planning and interpret the role of nursing to other disciplines. She then develops and implements policies and programmes based on available resources that support nursing practice and the mission of the organisation. These policies and procedures address not only patient care issues but also the development of education and research programmes. She also is responsible for evaluating nursing policies, programmes and services for effectiveness and consistency with the organisation's mission, goals and objectives. Another important role is the mentoring and career development of other nurse managers. Through acting as a role model, meetings and education, Noreen provides examples of leadership and professionalism.

Leadership in the National Health Service

Styles and approaches to leadership in the NHS have evolved as the service has changed. Prior to the health reforms of the 1990s, emphasis was placed on managing and controlling the service and bureaucratic styles of leadership were common. With the new emphasis on collaborative working between professionals, partnership between organisations and patient involvement, leaders and managers have had to develop skills in participative management and team working. Business skills are also needed to ensure that the trust competes for and wins contracts for services and then delivers the quality and service to ensure a positive patient experience.

Because of this complex range of leadership challenges emerging, the NHS Leadership Centre undertook research to define the personal characteristics skills and behaviours needed for successful leadership in the NHS and published these as the *NHS leadership qualities framework* (Figure 2.5) (NHS Institute of Innovation and Improvement, 2006). The framework was developed from observations and interviews of successful leaders in chief executive and director roles. Since the original research, the framework has been further validated for use with people in other leadership roles throughout the NHS. There are 15 qualities within the framework, arranged in three clusters: personal qualities, setting direction and delivering the service.

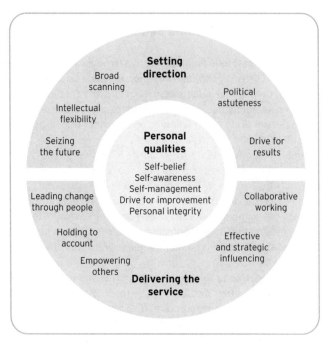

Figure 2.5 The NHS Leadership Qualities Framework.

Source: NHS Leadership Qualities Framework, 2006, Department of Health.
http://www.nhsleadershipqualities.nhs.uk/portals/0/the-framework.pdf.

The framework may be a useful tool for nurses in the NHS to reflect on their personal qualities and to develop skills for successful leadership.

What you know now

- Management and leadership are complementary activities; both are needed for successful goal achievement in complex health care organisations.
- Management is about accomplishing the goals of the organisation through managing complexity so as to consistently ensure high standards, good practice and efficiency.
- Leadership is the intention to set direction, align efforts and motivate people to achieve results, which might involve managing change.
- Management and leadership approaches are not static; they can be adapted for different situations, tasks, individuals and future expectations.
- Management and leadership theories are plentiful. Each theory is an attempt to enhance our understanding of these complex undertakings, and to help guide our actions for success.
- Formal management roles always have an element of leadership in them. Effective leadership and management are needed at all levels of the organisation.
- There are many opportunities to exercise leadership in nursing.

> ## Questions to challenge you
>
> 1. Think about people you know in management positions. Are any of them leaders as well? Describe the characteristics that make them leaders.
>
> 2. Think about people you know who are not in management positions but are leaders nonetheless. What characteristics do they have that make them leaders?
>
> 3. Think about the manager to whom you report. (If you are not employed, use the first-level manager on a clinical placement site.) How would you describe this person using the behavioural leadership styles (autocratic, democratic, laissez-faire or bureaucratic)? Where are they on the continuum suggested by Crail? What impact does this have on you and the rest of the team?
>
> 4. Think about yourself as a manager, whether you are in a management position or not. What skills do you possess that help you? What skills would you like to improve?
>
> 5. Evaluate yourself as a leader using the NHS Leadership Qualities Framework. Which of the personal qualities are your strengths? Which other qualities and skills do you have? Which might you need to develop?

References

Alimo-Metcalfe, B. (2008) Cast in a new light. *People Management Magazine Online*, 24 January, 38.

Alimo-Metcalfe, B., Alban-Metcalfe, J., Samele, C., Bradley, M. and Mariathasan, J. (2007) *The Impact of Leadership Factors in Implementing Change in Complex Health and Social Care Environments: NHS plan clinical priorities for mental health crisis resolution teams*. London: Department of Health NHS NIHR SDO, Project 22/2002.

Antrobus, S. and Kitson, A. (1999) Nursing leadership: influencing and shaping health policy and nursing practice. *Journal of Advanced Nursing*, **29**(3), 746-753.

Crail, M. (2001) *Leadership in the NHS*. London: Emap Public Sector Management.

Department of Health (DoH) (2008a) *High Quality Care for all*: NHS next stage review final *Report*. London: Department of Health.

Department of Health (DoH) (2008b) *A High Quality Workforce: NHS next stage review*. London: Department of Health.

Drucker, P. and Stone, N. (1998) *Peter Drucker on the Profession of Management*. Boston, MA: Harvard Business School Publishing.

Fayol, H. (1916) Administration industrielle et générale. *Bulletin de la Société de Industrie Minerale*, **10**, 5-16.

Fiedler, F. E. (1967) *A Theory of Leadership Effectiveness*. New York: McGraw-Hill.

Greenleaf, R. K. (1991) *The Servant as Leader*. Westfield, IN: The Robert K. Greenleaf Center.

Hersey, P., Blanchard, K. H. and Johnson, D. E. (2001) *Management of Organisational Behaviour*. Escondido, CA: Centre for Leadership Studies, 189, 196.

Jenkins, R. L. and Henderson, R. L. (1984) Motivating the staff: what nurses expect from their supervisors. *Nursing Management*, **15**(2), 13-14.

Kotter, J. P. (1990) What leaders really do. *Harvard Business Review*, **79**(11), 85–98.

Lewin, K., Lippitt, R. and White, R. K. (1939) Patterns of aggressive behaviour in experimentally created social climates. *Journal of Social Psychology*, **10**, 271–301.

NHS Institute of Innovation and Improvement (2006) *NHS Leadership Qualities Framework*. Available at http://www.nhsleadershipqualities.nhs.uk.

Porter-O'Grady, T. and Malloch, K. (2002) *Quantum Leadership: A textbook of new leadership*. Gaithersburg, MD: Aspen.

Taylor, F. W. (1911) *Principles of Scientific Management*. New York and London: Harper and Brothers.

Timmereck, T. C. (2000) Use of the classical functions of management by health services midmanagers. *Health Care Manager*, **19**(2), 50–67.

Ward, K. (2002) A vision for tomorrow: transformational nursing leaders. *Nursing Outlook*, **50**(3), 121–126.

Weber, M. (1905) *The Protestant Ethic and the Spirit of Capitalism: And other writings*. New York: Penguin Group.

Chapter 3
How Organisations Shape Leadership and Management

Introduction

Understanding the health care system, a crucial element of effective management and leadership, begins with understanding how the structure, culture and function of organisations shape the behaviour of those who work within them. Organisational theory helps us to understand how hospitals, primary care trusts, mental health trusts, health authorities and other health care organisations have changed in an effort to deliver high-quality health care.

Within our society there are numerous organisations, schools, businesses and community groups, to name only a few. An **organisation** is a collection of people working together under a defined structure to achieve predetermined outcomes using financial, human and material resources. Organisations coordinate the efforts of individuals, allowing them to gather more information, develop knowledge, purchase supplies, equipment and technology and produce more goods, services, opportunities and security than individual efforts alone.

Imagine

The organisation you work in has announced plans to change how it is structured in order to become more efficient whilst improving the quality and diversity of services provided. You are wondering what that will mean for you and the team you work with, and how the change will affect patient care. What will you need to understand to prepare them for the future, and to ensure that the quality of care remains high?

Organisational theories and models

The earliest recorded example of organisational thinking comes from the ancient Sumerian civilisation, around 5000 BC. The early Egyptians, Babylonians, Greeks and Romans also gave thought to how groups were organised. Later, Machiavelli in the 1500s and Adam Smith in 1776 established the management principles we know as specialisation and division of labour (Cannon, 1925). Nevertheless, organisational theory remained largely unexplored until the Industrial Revolution. During the late 1800s and early 1900s, a number of approaches to the structure and management of organisations developed. These approaches, or schools of thought, are traditionally labelled classical theory, human relations theory, systems theory, contingency theory and chaos theory.

Classical theory

The classical approach to organisations focuses almost exclusively on the formal structure of the organisation and is closely aligned with **scientific management** (see Chapter 2), which believes that standard methods should be used for each job, and that variation should be eliminated. The main premise is efficiency through design. People are seen as operating most productively within a rational and well-defined organisational structure that spells out each person's tasks and defines the relationship between employees. Therefore, one designs an organisation by specifying tasks to be done, dividing up those tasks and only then fitting people into the plan. Classical theory is built around four main elements: division and specialisation of labour, chain of command, organisational structure, and span of control.

- **Division and specialisation of labour.** Dividing the work reduces the number of tasks that each employee must carry out, and it also reduces the range of tasks to be done. This results in specialisation, wherein only certain employees do certain things. Division of labour and specialisation make sense for a number of reasons. Instead of having to train everyone to do everything, employees can be trained in a small range of tasks and those tasks can be standardised more easily. This provides greater control over work and normally leads to greater consistency of outcomes, and lower costs.

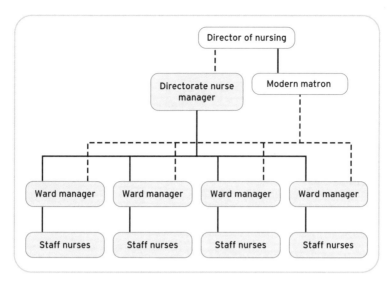

Figure 3.1 Directorate lines of authority.

- **Chain of command.** The chain of command is the hierarchy of authority and responsibility within the organisation. Authority is the right or power to direct activity, whereas responsibility is the obligation to attain objectives or perform certain functions. Both are linked to one's position within the organisation; higher levels of management delegate work to those below them in the organisation.

   One type of authority is line authority, the hierarchy through which activity is directed and which defines who is accountable to whom. Staff authority is an advisory relationship; recommendations and advice are offered, but responsibility for the work is assigned to others. In Figure 3.1, the relationships among the directorate manager, ward managers and staff nurses are shown as line relationships: in other words, the ward manager reports to the directorate manager, and the ward manager has formal authority over the staff nurses. The relationship between the modern matron and the ward manager illustrates staff authority; the modern matron gives advice to the ward manager, who is responsible to the directorate manager for implementing changes on the ward. The modern matron reports to the assistant director of nursing. Neither the modern matron nor the ward manager is responsible for the work of the other; instead, they work together to improve ensure the safe and effective delivery of care on the ward.

- **Organisational structure.** Organisational structure describes the division of labour and the relationship between and among work groups. Classical theorists developed the idea of creating discrete departments as a means to allocate responsibility, reinforce authority and provide a formal system for communication. The design of the organisation is intended to foster the organisation's survival and success.

   Characteristically, the structure takes shape as a set of different but related functions. Max Weber proposed the term **bureaucracy** to define the ideal organisation, which he believed to be a logically structured, rational and efficient form of organisation (Gerth and Mills, 1948). Now the word bureaucracy has a negative connotation, suggesting long waits, inefficiency and red tape.

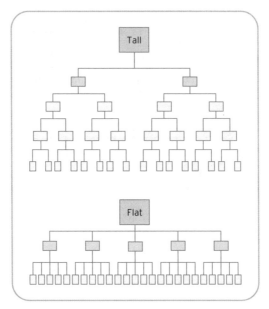

Figure 3.2 Contrasting span of control.

From *Managing Health Services Organizations and Systems*, 4th edn, p. 124, by B. B. Longest, J. S. Rakich and K. Darr, 2000, Baltimore, MD: Health Professions Press, Inc.

- **Span of control.** Span of control is a concept related to how many employees a manager can supervise effectively. Complex organisations differ enormously. Some are structured with numerous small and highly specialised departments and several layers of management, resulting in a tall organisational structure. Other organisations have flat structures, with several managers supervising large work groups. Figure 3.2 depicts the differences.

Human relations theory

Classical organisational theory and particularly scientific management were criticised for focusing too much on structure and not enough on the human element of groups working together. This led to the emergence of human relations theory, which sought to keep the basic structural understanding of organisations and add the ideas that emerged from the human relations movement of the 1930s. Human relations thinkers proposed that organisations would be more productive if staff were encouraged to contribute ideas and participate in decision-making, thereby building cooperation and tapping into the motivation of the individual.

The belief underpinning this theory is that people want personal fulfilment, good social relationships and to be an accepted member of a group. These ideas emerged as a result of a series of studies conducted by Elton Mayo at the Western Electric Company's Hawthorne plant in Chicago. The first study was conducted to examine the effect of lighting on productivity. The study found no relationship between the brightness of the light and productivity. In most groups, productivity varied at random, and in one study productivity actually rose as the lighting levels declined. The researchers concluded that unforeseen 'psychological factors' were responsible for the findings. Further studies of working conditions, such as rest breaks and the length of the working week, still failed to reveal a relationship to productivity. The researchers concluded that the social setting created by the research itself – that is, the special attention given to workers as part of the research – was what enhanced productivity. This tendency for people to perform better because of special attention being paid to them became known as the **Hawthorne effect** (Mayo, 1949).

Although the findings are controversial, they led organisational theorists to focus on the social aspects of work and organisational design. One important contribution of this school of thought was that individuals cannot be coerced or bribed to do things they consider unreasonable: formal authority does not work without willing participants (Barnard, 1938).

Systems theory

Supporters of systems theory believe that productivity results from the interplay between structure, people, technology and the environment. Organisational theory defines a system as a set of interrelated parts arranged in a unified whole (Robbins, 1983). Systems can be closed or open. Closed systems are self-contained and are actually quite rare because they do not interact with the environment. An open system, in contrast, interacts both internally and with its environment.

In organisational systems theory, an organisation is defined as a **complex open system**. According to Katz and Kahn (1978), resources, or input, such as employees, patients, materials, money and equipment, are imported from the environment. Within the organisation, energy and resources are transformed by work (a process called throughput) into a product. The product, or output, is then exported to the environment. An organisation, then, is a recurrent cycle of input, throughput and output. Every health care organisation, a hospital, outpatient clinic, primary care trust or strategic health authority, requires human, financial and material resources (inputs). Each organisation also provides a variety of services (throughput) to treat illness, restore function, provide rehabilitation and protect or promote wellness. The result (output) is better physical, mental and emotional health and well-being.

In organisational systems model, the manager is the catalyst for the input-throughput-output process and also the interface with the environment. Managers are responsible for integrating information and resources from the environment and for coordinating and facilitating the work of the organisation. Figure 3.3 depicts a systems model of a health care organisation.

Other systems theorists include March and Simon (1958), who viewed an organisation as an information-processing network with many decision points for both individual members and the organisation. Galbraith (1977) saw the organisation as a large communication system. He proposed a number of strategies for increasing capacity and decreasing uncertainty within the system. Though systems theorists have provided great insight into important organisational and human variables, systems theory does not recognise the vast complexity of organisations or the interactive effects of many variables.

Contingency theory

Contingency theorists believe that organisational performance can be enhanced by matching an organisation's structure to its environment. This system implies that as the environment or its constituents change, the organisation needs to react in order to retain its role in the grand scheme of things. The **organisational environment** is defined as the people, objects and ideas outside the organisation that influence the organisation. The environment of a health care organisation includes patients and the public; the government through health policy; regulators

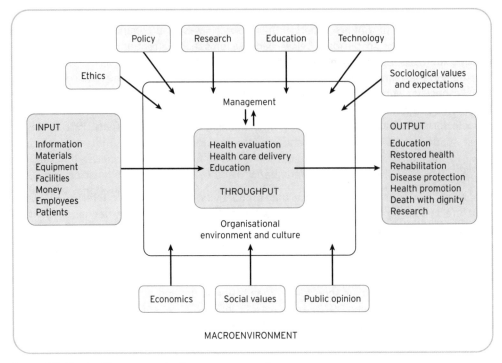

Figure 3.3 The health care organisation as an open system.

such as the Care Quality Commission; voluntary and community organisations; and suppliers of people (such as schools of nursing and medicine), equipment, drugs and supplies.

Health care organisations are shaped by external and internal forces. These forces emerge from economic and social factors, the technologies used in patient care, organisational size and the abilities and limitations of the people involved in the delivery of health care, including nurses, doctors, allied health professionals, support staff, managers and of course, patients and informal carers.

Given the variety of health care services and patients served today, it should come as no surprise that organisations differ with respect to the communities they serve, the levels of training and skills of their caregivers, and the emotional and physical needs of patients. It is naive to think that the form of organisation best for one type of patient in one type of environment is appropriate for another type of patient in a completely different environment. We would not expect to see the same staffing, rules, procedures or chain of command in a university teaching hospital as in a district general hospital. Thus, the optimal form of the organisation is contingent on the circumstances faced by that organisation.

Chaos theory

Chaos theory, which was inspired by the discovery of quantum mechanics, challenges us to look at organisations and the nature of relationships and proposes that the natural world does not follow a straight line. The elements of nature often move in fluid ways, ebbing and flowing differently each time. Natural systems such as meadows or ponds are good examples of chaos theory. A stream destined for the ocean, for example, never takes a straight path. In fact, very little in life operates as a straight line; people's relationships to each other and to their work certainly do not. This notion challenges traditional thinking regarding the design of organisations. Organisations are living, self-organising systems that are complex and self-adaptive.

The life cycle of an organisation is fully dependent on its adaptability and response to changes in its environment. The tendency is for the organisation to grow. When it becomes a large entity, it tends to stabilise and develop more formal standards, policies and procedures. From that point, however, the organisation tends to lose its adaptability and responsiveness to its environment. Its new challenge is to remain flexible and redesign the structure and culture that support the evolving nature and expectations for patient care. The set of rules that guided the industrial notions of organisations are no longer effective: newer principles that ensure flexibility, fluidity, speed of adaptability and cultural sensitivity must emerge. Chaos theory therefore suggests that the drive to create permanent organisational structures is doomed to fail.

The role of leadership in these changing organisations (often called quantum leadership) is to build resilience in the midst of change; to maintain the balance between tension and order that promotes creativity and prevents instability. In practice, this means that we must be open to creative and flexible ways within organisations that can be quickly adjusted and changed as the organisation's realities shift.

Complexity theory

Complexity theory originated when scientists noted that random events interfered with the expected outcomes of computer experiments. Linear cause and effect could no longer explain some outcomes. They realised it was more difficult to solve a problem than to check if the solution was correct: that is, it was easier to work backward than forward. The more complex the task, the less likely there was to be one clear solution (Goldreich, 2005).

This theory is useful in health care because there are no end of random events and complexity. Patients' conditions can change in an instant; equipment fails, staff are unavailable, or urgent admissions disrupt the planned care. Tasks involve intricate interactions between and among staff, patients and the environment. Managing in those situations requires considering every aspect of the system as it interacts and adapts to change.

Hierarchy is not particularly important in complexity theory. Every encounter between a patient and a carer offers information for a possible solution to problems (Bleich and Kosiak, 2007). Encouraging the flow of information between and among all members of the team, leaders and staff, whether top-down, bottom-up or sideways, is the leader's task. All theories that consider an organisation as a total system, including contingency, chaos and complexity theory, value individual contribution to the organisation.

Effective modern organisations

Effective modern organisations are adaptations of design, structure and function that best fit their purpose and goals. Organisations will continue to evolve to remain most effective. Together with organisational change, there will also continue to be evolution of roles and responsibilities.

Organisational structure

Mintzberg (1989) described five classic organisational structures: simple, machine bureaucracy, professional bureaucracy, divisional form and adhocracy. The differences between these structures are in the relationship between:

- executive management (called the strategic apex by Mintzberg);
- the individuals responsible for doing the work (Mintzberg's operating core);
- the managers;
- the individuals who help standardise and improve the work (such as the clinical governance team, audit department, finance, and training and development, called the technostructure);
- the support staff, individuals supporting others who provide the basic work, such as maintenance, housekeepers, cleaners and ward secretaries.

Simple

An organisation with a simple structure consists of only a strategic apex and an operating core. Though less common than in the past, an example of this is a single-handed GP practice. The GP is the strategic apex and the practice nurse, office manager and secretary are the operating core.

Machine bureaucracy

The machine bureaucracy is an example of the ideal bureaucracy that Weber found so attractive. Typically, these are tall, multilayered organisations with centralised decision-making and separate specialised departments. Central government organisations such as the Department of Health are machine bureaucracies, though there has been an effort to decentralise decision-making in recent years.

Professional bureaucracy

In the professional bureaucracy, the distinguishing feature is that the operating core consists of groups of professionals. Schools, hospitals, social services and some specialised businesses such as law firms or engineering companies are good examples of this type of structure. Unlike machine bureaucracies, in professional bureaucracies most decisions are made by professionals, and the executive team's authority to make decisions is limited. In hospitals, for example, individual clinicians make treatment decisions, not the medical director. The medical director makes decisions that affect the organisation as a whole with the intention of creating the circumstances in which professionals can exercise professional judgement in the patients' best interests.

Divisional

The divisional form of organisation is one where a number of independent work units are under a single overarching executive team. In these organisations, most decision-making is decentralised to the divisions. A primary care trust would be a good example of this structure, where there are a number of GP practices, a range of community services and a commissioning arm all under the same executive team. Many foundation trusts are adopting a form of divisional structure, calling their various parts clinical business units, directorates or simply divisions. These sections of the organisation are responsible for running the services in their division, within budget, and also developing new services. Support to the divisions is often provided by centralised services such as finance, human resources and the executive.

Adhocracy

Adhocracy represents a fluid structure in which management, staff and professionals work together on teams. Power, coordination and control are constantly shifting. A good example of this type of structure in the NHS would be an interprofessional or multiprofessional team put together to develop a care pathway for a specific patient group. The professionals would provide the information on clinical care needs whilst the managers would offer financial and systems support to the pathway design. Another example of an organisation that may take this form is a volunteer organisation such as a community support group for people with cancer, where family members meet to discuss their concerns and give support to each other. Group members share the work of the group by providing a venue for meeting, shopping or cooking for each other, or simply providing emotional support.

Working arrangements within structures

Authority in organisations can be centralised or decentralised, or more typically a mixture of both. **Centralised authority** means that decisions are taken 'up the line' to be made and then passed back down the line. **Decentralised authority** is when decisions are made by the individuals involved, at the bedside rather than in the board room. Clinical decisions are usually made in a decentralised way, meaning that nurses, doctors and other registered professionals, along with the patient and carers, decide the best treatment for the patient without consulting 'up the line'. Other decisions such as purchasing supplies and equipment, building maintenance and contracting with outside agencies are usually made centrally because they affect everyone and have significant cost implications. Whilst there is an argument that individual ward managers should be able to decide how many nurses are needed to deliver safe care, in reality, staffing is the single most expensive factor in care and must be considered as a part of the overall budget. Individual ward managers can often take decisions within a staffing establishment whereas changing the establishment as a whole is usually a centralised decision.

Functional working arrangements

In functional working arrangements (Figure 3.4), employees are grouped in departments by discipline, with similar tasks being performed by the same group, similar groups operating out of the same department and similar departments reporting to the same manager. This structure was widely used prior to the recent reforms in health care. Nursing departments stood separate from physiotherapy, occupational therapy, laboratory, estates and others, each department had a lead and each department managed the budget for its staff. This arrangement was popular with professional groups in that it supported professional autonomy and authority over standards of practice.

Unfortunately, functional working arrangements have several weaknesses. Coordination across functions is poor. Decision-making responsibilities can pile up at the top and overload senior managers, who may be uninformed regarding day-to-day operations. Responses to the external environment that require coordination across functions are slow. This makes functional

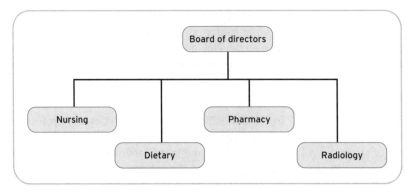

Figure 3.4 A functional structure.

structures particularly unsuited to modern models of care. Pathway commissioning and long-term condition management in the community need an integrated approach across disciplines and a common set of goals.

Functional working is sometimes still seen in the NHS, particularly where patients may be under the care of only one service. For example, well families with young children in the community may be under the care of the health visitor. An older person with Alzheimer's disease and depression at home with a carer may be under the exclusive care of a community mental health nurse.

Service-line working arrangements

In service-line working, all functions needed to produce a service are grouped together in self-contained units (Figure 3.5). The service-line structure is decentralised; units are based on service, geographical location or type of patient. Most acute services are now modelled in this way. Hospitals have directorates or divisions specially designated for certain services. For example, the musculoskeletal service includes consultants, nurses, physiotherapists, occupational therapists, podiatry, prosthetics and others working together to provide assessment, diagnosis and treatment of a wide range of conditions involving bones and muscles.

Community services are also beginning to develop this structure. Traditionally community services consisted of health visiting, school nursing, district nursing, general practice, midwifery and other functional units. There is now a movement to create community teams based on patient need such as diabetes teams, asthma services and sexual health teams.

One of the strengths of the service-line structure is its potential for rapid change in an unstable environment. Because each directorate or community team is specialised, its services can be tailored to the situation. For example, a patient who is referred for hip replacement may initially be seen by a physiotherapist, who will instruct the patient about strengthening and pain control prior to surgery. When non-surgical treatment becomes ineffective, the patient will be evaluated for surgery and the joint replacement done. Follow-up after surgery can be coordinated by the same team that saw the patient before surgery, who, because they are now familiar with the social and home conditions of the patient, are in a good place to set up community support at home.

Coordination across function occurs more easily in directorate or team models; work partners can collaborate with other disciplines to meet service goals and deliver a good care experience. Service goals such as meeting waiting time targets or treatment times are more easily

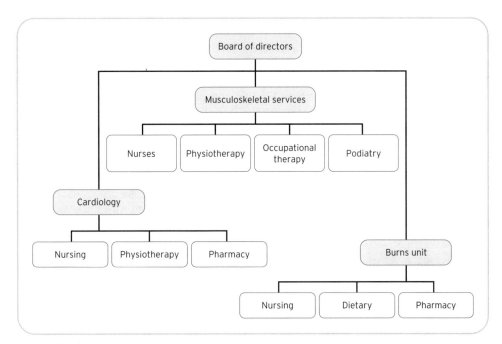

Figure 3.5 A service-line structure.

achieved in this structure because staff see themselves as having more control over and commitment to their own success.

The major weaknesses of service-integrated structures include possible duplication of resources (having to have a physiotherapy assessment area in more than one place) and lack of in-depth technical training and specialisation. Coordination across directorates (oncology, cardiology and the burns unit, for example) is difficult; services operate independently and can end up in competition with each other. Each directorate, which is independent and autonomous, has separate and often duplicate staff and competes with other service areas for resources.

With a directorate structure, nursing as a distinct department will not usually feature. Instead, nursing becomes a part of each directorate and will have line accountability to a directorate manager. Nurses in the directorates will have a professional (staff authority) relationship to the director of nursing, but he or she will not directly manage nurses. This presents a challenge to nursing directors and managers to maintain nursing standards across service lines (Fitzpatrick, McElroy and DeWoody, 2001).

The optimal organisational structure is one that best achieves its outcomes by choosing a structure and working arrangements that take into consideration its size, technology and the social, cultural and political environment in which it operates. When an organisation is poorly structured, the organisation's response to environmental change diminishes; decisions are delayed, overlooked or poor; conflict results; and performance deteriorates (Porter-O'Grady, 1994).

Organisational structure is an important tool through which managers can increase organisational efficiency. Reorganisation occurs when performance needs to improve and when the current structure is seen as unsuited to success in the future.

Organisational culture

The environment within an organisation can be defined in terms of its culture; that is, the norms and traditions maintained or, in layperson's terms, 'The way we do things around here'. **Organisational culture** affects the way things are done in the organisation and is often different from the formal policies and communication channels outlined. Organisational culture varies from one institution to the next and subcultures and even countercultures, groups whose values and goals differ significantly from those of the dominant organisation, may exist. A subculture is a group that has shared experiences or similar interests and values – nurses form a subculture within health care environments. They share a common language, rules, rituals and dress. Individual units also can become subcultures. Besides organisational cultures differing between institutions, culture may differ between the organisation and its subculture. If the subculture's norms and traditions are in agreement with the organisation, then things work well; if not, dissonance occurs.

Cooke and Lafferty (1989) have identified three types of culture:

- Constructive or positive, where the focus is on self-actualisation, humanism, affiliation and achievement

- Passive or submissive, where the focus is on approval, dependence, convention and avoidance

- Aggressive or defensive, where the focus is on competition, perfectionism, power and opposition.

The presence of a constructive culture promotes staff retention and decreases patient mortality (Aiken *et al.*, 2002). The Confidence in Caring project undertaken by the Chief Nursing Officer (DoH, 2008a) also indicated that culture plays a role in the experience of care. A positive culture enhances the confidence of patients in the care they receive and the confidence of nurses in the care they give.

Evaluating an organisation's culture is essential when reorganisation is undertaken. Ignoring issues of organisational culture can result in a negative culture developing or, in the case of a merger, one organisation's culture will dominate and the other will become suppressed (McConnell, 2000). Unintended consequences may result, including poor morale and, ultimately, loss of staff.

Organisational functions

Organisations achieve their goals through management and leadership activities. The following activities are common to all successful organisations.

Strategic and service planning

Successful organisations have learned that they must focus their energies, resources and actions. **Strategic planning** involves projecting the organisation's goals and activities into the future, usually two to five years ahead, and is chiefly an activity undertaken at board level. Effective strategic planning involves consideration of the goals and targets set by the Department of Health, the nature of the contract with the PCT, the financial performance of the trust, the existing service use and projected use, the historical performance of a service and the changes to population need anticipated. Strategic planning is an ongoing process, not an end in itself. It requires a continual focus on the goal and meticulous attention to progress; the organisation's mission and vision must always guide activities.

Service planning

This is the operational plan for the delivery of a service and this feeds into the strategic plan of the organisation as a whole. Each service is expected to project the demand on the service into the future and to identify the resources that it will take to meet that plan. The strategic plan of the organisation seeks to reconcile **service planning** between areas and make adjustments where necessary.

A number of factors feature in the process of service and strategic planning.

Values

Values are the beliefs or attitudes one has about people, ideas, objects or actions that form a basis for behaviour. NHS organisations are expected to adhere to the values and principles of the NHS and to align their services with the values of the community. Many organisations translate the core values of the health service into their own words, making the values more easily understood for those who work there.

Vision

A **vision statement** describes the overarching goal to which the organisation aspires. The vision statement is designed to inspire and motivate employees to achieve a desired state of affairs. At its best, a vision statement is succinct, engaging and simple, conveying a message with interest. Not all NHS organisations have developed vision statements, and those that have sometimes focus these in a more operational way. 'Excellence through Partnership' is the summary of the vision statement for Gloucestershire Hospitals NHS Foundation Trust, which goes on to state that it will achieve the vision through excellent services, inclusive governance and being an employer of choice.

Mission

The **mission** of an organisation is a broad, general statement of the organisation's remit. The mission statement defines the areas of health care service offered and by exception those that are not offered. For example some mental health trusts offer services for learning disabilities whereas others do not. Clarifying the mission of the organisation is the necessary first step to designing a strategic plan. 'To provide a range of high-quality health care services in our hospitals clinics and at home to meet the needs of our local population and others who wish to make use of our services' is the mission statement of South Tyneside NHS Foundation Trust, for example. The mission statement guides decision-making for the organisation. South Tyneside's mission statement clearly identifies that its services are available to others outside its local population, and therefore its strategic plan is likely to include actions to attract patients from outside its area.

Goals

Goals are specific statements of what is to be achieved. They follow the mission and vision of the organisation. Goals are measurable and precise. 'Hospital-acquired infections will be managed effectively' is an example of a goal. Goals apply to the entire organisation and are statements of outcome to which the organisation aspires. **Objectives** are statements of outcome. An objective may be 'MRSA will be eradicated from Ward 5'. **Strategies** follow objectives and specify what actions will be taken. 'Alcohol solution will be available for use in all wards by visitors' is an example of a strategy to meet the hospital-acquired infection objective.

Types of health care organisation in the UK

Most health service organisations in the UK fall into one of three broad designations: strategic, provider or commissioning organisations. A **provider organisation** is one that provides services to the public, including hospitals, mental health facilities, community clinics, school nursing and health visiting.

A **commissioning organisation** is one that purchases services on behalf of the public. Primary care trusts are commissioning organisations. They receive an allocation from the Treasury with which they purchase health services for their community. Effective commissioning requires an ability to assess and predict the needs for health services accurately as well as contracting for services in such a way as to shape the quality and supply of services for the future.

Strategic organisations are those that provide guidance, oversight and advice to provider organisations and professionals. A number of these are designated as special health authorities, which means that they are independent agencies that report to the Department of Health and are therefore accountable to parliament. Special health authorities include among many the Health Protection Agency (setting standards for patient safety), the National Institute for Health and Clinical Excellence (reviews and approves and advocates the use or non-use of drugs and treatments), NHS Direct (telephone advice and support to the public) and the Mental Health Act Commission (protecting mentally ill people).

A number of strategic organisations are not associated with the Department of Health; they are independent non-departmental public bodies with a role within the process of national government. These include the Human Fertilisation and Embryology Authority (responsible for overseeing assisted conception), the Commission for Patient and Public Involvement in Health, the Care Quality Commission (the inspection agency for all organisations providing health care, including private, NHS and voluntary organisations) and Monitor (the inspection and regulatory body for foundation trusts).

Devolved government

Prior to the devolution of some aspects of government to Scotland, Wales and Northern Ireland in the 1990s, the responsibility for setting health policy and overseeing the NHS was done for the whole of the UK by the Department of Health offices in London. Now, Scotland, Wales and Northern Ireland determine their own health policies and priorities separate to England.

The NHS in Scotland

The Scottish government determines national objectives for health services and offers guarantees on behalf of patients. The Scottish Government Health Directorate is the equivalent body to the Department of Health in England and fulfils the health promotion and protection functions through agencies such as NHS Health Scotland and NHS 24, the telephone assistance service. It also provides a clear statutory and financial framework for NHS Scotland and holds it to account for its performance. The Chief Executive of NHS Scotland leads the central management of the NHS, is accountable to ministers for the efficiency and performance of the service, and heads the Health Department, which oversees the work of the 14 NHS boards responsible for planning health services for people in their area. These boards provide strategic leadership and performance management for the entire local NHS system in their areas and ensure that services are delivered effectively and efficiently. NHS boards are responsible for the provision and management of the whole range of health services in an area including hospitals and general practice.

In addition Scotland has a further eight special boards, which are the equivalent of special health authorities in England and perform functions such as quality monitoring, communicable disease monitoring and ambulance services (NHS Scotland, 2008).

The NHS in Northern Ireland

The Department of Health, Social Services and Public Safety is one of 11 Northern Ireland departments created in 1999 as part of the Northern Ireland Executive by the Northern Ireland Act 1998. The Department's mission is to improve the health and social well-being of the people of Northern Ireland. It endeavours to do so by ensuring the provision of appropriate health and social care services, both in clinical settings such as hospitals and GPs' surgeries, and in the community through nursing, social work and other professional services. It also leads a major programme of cross-government action to improve the health and well-being of the population and reduce health inequalities. This includes interventions involving health promotion and education to encourage people to adopt activities, behaviours and attitudes which lead to better health and well-being. The aim is a population which is much more engaged in ensuring its own health and well-being (Northern Ireland Department of Health, Social Services and Public Safety, 2008).

The Department has three main responsibilities: health and social care, which includes policy and legislation for hospitals, family practitioner services and community health and personal social services; public health, which covers policy, legislation and administrative action to promote and protect the health and well-being of the population; and public safety, which covers policy and legislation for fire and rescue services. There are currently four area boards in Northern Ireland. They are responsible for assessing the needs of their respective populations and commissioning services to meet those needs. They are charged with the establishment of key objectives to meet the health and social needs of their population and the development of policies and priorities to meet those objectives (Northern Ireland Department of Health, Social Services and Public Safety, 2008).

The NHS in Wales

The Government of Wales Act of 1998 gave powers over a number of areas, including education, agriculture, social services, local government and health and health services to the National Assembly for Wales. The Minister for Health and Social Services is the person within the Welsh Assembly Government who holds cabinet responsibilities for both health and social care. The health and social services committee, which is composed of assembly members from all of the political parties, contributes to the development and scrutiny of health and social care policy. Civil servants, including those with professional backgrounds, provide support to the minister and the government in formulating and implementing health and social care policy (NHS Wales, 2008).

The Health and Social Care Department supports politicians across the areas of health and social care, reflecting emphasis on partnership working at all levels. The Health and Social Care Department has responsibility for children and families' policy; older people and long-term care policy; community, primary care and health services policy; performance and operations; and quality standards and safety improvement. Other areas of responsibility include research and development, finance, information management and technology, human resources and capital and estates (NHS Wales, 2008).

Three regional offices act as agent of the chief executive NHS Wales on a day-to-day basis by holding to account the chief executives of the 36 statutory NHS bodies in Wales and managing their performance in line with the Performance Improvement Framework. The Specialised Health Services Commissioning Agency is an 'arm's length' organisation. It provides advice on specialised secondary and regional services commissioning; provides dedicated guidance and support more generally in relation to acute services commissioning; and is the first source of independent advice and guidance on commissioning issues that require determination (NHS Wales, 2008).

The NHS in England

The Department of Health

The Department of Health (DoH) is a department of state responsible for improving standards in public health and for leading and driving forward changes in the NHS and social care. It is accountable to the public and the government through the Secretary of State for Health and the health ministers appointed by the government. The DoH is responsible for implementing health policy set by the government and overseeing the overall function of the NHS. Its objectives include improving the capability, capacity and efficiency of health and social care systems, and ensuring that reforms create value for money and higher-quality service to the public. The Department of Health accomplishes its objectives through strategic agencies such as special health authorities, nondepartmental public bodies and strategic health authorities (DoH, 2008b).

Whilst many of the activities of the Department of Health focus on the NHS, its overarching responsibility is for health protection and health improvement. Health protection includes policies and plans for the prevention and control of infectious diseases and other environmental threats to the population. This responsibility is historic, and arose from the challenges of diseases arising from poor housing, sewage and sanitation in centuries past. Immunisation programmes are in place for polio, measles, mumps, rubella, hepatitis, meningitis and diphtheria (DoH, 2008c). As vaccines become available in the future for human immunodeficiency virus (HIV) or other threats, it is expected that the Department of Health will include this protection in its plans.

The Department of Health's responsibility for health protection also includes planning for threats such as seasonal flu and the more worrying pandemic influenza. The UK and the rest of the world experience seasonal influenza caused by a common strain of the H1N1 virus, which can cause deaths, particularly among elderly people and people with underlying health problems, for whom there is an annual immunisation programme. Of greater concern is an outbreak of new strains of influenza, for which people have little resistance and that cause sickness and sometimes death on a wide scale; this is called a pandemic. The classic cited example is the Spanish flu outbreak of 1918 in which many millions of people died worldwide. More recent examples of pandemic influenza threats include the avian influenza (bird flu H5H1) outbreak in 1998, which caused deaths among people in close contact with infected birds, mainly in Asia. In 2009 there was a swine flu pandemic resulting from a novel strain of the common flu virus (H1N1) that originated in Mexico and the southern USA. As the virus spread into the UK, the Department of Health activated a pandemic response plan involving a network of national information centres, antiviral medication distribution and targeted immunisation. The Department of Health also works with other agencies such as the Department of Food and Rural Affairs to identify potential threats to people that can result from infections in animals or contamination of food sources. The culling of sheep in response to outbreaks of foot and mouth disease and the slaughter of birds infected with bird flu are recent examples of interagency cooperation for public health protection.

Not all actions under the health protection responsibility are to do with communicable diseases. The nationwide ban on smoking in enclosed public places is a measure undertaken to protect workers and members of the public from the dangers of cigarette smoke. Protection from other health hazards such as electromagnetic fields and radiation also falls into this category.

Health improvement is also a responsibility of the Department of Health. The current focus for health improvement is based on the trends in health and disease that are being identified each year. Obesity, alcohol misuse, smoking, healthy eating and sexual health are of increasing concern, as these lifestyle choices also lead to an increase in serious illness (e.g. cancer, heart disease) and long-term conditions (e.g. diabetes, arthritis, respiratory problems). The NHS, which has historically been focused on treating illness, is now expected to take an active role in health improvement (DoH, 2008d).

Strategic health authorities

Strategic health authorities (SHAs) are extensions of the Department of Health working in eight areas around the country to ensure the delivery of the Department of Health priorities throughout the country. Strategic health authorities have three main functions: strategic leadership, developing organisations and the workforce, and ensuring that local health systems operate effectively and deliver improved performance. Primary care trusts are accountable to the SHA, particularly in respect of their commissioning role.

How services are commissioned will affect the function of provider organisations and will shape the supply and quality of services in the local area. SHAs are also responsible for workforce planning and development, that is, ensuring there are sufficient trained professionals to meet the needs of the service. Finally, SHAs are responsible for assessing and performance managing the primary care trusts to ensure financial probity and best value for money for services purchased. The government has set ever-more ambitious targets for access, service and financial prudence in response to the expectations of the public, and it is the SHAs' responsibility to hold the PCTs to these ever increasing standards (DoH, 2008b).

Trusts

Almost all health provider organisations are now trusts, including primary care trusts, mental health trusts and acute hospital trusts. Prior to the establishment of health trusts in the 1990s, hospitals and community providers were funded from the Department of Health through a series of regional departments. In this centralised system, the individual hospital or community service was not financially accountable and the increasing complexity of service and rising public expectations made this system unworkable. Trusts enabled local health organisations to have greater control over their services and increased the local accountability for costs.

Trusts are a form of public corporation. In the case of a health or social care trust, the organisation is entrusted with public money collected as part of general taxation. Trust boards have executive and non-executive members. The non-executive members are appointed to the board and are responsible through the chair to the DoH. Their role is advisory, and they are also there to ensure that the interests of the public are protected and that the executive members do their jobs well. Executive members of the board are those hired into specific senior management roles and these managers are accountable through the chief executive to the chair of the board.

Trusts are accountable through SHAs that monitor and regulate their actions. They are given a budget every year based on prior spending and projected changes to service. The trust is then accountable for meeting the budget set out, and for ensuring that quality of service is also achieved (DoH, 2008b).

Because trusts are given their budget allocation yearly, it is very hard for them to plan services for the future. It is also very difficult for the trust to meet its budget every year as there is a need in some years to invest in order to save in future years. Health trusts are also forbidden from raising funds outside of the budget allocated from the Department of Health, making any cost overruns due to increasing demand impossible to recover.

Foundation trusts

Foundation trusts are a refinement of health trusts, giving the organisation even more independence and autonomy over the provision of services. The first **foundation trusts** were established in 2004 under the Health and Social Care Act 2003 as legally independent organisations called public benefit corporations. Whilst they are fully part of the NHS, foundation trusts are no longer subject to the direction of the Secretary of State for Health. Instead, foundation trusts are accountable to the local community through a membership arrangement not unlike a cooperative. Membership in the foundation trust entitles an individual to stand and vote to elect representatives to serve on the board of governors. Governors are responsible for representing the interests of the members and partner organisations in the local area. The board of governors works with the board of directors, which is responsible for the day-to-day running of the trust to ensure that the foundation trust acts responsibly and in accordance with its terms of authority. Therefore local people and staff have a bigger say in the management and service provision in their area (DoH, 2008e).

Foundation trusts remain largely funded through general taxation, though they have additional financial freedoms. They can raise capital from public or private sources based on their financial strength. They can also retain financial surpluses from year to year to make investment in improvements and more long-term planning possible.

Foundation trusts are no longer performance managed by SHAs. As free-standing, self-regulating organisations, foundation trusts are free to determine their own future within the core principles of free care, based on need and not ability to pay. Foundation trusts are accountable for quality and service to Monitor, the independent oversight organisation for foundation trusts.

The first organisations to be granted foundation trust status are large acute trusts, typically comprising a collection of hospitals including teaching and district general hospitals. Mental health and learning disability trusts are now eligible to apply for foundation trust status and primary care trusts are also expected to become eligible soon.

Primary care trusts

Primary care trusts (PCTs) have three main functions: engaging with the local population to improve health and well-being, commissioning a comprehensive and equitable range of high-quality, responsive and efficient services within allocated resources, and directly providing high-quality responsive and effective and efficient services (DoH, 2006). PCTs are unique amongst NHS organisations in that they are both a commissioner and a provider organisation. PCTs continue to offer a range of services such as health visiting, district nursing and school services in most areas. The commissioning and provider functions are required to be strictly separate from the board level down, and the providers are responsible to the commissioners. It is likely that the provider functions will eventually separate from the PCT and will become the local health care assessment and commissioning organisation. The services currently provided by the PCT will be offered by existing foundation trusts or newly formed social enterprises. A social enterprise is a smaller version of a public benefit corporation in that it will require membership, effective governance and a financial model that is sustainable and delivers services effectively.

Private, voluntary and social enterprises

Not all health services are now, or will be in the future, delivered by NHS organisations. Most private health care organisations such as BUPA offer health insurance that allows subscribers to access a range of health screening and treatment services. Most people who buy private health insurance do so in an effort to avoid queuing for appointments with a specialist or for treatment such as joint replacement where the NHS has waiting lists. As waiting times and lists decrease in the NHS, it will be interesting to see if the purchase of private health insurance continues as its present level.

Since the end of 2008 the government's promise that nobody will wait longer than 18 weeks for treatment and will have a choice of providers has been in place (DoH, 2004). Those providers that cannot offer appointments within 18 weeks are therefore not being chosen and not receiving funding under the Payment by Results programme. Private hospitals are included on the provider panels for surgery, which means that patients can now choose to go to a private hospital even if they do not have insurance, and the private hospital will not cost them a penny. This has put pressure on NHS trusts to ensure that they have a reputation for compassionate, safe and effective treatment. If all patients choose private hospitals rather than trusts, the money for those services would go elsewhere, making it more difficult for trusts to be successful.

There are also a growing number of voluntary and charitable organisations that provide health care and social support to the public. Hospices and care homes are a good example of charitable organisations that work with vulnerable people in the community. PCTs can commission services from voluntary organisations and it is projected that voluntary and charitable organisations will begin to replace some of the services that NHS organisations now deliver.

Social enterprises are small or medium-sized independent businesses set up to tackle a social or environmental need (Social Enterprise Coalition, 2008). They are not allowed to take profits; any surplus after salaries and expenses are paid must be reinvested in the business. A social enterprise could be set up by a group of community staff who could then vie for contracts to deliver community services. A famous example of a social enterprise is the Eden Project in Cornwall. It was set up by public-spirited entrepreneurs and remains a model of an independent enterprise based on public service. The social enterprise model is an opportunity for nurses and others to take direct control of services, but many nurses have little experience in this kind of business skill and will be reluctant to move into this future.

Future health care organisations

The NHS has changed substantially since its inception and dramatically in the past 10 years. It is projected that things will continue to change as the population needs change and services develop. As more and more trusts attain foundation status, it is reasonable to assume that they will be regulated by Monitor and that the role of the SHA in overseeing trusts will diminish. As PCTs develop skill and experience in commissioning, it is also reasonable to assume that the SHA role in supervising these organisations may change. Therefore, many are predicting the demise of SHAs in their current form, and the emergence of different strategic organisations to replace them. The aim of creating a network of separate, independent providers, shaped by the commissioners to meet the expectations of the public, is getting closer.

The importance of commissioning

The future of the nature and delivery of services, and the role of nurses and other professionals, lies in the hands of the commissioners. In England commissioning (the contracting for services with providers on behalf of the patients and public) is done by PCTs, whilst in Northern Ireland, Wales and Scotland the health boards accomplish this important role. Commissioners have the authority to decide which organisations provide the services they need and can withdraw funding for services that no longer offer best value or meet the standards of safety, timely access or patient satisfaction.

Even more importantly, commissioners are beginning to require providers to work together across diagnostic, acute and community services to provide pathways of care for certain patient groups. A good example of pathway commissioning is in the area of cancer care. Commissioners expect that where cancer is suspected by a GP, the patient will be seen in consultation and have diagnostic tests within two weeks and, where cancer is diagnosed, surgery, chemical or radiotherapy initiated within the shortest time possible. The collaboration of providers that offers the most efficient, timely, safe and effective pathway will be successful in receiving the funding for that service.

The commissioning of care for patients with long-term conditions such as asthma, diabetes or arthritis is also changing. Commissioners are requiring that the care of these patients is closely coordinated between GPs and community services so as to prevent the need for acute admission and to decrease the likelihood of deterioration of the individual's health. This shift presents unprecedented opportunity for nurses in the community to lead care. Nurse specialists in long-term condition management are growing in number and are likely to become even more important members of the health care team in the future.

Social conditions are known to effect health (DoH, 2008d), and a number of health problems are linked to poor social and environmental conditions: mental illness, drug use, teenage pregnancy, obesity and smoking are a few. This explains the recent shift in aligning social services more closely with health services. Commissioners are seeking to encourage community partnerships such as those between the police, the local authority, health and social care specifically to encourage a joint approach to these complex issues. Partnerships that deliver targeted improvements in health will receive the most funding and be most successful in the long run.

In summary, organisations that continue to examine their structures, relationships and jobs, and modify those to meet the challenges of equity, accessibility, quality and responsiveness, are most likely to be successful in the long term. Systems that allow for autonomy of clinical judgement within a clear and supportive framework are the ideal. These organisations are more likely to attract and retain independent, accountable professionals and to meet the expectations of the public in their local community. Success in the future depends not only on sound financial management and planning, but on the sustained commitment and support of the staff and the communities served. As the health care environment continues to evolve, more and more organisations are adopting patient-centred cultures that require accountability and compassion from nurses and others who deliver care.

What you know now

- The schools of organisational theory are classical, human relations, systems, contingency and chaos.
- Organisations can be viewed as social systems consisting of people working in a predetermined pattern of relationships who strive toward a goal. The goal of health care organisations is to provide a particular mix of health services.
- The organisational structure determines the formal communication system and guides organisational activities.
- Organisations develop strategic and service plans based on the values, philosophy and mission of the organisation and the vision of its leaders.
- Organisational culture defines the environment of the organisation.

Questions to challenge you

1. Secure a copy of the organisational chart from your trust or clinical placement. Would you describe the organisation in the same way as the chart depicts it? If not, redraw a chart to illustrate how you see the organisation. What organisational structure would you prefer?

2. Organisational theories explain how organisations function. Which theory or theories describes your organisation's functioning? Do you think it is the same theory the senior managers in the organisation would use to describe it? Explain.

3. Have you been involved in service planning? If so, explain what happened and how well it worked in directing the organisation's activities.

4. What is the culture of your organisation (school or work)? What would you change about the culture? Do generational differences affect its culture?

References

Aiken, L. H., Clarke, S. P., Sloane, D. M., Sochalski, J. and Silber, J. H. (2002) Hospital nurse staffing and patient mortality, nurse burnout, and job dissatisfaction. *Journal of the American Medical Association*, **288**(16), 1987–1993.

Barnard, C. I. (1938) *The Functions of the Executive*. Cambridge, MA: Harvard University Press.

Bleich, M. R., and Kosiak, C. P. (2007) Managing, leading and following. In P. S. Yoder-Wise, *Leading and Managing in Nursing*, 4th edn. St. Louis, MO: Mosby Elsevier.

Cannon, E. (ed.) (1925) *Adam Smith: An inquiry into the nature and causes of the wealth of nations,* 4th edn. London: Methuen. (Original work published 1776.)

Cooke, R. A. and Lattery, J. L. (1989) *Organisational Cultural Inventory*. Plymouth, MI: Human Synergistics.

Department of Health (DoH) (2004) *The NHS Improvement Plan: Putting people at the heart of public services*. London: Department of Health.

Department of Health (DoH) (2006) *PCT and SHA Roles and Functions*. London: Department of Health.

Department of Health (DoH) (2008a) *Confidence in Caring: A framework for best practice*. London: Department of Health.

Department of Health (DoH) (2008b) *How the Department of Health Works*. Available at http://www.dh.gov.uk/en/Aboutus/HowDHworks/index.htm.

Department of Health (DoH) (2008c) *Public Health Map*. Available at http://www.dh.gov.uk/en/Sitemap/Publichealthmap/index.htm.

Department of Health (DoH) (2008d) *High Quality Workforce: NHS next stage review*. London: Department of Health.

Department of Health (DoH) (2008e) *NHS Foundation Trusts*. Available at http://www.dh.gov.uk/en/Healthcare/Secondarycare/NHSfoundationtrust/index.htm.

Fitzpatrick, M. J., McElroy, M. J. and DeWoody, S. (2001). Building a strong nursing organisation in a merged, service-line structure. *Journal of Nursing Administration*, **31**(1), 24–32.

Galbraith, J. R. (1977) *Organisational Design*. Reading, MA: Addison-Wesley.

Gerth, H. and Mills, C. W. (eds) (1948) *From Max Weber: Essays in sociology*. London: Routledge.

Goldreich, O. (2005) *A Brief Overview of Complexity Theory*. Available at http://www.wisdom.weizmann.ac.il.

Katz, D. and Kahn, R. (1978) *The Social Psychology of Organisations*. New York: Wiley.

March, J. G. and Simon, H. (1958) *Organisations*. New York: Wiley.

Mayo, E. (1949) *Hawthorne and the Western Electric Company: The social problems of an industrial civilisation*. London: Routledge and Kegan Paul.

McConnell, C. R. (2000) The manager and the merger: adaptation and survival in the blended organisation. *Health Care Manager*, **19**(1), 1–11.

Mintzberg, H. (1989) *Mintzberg on Management: Inside our strange world of organizations*. New York: Free Press.

NHS Scotland (2008) *The Scottish Government, Health and Community Care*. Available at http://www.scotland.gov.uk/Topics/Health/NHS-Scotland.

NHS Wales (2008) *NHS Wales Health and Social Care Department*. Available at http://www.wales.nhs.uk/sites3/page.cfm?pid=11615&orgid=452.

Northern Ireland Department of Health, Social Services and Public Safety (2008) *About the Department*. Available at http://www.dhsspsni.gov.uk/index/about_dept.htm.

Porter-O'Grady, T. (1994) Re-engineering the nursing profession. *Asper's Advisor for the Nurse Executive*, **9**(7), 7–8.

Robbins, S. P. (1983) *Organizational Theory*. Englewood Cliffs, NJ: Prentice Hall.

Social Enterprise Coalition (2008) *What is Social Enterprise?* Available at http://www.socialenterprise.org.uk/pages/about-social-enterprise.html.

Chapter 4
Understanding Power, Policy and Politics

Key terms

Power
Policy
Reward power
Punishment (coercive) power
Legitimate power
Expert power
Referent power

Information power
Connection power
Position power
Personal power
Power play
Politics

Introduction

The words power and politics (the exercise of power) are often associated with undesirable or unethical actions such as control, corruption and manipulation. The fact is that power itself is neutral; it is simply a source of energy, the potential to influence others to achieve goals. Power is a force for good in many cases. Patients have gained power through access to information formerly available only to health professionals. Information power allows patients to be more involved in their treatment and to make informed choices. Whether we like it or not, understanding and use of power are essential skills for effective leadership.

Policy is a statement of the decisions taken by those with authority. Some people see policy as a restriction of professional autonomy whereas others see that policies guide actions and help people to make decisions. Whichever way we see it, policies are everywhere. Nationally, the government makes health policy that affects the way the health service works and how much funding is allocated. Organisations also have many policies on practically every aspect of our work. It is important to understand how policy can support effective leadership.

Imagine

You have very strong views on a matter of patient care but another member of the team disagrees. How would you go about influencing others to come round to your way of thinking? In other words, what forms of power would you use?

Why power?

Power emerges in every human encounter, whether you choose to acknowledge it or not. Often, the content, meaning and purpose of power use or abuse are misunderstood or ignored. **Power** is the potential ability to influence (Hersey, Blanchard and Johnson, 2001) or the potential to achieve goals.

It is also important to understand why power is used. The most common reasons are to gain a competitive advantage, acquire information, motivate, communicate, improve performance and improve processes. By developing a power base, you gain the potential for maximum influence. The willingness to use power increases a nurse's ability to acquire the resources needed to improve patient care.

Regardless of when, why and where care takes place, power centres around an individual's ability to influence others or the behaviour of others. To acquire power, maintain it effectively and use it skilfully, nurses must be aware of the sources and types of power that they will use to influence and transform patient care.

Power and leadership

Real power - principle-centred power - is based on honour, respect, loyalty and commitment. Principle-centred power is not forced; it is invited (Covey, 1990). It is defined by the capacity to act and to make choices and decisions. How you choose and what you choose is based on deeply held values. If you choose to live up to your own values and potential, you have an infinite amount of power available. By recognising your power and the capacity to use it, you can influence and lead others in promoting and creating changes in health care and in your community.

Leadership power then becomes the capacity to create order from conflict, contradictions and chaos. Leadership power comes from the ability to influence because followers trust and respect the leader to do the right thing for the right reason. As leaders in health care, nurses must understand and select behaviours that activate principle-centred leadership:

- Get to know people. Understanding what other people want is not always simple.
- Be open. Keep others informed. Trust, honour and respect spread just as easily as fear, suspicion and deceit.
- Know your values and visions. The power to define your goals is the power to choose.
- Sharpen your interpersonal competence. Actively listen to others, and learn to express your ideas well.
- Use your power to enable others. Be attentive to the dynamics of power, and give attention to ground rules, such as encouraging dissenting voices and respecting disagreement.
- Enlarge your sphere of influence and connectedness. Power sometimes grows out of someone else's need.

How managers and leaders get things done

Classically, managers in health care organisations relied on authority to compel employees to perform tasks and accomplish goals. In contemporary health care organisations, effective managers use persuasion, enticement and inspiration to mobilise the energy and talent of a work group and to overcome resistance to change.

A leader's use of power alters attitudes and behaviour by addressing individual needs and motivations. There are seven generally accepted types of interpersonal power used in organisations to influence others (French and Raven, 1959; Hersey, Blanchard and Natemeyer, 1979).

Reward power is based on the inducements the leader can offer group members in exchange for cooperation and contributions that advance the leader's objectives. The degree of compliance depends on how much the follower values the expected benefits. For example, a ward manager may approve attendance at a conference as a way of rewarding staff nurses for their work as practice development leaders.

Punishment or **coercive power** is based on the penalties a manager or leader might impose on an individual or a group. Motivation to comply is based on fear of punishment or withholding of rewards. Punishments are often subtle. For example, the ward manager/team leader might give a disruptive nurse an undesirable job assignment or unfavourable off duty, or deny requests for leave or educational opportunities. Coercion is a bit different. Coercive power entails the ability to compel someone to do things they don't want to do by use of implied threats or manipulation. This type of behaviour is often called bullying. Staff nurses do what the manager wants through fear of the consequences of not cooperating.

Legitimate power stems from the manager's right to make a request because of the authority associated with job and rank in an organisational hierarchy. Followers comply because they accept a manager's prerogative to impose requirements, sanctions and rewards in keeping with the organisation's mission and aims. For instance, staff nurses will comply with a team leader's expectation to keep a log of home visits and mileage travelled because they know that the manager is charged with accounting for staff time, patient contact and expenses.

Expert power is based on possession of unique skills, knowledge and competence. Senior nurses such as modern matrons or nurse specialists by virtue of experience and advanced education are often the best qualified to determine what to do in a given situation. Others follow their advice because they respect the colleague's expertise. Expert power relates to the development of personal abilities through education and experience. Newly qualified nurses often rely on their more experienced colleagues when new clinical situations arise.

Referent power is based on admiration and respect for an individual. Followers comply because they like and identify with the leader. Referent power relates to how closely a person wants to be associated. For example, nurses may want to be on a task force for infection control because the task force leader is a nationally respected expert on health care-acquired infection. Alternatively, referent power could be associated with how well liked the person is. Students often seek jobs based on how well they were treated during a clinical placement. As a newly qualified nurse, they want to be in a situation where others treat them well and they feel supported in their development.

Information power is based on access to valued data. Followers comply because they are motivated by a desire for information that will meet personal needs and facilitate decision-making. Information power depends on a person's position, connections and communication skills. For example, ward sisters/team leaders are frequently privy to information that will affect nurses' work situations. A leader can therefore choose to exercise information power by either sharing or withholding information at staff meetings.

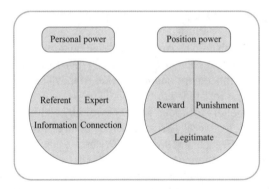

Figure 4.1 Personal and position power.

Connection power is based on an individual's formal and informal links to influential or prestigious persons within and outside an area or organisation. Followers comply because they want access to people who can further their purpose. Connection power relates to the status and visibility of the individual as well as the position. In some cases, managers or ward sisters have personal relationships with an organisation's board members that followers believe will protect or advance their work situation.

These power sources fall into two broad categories: personal power or position power (Figure 4.1). **Position power** is determined by the role and its accompanying responsibilities, recognition, advancement, authority, control of resources and scope for decision-making. Legitimate, coercive and reward power are position power because they relate to the 'right' to influence others based on rank or role. The extent to which managers mete out rewards and punishment is usually dictated by organisational policy. Information and legitimate power are directly related to the ward manager/team leader's role in the organisational structure.

Expert, referent, information and connection power are based, for the most part, on personal traits and the relationships in the work setting. **Personal power** refers to one's credibility, reputation, expertise, experience, knowledge, charm, personality and ability to build effective relationships. The extent to which one may exercise expert, referent, information and connection power relates to personal skills and positive interpersonal relationships, as well as employees' needs and motivations.

Leaders and managers often exercise power differently. Leaders tend to rely primarily on personal power sources to provoke interest, inspire commitment and instil confidence. Managers tend to use position power to ensure adherence to policies and standards and to complete work assignments. Managers also use position power to ensure orderly operation of their areas of responsibility. In reality the most effective managers are those who are also skilled in relating to people and will use personal power to handle 'people issues' such as resolving conflicts among members of the work group, changing an aspect of delivery, or to improve working relationships with other professionals, clients or organisational decision-makers. Managers also rely on personal power to sustain commitment and interest in highly routine jobs, as well as to maintain morale and motivation in trying times.

'Power is interdependent and a balancing act between managers and employees,' say King and Koliner (1999: 39). A manager must exercise position power judiciously, because the relationship between managers and staff is unequal. Managers always have more power than staff and therefore if power, particularly position power, is wielded liberally staff will feel vulnerable and resentful, causing distrust and lack of cooperation between colleagues.

A manager has both positional and personal power; the most effective balance depends on the manager's personality, the situation and the needs of followers. Box 4.1 provides guidelines for use of power in organisations.

All nurses must recognise that power helps them influence actions and decisions that will benefit staff as well as patients, families and communities. Power should be viewed as a valuable resource to be acquired, conserved and applied carefully. Power is best used to support organisational priorities, to facilitate important activities and decisions and to manage differences among interdependent organisation members. Interpersonal skills and technical and managerial competence are far more likely to generate genuine commitment than is the use of rewards and punishment.

Managers and leaders use power to motivate others, to strengthen their abilities, and to create alliances among diverse parties. Through the effective use of legitimate and expert power, a manager might require staff to develop skills and change ways of working in anticipation of service redesign. A manager also may use connection and referent power to bring conflicting parties together to solve problems or develop new programmes. This use of power is considered to be constructive politics, that is, the methods are morally and ethically appropriate as well as intended for the greater good of the organisation.

When an individual seeks power only to enhance their status or opportunity for advancement or to attain personal goals at the expense of others, this will be seen as negative politics and will generate cynicism, distrust, lack of cooperation and relationship breakdown. On the other hand, power used in the service of others - patients, staff, the community, the organisation – increases the status, confidence and effectiveness of all concerned.

Using power

In fast-paced, contemporary organisations, power flows to individuals who have the ability to help the organisation deal with complex, difficult tasks. Nurses have historically resisted the need to develop their personal and position power, reacting perhaps to their experience of negative politics in organisations. Power is, however, an important and essential tool for effecting change and ensuring that the voice of patients and staff in constructing humane, safe and satisfying health care organisations is considered.

Despite the benefit that can be achieved through the use of power and influence, some nurses still consider power unattractive. The association of power with aggression and coercion remains strong. In a profession that prides itself on care and compassion, power is viewed as alien. How, then, can nurses bridge the disparity between power as good versus power as bad?

Power grabbing, which has been the traditionally accepted means of relating to power for one's own self-interests and use, is how nurses often think of power. Rather, nurses tend to be more comfortable with power sharing and empowerment: power 'with' rather than power 'over' others. Although nurses need power to ensure that patients have access to quality care, they can help transform health care organisations by using power that embraces equality and caring.

Image as power

A major source of power for nurses is an image of power which comes from portraying themselves as confident and competent. Even if one does not have formal power from other

Box 4.1   Guidelines for the Use of Power in Organisations

Guidelines for Using Legitimate Authority

Make polite, clear requests.

Explain the reasons for a request.

Don't exceed your scope of authority.

Verify authority if necessary.

Follow proper channels.

Follow up to verify compliance.

Insist on compliance if appropriate.

Guidelines for Using Reward Power

Offer the type of rewards that people want.

Offer rewards that are fair and ethical.

Don't promise more than you can deliver.

Explain the criteria for giving rewards and keep it simple.

Provide rewards as promised if requirements are met.

Use rewards symbolically (not in a manipulative way).

Guidelines for Using Coercive Power

Explain rules and requirements, and ensure that people understand the serious consequences of violations.

Respond to infractions promptly and consistently without showing any favouritism to particular individuals.

Investigate to get the facts before using reprimands or punishment, and avoid jumping to conclusions or making hasty accusations.

Except for the most serious infractions, provide sufficient oral and written warnings before resorting to punishment.

Administer warnings and reprimands in private, and avoid making rash threats.

Stay calm and avoid the appearance of hostility or personal rejection.

Express a sincere desire to help the person comply with role expectations and thereby avoid punishment.

Invite the person to suggest ways to correct the problem, and seek agreement on a concrete plan.

Maintain credibility by administering punishment if non-compliance continues after threats and warnings have been made.

Guidelines for Using Expert Power

Explain the reasons for a request or proposal and why it is important.

Provide evidence that a proposal will be successful.

Don't make rash, careless, or inconsistent statements.

Don't exaggerate or misrepresent the facts.

Listen seriously to the person's concerns and suggestions.

Act confidently and decisively in a crisis.

→

> **Ways to Acquire and Maintain Referent Power**
>
> Show acceptance and positive regard.
>
> Act in a supportive and helpful way.
>
> Use sincere forms of ingratiation.
>
> Defend and back up people when appropriate.
>
> Do unsolicited favours.
>
> Make self-sacrifices to show concern.
>
> Keep promises.
>
> Adapted from *Leadership in Organizations*, 5th edn., pp. 146-152, by G. Yukl, 2002, Upper Saddle River, NJ: Prentice Hall. Reprinted by permission of Pearson Education, Inc.

sources, the perception by others that one is powerful bestows a degree of power. Images emerge from interactions and communications with others. If nurses present themselves as caring and compassionate experts in health care through their interactions and communications with the public, then a strong, favourable image develops for both the individual nurse and the profession. Nurses, as the ambassadors of care, must understand the importance and benefit of positive therapeutic communications and image. Developing a positive image of power is important for both the individual and the profession (DoH, 2008).

Individual nurses can promote an image of power by a variety of means. Introducing yourself appropriately by saying your name, using eye contact and shaking hands can immediately establish you as a powerful person. If nurses introduce themselves by first name to other professionals such as doctors who introduce themselves with their title and surname (Mr Smith, consultant orthopaedic surgeon), they have created an unequal power relationship. In Western cultures, eye contact conveys a sense of confidence and connection to the individual to whom one is speaking. These seemingly minor behaviours can have a major impact on whether the nurse is perceived as competent and capable and therefore powerful and worthy of attention.

Appropriate attire can symbolise power and success. Although nurses may believe that they are limited by the need to wear a particular uniform, it is in fact the presentation of the uniform that can hold the key to power. A senior nurse needs a powerful image with staff, senior managers and other professionals who are determining organisational strategy and policy. An astute senior nurse might wear a suit rather than a uniform to work on the day of a high-level multidisciplinary committee meeting. Certainly, attention to details of grooming and uniform presentation can enhance the power of the staff nurse as well.

Conveying a positive and energetic attitude sends the message that you are a 'doer' and someone to be sought out for involvement in important issues. Chronic complaining conveys a sense of powerlessness, whereas solving problems and being optimistic promotes a 'can do' attitude that suggests power and instils confidence in others. Pay attention to how you speak and how you act when you speak. Non-verbal signs and signals say more about you than words. Make sure your words are reflected in your body language. In other words, keep your facial expression consistent with your message. Stand erect and move energetically. Speak with an even pace and enunciate words clearly. Use only body movements and gestures necessary to make your point.

Use facts and figures when you need to demonstrate your point. Policy changes usually evolve from data presented in a compelling story. To position yourself as a powerful player requires the ability to collect and analyse data. Data can be obtained to describe care issues, activities or concerns. These include patient turnover, length of stay, delayed discharges, infection rates complaints and complements, staffing establishments and patterns, budget reports and any other data that reflect the contribution of your work. Remember that power is a matter of perception; therefore, you must use whatever data are available to support your judgement.

Knowing when to be at the right place at the right time is crucial to gain access to key people in the organisation. It means ensuring that you are invited to sit at the policy table when decisions affecting staffing and patient care are made. Influence is more effective when it is based on personal relationships and when people see others in person: 'If I don't see you, I can't ask you for needed information, analysis, and alternative recommendations.' Become visible. Be available. Offer assistance. You can be invaluable in providing policy-makers with information, interpreting data and teaching them about the patient's experience of health care.

In dealing with people outside of nursing, it is important to develop powerful partnerships. Be very careful to use 'we' instead of 'they'. Learn how to share both credit and blame. When working on collaborative projects, be clear about what is needed. If something isn't working well, say so. Never accept another's opinion as fact. Facts can be easily manipulated to fit one's personal agenda. Learn how to probe and obtain additional information. Don't assume you have all the information.

Make it a point to get to know the people who matter in your sphere of influence. Become a part of the power network so that when people are discussing issues or seeking people for important appointments of leadership, your name comes to mind. Be sure to deal with senior people. The more contact you have with the 'power brokers', the more support you can generate in the future should the need arise. The more power you use, the more you get.

Know who holds the power. Develop a strategy for gaining access to influential people through joining alliances and coalitions. Learn how to question others and how to become part of the organisational infrastructure. There is an art to determining when, what and how much information is exchanged and communicated at any one time and to determining who does so. Powerful people have a keen sense of timing. Be sure to position yourself to be at the right place at the right time. Any strategy will involve a good deal of energy and effort. Direct influence and efforts towards issues of highest priority or when greatest benefits are likely to result.

Use power appropriately to promote consensus in organisational goals, develop common means to achieve these goals and enhance a common culture to bind organisational members together. As the health care providers closest to the patient, nurses are in a unique position to represent patients' needs and wants. In the hospital, nurses are usually the first point of contact and thereafter for 24 hours a day, 7 days a week. In the outpatient setting, the nurse may be the person the patient sees first and most frequently. Patient power is increasing through the choice initiatives and formal requirements for involvement in policy and organisational goals (see foundation trusts in Chapter 3). By capitalising on the special relationship that nurses have with patients, they can gain influence with others as a voice for the patient.

Nursing plays an important role in the achievement of the objectives of health care organisations. Nursing care has a significant impact on patient experience, which is increasingly being seen as an indicator of an organisation's overall quality. Nursing also has an important impact on patient safety through management of the patient environment, ensuring care is coordinated and liaising with other health care professionals on their behalf. Regardless of the setting, quality nursing care is something that is desired and valued. Through understanding patients' needs and preferences for care, nurses become an important source of advice and direction for the organisation.

Using power appropriately

Using power not only affects what happens at the time but also has a lasting effect on your relationships. Therefore, it is best to use the least amount of power necessary to accomplish your goals. Also, use power appropriate to the situation (Sullivan, 2004).

Table 4.1 lists rules for using power.

Improper use of power can destroy a leader's effectiveness. Power can be overused or underused. Overusing power occurs when you use excessive power relative to the situation; if you fail to use power when it is needed, you are underusing your power. In addition to the immediate loss of influence, you may lose credibility for the future.

Power plays are another way that power is used inappropriately. Power plays are attempts by others to diminish or demolish their opponents. Table 4.2 describes several common power plays and their consequences. It is essential that nurses do not accept these statements at face value. Often, restating one's initial point in a firm manner is a useful strategy. It is not necessary to respond directly to statements such as those shown in Table 4.2.

Nursing must begin to recognise power for what it really is – the ability to mobilise and focus energy and resources. What better position can nurses be in but to assume power to face new problems and responsibilities in reshaping patient care to adapt to changing situations? Power is the means, not the end, to seek new ways for doing things in this uncertain and unsettling time in health care.

Power plus vision

The key to understanding and gaining power is to identify what you and other people really want. Once you have decided what you want, look at the big picture, the factors that influence

Table 4.1 Rules for using power

1. Use the least amount of power you can to be effective in your interactions with others.
2. Use power appropriate to the situation.
3. Learn when not to use power.
4. Focus on the problem, not the person.
5. Make polite requests, never arrogant demands.
6. Use coercion only when other methods don't work.
7. Keep informed to retain your credibility when using your expert power.
8. Understand you may owe a return favour when you use your connection power.

Adapted from: *Becoming Influential: A Guide for Nurses* (p. 35), by E. J. Sullivan, 2004, Upper Saddle River, NJ: Prentice Hall. Reprinted by permission of Pearson Education, Inc.

Table 4.2 Power plays

Power play	Recipient's response
'Let's be fair.'	Feelings of insecurity; insecure about choices because power game is played by someone else's rules.
'Can you support that with fact?'	Embarrassed by inability to prove 'that'.
'Be specific.'	Feelings of incompetence if facts and figures cannot be generated to support position.
'It's either this or that; which is it? Take your pick.'	Angered at being forced to choose between limited options.
'But you said . . . and now you say . . .'	Confused about what was meant; believe your position is illogical.

the attainment of your desired future. Take into account, for example, the whole organisation, not just your workplace or unit. What national policies are affecting the way your organisation responds? Determine who controls what you want and who or what stands in the way of achieving it. Identify the resources you control and the individuals who might desire those resources. Power resides not in aggressiveness or assertiveness but in the ability to make a conscious choice. Focus on the choice, not the action.

By making choices about what you want, you develop a strong sense of self-confidence and are aware of and feel good about your true capabilities. Your self-respect depends not on maintaining your role or position of power, but rather on your sense of purpose and direction. A clear vision pulls it all together by building consensus and support, identifying present capabilities, determining success factors and identifying resources of people, time and money.

Once you understand how power influences what choices are made and how these choices affect behaviours and feelings, you can appreciate its usefulness. In a constantly dynamic universe, power is a fundamental ingredient. You must ask yourself: are you willing to use your power to know yourself, set goals, ignite the imagination, direct nursing care, build teams and reach beyond the unknown into what could be? To use power to change and improve patient care is to recognise that power is natural and desirable.

Policy and politics

Policy can be defined as the decisions that govern action. Policies determine an organisation's relationships, activities and goals and result from political action either on a national or a local level.

There are many kinds of policy that affect nursing and patient care. In the UK, the government sets health policy, which is then implemented by the Department of Health (or health boards) through a variety of NHS, voluntary, private and arm's length organisations (see Chapter 3). Policies set by the government include those that determine how the NHS will operate, for example how the service is structured, the lines of responsibility and accountability within and across organisations and how funding is allocated and accounted for. There are also a number of policies that affect how the organisation functions as a workplace. These standards can relate to human resource matters, health and safety and employment regulation. The ban on smoking in enclosed public spaces is one example of a workplace policy in that the primary reason for implementing the ban was for the protection of workers.

Government policy also influences the service and care standards that the public can expect. Early in the most recent round of health reform, the focus was on policies to improve access, choice and equality in health services. Waiting time targets for hospital treatment were set by consultants, as were targets for episodes of care such as trolley waits in accident and emergency departments. Much energy has also been expended to make specialist treatment such as those for cancer available to all people fairly. The problem is often labelled the 'postcode lottery', which means that if you live in a large urban centre such as London or Birmingham it is easier to get specialist treatment than if you live in more rural communities. Another kind of postcode lottery also exists, where certain commissioners will pay for drug treatment whereas others will not. The National Institute for Health and Clinical Excellence (NICE) was set up partly to address this concern in that it makes recommendations on the cost-effectiveness and appropriateness of drugs for certain conditions. Once NICE has ruled, each commissioner is expected to apply the policy.

Having come a long way in achieving public expectations for access and equity, the focus has now shifted to quality. Standards for quality include safe care (prevention of hospital-acquired infection and injury caused by treatment) and positive patient experience (the experience of compassion, respect and dignity). There is also a policy expectation that health care service providers, and commissioners in particular, will move away from illness-based care to address more effectively the health and social issues that are of concern such as obesity, sexual health, mental illness and long-term conditions.

This kind of national policy often specifies what is to be achieved (specific reductions in hospital-acquired infection or rates of teenage pregnancy in a community, for example), but they seldom specify *how* to achieve the policy. This is where nurses have an opportunity to be involved. They can use their expertise and experience to help define the specific strategies for their organisation, community or situation. An approach that works in a sparsely populated rural area will be different from one chosen for an inner city community with an ethnically diverse population, but both strategies can achieve the quality standards set.

Sometimes a policy as mundane as what type of uniform is worn or restriction of visiting hours can become important when the consideration is given to the balance between allowing maximum contact for patients with their families, and decreasing traffic flow in ward areas in order to decrease the risk of infection from outside. Because nurses having a great deal of day-to-day experience of such matters, it is appropriate that they are very involved in policy setting for these issues.

Of course, the policies about how supplies and equipment are made available for nurses can affect care. For example, staff nurses in a clinic may waste precious time trying to locate one of the clinic's two tympanic thermometers. Why does the clinic have only two tympanic thermometers available? Why will the organisation spend money on expensive diagnostic equipment such as a nuclear magnetic imager but not on relatively inexpensive equipment that would facilitate cost-effective use of the nurses' time? In organisations where nurses are very involved in policy, these important questions are more likely to be addressed.

Working with policy

Working effectively with policy is a key skill for nurses. The question is how to work with policy to be sure that it achieves its purpose without being overly constraining. Some policies such as controlled drug policy have very little flexibility for interpretation, whereas other policies such as privacy and dignity in an outpatient clinic may be more open to different ways of working. The following questions and Case Study 4.1 will help you work with policy:

- What is the purpose of this policy? What is it trying to achieve?
- What actions are required by this policy?
- Where is there flexibility?
- What are the options for implementing the policy?
- What changes to day-to-day working will be needed as a result of this policy?
- What are your training and information needs regarding this policy?
- How will staff react to this change?
- How will compliance with the policy be measured?

Case Study 4.1

Your trust has recently issued a policy that all staff returning from sick leave will have a return-to-work interview. Using the questions above, identify how you as a ward manager or team leader would work with this policy.

Politics: the art of influencing

Although most people associate the word politics with government, it pertains to every aspect of life that involves competition for allocating scarce resources or influencing decision-making. As such, it is relevant to what nurses do in their daily work, whether as a community or district nurse, a midwife in a family planning clinic, or a ward manager in a hospital. What nurses do in their everyday role is influenced by, and in turn influences, what governments do, what professional organisations do and what communities do. What nurses do or do not do in one of these areas can have an effect on other areas and on their overall political power.

Politics is the art of influencing the allocation of scarce resources, which includes money, time, personnel and materials (Mason, Leavitt and Chaffee, 2002). Politics is a means to an end, a means for influencing events and the decisions of others. Nurses who renounce politics are essentially saying they do not want to influence events in their everyday work.

Politics

- is an interpersonal endeavour;
- is a collective activity;
- requires analysis and planning;
- involves image.

As an interpersonal endeavour, politics uses the skills of communication and persuasion. Nurses' communication skills make them particularly effective in political activities. Nurses understand the importance of rapport and how to create meaningful connections with people. They understand the importance of time in developing these connections. They also understand the need to appeal to the other person's needs and interests if the goal is going to be reached.

As a collective activity, politics often requires the support and action of many people to bring effective politics to bear on a situation or issue. Furthermore, working with others for political action can be invigorating, more creative and simply more effective because there are more people to do the work and provide the emotional support that may be needed to sustain long-term political action.

The politically astute nurse develops and carefully uses a support base that crosses the boundaries created by differences in discipline, position, role and organisation. In the workplace, this means developing connections to other nurses, support staff such as housekeepers, cleaners and porters, and other professional disciplines such as allied health professionals, doctors and social services. It is also important to develop relationships with staff nurses and other people close to the patient interface because these people are the ones who can bring the knowledge of practical solutions. Certainly this takes time, but it can and should be a part of the nurse's everyday work. For example, greet and speak to the person who is cleaning the floor every morning, sit with different people at lunch, and invite the new consultant for a cup of coffee. It involves going to professional nursing forums, interdisciplinary conferences and informal gatherings. It involves providing support for others' agendas, knowing that they may be able to support you on an issue in the future, and it involves being able to organise and mobilise groups of nurses and coalitions of diverse groups. Case Study 4.2 illustrates how a politically astute nurse can ethically use a support base to achieve personal goals that will also benefit the organisation.

It is helpful to have a target list of people with whom you would like to connect to build your support base, remembering that the personal assistant to the chief nursing officer in the organisation may be one of the most powerful people in the organisation by virtue of their ability to control access to senior people.

Effectiveness in politics arises from a careful and insightful political analysis of the situation, issue or problem. A political analysis includes assessing the structure and functioning of the area in which you are operating. What is the organisational structure? What are the formal and informal lines of communication? Who holds legitimate power? Who holds informal power? What are the stated and hidden missions and agendas of the organisation? What individuals are involved in the issue or situations that matter? From a systems perspective, one change in the system can have far-reaching effects on the rest of the system. What are the values and beliefs of people involved, and what are their personal and organisational interests, goals and priorities? What benefit would be realised by other people if your goals were to be achieved? What connections and power bases do they have? What is the current context of the situation or issue? What is the climate for change? What outside forces might be influencing the situation or potential solutions or changes? What recent events might influence how others view the situation and their openness to change?

A good political analysis also includes a thorough assessment of the issue or problem itself. Why does the issue exist? What are the contributing factors? Who is affected by the issue? Do efforts need to be devoted to creating an audience interested in the issue? What beliefs and feelings do people hold about the issue? Are more data needed?

Effective political action involves planning. Based on the analysis just described, a group trying to influence an issue or situation would brainstorm about alternative solutions and evaluate their risks and benefits. However, the group would also develop a plan for introducing its

Case Study 4.2 **Using Organisational Politics Ethically**

Karen Keller has been the ward sister on an elderly care ward in a large teaching trust for seven years. Two years ago, Karen completed her master's degree in nursing focusing her research on fall prevention for the elderly. Karen is well respected in her current role and is a member of committees on patient safety and experience.

Although Karen enjoys her work, she is very interested in the role of modern matron, where she feels she can work to improve the care of older people across the trust.

During her time at the hospital, Karen has developed good working relationships with nurses, managers and consultants within her division and across the trust. She is universally pleasant and professional with everyone she meets. Her work outside the hospital with elderly people in the community is well known, and Karen has featured in the trust newsletter several times alongside members of support groups for elderly people such as Help the Aged.

Karen decides to discuss her interest in the matron role with the divisional nurse lead. She makes an appointment and asks the divisional nurse lead for advice on preparing an application. Karen wants to know what will be important to the people on the appointing panel and how she can best put her case forward. Karen receives good advice from the divisional manager and leaves with a better understanding of the role. Karen is ultimately successful in her application for matron.

In summary, the ethical use of power involves:

- knowing and understanding the reporting relationships and authority in the roles within the organisation;
- identifying key stakeholders and understanding their priorities and how those priorities affect any new initiatives;
- understanding the importance of timing when initiating change;
- being in the right place at the right time to take advantage of new opportunities;
- building strong and credible working relationships with decision-makers;
- exhibiting a willingness to take on new and challenging tasks that may lead to more responsibility.

alternative and persuading others to support its position. Political analysis tells you who can be counted on to play what role in this process. For example, who should introduce the alternative to the person with the formal authority to make the decision to adopt it? Sometimes, the most politically astute approach is to have not the originator of the alternative introduce it but rather the individual who is most likely to be accepted by the decision-maker(s). Is collective action needed? What coalitions need to be formed? The political analysis also will suggest strategies related to timing. Should the alternative be proposed now or in two months? Should it be proposed as a pilot project or demonstration project? Should it be gradually phased in or implemented fully at one time? Should group pressure be brought to bear now or later? Timing is often crucial to the effectiveness of political action. People usually are more willing to accept something as a trial or test and pilot projects also enable those affected to adjust to the change gradually.

Politics is also about image and perception. Do people think you can make the change? Do people think the change will be harmful to them? Do people trust you? Do people identify positively with the coalition involved? Your future ability to be politically effective may hinge on

Table 4.3 Steps in political action

1. Determine what you want.
2. Learn about the others who will be affected by the change and what they want.
3. Gather supporters and form coalitions.
4. Be prepared to answer opponents.
5. Explain how what you want can help them.

From: *Becoming Influential: A guide for nurses*, p. 35, by E. J. Sullivan, 2004, Upper Saddle River, NJ: Prentice Hall. Reprinted by permission of Pearson Education, Inc.

the image that others have of you or the group. For example, it is well known that when a contract is settled in a collective-bargaining dispute, both the union and management sides try to come out of the negotiations with the appearance of having won the most. Even losses can be seen as victories, particularly if the effort resulted in the mobilisation and empowerment of nurses so that the whole group's power and likelihood of future success are enhanced. Defining the message you want others to receive and marketing that message effectively can create the image needed to further your political agenda.

Some of these guidelines for effective political action stem from long-standing political tenets based on how people (men, in particular) have operated in politics. Machiavelli's *The Prince* is the classic work advocating the use of cut-throat strategies for getting what one wants. Some nursing literature has addressed how to 'swim with the sharks', and certainly nurses need to be aware of how the game of politics traditionally is played. However, work by feminist scholars is suggesting that many women may be uncomfortable with cut-throat, Machiavellian politics. It is important for nurses to think about the ethics of their politics. According to Mason (1999), a new ethic is evolving in nursing based on women's ways of knowing and working together. This is particularly relevant to understanding what power is, how to get it and how it can be used and abused.

The steps in political action are shown in Table 4.3. You must first decide what you want to accomplish. Is it realistic? Will you have supporters? Who will be the detractors?

Try to find out what other individuals want. Maybe you could align your needs with their needs. Start telling your supporters about your idea and see if they will join with you in a coalition. This is not necessarily a formal group but intended for you to know who you can count on in the discussions. Find out exactly what objections your opponents have and try to figure out a way to alter your plan accordingly or help them understand how your proposal might help them. It is sometimes a good idea to meet with opponents before proposing your solution so that they feel respected and included and have had an opportunity to think through your ideas before having to meet publicly. Political action is never easy, but the most politically astute people accomplish goals far more often than those who don't even try.

Political action in the organisation

The type and quality of care received by a patient can also be influenced by politics. For example, the nurse may not find the time to sit with the elderly patient who needs to be fed but will unquestioningly take the time to give the tube feeding that has been ordered by the doctor for a patient who is not eating. The politics of this situation involves what values and policies the organisation has embraced. In this case, a technical procedure is valued more highly than humanistic, low-technology, personal care.

Politics in the workplace is often regarded with disdain, as reflected in the remark 'She plays politics.' This statement is used to imply that the individual got what they wanted because of personal connections rather than on merit, yet health care always involves different special-interest groups all competing for their piece of a limited pool of resources. A group's failure to recognise this fact ensures that the group's ability to influence decision-making within the organisation will be limited.

Staff nurses need to understand that they belong to a complex organisation that is continually confronted with limited resources and is in competition for those resources. With this understanding in mind, staff nurses can use their power when the limitations interfere with and place restrictions on patient care. Whether the restrictions come in the form of limited supplies, money or time, nurses can use their power and the political skills of artful negotiation, collaboration and networking to obtain the necessary resources to provide care. Speaking on behalf of patient care, access and quality are what drive the politics of nursing care.

What happens in the workplace both depends on and influences what is happening in the larger community, professional organisations and government. The effective leader understands the connections among these groups and uses them to the advantage of nursing, patients and the health care organisation. Developing influence in each of these three groups takes time and a long-range plan of action. Although the nurse's first priority should be to establish influence in the workplace, the nurse can gradually increase connections and influence with other groups and, later on, make these other groups a priority.

Using power and politics for improving health care in the future

How can nurses apply the principles of power and politics outside their organisations and influence the future of health care as a whole? Health care is in a state of constant change. There is a shift away from hospital-based services to care in the community and an expansion of primary care services, urgent care centres and community clinics.

Nurses know the problems and have many of the solutions. Making a case for nursing input into health care policy is no longer an option for nurses. Nurses must be prepared to demand a seat at the policy table, whether that seat is in the board room, at national or local levels of government, or in any other setting where nurses remain a strong, vital component in health care delivery.

Nurses can have a tremendous impact on health care policy. The best impact is often made with a bit of luck and timing, but never without knowledge of the whole system. This includes knowledge of the policy agenda, the policy-makers and the politics that are involved. Once you gain this knowledge, you are ready to move forward with a political base to promote improvements to patient care.

To convert your policy ideas into political realities, consider the following power points:

- Use persuasion over coercion. Persuasion is the ability to share reasons and rationale when making a strong case for your position while maintaining a genuine respect for another's perspective.
- Use patience over impatience. Despite the inconveniences and failings caused by health care restructuring, impatience in the nursing community can be detrimental. Patience, along with a long-term perspective on the health care system, is needed.

- Be open-minded rather than closed-minded. Acquiring accurate information is essential if you want to influence others effectively.
- Use compassion over confrontation. In times of change, mistakes and poor decisions are easy to pinpoint. It takes genuine care and concern to change course and make corrections.
- Use integrity over dishonesty. Honest discourse must be matched with kind thoughts and actions. Control, manipulations and malice must be pushed aside for change to occur.

To support high-quality patient care in the future, nurses must come to realise that nursing expertise and clinical judgement are the best combination to effectively influence nursing practice and policy changes. By applying power and politics to the workplace, nurses increase their professional influence. Using influence, knowledge and expertise can make the health care delivery system work.

What you know now

- Power enables individuals and organisations to accomplish their goals.
- Exercise of power is an essential aspect of leadership. Power is positional or personal and is based on several different sources, including control over rewards, punishment, information, institutional authority, expertise, personal likeability and connections.
- Nurses must perceive power for what it really is – the ability to mobilise and focus energy and resources.
- Effective use of power is using it appropriately.
- Image is a source of power.
- Politics is the ability to influence the allocation of scarce resources and events in our everyday world.
- Nurses can use political action to influence policies in a variety of areas.

Questions to challenge you

1. Consider a person you believe to have power. What are the bases of that person's power?
2. Evaluate how the person you named uses their power. Is it principle-centred and enabling (power to accomplish a purpose), or self-centred and manipulative (power over others).
3. Have you observed people using power inappropriately? Describe what they did and what happened as a result.
4. Assess your own power using the seven types of power discussed in this chapter. Name three ways you could increase your power.
5. Have you been involved in developing policies or political activities? Explain.

References

Covey, S. (1990) *Principle-centered Leadership*. New York: Simon and Schuster.

Department of Health (DoH) (2008) *Confidence in Caring: A framework for best practice*. London: Department of Health.

French, J. R. P. and Raven, B. (1959) The bases of social power. In C. Cartwright and A. Zander (eds), *Studies of Social Power*. Ann Arbor, MI: Institute for Social Research.

Hersey, P., Blanchard, K. and Johnson, D. E. (2001) *Management of Organizational Behavior*. Upper Saddle River, NJ: Prentice Hall.

Hersey, P., Blanchard, K. and Natemeyer, W. E. (1979) Situational leadership perception and the impact of power. *Group and Organisational Studies*, **4**(4), 418-428.

King, C. and Koliner, A. (1999) Understanding the impact of power in organisations. *Seminars for Nursing Managers*, **7**(1), 39-46.

Mason, D. J. (1999) Nurses dancing with wolves. *American Journal of Nursing*, **99**(8), 7.

Mason, D. J., Leavitt, J. K. and Chaffee, M. W. (2002) *Policy and Politics in Nursing and Health Care*, 4th edn. St Louis, MO: Saunders.

Sullivan, E. J. (2004) *Becoming Influential: A guide for nurses*. Upper Saddle River, NJ: Prentice Hall.

Part 2

Practical Skills for Leading and Managing

Chapter 5
Leading and Managing in Teams

Key terms

Group
Teams
Formal group
Informal group
Real (command) group
Task groups
Committees
Competing groups
Ordinary interacting groups
Forming
Storming
Norming
Performing

Adjourning
Reforming
Hidden agendas
Norms
Role
Status
Status incongruence
Productivity
Cohesiveness
Formal committees
Informal committees
Task groups

Introduction

What distinguishes a group from a team? To understand the concept more clearly, think about an orchestra. The very first day the musicians come together, they are a group of people, each with individual skills and knowledge. The conductor, their leader, gives them a framework: the musical score. To achieve their goal, creating music, the musicians must learn to cooperate and rely on each other as a team. The orchestra analogy is not unlike health care, a team-oriented profession with many different types of player. This chapter looks at the different types of group and group dynamics and offers strategies for working effectively in teams.

Groups of people that share common objectives and function in a harmonious, coordinated, purposeful manner are known as teams. High-performance teams require expert leadership skills. In a health care system integrated across settings, a team environment becomes increasingly essential. Team leaders, ward managers, modern matrons and directors of nursing find themselves needing to lead interdisciplinary teams as well as nursing teams. Understanding the nature of groups and how groups are transformed into teams is essential for effectiveness.

Because people who take care of patients work in close proximity and frequently depend on each other to perform their work, the quality of group leadership and interaction is vital. A positive climate is one in which there is mutual high regard and in which group members openly discuss work-related concerns, critique and offer suggestions about clinical practice and experiment comfortably with new behaviours. Maintaining a positive climate and building a team is a complex and demanding leadership task.

Imagine

Think about the people you generally work with. Do they work as a team, share common goals and work cooperatively even though they might have different parts to play? Perhaps they are a group, a collection of people working alongside each other, but with their own goals, sometimes in competition? It is very important to consider this distinction; there is evidence that effective teams get better patient care results.

Differentiating groups from teams

A **group** is an aggregate of individuals who interact and influence each other; both formal and informal groups exist in organisations. **Formal group**s are clusters of individuals designated temporarily or permanently by an organisation to perform specified organisational tasks. Formal groups may be structured laterally, vertically or diagonally. Teams, task groups and committees may be structured in all of these ways, whereas command groups generally are structured vertically.

Groups may be permanent or temporary. Command groups, teams and committees are usually permanent although their constituent membership may alter, whereas problem-solving groups and task groups are often temporary. **Informal group**s evolve naturally from social interactions; groups are informal in the sense that they are not defined by an organisational structure. Examples of informal groups include individuals who regularly eat lunch together or who get together to discuss a clinical issue.

Real (command) groups are regularly assigned staff who work together under the direction of a single manager. Its members are interdependent, share a set of norms, generally differentiate roles and duties among themselves, are organised to achieve ongoing organisational goals, and are collectively held responsible for measurable outcomes. The group's manager has line authority in relation to group members individually and collectively. The group's assignments are usually routine and designed to fulfil the specific mission of the agency or organisation.

A **task group** is composed of several people who work together, with or without a designated leader, and are charged with accomplishing specific time-limited assignments. A group of nurses selected by their colleagues to plan an induction programme for new staff constitutes a task group. Usually, several task groups exist within a service area and may include representatives from several disciplines. A task group consisting of nurses, doctors, dieticians and social services may be formed to develop a care pathway for nutrition management for the elderly.

Other special groups include **committees** formed to deal with specific issues involving several service areas. Most organisations have standing committees, such as the safety committee or the clinical governance committee which meet regularly and do important continuing work within the organisation. Committees can also be formed to address a specific need such as selection of a new information technology system or service reconfiguration. Health care organisations depend on numerous committees, which nurses participate in and often lead.

Teams are real groups in which individuals must work cooperatively with each other in order to achieve some overarching goal; they demonstrate healthy interdependence. Morhman, Cohen and Morhman (1995) define a team as a group of individuals who work together to produce products or deliver services for which they are mutually accountable. Team members share goals and are mutually held accountable for meeting them, they are interdependent in their accomplishment, and they affect the results through their interactions with one another.

Teams have authority to perform tasks, and membership is based on the specific skills required to accomplish the tasks. Similar to groups described above, teams may include individuals from a single work group or individuals at similar job levels from more than one work group, individuals from different job levels, or individuals from different work groups and different job levels in the organisation. They may have a short lifespan or exist indefinitely.

Not all work groups, however, are teams. Groups of individuals who perform their tasks independently of each other are not teams. For example, a GP group may have six GPs who work alongside each other but do not need to work as a team to take care of the patients in that practice. Their office staff, however, may need to work as a team to ensure appointments are made, records are available, and patient referrals are done efficiently.

Competing groups, in which members compete with each other for resources to perform their tasks or compete for recognition, are also not teams. This type of group is rare in health care, and more typically you will see them involved in sales, particularly telephone marketing.

A work group becomes a team when the individuals must apply their skills within the group skills to achieve specific results. They must exchange ideas, coordinate work activities, and develop an understanding of other team members' roles in order to perform effectively. Members appreciate the talents and contributions of each individual on the team and find ways to capitalise on them. Most work teams have a leader who maintains the integrity of the team's function and guides the team's activities, performance and development.

Unfortunately, research indicates that managers and leaders can experience difficulty in transforming work groups into effective teams (Aston Centre for Health Service Organisation Research, 2001). Some lack the critical thinking skills to plan, organise, focus and manage group process to achieve performance goals. Others struggle with the communication and influencing skills for working with group members to identify goals, distribute tasks and gain the cooperation and motivation of the members.

Leaders may lack skills in conflict management. Although conflict within any work group is inevitable, the manner in which conflict is managed depends on the individual's skill in helping others to sort out personal differences and improving their understanding and acceptance of differing views and styles (see Chapter 9).

Some people have difficulty managing the interpersonal relationships with group members. A group leader will naturally find some people easier to work with than others, and this can result in the appearance of favouritism or the exclusion of some members who are withdrawn or have challenging behaviours. Achieving balanced relationships with even the most difficult members is part of successful group leadership and is essential to the work group's function.

Many groups formed in health care organisations fall into the category of **ordinary interacting groups**. Most interdisciplinary teams, task groups and committees are ordinary interacting groups. These groups usually have a designated formal leader, but not always. Sometimes the group selects the leader or works on a rotating or informal leader basis. Group meetings generally occur in the following way. Discussions usually begin with a statement of the problem by the group leader, followed by an open, unstructured conversation. Normally, the final decision is made by consensus (without formal voting; members indicate concurrence with a group agreement that everyone can live with and support publicly). The decision also may be made by the leader or someone in authority, majority vote, an average of members' opinions, minority control, or an expert member. Interacting groups enhance the cohesiveness and esprit de corps among group members. Participants are able to build strong social ties and will be committed to the solution decided on by the group.

Ordinary interacting groups often are dominated by one or a few members. If the group is highly cohesive, its decision-making ability may be affected by 'groupthink'. Members may spend excessive time dealing with social relationships, reducing the time spent on the problem and slowing consensus. Ordinary groups may reach compromise decisions that do not really satisfy any of the participants. Because of these problems, the functioning of ordinary groups is very dependent on the leader's skills.

The value of teamworking to patient care and staff well-being

The leader's influence on group processes, formal or informal, and the ability of the group to work together as a team often determine whether the group accomplishes its goals. Ward sisters and team leaders can turn work groups into teams by understanding principles of group processes and applying them to group decision-making, team building and leading committees and task groups.

An important study called the Health Care Team Effectiveness Project was undertaken by a collection of universities to determine the impact of teamworking on patient care. The results were published in 2001 in a document called *Team Working and Effectiveness in Health Care: Findings from the Health Care Team Effectiveness Project* (Aston Centre for Health Service Organisation Research, 2001). The findings identified a number of important positive relationships between effective teamworking, patient outcome and staff well-being. The study drew the following conclusions:

- Health care teams that have clear objectives, high levels of participation, emphasis on quality and support for innovation provide high-quality patient care. Such teams also introduce innovation in patient care.
- Members of teams that work well together have relatively low levels of stress.
- The quality of meetings, communication and integration processes in health care teams contributes to the introduction of new and improved ways of delivering patient care.
- People working in teams perceive that there is generally more cooperation in the organisation, which leads to more positive work attitudes.
- Clear leadership contributes to effective team processes, to high-quality patient care and to innovation.

Borrill and West (2001) went on to develop a guide for managers for developing team working in health care based on the Health Care Team Effectiveness Project. They identified the following conditions for effective teamworking:

- the extent to which the organisational context supports team working;
- types and levels of leadership available to the team;
- team composition – the members must have an appropriate mix of skills, knowledge and experience;
- the extent to which the teams work well together, that is, members have common objectives, communicate, make decisions jointly, support innovation and review progress.

Leadership of the team is critical for effective team working:

The role of the team leader is to maximise the potential benefits of team working while minimising the weaknesses. There are three complementary tasks that leaders must carry out: managing the team, coaching the members and leading the team [see Table 5.1]. These tasks can be the responsibility of one person, or shared. What is important is that those in the leadership role, and team members are clear about who is responsible for carrying out these tasks, and that the tasks are performed effectively.

(Borrill and West, 2001: 9)

Table 5.1 Sample actions used to manage a team, coach an individual and lead a team

Managing the team	Coaching individuals	Leading the team
Setting clear, shared objectives	Listening	Creating favourable performance conditions such as facilitating links, cooperation and information sharing
Clarifying the roles of the team members	Recognising and exploring feelings of others and comfortable revealing own feelings	Building and maintaining the team
Developing individual tasks	Giving feedback	Coaching and supporting the team
Evaluating individual contribution	Agreeing goals	Directing change for and within the team
Providing feedback on team performance	Developing individuals	
Reviewing team processes, strategies and objectives		

Adapted from Borrill and West (2001).

Group and team processes

The modified version of Homans' (1950, 1961) social system conceptual scheme presented in Figure 5.1 provides a framework for understanding group inputs, processes and outcomes. The schematic depicts the effects of organisational and individual background factors on group leadership, including dynamics (tasks, activities, interactions, attitudes) and processes (forming, storming, norming, performing, adjourning). Elements of the required

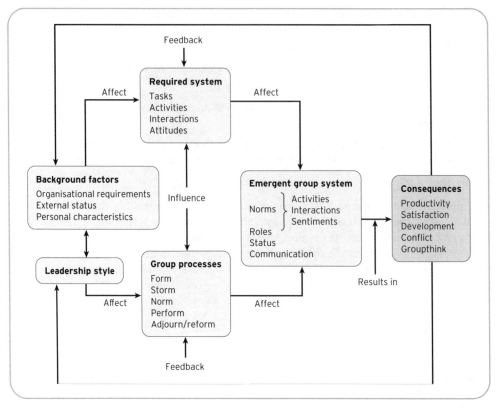

Figure 5.1 Conceptual scheme of a basic social system.
Adapted from Homans (1950) and Homans (1961).

group system and processes influence each other and the emergent group system and social structure.

This system determines the productivity of the group as well as members' quality of work life, such as job satisfaction, development, growth and similarity in thinking. The framework distinguishes required factors that are imposed by the external system from factors that emerge from the internal dynamics of the group.

According to Homans' framework, the three essential elements of a group system are activities, interactions and attitudes. Activities are the observable actions of group members. Interactions are the verbal or non-verbal exchanges of words or objects among two or more group members. Attitudes are the perceptions, feelings and values held by individual group members, which may be both positive and negative. To understand and guide group functioning, a manager should analyse the activities, interactions and attitudes of work group members.

Homans' framework indicates that background factors, the manager's leadership style and the organisational system influence the normal development of the group. Groups, whether formal or informal, typically develop in the phases: form, storm, norm, perform, and adjourn or reform. In the initial stage, **forming**, individuals assemble into a well-defined cluster. Group members are cautious in approaching each other as they come together as a group and begin to understand requirements of group membership. At this stage, the members often depend on a leader to define purpose, tasks, and roles.

As the group begins to develop, **storming** occurs. Members wrestle with roles and relationships. Conflict, dissatisfaction and competition arise on important issues related to procedures and behaviour. During this stage, members often compete for power and status, and informal leadership emerges. During the storming stage, the leader helps the group to acknowledge the conflict and to resolve it in a win-win manner.

In the third stage, **norming**, the group defines its goals and rules of behaviour. The group determines what are or are not acceptable behaviours and attitudes, and group structure, roles and relationships become clearer. Cohesiveness develops. The leader explains standards of performance and behaviour, defines the group's structure and facilitates relationship building.

In the fourth stage, **performing**, members agree on basic purposes and activities and carry out the work. The group's energy becomes task-oriented. Cooperation improves and emotional issues subside. Members communicate effectively and interact in a relaxed atmosphere of sharing. The leader provides feedback on the quality and quantity of work, praises achievement, critiques poor work and takes steps to improve it and reinforces good interpersonal relationships within the group.

The fifth stage is either **adjourning** (the group dissolves after achieving its objectives) or **reforming**, when some major change takes place in the environment or in the composition or goals of the group that requires the group to refocus its activities and recycle through the four stages. When a group adjourns, the leader must prepare group members for dissolution and facilitate closure through celebration of success and leave-taking. If the group is to refocus its activities, the leader will explain the new direction and provide guidance in the process of reforming.

Characteristics of groups

Norms are the informal rules of behaviour shared by group members. Norms emerge whenever humans interact. Groups develop norms that members believe must be adhered to for fruitful, stable, group functioning. Nursing groups often establish norms related to how members deal with absences that affect the workload of colleagues. Norms may include not calling in sick on Fridays, readily accommodating requests for trading shifts and returning from breaks in a timely manner. In a team environment, norms are more likely to be linked to each team member's expected contribution to the performance and products of the team's efforts. If an individual agrees to take on a specific assignment on the team's behalf and fails to complete the assignment on time, a group norm has been violated.

Group norms are likely to be shared if they serve to facilitate group survival, ensure predictability of behaviour, help avoid embarrassing interpersonal problems, express the central values of the group and clarify the group's distinctive identity. Groups go through several stages in enforcing norms with deviant members (Leavitt and Bahrami, 1988). First, members use rational argument or present reasons for adhering to the norms to the deviant individual. Second, if rational argument is not effective, members may use persuasive or manipulative techniques, reminding the deviant of the value of the group. The third stage is coercion, an attempt to force the deviant to conform. This may take the form of personal attacks against the character or working practices of the deviant, or even sabotaging the deviant's work. The final stage is ignoring the deviant.

It becomes increasingly difficult for a deviant to comply with expectations and to be accepted back into the group as these strategies escalate. Agreeing to rational argument may be easy, but agreeing after coercion or personal attacks have been made is very difficult. When the final stage (ignoring) is reached, reconciliation with the group may be impossible because group members refuse to allow the deviant back in. A leader has a responsibility to help groups deal with members who violate group norms. If the team leaders or ward manager fail to deal effectively with group members that have fallen out with the group, it leaves the door open for disruptive conflict. Eventually, the deviant may feel obliged to leave the group altogether.

Group roles

A **role** is a set of expectations about behaviour ascribed to a specific position in society or at work. Dr Meredith Belbin demonstrated that balanced teams comprising people with different capabilities performed better than teams that are less well balanced. Belbin's key book, *Management teams: why they succeed or fail*, was first published in 1981 and his work on team roles has been widely used in the UK ever since.

Belbin initially identified a set of eight roles, later increased to nine, and the labels for some roles changed to reflect new language usage (Table 5.2). Belbin suggested that there are no 'good' or 'bad' roles. People are as they are, and all roles play important parts in successful teams. Belbin also suggested that certain roles tend to be more extraverted (outgoing, proactive, outward-looking) while other roles tend to be more introverted (inward-looking, reactive). An individual in a team can play more than one role, but to be effective, the team needs all roles to be undertaken.

Table 5.2 Belbin team roles and descriptions

Role name	
Coordinator (CO)	Able to get others working to a shared aim; confident, mature
Shaper (SH)	Motivated, energetic, achievement-driven, assertive, competitive
Plant (PL)	Innovative, inventive, creative, original, imaginative, unorthodox, problem-solving
Monitor–evaluator (ME)	Serious, prudent, critical thinker, analytical
Implementer (IMP)	Systematic, common sense, loyal, structured, reliable, dependable, practicable, efficient
Resource investigator (RI)	Quick, good communicator, networker, outgoing, affable, seeks and finds options, negotiator
Teamworker (TW)	Supportive, sociable, flexible, adaptable, perceptive, listener, calming influence, mediator
Completer–finisher (CF)	Attention to detail, accurate, high standards, quality orientated, delivers to schedule and specification
Specialist (SP)	Technical expert, highly focused capability and knowledge, driven by professional standards and dedication to personal subject area

http://www.belbin.com

Status is the social ranking of individuals relative to others in a group based on the position they occupy. Status comes from factors that the group values, such as achievement, personal characteristics, the ability to control rewards, or the ability to control information. Status is usually enjoyed by members who most conform to group norms. Higher-status members often exercise more influence in group decisions than others.

Status incongruence occurs when factors associated with group status are not congruent, such as when a younger, less experienced person becomes the group leader. Status incongruence can have a disruptive impact on a group. For example, some groups contain individuals with high external status and different backgrounds from regular group members. They usually work at acceptable levels but are isolated from the group because they do not fit the group member profile. Sometimes status incongruence occurs because the individual does not need the group's approval and makes no effort to obtain it. For example, imagine that a ward has been having problems with MRSA. Working with infection control, alcohol gel bottles have been installed at the door. The nurses have all agreed to use the gel; however, the consultant refuses. The consultant's actions are based on her perception that she does not need the nurse's approval, and her status puts her outside the group norms.

The most important role in a group is the leadership role. Leaders are appointed for most formal groups, such as command groups, teams or committees. Leaders in informal groups tend to emerge over time and in relation to the task to be performed. Some of the factors contributing to the emergence of leadership in small groups include the ability to accomplish the group's goals, sociability, good communication skills, self-confidence and a desire for recognition.

Communication in groups

Groups provide an important channel of communication in organisations. Members of high-performance work teams generally communicate openly, candidly and clearly with one another about procedures, expectations and plans. Communication is influenced by the status and roles of the individuals who dominate team discussions. High-status members who are fulfilling key roles in relation to a team's priorities are likely to exercise considerable control over communication in the group by determining topics, setting the tone of the discussion and influencing how decisions are made.

Effective leaders can facilitate communication in groups by maintaining an atmosphere in which group members feel free to discuss concerns, make suggestions, critique ideas and show respect and trust. An important leadership function related to communication is gatekeeping, that is, keeping communication channels open, refocusing attention on critical issues, identifying and processing conflict, fostering self-esteem, checking for understanding, actively seeking the participation of all group members and suggesting procedures for discussing group problems.

How groups affect individuals

Group relationships affect individual behaviour in many ways. Organisational work groups affect the beliefs, knowledge, attitudes, values, emotions and social behaviour of individuals. Groups profoundly affect the nature and process of communication and interpersonal relationships. On the one hand, they may engender a higher degree of competition and political activity than individual behaviour.

Group influence is greater than the sum of its parts. A group can bring out the best and the worst in individuals due to the stimulating presence of others. Frequently, this stimulation increases motivation, especially when an individual's potential contribution to the task is fairly clear or easily measured. On the other hand, groups can lead to inordinate conformity among group members. Groups may be tyrannical towards members and ruthless toward non-members and thereby contribute to conflict in the organisation. Some issues involved in intra-group, intergroup and intra-organisational conflict are discussed in Chapter 9.

Group productivity and cohesiveness

Productivity represents how well the work group or team uses the resources available to achieve its goals and produce its services. If patient care is satisfactorily completed at the end of each shift in relation to the levels of staffing, supplies, equipment and support services used, the group has been productive. Productivity is influenced by work-group dynamics, especially a group's cohesiveness and collaboration.

Cohesiveness is the degree to which the members are attracted to the group and wish to retain membership in it. Cohesiveness includes how much the group members enjoy participating in the group and how much they are willing to contribute. Cohesiveness is also related to homogeneity of interests, values, attitudes, and background factors. Strong group cohesiveness leads to a feeling of 'we' as more important than 'I' and ensures a higher degree of cooperation and interpersonal support among group members.

Group norms may support or subvert organisational objectives, depending on the level of group cohesiveness. High group cohesiveness may foster high or low individual performance, depending on the prevailing group norms for performance. When cohesiveness is low, productivity may vary significantly. Although groups, in general, tend towards lower productivity, nursing education and practice have especially high standards of performance that help to counter this tendency.

Groups are more likely to become cohesive when members:

- share similar values and beliefs;
- are motivated by the same goals and tasks;
- must interact to achieve their goals and tasks;
- work in proximity to each other (on the same unit and on the same shift, for example);
- have specific needs that can be satisfied by involvement in the group.

Group cohesiveness is also influenced by the formal reward system. Groups tend to be more cohesive when group members receive comparable treatment and pay and perform similar tasks that require interaction among the members. Similarities in values, education, social class, gender, age and ethnicity lead to similar attitudes and strengthen group cohesiveness.

Cohesiveness can produce intense social pressure. Highly cohesive groups can demand adherence to norms regardless of their practicality or effectiveness. In this circumstance, the nurse manager may have a very difficult time influencing individual nurses, especially if the group norms deviate from the manager's values or expectations. For example, a clinical team may be in the habit of chatting during handover, making the process last longer than necessary.

The manager believes that handover should be done quickly so as to spend more time with the patients. If the current system for handover is long-standing, and well liked by the staff, the manager may have little hope of changing it. Group cohesion can also affect absenteeism and turnover. Groups with high levels of cohesiveness exhibit lower turnover and absenteeism than groups with low levels of cohesiveness.

For most individuals, the work group provides one of the most important social contacts in life; the experience of working on an effective work team contributes significantly to one's professional confidence and to the quality of work life and job satisfaction. Work-group relations influence the satisfaction of staff with their jobs, the overall quality of work life, and the quality of the environment for patient care. The work group often provides the primary motivation for returning to the job day after day even when employees are dissatisfied with the employing organisation or other working conditions.

Groups can provide learning opportunities by increasing individual skills or abilities. The group may facilitate socialisation of new employees into the organisation by 'showing them the ropes'. The nurse manager must establish an atmosphere that encourages learning new skills and knowledge, creating a group-oriented learning environment by continuously en-couraging group members to improve their technical and interpersonal skills and knowledge through training and development. Group cohesiveness and effectiveness improve as staff members take responsibility for teaching each other and jointly seeking new information or techniques.

Group size and composition

Groups with five to ten members tend to be optimal for most complex organisational tasks, which require diversity in knowledge, skills and attitudes and allow full participation. In larger groups, members tend to contribute less of their individual potential while the leader is called on to take more corrective action, do more role clarification, manage more disruption and make recognition more explicit. Groups tend to perform better with competent individuals as members. However, coordination of effort and proper utilisation of abilities and task strate-gies must occur as well. Homogeneous groups tend to function more harmoniously, whereas heterogeneous groups may experience considerable conflict.

Evaluating team performance

The manager may be accustomed to evaluating individual performance, but evaluating how well a team performs requires different assessments. Patient outcomes and team functioning are the criteria by which teams can be evaluated (Barter, 2002). Using clinical pathway data, complication rates, falls and medication errors are examples of outcome data that can help the manager evaluate team performance.

Group functioning can be assessed by the level of work-group cohesion, involvement in the job and willingness to help each other. Conversely, aggression, competition, hostility, aloof-ness, shaming and blaming are characteristics of poorly functioning groups. Stability of mem-bers is an additional measure of group functioning.

See how one nurse handled his new assignment as manager for a multidisciplinary team in Case Study 5.1.

Case Study 5.1   Introducing Multidisciplinary Teams

Tom Johnson was promoted six months ago to assistant director of nursing with responsibility for the stroke rehabilitation service. Patient care delivery systems have been under intensive review, and major changes in staffing are expected. Previously, physiotherapists and occupational therapists were in a separate department and reported to the director of therapy services. Now all therapists will be ward-based and report to Tom. Care pathways have been developed and a multidisciplinary patient record based on the pathway will now be used rather than separate notes for each discipline.

Janice Simpson has been a physiotherapist for 25 years and has been at the hospital for the past 6 years. She worked as a senior therapist team leader for physiotherapy until the structure was implemented. Janice has been assigned to the stroke rehab service and will be reporting to Tom. She is feeling uncomfortable in her new role and is concerned about how she will fit in with the nursing team, and she is reluctant for the therapy team to be dispersed. Janice is also concerned about the new multidisciplinary care pathway notes and believes that the detailed physiotherapy assessment document should remain as a separate part of the patient record.

Tom is eager for Janice to become a member of the stroke service team. He schedules individual meetings with Janice and the three other therapists who will be assigned to the service. Tom outlines the roles and expectations of staff on the unit and listens attentively to their questions and concerns. At the monthly staff meeting, Tom invites the therapists to come along and to discuss their roles and responsibilities with the nurses and to invite the nurses to share the focus of their work. Tom sets up a working group of nurses and therapists to look at role integration. Social activities are set up to allow nurses and therapists to get to know each other on an informal basis. A team facilitator is brought in to work with the interdisciplinary team once a month to manage any differences that might emerge, build relationships and to head off any disruptive conflict. Tom also arranges for clinical supervision by the therapists by another therapist so as to provide professional support.

Manager's Checklist

In this situation Tom is responsible for the following:

☐ Understanding the new structure and the impact on the unit.

☐ Familiarising himself with occupational and physiotherapy work and any regulatory or statutory responsibilities.

☐ Easing the transition of new staff into the existing staff group to help build trust and respect.

☐ Ensuring that all staff attend training on the care pathway and documentation.

☐ Auditing patient records against the new care pathway standards.

☐ Reviewing and defining roles for the therapists and the nurses in the new structure.

☐ Facilitating open communication between and among therapists and nurses to discuss concerns or suggestions.

☐ Providing information and feedback to staff and to those above in the organisation.

Leading committees and task groups

Committees are generally permanent and deal with ongoing work. Membership on committees is usually determined by organisational position and role. **Formal committees** are part of the organisation and have authority as well as a specific role. **Informal committees** are primarily for discussion and have no delegated authority. **Task groups** are ad hoc committees appointed for a specific purpose and a limited time. Task groups work on problems or projects that cannot be readily handled by the organisation through its normal activities and structures and often deal with issues crossing departmental boundaries. They tend to generate recommendations and then disband.

Guidelines for conducting meetings

Although meetings are vital to the conduct of organisational work, they should be held principally for problem-solving, decision-making and enhancing working relationships. Other uses of meetings such as giving or clarifying information or soliciting suggestions must be thoroughly justified as these objectives may be better accomplished in different ways. Meetings should be conducted efficiently and should result in relevant and meaningful outcomes.

Preparation

The first key to a successful meeting is thorough preparation. Preparation includes clearly defining the purpose of the meeting. The leader should prepare an agenda, determine who should attend based on the purpose of the meeting, distribute relevant material, arrange for recording of minutes and select an appropriate time and place for the meeting. The agenda should be distributed well ahead of time, 7 to 10 days prior to the meeting, and it should include what topics will be covered, who will be responsible for each topic, what pre-work should be done, what outcomes are expected in relation to each topic and how much time will be allotted for each topic.

Participation

In general, the meeting should include the fewest number of people who can actively and effectively participate in decision-making, who have the skills and knowledge necessary to deal with the agenda and who can represent adequately the interests of those who will be affected by decisions made. Too few or too many participants may limit the effectiveness of a committee or task group.

Place and time

Meetings should be held in places where interruptions can be controlled and at a time when there is a natural time limit to the meeting, such as late in the morning or afternoon, when lunch or dinner makes natural time barriers. Meetings should be limited to 50 to 90 minutes, except when members are dealing with complex, detailed issues in a one-time session. Meetings that exceed 90 minutes should be planned to include breaks at least every hour. Meetings should start and finish on time. Starting a meeting late rewards those who arrive late, while penalising those who arrive on time or early. If sanctions for late arrival are indicated, they should be applied respectfully and objectively. If it is the leader who is late, the cost of starting meetings late should be reiterated and an appropriate designee should begin the meeting on time.

Member behaviours

The behaviour of each member may be positive, negative or neutral in relation to the group's goals. Members may contribute very little, or they may use the group to meet personal needs. Some members may assume most of the responsibility for the group action, thereby enabling less participative members to avoid contributing.

Group members should:

- be prepared for the meeting, having read pertinent materials ahead of time;
- ask for clarification as needed;
- offer suggestions and ideas as appropriate;
- encourage others to contribute their ideas and opinions;
- offer constructive criticism as appropriate;
- help the discussion stay on track;
- assist with implementation as agreed.

These behaviours facilitate group performance. All attendees should be familiar with behaviours that they may employ to facilitate well-managed meetings. All meeting participants must be helped to understand that they share responsibility for successful meetings.

A leader can increase meeting effectiveness greatly by not permitting one individual to dominate the discussion; separating idea generation from evaluation; encouraging members to refine and develop the ideas of others (a key to the success of brainstorming); recording problems, ideas and solutions on a flip chart; checking for understanding; periodically summarising information and the group's progress; encouraging further discussion; and bringing disagreements out into the open and facilitating their reconciliation. The leader is also responsible for drawing out the members' hidden agendas (personal goals or needs). Revealing hidden agendas ensures that these agendas either contribute positively to group performance or are neutralised. Guidelines for leading group meetings are provided in Box 5.1.

Managing task groups

There are a few critical differences between task group and formal committees. For example, members of a task group have less time to build relationships with each other and, because task groups are temporary, there may be little motivation to build longer-term relationships. Formation of a task group may suggest that the organisation's usual problem-solving mechanisms have failed. This perception may lead to tensions among group members and between the task group and other parts of the organisation. The various members of a task group usually come from different parts of the organisation and therefore have different values, goals and viewpoints. The leader will need to take specific action to build effective working relationships in a short space of time.

Preparing for the first meeting

Prior to the task group's first meeting, the leader must clarify the objectives of the task group in terms of specific measurable outcomes, determine its membership, set a task completion date,

> ### Box 5.1   Guidelines for Leading Group Meetings
>
> - Begin and end on time.
> - Create a warm, welcoming and accepting atmosphere.
> - Arrange seating to minimise differences in power, maximise involvement and allow visualisation of all meeting activities: a U-shape is optimal.
> - Use interesting and varied visuals and other aids.
> - Clarify all terms and concepts. Avoid jargon.
> - Foster cooperation in the group.
> - Establish goals and key objectives.
> - Keep the group focused.
> - Focus the discussion on one topic at a time.
> - Facilitate thoughtful problem-solving.
> - Allocate time for all problem-solving steps.
> - Promote involvement.
> - Facilitate integration of material and ideas.
> - Encourage exploration of implications of ideas.
> - Facilitate evaluation of the quality of the discussion.
> - Elicit the expression of dissenting opinions.
> - Summarise discussion.
> - Finalise the plan of action for implementing decisions.
> - Arrange for follow-up.

plan how often and to whom the task group should report while working on the project, and ascertain the group's scope of authority, including its budget, availability of relevant information and decision-making power. The task group leader should communicate directly and regularly with the administrator or governing body that commissioned the task group's work so that ongoing clarification of its charge and progress can be tracked and adjusted.

Task group members should be selected on the basis of their knowledge, skills, personal concern for the task, time availability and organisational credibility. They should also be selected on the basis of their interpersonal skills. Those who relish group activities and can facilitate the group's efforts are especially good members. The group leader should also plan to include one or two individuals who potentially may oppose task group recommendations in order to solicit their input, involve them in the decision-making process and win their support. By holding personal conversations with task group members before the first meeting, the group leader can explore individual expectations, concerns and potential contributions. It also provides the leader with an opportunity to identify potential needs and conflicts and to build confidence and trust.

Conducting the first meeting

The goal of the first meeting is to come to a common understanding of the group's task and to define the group's working procedures and relationships. Task groups must rely on the general norms of the organisation to function. The task group leader should legitimise the representative nature of participation on the task group and encourage members to discuss the task group's process with the other members of the organisation.

During the first meeting, a standard of total participation should be well established. The leader should remain as neutral as possible and should prevent premature decision-making. Working procedures and relationships among the various members, subgroups and the rest of the organisation need to be established. The frequency and nature of full task group meetings and the number of subgroups must be determined. Ground rules for communicating must be established, along with norms for decision-making and conflict resolution.

Managing subsequent meetings and subgroups

In running a task group, especially when several subgroups are formed, the leader should hold full task group meetings often enough to keep all members informed of the group's progress. Unless a task group is small, subgroups are essential. The leader must not be aligned too closely with one position or subgroup. A work plan should be developed that includes realistic interim project deadlines, and the task group and subgroups should be held to these deadlines. The leader plays a key role in coaching subgroups and the task group to meet its deadlines.

The leader must also be sensitive to the conflicting loyalties sometimes created by belonging to a task group. One of the leader's most important roles is to communicate information to both task group members and the rest of the organisation in a timely and regular fashion. The leader should solicit feedback from other key organisational representatives during the course of the task group's work.

Completing the task group's report

In bringing a project to completion, the task group should prepare a written report for the commissioning administrators that summarises the findings and recommendations. Drafts of this report should be shared with the full task group prior to presentation. To identify any overlooked or sensitive information and reduce defensive reactions, it is especially important that the task group leader personally brief key administrators prior to presenting the report. This gives administrators a chance to read and respond to the report before making recommendations. The leader should consider involving a few task group members in the administrative presentation.

Patient care conferences

Patient care conferences are held to address the needs of individual patients or patient populations. The purpose of the conference determines the composition of the group. Patient care meetings are usually multidisciplinary and used for case management or to discuss specific patient care problems. For example, a multidisciplinary team meeting may be formed to discuss the care programme approach (CPA) for a mental health patient prior to discharge.

Often nurses are involved in activities associated with improving the quality of care for various patient groups and their families. For example, a modern matron might organise meetings with local GPs to discuss how to improve discharge planning, to explore strategies to reduce emergency admissions, or to improve the coordination of care for patients with long-term conditions at home.

The leader of a patient care conference is often not a manager with authority to require professional staff to take a certain decision. More often, the leader of a care conference is an equal peer to the other professionals participating and therefore benefits from good leadership skills. The style of leadership used is dependent on the experience and capability of other members of the team. Highly skilled and experienced nurses, for example, would not require, or appreciate, a leader who tries to direct professional aspects of their work, whereas less-experienced individuals may benefit from more advice, coaching and support (Barter, 2002).

What you know now

- A group is an aggregate of individuals who interact and mutually influence each other.
- Groups may be classified as real or task, formal or informal, permanent or temporary.
- A team is a group of individuals with complementary skills, a common purpose and performance goals who are mutually accountable for the achievement of the goals.
- Groups have an impact on cohesiveness and productivity, as well as individual development and growth.
- A group's norms and roles directly influence the productivity and satisfaction of group members and their ability to develop and grow.
- Groups come together, build cohesiveness, complete their task and disband or reform.
- Leading teams requires good communication and conflict resolution skills as well as the ability to plan, organise, facilitate and evaluate group performance.
- Managing meetings involves preparing thoroughly, facilitating participation and completing the group's work.

Questions to challenge you

1. Identify the groups that include you in your work or school. How are they different? Similar? Explain.
2. Describe an example of effective group leadership and an example of poor leadership.
3. Evaluate your own leadership performance. How could you improve?
4. Have you been involved in team building at work or school? Was it effective? Explain.
5. What roles do you usually play in a group meeting (or class)? What role would you like to play? Describe it.

References

Aston Centre for Health Service Organisation Research (2001) *Team Working and Effectiveness in Health Care: Findings from the Health Care Team Effectiveness Project*. Birmingham: Aston Centre for Health Service Organisation Research.

Barter, M. (2002) Follow the team leader. *Nursing Management*, **33**(10), 54–57.

Belbin, R. M. (1981) *Management Teams: Why they succeed or fail*. Oxford: Butterworth-Heinemann.

Borrill, C. and West, M. (2001) *Developing Team Working in Health Care: A guide for managers*. Birmingham: Aston University Centre for Health Service Organisation Research.

Borrill, C. S., Casletta, J., Carter, A. J., Dawson, J. F., Garrod, S., Rees, A., Richards, A., Shapiro, D. and West M. A. (2001) *The Effectiveness of Health Care Teams in the National Health Service*. Birmingham: Aston Centre for Health Service Organisation Research.

Homans, G. (1950) *The Human Group*. New York: Harcourt Brace Jovanovich.

Homans, G. (1961) *Social Behaviour: Its elementary forms*. New York: Harcourt Brace.

Leavitt, H. J. and Bahrami, H. (1988) *Managerial Psychology*, 5th edn. Chicago, IL: University of Chicago Press.

Morhman, S. A., Cohen, S. G. and Morhman, A. M. Jr (1995) *Designing Team-Based Organizations*. San Francisco, CA: Jossey-Bass.

Chapter 6
Leading through Communication

Introduction

As one of the most fundamental human activities and one of the most basic tools of management and leadership, communication encompasses so much that it nearly defies definition. We communicate to relay information, to influence, to teach and to express emotion. Successful and effective management and leadership depend on well-developed communication skills. Communication skills are needed to facilitate team building, manage conflict, and demonstrate insight, empathy, caring and trustworthiness. This chapter discusses the importance of communication in management and leadership in nursing.

Imagine

Think about a recent situation in which you became aware of how complex communication can be. Perhaps it is a situation in which there was a mismatch between what was intended and what was actually communicated. Effective leadership depends on communication and is often the difference between success and failure.

Communication

Communication is a complex, ongoing, dynamic process in which the participants simultaneously create shared meaning in an interaction. The principal goal of communication is to approach, as closely as possible, a common understanding of the message sent and the one received. At times, this can be difficult because both participants are influenced by past conditioning, the present situation, each person's purpose in the current communication, and each person's attitudes toward self, the topic and each other (see Figure 6.1). It is important that participants construct messages as clearly as possible, listen carefully, monitor each other's response and provide feedback.

The role of communication in management and leadership

As we saw in Chapter 2, management and leadership are complementary processes; management is concerned with planning, organising, coordinating, supervising, staffing and evaluating, whilst leadership is concerned with persuasion, energising, forging links, creating connections, empowering others, creating meaning and facilitating learning. Managers use communication to inform, clarify, direct, develop plans and evaluate outcomes. Leaders use communication to motivate people, create a common vision and goals, and create alignment between different perspectives.

In reality, nurses use both forms of communication to be successful. Situational leadership theory, mentioned in Chapter 2, identifies directing and supporting as essential leadership actions. There are times when what is needed is clear instruction (direction) that sets standards and guides effective care. Communicating policies and procedures, teaching students, delegation and directing the actions of new staff are all examples of communicating from a management perspective.

Communication from a leadership perspective is more likely to be needed when people are capable but unwilling. For example, there may be a need to introduce an electronic record to replace a paper-based one. There will be some people in the group who resist the change because they are not comfortable with computers, or they think it will take too long, or they are simply happy with the current system. This situation requires the leader to listen carefully to the concerns raised, discuss the benefits and drawbacks, discuss training needs and support people to feel valued through the change. The purpose is to use good interpersonal skills to move people towards cooperation with the new electronic system. Changes like this are seldom accomplished by simply telling people it will happen.

Factors that can affect communication

A message is conveyed through words, sounds (such as the tone, volume and speed of speech) and what is seen. Mehrabian (1969) in his classic study of communication found that the total impact of a message is about 7 per cent verbal (words only), 38 per cent vocal (tone, of voice, inflection and other sounds) and 55 per cent non-verbal. **Non-verbal communication**

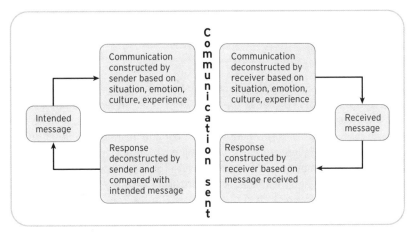

Figure 6.1 A communication model.

is a method of sending a message without using words and can take the form of gestures, facial expressions, body positioning and actions. In person, body language conveys the greatest part of the message, whilst on the phone, the tone of voice is most important. Written communication depends heavily on the choice of words, how sentences are constructed and the clarity of the message.

Body language

Body language can affect the meaning of the words spoken. When speaking to someone in person, verbal messages are accompanied by a number of non-verbal messages. These behaviours include head position, facial expression, eye contact, gestures of the shoulders, arms, hands or fingers, body posture and position, dress and appearance. These factors combine to create an impression in the mind of the receiver, causing the meaning of the words themselves to be reinterpreted (Pease, 1997).

Non-verbal communication can also take the form of actions. When a verbal message is incongruent with the non-verbal message, the recipient has difficulty interpreting the intended meaning. For example, a manager who states 'Come talk to me any time' but keeps the office door closed sends a conflicting message to the staff. Similarly, the organisation may encourage a nurse to report errors, whereas the manager is known to be very judgemental of errors and will implement the disciplinary process at the least infraction. The nurse is caught between conflicting messages from the two sources of authority, the policy and the manager's actions.

Vocal sounds – tone, volume and inflection of the voice

It is important that the way words are spoken is congruent with the intended message. An insult delivered with a smile and light-hearted tone of voice is more often taken as a joke than an insult. Conversely, praise offered in a deadpan voice lacking enthusiasm can be seen as insincere or as sarcastic.

Sounds other than tone and inflection can also have a significant impact. We are all familiar with squeals of delight and hurrahs as a sign of pleasure. Gasps can signal surprise or horror and sighs are often a signal of boredom or disinterest. Tutting, clicking of the tongue, and blowing noisily through the lips can all be signs of frustration or disapproval, while laughter, depending on its tone, can in itself convey every emotion from delight to derision. Many people are not familiar with the sounds they make; it can be very enlightening to hear a tape record-ing of yourself in conversation taking note of how you sound as much as what you say.

Words

The choice of words can significantly affect the intended message. You will know that using medical jargon with patients can cause them not only to misunderstand but also to feel as if you are not like them; you are different and perhaps superior. Nurses get into the habit of using their own form of words that can also distort communication with other disciplines.

Some words are 'value-laden' and can convey a judgemental view of other people. If a man-ager describes a staff member as 'not a team player', this description implies that the person has undesirable attributes and the manager is more likely to show that disapproval in the tone of voice or choice of words. This can set up tension with the other person and could lead to conflict. Reframing those judgemental words into descriptions such as 'Mary prefers to work independently' conveys respect, and interactions with Mary are more likely to be productive.

Culture

Cultural attitudes, beliefs and behaviours all affect communication. Cultural differences in communication are seen within the UK as well as abroad; elements such as colloquial expres-sions, greetings, tone of voice and accent change, and with that change comes a difference in perception. A great many problems result from people's lack of understanding of each other's cultural norms. Gestures are a good example of this. Whilst making a circle with your thumb and finger may in some cultures indicate that everything is okay, in others, it simply signifies zero or 'nothing' (Pease, 1997).

Understanding the cultural heritage and learning to interpret cultural messages is essential for the manager to communicate effectively with staff from diverse backgrounds. Diversity train-ing is available, as are information sessions on particular cultural groups to help staff to be more sensitive and effective. It is important to recognise, however, that subcultures exist within all cul-tures; therefore, what applies to one individual will not be true for everyone else in that culture.

Power

As we discussed in Chapter 4, people naturally place themselves into a power dynamic. As a nurse, you are in a more powerful position than the patient. As a staff nurse you are in a less powerful position than the ward manager or team leader. Power dynamics affect communica-tion in that a person who feels less powerful in relation to others will tend to communicate from a less confident position. There may be a reluctance to express opinions, offer honest feedback or disagree. Recognising that this dynamic is at play in every interaction can help you to choose an approach that creates safety for each person in the interaction (Oshry, 2007).

Modes of communication

Choosing the appropriate mode of communication can be an important leadership and man-agement skill. Written communications (memos, emails, faxes, letters) are an important man-agement tool in that the information can be stored and referred back to when needed. Verbal communications such as telephone calls, conversations and meetings are more suited to situations needing discussion, sharing of ideas, or developing relationships and understanding.

In general, the more important or delicate the issue, the better it is to use a close, personal approach. Any difficult issue should be communicated face to face, such as return-to-work interviews following sickness, performance reviews and clinical supervision. Situations where conflict exists are also usually best handled in person so that the individual's response can be seen and answered appropriately.

A telephone conversation is slightly less personal than a face-to-face conversation. Whilst body language cues are not available over the phone, tone of voice is, and it conveys a much richer message than words alone. Email has largely replaced voice mail for non-urgent communication, but leaving a voice message can still be the best choice in some situations. Voice mail is useful to relay a message that you would have done by conversation if the person had answered the phone. Voice mail allows you to use your tone of voice and choice of words to have greater impact than an email message. Voice mail is therefore particularly well suited to situations such as offering congratulations, conveying excitement or offering support.

Many of the routine messages that used to be delivered by telephone or voice mail are now sent by email; routine meeting times and places, policy information, minutes, reports, requests for information and other messages are common examples. Email has the advantage of being traceable (records can be kept of when messages were sent and received), recordable (messages that are sent or received can be stored electronically), instantaneous and easily sent to groups or individuals. Unfortunately, the advantages of email are also its disadvantages. It is not unusual now for dozens of messages to be received every day; and a number of those messages will not apply to the recipient or will be of low priority. The use of mailing lists has also caused some organisations to fall into the habit of sending email to everyone on the list rather than selecting the few people who really need to know. Managing this volume of messages is time-consuming and can lead to information overload. An important message may be missed because the recipient is distracted by low-priority messages.

There is also a worrying trend in some organisations of using email when personal communication should be undertaken. A recent exchange happened between two community matrons who were jointly responsible for compiling a report. Matron A felt that Matron B was not fulfilling her responsibility. Instead of picking up the phone to ask what was happening and to try to solve the problem together, Matron A sent a critical email to Matron B, copying in Matron B's boss. The result as you can imagine is that the two matrons got into conflict, and the trust and respect for all involved were damaged.

The level of formality of the communication also affects the mode used. Applying for a post usually requires a written application delivered in person or in the post. Correspondence about human resource matters such as sickness, pay increments, role changes, secondments, suspension or extended leave are commonly written and posted, sometimes via registered mail.

Directions of communication

Formal or informal communication may be downward, upward, lateral or diagonal. **Downward communication** (manager to staff) is often directive. The staff members are told what needs to be done or given information to facilitate the job to be done. **Upward communication** occurs from staff to management or from lower management to middle or upper management. Upward communication often involves reporting pertinent information to facilitate problem-solving and decision-making. **Lateral communication** occurs between individuals or departments at the same hierarchical level (ward managers, team leaders). **Diagonal communication** involves individuals or departments at different hierarchical levels or external to the organisation (ward manager to head of estates or modern matron to PCT nurse lead). Both lateral and diagonal communications involve information-sharing, discussion and negotiation.

An informal channel for communication commonly seen in organisations is the 'grapevine' (i.e. rumours and gossip). Grapevine communication is usually rapid, haphazard and prone to distortion. It is also useful. Sometimes the only way you learn about a pending change is through the grapevine. One problem with grapevine communication is that no one is accountable for the misinformation relayed. Keep in mind also that information gathered this way has undergone subtle changes as the message has passed from person to person. It is a slightly altered version of the truth.

Communicating downwards to staff

Communication with staff that report to you, either as members of your team or as health care support workers that assist in care, is probably the single most important part of being a team leader. Staff rely on the team leader or manager for information to get the job done, feedback on how they are performing and support for their development. Much of the information provided by a team leader or manager is routine, such as which patients to attend to first, posting the rota, making assignments, or notifying staff of changes to policy. Communication can become more sensitive when the manager is reviewing performance, giving feedback or offering development advice.

It is important to remember that you as a team leader or manager are in a more powerful position than your staff. Staff are often particularly sensitive to communications from their manager. The manager has formal authority over staff and that will affect how communication is received. The principles of effective communication are especially important when communicating with staff, because good communication is the adhesive that builds and maintains an effective work group.

Communicating upwards to those above you in the organisation

The ward manager or team leader's interaction with people above them in the organisation is comparable to the interaction between the manager and a staff member, except that the manager is now the one in the less powerful position. The principles for effective communication are equally important in upward communication. Communicating in a clear and concise manner will inspire confidence in those to whom you report, and enable them to fulfil their responsibilities. It helps to be organised and prepared to state needs clearly, explain the rationale for requests, and to suggest benefits for the larger organisation. Be prepared to listen objectively to the other person's assessment of the situation and be willing to consider reasons for possible conflict with needs of other areas.

Managing upwards is a crucial skill for nurses in management and leadership positions. To manage upwards, remember that the relationship requires participation from both parties.

> ### Box 6.1   Guidelines for Managing Upwards
>
> Give immediate feedback for things the other person does that support you or your service; feedback, praise and gratitude are often a welcome change.
>
> Never let those above you be caught off guard; keep them informed.
>
> Always tell the truth. Admit when you are wrong.
>
> Find out what the other person's priorities and goals are. Try to align your goals with theirs. Show them how your ideas will have a positive impact on the priorities they have responsibility for.
>
> Keep those above you informed on the successes you achieve; don't assume they will find out on their own. At each meeting be sure to describe progress towards goals, problems solved and important outcomes such as positive patient comments.
>
> Be aware of the other person's achievements and acknowledge them. If your manager asks you to do something, do it well and ahead of the deadline if possible. If appropriate, add some of your own suggestions.

Managing upwards is successful when power and influence move in both directions. Guidelines for managing upwards are found in Box 6.1.

One very important aspect of managing upwards is to understand the other person's particular perspective. This will make it easier to propose solutions and ideas that will be accepted. Understand that the people above you have even more responsibility and pressure than you do. For example, modern matrons in an acute facility generally have responsibility for ward cleanliness. When you meet with that modern matron it is important to remember that their success depends on how well your ward meets its environmental standards. Be aware that the modern matron will be reluctant to agree to support an idea that would put that standard in jeopardy.

Getting to know the other individual on a personal and professional level is also important. How does the person respond to stress? What previous experiences are liable to affect today's issues? This assessment will allow you to identify ways to help you to support the person with their job and for them to help you with yours.

Influencing upwards

Managers and leaders need to be willing and able to exert influence on a variety of issues and problems such as changes in staffing levels, implementing policy or changing service provision. Timing, rationale, methods and possible objections all are important factors to consider as you prepare to make such a request. Timing is critical; choose an opportunity when the other person has time and appears receptive. Also, consider the impact of your ideas on other events occurring at that time.

Should ideas be presented in spoken or written form? Usually some combination is used. Even if you have a brief meeting about a relatively small request, it is a good idea to follow up with an email or briefing paper detailing your ideas and the plans to which you both agreed. Sometimes the procedure works in reverse. If you provide the other person with a written proposal prior to a meeting, both of you will be familiar with the idea at the start. In the latter case, careful preparation of the written material is essential.

What can be done if, in spite of careful preparation, your manager says no? First, make sure you have understood the objections and associated feelings. Carefully restate what you have understood from the other person. For example: 'I have asked you to consider adding another qualified nurse to my establishment. You are unable to support that request because the trust has to make cost improvements, and therefore adding to the establishment is not possible now.' Once the other person has agreed that this is an accurate summary, you then have an opportunity to rephrase your idea. 'I realise the cost improvements are a priority. What I want you to understand is that I have been using a lot of bank staff to meet the increased activity on my ward. Hiring another staff member would be a lower-cost option than bank staff. What further information would you need from me to support this proposal?' This approach lets the other person know that you support their priority (cost improvement) and you also see your proposal as important.

The approach is assertive as well as clear. If the answer is still no, then ask to revisit the idea at a set point in the future.

Afterward ask yourself: 'What new information did I get from my manager?' 'What are ways I can renegotiate?' 'What do I need to know or do to overcome objections?' This information will help you to design your approach for the follow-up meeting you have arranged. Managers often succeed in influencing through persistence and repetition, especially if supporting data and documentation are supplied. Keep an open mind, listen, and try to meet objections with suggestions of how to solve problems. Be prepared to compromise, which is better than no movement at all, or to be turned down.

Taking a problem upwards

No one wants to hear about a problem, and your manager is no different. Nonetheless work involves problems, and the manager's job is to solve them. Approach your manager with the goal of solving the problem together. Have some ideas about solving the problem in hand if you can but do not be so wedded to them that you are unable to listen to other ideas. Use the following steps to take a problem to your supervisor:

- Find an appropriate time to discuss a problem, scheduling an appointment if necessary.
- State the problem succinctly and explain why it is interfering with work.
- Listen to your supervisor's response and provide more information if needed.
- If you agree on a solution, offer to do your part to solve it. If you cannot discover an agreeable solution, schedule a follow-up meeting or decide to gather more information.
- Schedule a follow-up appointment to review the impact of the solution or to agree further action.

By solving the problem together and, if necessary, by taking active steps together, you and your manager are more likely to accept the decision and be committed to it. Setting a specific follow-up date can prevent a solution from being delayed or forgotten.

Peers

Relationships with peers can vary from comfortable and easy to challenging and complex. Because peers often have much in common with respect to authority and power, they can share similar concerns. Camaraderie may be present; peers can exchange ideas and address problems creatively. Peers can provide support, and the strengths of one can be developed in the other. Conversely, there may also be competition or conflicts (e.g. battles over territory, personality clashes, difference of opinion). Interactions with peers are inevitable. Even when there are conflicts, peers should interact on a professional level.

Other disciplines and support staff

The ward manager or team leader has the responsibility for coordinating the activities of a number of people with varied levels and types of preparation and different kinds of tasks. The patient may receive care from a nurse, consultant, care assistant, physiotherapist, occupational therapist and others. Non-clinical support staff such as ward clerks, housekeepers, cleaners and secretaries also contribute to patient care and to the effectiveness of the team, though it is not uncommon that the importance of effective communication with them is overlooked. The manager must use considerable skill to communicate effectively with this diverse collection of people. When interacting with people from other departments or disciplines, the manager must recognise and respond to differences between the perspectives, pressures, goals and practices each person brings. Recognising this helps both parties to identify their commonalities and to deal with their differences.

To support greater collaboration between nurses and people from other disciplines and to improve patient care, keep these principles in mind:

- Develop mutual respect, that is, understand that other disciplines make an important contribution to care. They have different skills, knowledge and perspectives that are needed in situations where care is complex.
- Consider yourself and your staff equal partners with other disciplines.
- Build your staff's clinical competence and credibility. Ensure that your staff members have the clinical preparation necessary to meet required standards of care.
- Actively listen and respond to comments made by other disciplines.
- Create a problem-solving structure that involves participation by all those involved.
- Build effective relationships. Use every opportunity to increase your staff's contact with other disciplines through ward rounds, multidisciplinary meetings and committee work. Remember that limited interactions contribute to poor communication.
- Serve as a role model to your staff in respectful, assertive communication.

Patients and families

The patient, their families and the public are becoming equal partners with health care professionals in the design and delivery of care. Many of the complaints from the public are about problems with communication, specifically incomplete information, lack of opportunity to talk to doctors about their care, and finding someone to discuss their worries and concerns with (Picker Institute, 2008). Here are a few tips for effective communication with patients and the public:

- Most individuals are unfamiliar with medical jargon. Use simple words that are appropriate to the recipient's level of understanding without speaking down to the patient.
- As much as possible, maintain privacy. Try to hold your conversations where they cannot be overheard by others.
- Recognise cultural differences in communicating with patients and their families. People in some cultures do not ask questions for fear of imposing on others. Some cultures prefer interpreters from their own culture; others do not.
- Provide information verbally and in writing wherever possible. This will give the person something to remind them of the key points of information.

Approaches to communication

How powerful, comfortable or confident you feel in relation to the other person in the conversation will affect how you approach him or her. There are four styles of approach: passive, aggressive, passive-aggressive and assertive.

A **passive approach to communication** is where the sender approaches the receiver in a subservient way and communicates through body language, tone of voice and choice of words that there is respect for the receiver but not for self. Emma, a newly qualified nurse, may approach an experienced nurse who is known to be gruff with the following request. 'Mary, would you please, when you have time, come and look at Mrs Turner with me. I am worried about her and not sure if I should call someone. I know you are busy, but I really need your help. Please.' It is likely that the newly qualified nurse would use a pleading tone of voice. Emma has inadvertently communicated weakness and insecurity and, as a strong character, Mary is not likely to respect that kind of approach.

An **aggressive approach to communication** is where the sender has respect for self but not for the receiver. Anger often accompanies aggression, such as anger about being criticised, treated unfairly or put down. The speaker often attributes some negative attribute to the receiver such as stupidity, incompetence, unfriendliness, rudeness or simply that they are somehow 'less worthy' than the sender. In the above example, Mary may take an aggressive approach with Emma in response to her request. 'You again, every time I turn around you want something. You are a fully qualified nurse now, not a student, and you should be able to look after your patients without always bothering me. I am tired of doing your job for you.' Mary clearly sees Emma as a problem and a bother, and has little respect for her as a colleague.

A **passive-aggressive approach** is one in which an individual disagrees with the speaker but fails to voice their disagreement, or resists an idea through inaction. Instead of voicing a concern about an idea, the passive-aggressive person may simply stay quiet. The sender of the message believes the receiver is in agreement because they have no information to the contrary, but in fact the receiver disagrees. In the example above, Emma may respond to Mary's aggressive reply with passive-aggressive actions. Emma may simply walk away and, without giving Mary any feedback directly, go to the ward manager to complain about Mary. Emma is hurt and angry and wants to get Mary into trouble.

An **assertive approach** is reciprocal, one that respects both the sender and the receiver (Dickson, 2004). Being assertive requires personal confidence as well as careful planning. In the situation above, Emma would have been better to approach Mary assertively, not only conveying respect for herself but also using a common value as a basis for her approach. 'Mary, I am concerned about Mrs Turner. My experience in caring for someone in an unstable position is limited. I trust your judgement and experience and I would like your professional opinion. I want Mrs Turner to be safe and to receive the best care possible.' By phrasing her request in this way, Emma recognises her limitations and makes it clear that she has Mrs Turner's safety as a primary concern. Mary is much more likely to respect Emma and to assist her in the situation.

Using an assertive approach to professional situations is normally the best option. Assertive communications build professional relationships and teamworking from a position of mutual respect.

Box 6.2 provides guidelines for effective communication that supports understanding and respect.

Box 6.2	**Steps in Effective Communication**

Speaking or writing a message is not, in itself, communication. Communication is achieved when the message has been accurately sent and an appropriate response received. Purposeful and effective communication does not happen by itself. The following steps are recommended when planning important communications.

Be clear about exactly what you want to happen. Be certain you know exactly what you want from the other individual, within what time frame, and what steps should be followed to do it. Be clear in your own mind what information the person needs to be able to achieve your expectation, what the outcome will be if the expectation is achieved, and how that outcome can or will be evaluated. When you have thought through these questions, you are ready to communicate.

Get positive attention. The first step in face-to-face communication is to enable listening. Avoid factors that interfere with effective listening such as noise, distraction and competing commitments. Depending on the nature of communication, be prepared to supply the background to the situation and explain its importance; indicating the importance of the instructions also may be appropriate.

Give clear, concise information. Use an inoffensive and non-defensive style and tone of voice. Be precise, and give all the information receivers need to carry out your expectations. Follow a step-by-step procedure if several actions are needed.

Verify understanding. Make sure the receiver has understood your specific request for action. Ask them to describe back to you their understanding. Give them the opportunity to clarify.

Give follow-up communication. Understanding does not guarantee performance. Follow up to determine the outcome of your communication and give feedback to the receiver.

Situations that challenge effective communication

In which situations do you find it most difficult to communicate? When you need to tell someone that they are not up to standard? Or when you find the other person intimidating? What subjects do you find hard to raise with another person? Timekeeping? Personal hygiene? Poor teamworking? Mistakes? Disrespect? Incompetence? If you find these difficult, you are not alone.

An important study called 'Silence Kills' was undertaken (VitalSmarts, 2005) to discover the types of message that were difficult for managers, nurses and doctors to address with each other. They are:

- broken rules;
- mistakes;
- lack of support;
- incompetence;
- poor teamwork;
- disrespect;
- micro-management.

The study found that less than 10 per cent of people who witnessed these situations felt able to address these issues, and that most of the time, the issues have persisted for more than a year. They are a serious barrier to teamworking and can have consequences for the patient.

These are the issues that could lead to the undertaking of **difficult conversations**, conversations that involve risk to one or more of the participants. The nature of the risk varies. In conversations where a manager is bringing an issue of poor teamwork to a staff member, the staff member may feel at risk, because the manager has the legitimate authority to impose disciplinary action on the employee. However, the manager may also feel at risk. If the employee has a reputation for having a short temper, the manager may fear being yelled at or accused of bullying.

Feeling at risk is even more common when a ward manager or team leader feels the need to raise concern with a member of another discipline or a peer on another ward. In these situations, the manager has no legitimate authority and will be concerned about being accused of 'sticking their nose in where it doesn't belong'.

Difficult conversations are often avoided because of fear: fear of feeling awkward, fear of hurting the other person, fear of retaliation, fear of making the situation worse and sometimes fear of personal safety. The fear stops us from addressing the situation, and somewhere down deep we hope the situation will get better. The problem is that avoidance fails to respect either party, the sender of the message continues to be frustrated by the situation, and the receiver of the message has no awareness and therefore no opportunity to change (Dickson, 2004).

The intention in holding a difficult conversation is to communicate a sensitive or unwelcome message whilst maintaining or improving the relationship between two people. In order to accomplish this noble aim, planning for a difficult conversation is essential. Dickson (2004) recommends starting with three questions for reflection:

1. What is happening?

2. How do I feel about it?

3. What would I like to be different?

Asking yourself 'What is happening?' gives you the opportunity to describe and gather evidence about the situation. For example, if you have an employee who has been late a number of times in the past two months, you need to know the exact nature of the lateness. Take time to review the evidence. How many times, how late and on what shift are all essential objective facts, but it is also important to collect evidence about the *impact* of the lateness on colleagues and on patient care. Gathering evidence on the impact answers the 'So what?' objection, where

---

Box 6.3	**Effective Feedback**

Feedback is the gift of information. It is neither criticism nor praise. Criticism is a negative judgement on the actions of motives of the other person. Universally, people respond to criticism with defensiveness and that makes criticism an ineffective tool for communicating desired changes.

Praise is a positive judgement on the actions or motives of the other person. People generally respond to praise with pleasure and pride especially if they value and respect the person offering the praise. Feedback is information, offered in the form of evidence and impact. It offers the receiver the objective evidence (what, when, where, how often), the subjective evidence (how people reacted) and why it is important. Feedback is intended to inform and, through the development of insight into the situation, motivate the person to change.

the person you are speaking to dismisses their lateness as unimportant. These two pieces of information, evidence and impact, are the components of effective feedback (Box 6.3).

Table 6.1 shows some examples of situations where praise, feedback and criticism may be used.

The second question to ask yourself when preparing for a difficult conversation is 'How do I feel about it?' Identifying your emotional response to a situation is an important step in preparing for a difficult conversation. As stated above, fear is the most common emotion to

Table 6.1 Examples of praise, feedback and criticism

Situation	Praise	Feedback	Criticism
Staff member with a history of lateness has been on time for the past two weeks	Good job for getting here on time!	You've been on time every shift for the past two weeks. That has made it possible for handover to go smoothly and for the night shift to get home on time	I knew you could get here on time if you tried hard enough
Consultant interrupts breakfast on the ward insisting on doing rounds		Breakfast is served on this ward at 8:00. There are a number of patients that need assistance from the nurses at this time. Holding ward rounds then is putting nutrition needs at risk	Your ward rounds interfere with breakfast. The nurses are following around after you rather than feeding the patients. Aren't the patients important to you?
A staff nurse is often heard complaining about nurses on other shifts		On three occasions in the past week, I have heard you commenting on the night staff, saying things like 'They sit around all night not doing anything.' These comments are causing me to feel uncomfortable, and concerned about how we work together as a team	You are always complaining about night staff. They work just as hard as you do, even harder I expect if you have so much time for complaining
A staff member receives special mention in a patient letter	Well done	Mr Scholes commented that you took extra time with him explaining his tests and that it really made him feel less anxious. That was clearly an important part of his care	He liked you, didn't he? No wonder you spent so much time with him

get in the way of difficult conversations, though not the only one. If you feel angry about the situation, you may be inclined to become aggressive. This feeling in itself could be enough to prevent you from addressing an important issue in that you worry that you will lose your temper and yell or criticise. If you feel hurt, you may worry that you will cry or whinge, and that the expression of those emotions will be seen as unprofessional.

The third question is 'What do you want to be different?' In this step of preparation, you are challenged to consider what you want the future to be like. Be careful to state what you want, not what you *don't* want. For example, if a staff nurse is rude, it is tempting to answer this question by saying 'I want her to stop being rude.' This reply doesn't describe what is wanted, which is a much better message to give. Instead, say 'I want her to be polite in all conversations with staff, patients and families.' This sets a positive standard and will hopefully focus the person on the desired behaviour.

Table 6.2 gives some examples of how to use the three questions for reflection to prepare for a difficult conversation.

Preparation for a difficult conversation by answering these three questions then leads into planning for the conversation itself. Two more things need to be considered before actually holding the discussion.

Timing

Timing the conversation is important. Be sure to set time aside in a private place. It is best to hold the conversation as close to the time of the event occurrence as practical, though not

Table 6.2 Preparing for a difficult conversation

What is happening?	How do I feel about it?	What do I want to be different?
When Sandra has been scheduled for a Saturday shift, she has phoned in sick the past three occasions and the ward has been short-handed. This has caused other staff to work harder and to feel angry with Sandra	I feel frustrated and concerned about how the team is feeling about Sandra. The discontent could affect care	I want Sandra to come to work on the Saturdays she is assigned
On two occasions in the past month a senior registrar Dr Singh has yelled at a nurse in front of the patients. Both nurses have complained to you about the registrar and said they don't want to work with him any more	I am concerned that the staff will avoid the registrar and that patient care will suffer. I am also afraid that he will yell at more nurses or at me	I want him to speak courteously to all staff members
On three occasions over the past week, a dressing applied on the night shift has had to be redone within a few hours. All three dressings were done by Barbara, the senior staff nurse on nights	I am worried about this staff member's competence in dressing technique	I want to feel confident that her dressing technique is up to standard

when emotions are running high. When emotions are high, it is easy to get into aggressive or critical approaches which will damage the relationship for the future. Tell the person you need to discuss the situation in the near future, but for now, it is best to calm down and reflect on the situation. Make an appointment to address the issue within the next 24 hours if possible, as this breaks the cycle of worry about when the matter will be discussed.

Setting the tone of the conversation

The first part of any difficult conversation is about setting the tone and creating safety or rapport with the other person. It is important to thank the person for meeting with you, and to let them know how much time has been set aside for the conversation. The next step is to tell them how you feel about the situation. This may seem risky at first glance, but generally it will serve to diffuse tension and make way for an assertive approach.

Opening a difficult conversation

The five-step approach to opening a difficult conversation shown in Table 6.3 overleaf usually works.

After opening the conversation, it is their turn to tell you their perspective. Because you have used assertive communication and objective description and given a clear statement of what you want to happen, it is common that the other party will respond reasonably and you will then be able to problem-solve the situation together. There are, however, other types of response that can occur.

Explanations

It is possible that the person involved will offer a reasonable explanation, or disclose some personal circumstances that are affecting the situation. If you feel like the response is genuine, then it is wise to listen and feed back the reasons as accurately as you can. 'I am having some problems at home that make it hard for me to come to work on time.' It is important that you are not drawn in to solving the problem for them. Keep the momentum with them by reflecting back their concern whilst keeping the responsibility for solving the problem with them. 'As I understand it you are having some problems at home. It remains important for you to be at work on time as it affects both the service we offer and the team. What needs to happen to ensure you can get to work on time?'

This response keeps the accountability for timekeeping with them and conveys that you believe that they can solve the problem as a responsible adult. This should ensure that the person involved stays focused and conveys the importance of the situation.

Deflections

It is possible that the person will try to deflect you from the issue at hand by providing an excuse or attacking your credibility. These deflections can be successful in the right hands. The key is to recognise them as deflections and to return to the issue at hand. For example: 'I've heard it all before.' 'Here we go again.' 'You just don't understand.' 'I don't have time.' 'I've tried that and it doesn't work.'

Effective responses to these deflections consist of two parts: acknowledgement and redirections. The first step is to acknowledge the concern using the person's own words and then bring the situation back to the topic at hand. If for example a staff member were to reply to your suggestion about changing handover by saying 'We tried that and it didn't work', you

Table 6.3 Opening a difficult conversation

Step	Example 1	Example 2	Example 3
1. Thank the person for meeting	Sandra, thanks for agreeing to meet with me today.	Thanks for meeting with me today.	I'm glad you agreed to meet today. This is important.
2. Tell them how you are feeling, using the feelings section from your preparation	I have been feeling very frustrated lately.	I have been nervous about bringing this up with you.	I have been feeling concerned about you and I want you to understand that I am also concerned about patient care.
3. Describe the situation from your 'what is happening?' section	The past three times you were scheduled to work on a Saturday you have phoned in sick. Because it is difficult to back-fill weekends, your colleagues often have to work short-handed, which has led to resentment from your colleagues and puts a strain on patient care	Within the past week, two nurses have come to me upset about the way you spoke with them. They are so upset that they have said they no longer want to work with you.	Three times in the past month a dressing you applied has had to be redone on day shift. That creates more work for those staff and also makes me wonder about your technique.
4. Tell them what you want to happen from your preparation	I want to be confident that you will be at work on the Saturdays you are assigned.	I want to have good relationships between you and the nurses and for the communication between you to be professional and courteous.	I want the dressings you apply to last as they are intended.
5. Invite a response	Tell me about those Saturdays so I can better understand the situation.	Tell me about the situation from your point of view.	Tell me what you think is happening.

could respond by saying 'I know that has been tried before [acknowledgement], but the situation has changed and I think it is a good time to give it a try [redirection]'.

When responding to a deflection, it is important to stay calm and avoid the tendency to get emotional. Remember, deflections are intended to draw you off topic so if that can be accomplished using emotion laden words or phrases, it will be tried.

The diatribe

The diatribe (or rant) is an explosion of anger typically including indignation or criticism. It is important that the diatribe is halted, and that the person is treated with respect. The following method is suggested.

1. Interrupt the speaker by repeating their name firmly and loudly without anger in your voice.

2. Once they stop speaking say: 'I want to hear your point of view, and I cannot concentrate on what you are saying when you are speaking like that. Please tell me your concern.'

Tears

Tears can be a deflection, but more often it is a sign of emotional intensity. It is best to stay in the room, with the person, staying quiet and letting them compose themselves. When the tears stop, say, 'I realise this is difficult. I don't intend to upset you. It is important to talk about [the issue].'

Silence

Silence can be an expression of resistance or defiance, or it can be a sign of fear about telling the truth. It is most important to allow silence to occur without jumping in. Remain relaxed, attentive and expect an answer. If the silence persists, say 'You have been silent for some time now, and I think you have something to say. What is on your mind?' Wait for another reasonable time. Try asking again 'What is it you want to say?' If the silence persists, it may be useful to reschedule the conversation for later in the day, or soon thereafter to resume the conversation. Say 'I would like to resolve this situation. You seem in need of some time to think. Shall we start again after lunch?'

Storming out

It is never safe or helpful to hold someone in a meeting if they are determined to leave. If a person announces their intention to leave, you cannot stop them. If possible, tell the person that you will set up another meeting as this is an important issue and it needs to be addressed. If the leaving is very sudden, contact the person within a day or so to set up a continuation.

Other responses

When tackling difficult conversations, or those that carry a lot of risk, it is not always easy to predict the other person's response. Be sure you plan well, practise and alert those who need to know of your intentions. If caught off guard, don't be afraid to say you are unsure how to respond and that you need some time to think about it. Call a break and return when you have had time to think and know what to say.

In the interaction in Box 6.4, one of the most important things the team leader did early on was to set aside her judgement that Ann was 'not pulling her weight'. Approaching Ann from that perspective could have led the team leader to become aggressive or lecturing. Approaching the situation in an assertive, non-judgemental way was the key to success.

The effort to develop excellent communication skills is well worth the manager's effort. As Porter-O'Grady (2003) reminded us, today's relationship-oriented environments require superb interpersonal skills. A facilitative leadership style encourages others, empowers them to do their best work, and supports them when problems and conflict inevitably emerge.

Successful leaders are able to persuade others and enlist their support. The most effective means of persuasion is the leader's personal characteristics. Competence, emotional control, assertiveness, consideration and respect promote trustworthiness: credibility and good communication skills are the key.

| Box 6.4 | **A Difficult Conversation from Beginning to End** |

You are the district nurse team leader. One of your team keeps her patients on service much longer than other nurses, and has therefore had fewer new cases added to her caseload than the rest of the team. New patients take more time than patients who have been on service for a while and the other members of the team are beginning to feel like Ann is not pulling her weight. There is tension in the team and you are concerned that patient care will suffer.

- Planning – in order to get ready for the conversation you undertake the three questions above:
  - What is happening? The average length of service for patients is 10 weeks. Ann's patients are on service 16 weeks on average. The team average for new patients is 24 a year, whilst Ann has had only 15. The other members of the team are getting frustrated with Ann, and there is a waiting list for service.
  - How do you feel? I feel frustrated with Ann. I have tried to raise this issue before but Ann has put me off by saying her patients are sicker and need more service. It is important that Ann's care falls into line with others on the team and that the waiting list is reduced.
  - What do you want to happen? I want Ann to bring her caseload into line with others on the team. I also want Ann to be a respected member of the team and for the team to work well together.
- Opening the conversation:
  - *Team leader* 'Thanks for meeting with me, Ann. I invited you here today to talk about your caseload. I have been concerned for a while that your patients stay on service much longer than others on the team and that you take fewer patients than the rest. This is not only causing friction in the team, it is contributing to our waiting list for service going up. People out there need our help and they are not able to get a place on service. I asked you here today to see what can be done to bring your caseload in line with expectations. How do you see the situation?
  - *Ann* I have told you before that my patients are sicker than the other nurses' patients [explanation]. I'm not like the other nurses who do the bare minimum for their patients – I am a good nurse [deflection].
  - *Team leader* Yes, Ann, you are a good nurse [acknowledgement] and your patients receive good care. What I hope to accomplish today is to work with you to get your time on service down for your existing patients and therefore make space for you to take on some of the people on the waiting list [redirection].
  - *Ann* I know there are people waiting and they need care too. I care a lot about my patients. Most of them live alone and I am the only person they see all week. If I discharge them they will be lonely, and their health may slip back [explanation].
  - *Team leader* You are right to be concerned. I am sure you can work out a way to get other people involved with those who live alone earlier so they will have support when you are no longer there for them [supportive and problem-solving].
  - *Ann* I'm sure you are right. Maybe I can sort this out [agreement].
  - *Team leader* I have confidence in you. What support do you need from me? [offer of help].
  - *Ann* Jayne always seems to be able to get her patients involved with community activities. Would you be happy for me to work with Jayne for a couple of days to see how she does it?
  - *Team leader* Absolutely. Let's meet in a month to see how things are going.
  - *Ann* Okay.

What you know now

- Communication is a complex, ongoing, dynamic process in which participants simultaneously create meaning in an interaction.
- Expert communication skills are essential for a nurse manager's success. Gender, cultural background and the organisational culture influence communication and its outcome.
- Messages can be distorted or misconstrued. Your job is to be as clear as possible and ensure that you have been understood.
- Communication strategies vary according to the situation and the roles of people involved.

Questions to challenge you

1. What are the communication channels in your workplace or clinical site? Are they congruent with the published organisational chart? How well does communication flow both upwards and downwards?
2. Are messages received in a timely fashion?
3. Is the medium (in person, phone, email, etc.) appropriate to the message?
4. Are messages worded appropriately? For example, bad news is suitably serious, good news more positive.
5. Are messages negative in tone? For example, 'Everyone must . . .' rather than 'The requirements are . . .' (The difference is subtle, but important.)

References

Dickson, A. (2004) *Difficult Conversations*. London: Piatkus.

Mehrabian, A. (1969) *Tactics in Social Influence*. Englewood Cliffs, NJ: Prentice-Hall.

Oshry, B. (2007) *Seeing Systems: unlocking the mysteries of organizational life*, 2nd edn. San Francisco, CA: Berrett-Koehler.

Pease, A. (1997) *Body Language: How to read others' thoughts and gestures*. London: Sheldon Press.

Picker Institute (2008) *The Key Findings Report for the 2007 Inpatient Survey*. Oxford: Picker Institute Europe.

Porter-O'Grady, T. (2003) A different age for leadership, part 1: new context, new content. *Journal of Nursing Administration*, **32**(**2**), 105-110.

VitalSmarts (2005) *Silence Kills*. Available at http://www.silencekills.com.

Chapter 7
Delegating Successfully

Introduction

Delegation is the act of entrusting and empowering another with responsibility. It is a dynamic process that can often be difficult to learn but is an essential part of a manager's job. Effective delegation is a tool that benefits both the individual and the organisation. This chapter outlines the process of delegation, dealing with both authority and acceptance, and the obstacles faced by those who delegate.

You have just arrived at work. Where do you begin? You have a report to prepare for the audit committee. You need to change the rota to schedule staff for their annual safety review. Staff reviews are coming up and a number of staff have yet to arrange their clinical supervision sessions. Several admissions are scheduled for today, and beds are tight. Have you ever felt this way? How can you get it all done, be efficient, provide quality care and survive the day? Delegate!

It is easy to say delegate, but delegation is a difficult leadership skill for nurses to learn. With changes in health care delivery, both newly qualified and experienced nurses are struggling to develop their delegation skills. Never before has delegation been as critical a skill for nurses to perfect as it is today, with the emphasis on doing more with less. This chapter describes the delegation process, the benefits and barriers to delegation, and tips on how to avoid ineffective or inappropriate delegation.

Imagine

Think about the last time you delegated responsibility to someone else: perhaps you asked a nursing assistant to help a patient with her meal, or to ambulate a patient recovering from surgery. Were you clear in your instructions, and did you follow up with the assistant later to find out how the delegated responsibility went? Whenever you ask someone to take on your responsibilities, you are delegating.

Defining delegation

Delegation is the process by which responsibility and authority for performing a task (function, activity, or decision) is transferred to another individual who accepts that authority and responsibility. Although the delegator remains accountable for the task, the delegate is also accountable to the delegator for the responsibilities assumed. Therefore, delegation is a dynamic process that involves responsibility, accountability and authority. As a process, delegation empowers others and builds trust, enhances communication and leadership skills and develops teamwork.

Delegation is also a management tool. With effective delegation a manager can accomplish more tasks, and productivity increases. Delegation can also be a tool to develop the skills and abilities of others giving them the opportunity for advancement, increasing morale and promoting job satisfaction.

Effective delegation is both an art and a skill involving critical thinking and planning. The critical thinking part of delegation involves a careful assessment of the task or decision to be delegated, the capability of the delegate, and the devising of a plan to communicate clearly and follow up the delegation. Underpinning effective delegation is a clear understanding of the concepts of responsibility, accountability and authority.

Responsibility, accountability and authority

Although the terms responsibility and accountability are often used interchangeably, the words represent different concepts that go hand in hand. **Responsibility** is an obligation to accomplish a task, whereas **accountability** is accepting ownership for the results whatever they are.

Responsibility

The first principle of delegation is that you can delegate only those tasks for which you are responsible and are within your scope of practice and job description. If you have no direct responsibility for the task, then you can't delegate that task. For instance, if a manager is responsible for bringing bank and agency staff to cover shortages, the manager can delegate this responsibility to another individual. However, if bank staff use is centrally coordinated, the manager can make their needs known, request particular staff and otherwise influence the coordinator, but cannot delegate the task.

Similarly, if a porter who is responsible for transporting a patient from medical admissions to the ward is delayed, and a nurse asks a care assistant to get the patient, then it is not delegation as the nurse is not responsible for transport. However, if the porter (the person responsible for the task) had asked the care assistant to help, this could be an act of delegation if the other principles of delegation are met.

This principle is reinforced within *The Code: Standards of conduct, performance and ethics for nurses and midwives* (Nursing and Midwifery Council, 2008a), which states:

The nurse or midwife when delegating, is authorising that person to perform aspects of care normally within the nurse/midwife scope of practice.

Many leadership or management responsibilities are not specifically within the scope of practice of a nurse. That means that some of the management or leadership responsibilities, such as planning a duty roster or chairing a committee, are not specifically covered by *The Code*. Managerial responsibilities that can relate to *The Code* are those that involve staffing, education and training, and staff supervision and support.

Accountability

In delegation, responsibility is transferred whereas accountability is shared. For example, a nurse may ask a nursing assistant to do the observations on a patient and to report back to the nurse. The nursing assistant is now accountable for doing the observations to the appropriate standard of accuracy, to record those observations and to report back to the nurse. The nurse is accountable for the delivery of the care plan and for ensuring that the overall objectives of the plan are achieved (Nursing and Midwifery Council, 2008b). In this example that means the nurse remains accountable for the overall care of the patient and for following up on the observations taken by the care assistant. If the patient has a fever, it is the nurse's responsibility to take appropriate action, not the care assistant.

To clearly understand responsibility and accountability, it is most important to look first to the standards within *The Code* (Nursing and Midwifery Council, 2008a). *The Code* refers principally to the delegation of aspects of clinical care though it has implications for nurses in formal management positions. In particular, if the delegate is in employment, it is the employer's responsibility to ensure that they have undertaken sufficient training and education to undertake all aspects of care competently. Ensuring that staff attend training, that they are reviewed and that clinical supervision is undertaken is often a responsibility of the ward manager/sister or team leader.

The statements from within *The Code* and its accompanying advice are presented in Box 7.1. *The Code is a dynamic document, updated and reviewed periodically, and the most recent version should always be used as your guide to delegation.*

The Code is further supported by employment documents such as job descriptions and policies. These documents represent the employer position on delegation and outline the responsibilities within each role. What may have been allowed at one organisation may not be permitted at another, so being knowledgeable about your organisation's position is essential to safe and effective delegation for managers and leaders.

Authority

The second principle of delegation is that, along with responsibility, you must transfer authority. **Authority** is the right to act. Therefore, by transferring authority, the delegator is empowering the delegate to accomplish the task. Too often this aspect of delegation is unclear leaving the delegate unsure about the extent to which they can act, or the manager exercising too much control, crippling the delegate's abilities to accomplish the task, setting the individual up for failure and impairing efficiency and productivity. This pitfall is discussed later in this chapter.

Box 7.1	**The Code**

The Code: Standards of conduct, performance and ethics for nurses and midwives (Nursing and Midwifery Council, 2008a) provides the standards to which a nurse or midwife is held to account in respect of delegation. The overarching principle within *The Code* is that delegation must be appropriate, safe and in the best interests of the person in the care of the nurse or midwife.

The Code states:

● You must establish that anyone you delegate to is able to carry out the instructions

● You must confirm that the outcome of any delegated task meets the required standards

● You must ensure that everyone you are responsible for is supervised and supported.

Advice on delegation for registered nurses and midwives (Nursing and Midwifery Council, 2008b) further clarifies *The Code* by the following statements:

● Where a nurse or midwife has authority to delegate tasks to another, *they will retain responsibility and accountability for that delegation.*

● A nurse or midwife may only delegate an aspect of care to a person whom they deem competent to perform the task and they should assure themselves that the person to whom they have delegated fully understands the nature of the delegated task and what is required of them.

● Where another such as an employer has the authority to delegate an aspect of care, the employer becomes accountable for that delegation. The nurse or midwife will however continue to carry responsibility to intervene if she feels that the proposed delegation is inappropriate or unsafe.

● The decision whether or not to delegate an aspect of care and to transfer and/or to rescind delegation is the sole responsibility of the nurse or midwife and is based on their professional judgement.

● The nurse or midwife has the right to refuse to delegate if they believe that it would be unsafe to do so or if they are unable to provide or ensure adequate supervision.

● Those delegating care and those employees undertaking delegated duties should do so in accordance with local policies.

● The decision to delegate is either made by the nurse or midwife or the employer and it is the decision-maker who is accountable for it.

● Health care can sometimes be unpredictable. It is important that the person to whom an aspect of care is being delegated understands their limitations and when not to proceed should the circumstances within which the task has been delegated change.

● No one should feel pressured into either delegating or accepting a delegated task. In such circumstances advice should be sought from the nurse's professional line manager and if necessary from the Nursing and Midwifery Council.

Source: Nursing and Midwifery Council (2008a, 2008b)

Differentiating delegation from work allocation

Delegation is often confused with work allocation. Delegation is the transfer of *your* responsibility and authority that occurs on the basis of competence and trust. A ward manager may delegate responsibility for completing a safety audit to a staff nurse because safety audits are within the ward manager role. A nurse may delegate aspects of care to an unqualified staff member. In delegation, overall accountability for the function remains with the delegator.

Work allocation is a coordination function in which work is distributed to people over whom you have management responsibility. A team leader, for example, decides which patients will be cared for by which nurses on a shift. The nurse is responsible and accountable for the patients assigned, not the person who makes the assignment. The team leader has a responsibility for the appropriateness of the assignment, not the care of the patient. This is an important distinction to understand, and we will explore this in more detail later.

Benefits of delegation

Effective delegation benefits both the individual and the organisation. Some of these benefits have been previously mentioned. This section describes the benefits to the manager, delegate and the organisation.

Benefits to the ward manager/team leader

Delegation yields a number of benefits for the ward manager or team leader. Importantly, the leader will be able to devote more time to those tasks that cannot be delegated. With more time available, the front-line manager can invest time and energy into developing practice, improving standards and influencing decisions that affect their service. Developing others through delegation increases the chances that the standards of leadership will be consistent in the ward manager's or team leader's absence and important work continues.

Benefits to the delegate

The delegate also benefits from delegation. The delegate gains new skills and abilities that can enhance effectiveness in their role and provide for advancement opportunity. Delegation often builds trust and respect, thereby building self-esteem and confidence. Job satisfaction and motivation are enhanced as individuals feel valued and challenged by new responsibilities. Morale improves; a sense of pride and belonging develops, as well as greater awareness of responsibility. Individuals feel more appreciated and learn to appreciate the roles and responsibilities of others, increasing cooperation and enhancing teamwork.

Benefits to the organisation

As individuals become able to fulfil a wider range of responsibilities and work flexibly, the organisation benefits by achieving its goals more efficiently. Delegation can also improve morale and work satisfaction, which is linked to quality, safety and patient satisfaction.

The delegation process

The delegation process has five steps:

1. **Decide what to delegate** Delegate only an aspect of your own work for which you have responsibility and authority. These include:
   - routine tasks that others are trained and competent to perform;
   - tasks for which you do not have time;
   - tasks that have moved down in priority.

   Define the nature of the task. Ask yourself:
   - Does the task involve technical skills or special knowledge?
   - Are specific qualifications necessary?
   - Is delegation of this task restricted by scope of practice, standards or job descriptions?
   - How complex is the task?
   - Is training or education required?
   - Is the task required to be done in a particular way or is there room for creativity?
   - Would a change in circumstances affect who could perform the task?

   While you are trying to define the complexity of the task and its components, it is important not to fall into the trap of thinking no one else is capable of performing this task. Often others can be prepared to perform a task through education and training, or mentoring by an experienced person. The time taken to prepare others can be recouped many times over.

   An alternative would be to subdivide the task into component parts and delegate the components congruent with the available delegate's capabilities. For example, developing a service plan is a managerial responsibility that cannot be delegated, but someone else could gather information needed for the plan such as bed occupancy data, new admissions and time on service, and the staff could develop, and manage, the design and running of a patient experience (satisfaction) programme. The ward manager then consolidates all this into the service plan.

   What can be delegated? Before a task is delegated, two questions must be asked. First, what authority (what decisions will need to be made, what actions taken), and what resources (time, money, information) must the person control to achieve the expected results? Second, what are the limits, boundaries or parameters for each area of authority or resource to be used? A ward manager who is responsible for maintaining adequate supplies needs the authority to spend money on supplies within the supply budget allocation. The ward manager does not usually have authority to spend outside the budget; that authority rests with their manager.

   Certain tasks should never be delegated. Never delegate something that has been specifically delegated to you. If for example your boss asks for a report on a patient complaint, it would be inappropriate to ask another person to prepare that report. Your boss expects the report to be your work, not the work of another person. Disciplinary issues and ongoing performance or conduct issues should not be delegated. Issues involving confidential personal circumstances should not be delegated to others.

2. **Decide on the delegate** Match the task to the individual. It is important to analyse individuals' abilities to perform the various tasks involved in the delegation and to determine factors that might prevent them from accepting responsibility for the task. Conversely

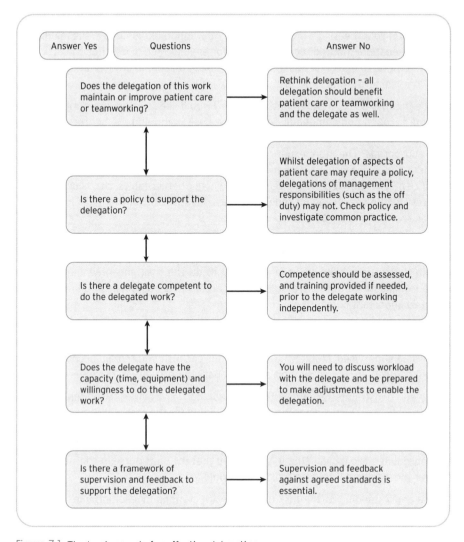

Figure 7.1 The 'yes' cascade for effective delegation.

experience and individual characteristics, such as initiative, intelligence and enthusiasm, can expand the individual's capabilities. A rule of thumb is to delegate to the lowest person in the hierarchy who has the requisite capabilities and who is allowed to do the task legally and by organisational policy (see Figure 7.1).

Next determine availability. For example, Charles might be the best candidate, but he goes on leave tomorrow and won't be back before the project is due. Some potential delegates may have more difficulty fulfilling the delegated responsibility because of current workload. A potential delegate already under pressure for delivering another piece of work may not be the best choice. One strategy that is very useful is to invite potential delegates to express interest in the delegation. A delegate with interest and motivation to add to capability is often the best candidate.

3. **Define the task**   The next step in delegation is clearly defining your expectations for the delegate. Plan your meeting with the delegate. Attempting to delegate in the middle of a crisis is not delegation; that is directing. Provide for enough time to describe the task and your expectations and to entertain questions. Communication should be clear and complete.

Key behaviours in delegating tasks are:

(a) Describe the task using 'I' statements, such as 'I would like . . .' and appropriate non-verbal behaviours — open body language, face-to-face positioning and eye contact. The delegate needs to know what is expected, when the task should be completed and where and how, if that is appropriate. The more experienced delegates may be able to define for themselves the where and how. Decide whether written reports are necessary or if brief oral reports are sufficient. If written reports are required, indicate whether tables, charts or other graphics are necessary. Be specific about reporting times. Identify critical events or milestones that might be reached and brought to your attention.

(b) Provide the delegate with a reason for the task. Describe the importance to the organisation, you, the patient and the delegate. Provide the delegate with an incentive for accepting both the responsibility and the authority to do the task. Incentives might include a release from routine duties for a time period, access to a training programme or membership on an important committee.

(c) Identify the standard by which the task will be evaluated and how often. Clearly describe the expected outcome and the timeline for completion. Establish how closely the assignment will be supervised. Monitoring is important because you remain accountable for the task, but controls should never limit an individual's opportunity to grow.

(d) Identify any constraints for completing the task as well as risks. Also identify any situational variables by which authority and responsibility for the task will change. For example, you may ask a staff nurse to manage the staffing for the weekend, but if the core staffing is at risk of dropping below an agreed level, then the task must be referred back. In this case you would make it clear that it is expected that the staff nurse in charge would phone you over the weekend if this circumstance should arise.

(e) Validate understanding of the task and your expectations by eliciting questions and providing feedback.

4. **Reach agreement**   Once you have outlined your expectations, you must be sure that the delegate agrees to accept responsibility and authority for the task. You need to be prepared to equip the delegate to complete the task successfully. This might mean providing additional information or resources or informing others about the arrangement as needed to empower the delegate. Before meeting with the individual, anticipate areas of negotiation, and identify what you are prepared and able to provide.

5. **Monitor performance and provide feedback**   Monitoring performance provides a mechanism for feedback and control that ensures that the delegated tasks are carried out as agreed. Give careful thought to monitoring efforts when objectives are established. When defining the task and expectations, clearly establish the where, when and how. Remain accessible. Support builds confidence, reassures the delegate of your interest in them and negates any concerns about dumping undesirable tasks.

Monitoring the delegate too closely, however, conveys distrust. Analyse performance with respect to the established goal. If problem areas are identified, they should be

Case Study 7.1 — Delegation

Eilish Doherty is the team leader for a large community nursing team. The team consists of district nurses, health visitors and school nurses. Eilish has a background in health visiting, and has a number of senior experienced nurses with backgrounds in school nursing and district nursing. The staff is quite large, and Eilish feels that it would be best that staff reviews are conducted by people with the same clinical background as the person being reviewed. Eilish approaches Mary, a school nurse, to ask her to take on the school nurse staff reviews. Mary has been a preceptor for newly qualified staff and has been praised by the newly qualified staff as a valuable colleague and good role model. Mary is interested but has a number of concerns. She has never done this type of review before and has not trained as a reviewer. She is also nervous about reviewing some of the nurses on the team because they are as experienced as she is, and she has worked with them for a long time. She doesn't feel like she has the credibility to conduct their reviews. Eilish agrees to send Mary on reviewer training, and to find her a mentor from another team of school nurses to help her get prepared. Eilish also agrees that for now, Mary will only be responsible for the reviews of the junior staff, and once she is more confident they will discuss her taking on reviews for her more experienced colleagues.

Eilish's Checklist for Successful Delegation

- ☐ Investigating *The Code* and advice for delegation to identify any application to this situation.
- ☐ Checking organisational policy about staff reviews.
- ☐ Sourcing a training programme for staff reviewers approved by the organisation and scheduling Mary to attend.
- ☐ Finding and agreeing mentorship for Mary and ensuring that Mary obtains supervision for her clinical and staff review roles.
- ☐ Freeing Mary from clinical duties to make time for review preparation and review sessions.
- ☐ Setting up and holding review meetings with Mary.
- ☐ Auditing staff review attendance and completion.
- ☐ Offering Mary feedback on her staff review work.

addressed quickly using feedback, and develop a problem-solving approach with the delegate. Be sure to give the praise and recognition due, and don't be afraid to do so publicly.

See how a team leader handled delegation in Case Study 7.1.

Accepting delegation

When you accept delegation, it is important to understand what is being asked of you. First, acknowledge the delegator's confidence in you, but examine realistically whether you have the skills and abilities for the task and the time to do it. If you do not have the requisite skills, it is your responsibility to inform the delegator. However, it does not mean you cannot accept the responsibility. See whether the person is willing to train or otherwise equip you to accomplish the task. If not, then you need to refuse the offer.

Accepting delegation means that you accept responsibility for doing what was asked of you, and you share accountability for the outcome with the delegator. Just as the delegator has the option to delegate parts of a task, you also have the option to negotiate for those aspects of a task you feel you can accomplish. Recognise, however, that this may be an opportunity for growth. You may decide to capitalise on it, obtaining new skills or experiences in the process.

Once you agree on the responsibilities you are to assume, make sure you are clear on the time frame, feedback mechanisms and other expectations. Don't assume anything. As a minimum, repeat to the delegator what you heard said; better yet, outline the task in writing.

In the event you are not qualified or do not have the time, do not be afraid to say no. Thank the delegator for the offer and clearly explain why you must decline at this time. Express your interest in working together in the future.

Obstacles to delegation

Although delegation can yield many benefits, there are potential barriers. Some barriers are situational; others are the result of the delegator's or delegate's beliefs or inexperience. Table 7.1 summarises potential obstacles to delegation.

Situational factors

Factors both within and external to the organisation may present obstacles to delegation.

Organisational culture

The culture within the organisation may restrict delegation. Hierarchies, management styles and norms may all preclude delegation. Rigid chains of command and autocratic leadership styles do

Table 7.1 Potential obstacles to delegation

Environmental	Delegator	Delegate
Scope of practice	Lack of trust and confidence	Inexperience
Standards	Believe others incapable	Fear of failure and reprisal
Job descriptions	Believe self indispensable	Lack of confidence
Policies	Fear of others doing it better	Overdependence on others
Organisational structure	Fear of criticism	Avoidance of responsibility
Management styles	Fear of blame for others' mistakes	
Resources	Fear of loss of control	Fear of overburdening
		Fear of decreased job satisfaction
		Insecurity
		Inexperience in delegation
		Inadequate organisational skills

Adapted from Delegation: How to deliver care through others, R. Hansten and M. Washburn, 1992, *American Journal of Nursing*, **92**(3), 87-88.

not facilitate delegation and rarely provide good role models. The unspoken assumption is that others are not capable or skilled so the work is done by the managers. An atmosphere of distrust prevails as well as a poor tolerance for mistakes. Additional environmental factors include a norm of crisis management and poorly defined job descriptions or chains of command.

Personal qualities

Poor communication and interpersonal skills can also be a barrier to delegation. Thomas and Hume (1998) note that in addition to good communication skills and respecting and treating staff fairly, a willingness to work with the other, to be open to suggestions, to provide feedback and acknowledgment for work well done is essential. They also note that delegates must be reliable and willing to follow instructions.

Resources

Another difficulty frequently encountered is a lack of resources in the broadest sense: people, equipment, supplies and time. For example, there may be no one to whom you can delegate. This can happen due to staffing shortages or simply because of the structure of the service. Another limiting factor may be money to send someone on a training course or to buy a software program to support the project.

Time is often the most difficult resource to find. Whilst a team leader may want to delegate in order to free up their time to undertake a delegation from their manager, the patient needs on their team may be so acute that they are unable to free up enough time from clinical duties to enable a staff nurse to undertake the delegation.

An insecure delegator

The majority of the barriers to delegation arise from the delegator. Three conflicts have been identified by del Bueno (1993):

1. Trust versus control
2. Approval versus affiliation
3. Democratic ideal versus the classical hierarchy.

Trust is paramount to delegation, but to trust another individual means to give up some control. Everyone has the need for both approval and affiliation, but which is more important – the need to be liked, or the need to belong and be accepted? Which is more valued – teamwork and empowerment, or control and the established hierarchy? These are difficult to address.

Commonly voiced concerns about delegation are:

'I can do it better.'

'I can do it faster.'

'I'd rather do it myself.'

'I don't have time to delegate.'

Often underlying these statements are unexamined beliefs, fears and inexperience in delegation. In fact, a delegator should delegate those things that the delegator can do well. Therefore, there is a degree of truth in the first three statements. Most people find it satisfying to do a task well and it is tempting to keep the tasks you enjoy and do with ease to yourself. However, one of the roles of a manager is to develop staff; that may mean trusting someone else to take on a cherished activity and supporting them to gain the necessary expertise to do it well.

Unfortunately, by failing to delegate, you may be sending an unintended message to those around you. You may be conveying a lack of trust or confidence in others, or perhaps even that you see them as incapable or yourself as indispensable. In the process the staff are demoralised, and the manager loses commitment. More often than not, these statements are smokescreens for the delegator's own fears and weaknesses.

The following are some common fears:

- Fear of competition or criticism. What if someone else can do the job better or faster than me. What will others think? Will I lose respect and control? This fear is unfounded if the delegator has selected the right task and matched it with the right individual. In fact, the delegate's success in the task provides evidence of the delegator's leadership and decision-making abilities.

- Fear of accountability. Some individuals are not risk-takers and shy away from delegation for this reason. There are risks associated with delegation, but the delegator can minimise these risks by following the steps of delegation, as previously described. A related concern is a fear of being blamed for the delegate's mistakes. If the delegator used good judgement in selecting the task and delegate, and followed the steps in delegation, then the responsibility for any mistakes made are those of the delegate; it is not necessary to take on guilt for another's mistakes. To help keep this issue in perspective, it is important to recall the benefits of delegation and balance the rewards with the risks while making the delegation decision.

- Fear of loss of control. Will I be kept informed? Will the job be done right? How can I be sure? The more one is insecure and inexperienced in delegation, the more this fear is an issue. This is also a predominant concern in individuals who tend towards autocratic styles of leadership and perfectionism. The key to retaining control is to clearly identify the task and expectations and then to monitor progress and provide feedback.

- Fear of overburdening others. They already have so much to do; how can I suggest more? Everyone has work to do. Such a statement belittles the decisional capabilities of others. Remember that delegation is a voluntary, contractual agreement; acceptance of a delegated task indicates the availability and willingness of the delegate to perform the task. Often, the delegate welcomes the diversion and stimulation, and what the delegator perceives as a burden is actually a blessing. The onus is on the delegator to select the right person for the right reason.

- Fear of loss of personal satisfaction. Because the types of task recommended to delegate are those that are familiar and routine, the delegator's job satisfaction should actually increase with the opportunity to explore new challenges and obtain other skills and abilities.

Additional hindrances to delegation include inadequate organisational skills, such as poor time management, and inexperience in delegation.

An unwilling delegate

A delegate may be unwilling for a range of reasons. Fear of failure is the most common reason people are reluctant to accept a delegation, but they may also see themselves as incapable or overburdened. Reassurance and support are needed, and the manager should be prepared to invest time to equip the delegate for the new responsibility. If proper selection criteria are used and the steps of delegation followed, then the delegate should be successful.

Failed delegation

When the steps of delegation are not followed or barriers remain unresolved, the delegation may fail, meaning the delegate is unable to achieve the outcomes expected within the delegation. The most common reason for **failed delegation** is that the initial steps in delegation are not followed, or that the delegator meddles in the process once undertaken. Here are some common situations that can lead to failed delegation.

Unnecessary duplication

If staff are duplicating the work of others, the manager may have given related tasks to too many people (Barter, 2002). To avoid unnecessary duplication, try to delegate associated tasks to as few people as possible. This allows the person to complete the assignment without spending time negotiating with others about which task should be done by which person. Reporting is also simplified for both the employee and the manager.

Reverse delegation

In **reverse delegation**, someone who has accepted a delegation gives it back to the delegator. This can happen when things get difficult or controversial, or when the delegate's confidence or willingness flags. Imagine a community team that uses a self-rostering system. Self-rostering is a form of delegated responsibility from the team leader to the team. The success of self-rostering is dependent on high levels of trust and cooperation between staff. An example of reverse delegation in this team would be the team asking the manager to do the Christmas off-duty because the team does not want to undertake the tough negotiations that may be needed. Faced with this situation, the manager must think through the consequences of accepting the reverse delegation. Am I doing this to avoid conflict? Do the staff have the skills to manage conflict amongst themselves? Is the situation so different that self-rostering should be suspended? Passively accepting a reverse delegation could signal a barrier to effective delegation in the future. Managers that are uncomfortable with conflict may passively accept this reverse delegation, causing the delegation to fail by their actions.

Wrong reasons

The delegator needs to be delegating for the right reasons: not to gain personal prestige or dump undesirable tasks, but to accomplish the goals of the organisation more efficiently. Staff will soon lose respect for a manager who delegates difficult and demanding work to free up time for personal benefit or to avoid accountability.

The importance of delegation to leadership and management

Delegation is a skill that can be learned, but not easily (Jones, 2003). Like other skills, delegating successfully requires practice. Sometimes it seems it might be easier to do it yourself, but it is not. Once you learn how to delegate, you will extend your ability to accomplish more by using others' help. No one in health care today can afford to fail to delegate.

What you know now

- Delegation is a process by which authority and responsibility for a task is transferred by the person accountable for the task to another individual.
- Delegation involves skill in defining the responsibility to be delegated, determining who has the requisite skills and abilities, describing expectations clearly, reaching mutual agreement, monitoring performance and providing feedback.
- Delegation benefits the manager, delegate, organisation and patients.
- Various barriers to effective delegation reside within the organisation, the delegator and the delegate.
- Failed delegation can result from inadequate or inappropriate initial transference of authority or responsibility, or from a failure to equip, supervise or support the delegate.
- Adhering to the steps of delegation – in particular, prudently selecting a qualified person as delegate and providing appropriate supervision – minimises the risk.
- All managers must learn to delegate in order to be successful in their positions.

Questions to challenge you

1. Download a copy of *The Code* and a copy of the advice for delegation from the Nursing and Midwifery Council. Draw up a list of the responsibilities you believe would be appropriate to delegate to an unqualified member of the team.
2. What are your organisation's policies on delegation?
3. Describe a situation in which you delegated a task to someone else. Did you follow the steps of delegation explained in this chapter? What was the outcome? Did the delegate complete the task to expected standard? How did you feel whilst delegating - confident, concerned, in control?
4. Describe a situation when someone else delegated a task to you. Did your delegator explain what to do? Did you receive too much information? Not enough? Was supervision appropriate to the task and to your abilities? What was the outcome?

References

Barter, M. (2002) Follow the team leader. *Nursing Management*, **33**(10), 54-57.

del Bueno, D. J. (1993) Delegation and the dilemma of the democratic ideal. *Journal of Nursing Administration*, **23**(3), 20-21, 25.

Hansten, R. and Washburn, M. (1992) Delegation: how to deliver care through others. *American Journal of Nursing*, **92**(3), 87-90.

Jones, R. (2003) Perspectives in leadership: the art of delegation. *Nursing Spectrum*, **13**(6), 7.

Nursing and Midwifery Council (2008a) *The Code: Standards of conduct performance and ethics for nurses and midwives*. London: Nursing and Midwifery Council.

Nursing and Midwifery Council (2008b) *Advice on Delegation for Registered Nurses and Midwives*. London: Nursing and Midwifery Council.

Thomas, S. and Hume, G. (1998) Delegation competencies: beginning practitioners' reflections. *Nurse Educator*, **23**(1), 38-41.

Chapter 8
Motivating and Developing Others

Key terms

Motivation
Content theories of motivation
Process theories of motivation
Reinforcement theory
Operant conditioning
Positive reinforcement
Negative reinforcement
Extinction
Shaping
Expectancy theory
Equity theory
Goal-setting theory

Staff development
Life-long learning
Training and development needs
 assessment
Development planning
Social learning theory
Relapse prevention
Adult learning theory
Induction
Preceptor
On-the-job instruction
Evaluation of staff development

Introduction

The performance of individuals within an organisation determines how successfully an organisation operates. Important factors influencing performance are the skill and knowledge of the staff (ability) and the commitment to the work to be done (motivation). A common and troublesome question facing leaders and managers today is why some people perform better than others. Each person is different and, in order to get the best out of people, it is important to know how such differences influence the behaviour of the team members and their performance in the requirements of the job. Employee performance literature ultimately reveals two major dimensions as determinants of job performance: motivation and ability (Hersey, Blanchard and Johnson, 2001). This chapter presents techniques for motivating and developing others.

> ### Imagine
>
> Think about a time when you have been entirely focused, committed, energised and enthused about accomplishing a task. Now think about a time when you put off doing a task until it was inevitable, and you accomplished the task painfully, through gritted teeth. The difference between these two situations is often down to one of two things - motivation or ability.

Motivation

Motivation is the energy behind performance, the focusing of interest in the activity. Because individuals bring different needs and goals to the workplace, the type and intensity of motivators vary among employees. Motivated people are more likely to be productive than are unmotivated workers. This is one reason that motivation is an important consideration for those who lead and manage.

Motivational theories

Historically, motivational theories were concerned with three things:

- what mobilises or energises human behaviour;
- what directs behaviour toward the accomplishment of some objective;
- how such behaviour is sustained over time.

The usefulness of motivational theories depends on their ability to explain motivation adequately, to predict with some degree of accuracy what people will actually do and, finally, to suggest practical ways of influencing employees to accomplish organisational objectives. Motivational theories can be classified into at least two distinct groups: content theories and process theories.

Content theories

In general, **content theories of motivation** emphasise individual needs or the rewards that may satisfy those needs. There are two types of content theory: instinct and need. Instinct theorists characterised instincts as inherited or innate tendencies that predisposed individuals to behave in certain ways. Whilst explaining some instinctive behaviour such as flight or fight response when faced with danger, it was less useful for explaining why an individual would put themselves in a dangerous position such as rescuing a child from a swollen river. It was recognised that instinct is stronger in some individuals than others and could not be relied on to predict behaviour or to motivate others.

Need theories have some advantages over instinct theories and went some way to explaining the variation between individuals. For example, whilst all people need to eat to live, some people are more motivated by food than others. An individual's needs can change over time, and can be influenced by the situation. Behaviours that occur in response to a need can be learned. For example, two employees may both need time off on Saturday. One employee makes an honest request, is willing to negotiate and has the best interests of the ward in mind. Another employee may choose to keep quiet and to phone in sick on the day. In this case the behaviours chosen in response to the need are very different.

Perhaps the most noted of the need theorists were Abraham Maslow, Clayton Alderfer and Frederick Herzberg. Maslow (1943, 1954) identified five groups of needs arranged in a hierarchy and often illustrated as a pyramid. He suggested that the lowest level of need drives behaviour until those needs are satisfied, and then the next level of need takes over, directing behaviour. This pattern repeats itself until the highest level of needs, self-actualisation (reaching full potential), is achieved. Maslow's hierarchy of needs theory is often used to explain extremes of behaviour that would not normally be seen. For example, a group of ordinary people who would never consider killing an animal, when they become stranded in the forest without food, will hunt to survive or kill an animal to protect themselves.

This hierarchy, from the lowest to the highest level, is as follows:

- physiological needs, such as hunger and thirst, sleep, warmth;
- safety needs, that is, bodily safety;
- belongingness or social needs, such as friendship, affection and love;
- esteem needs, such as recognition, appreciation and self-respect;
- self-actualisation, that is, developing one's whole potential.

The three content theorists are compared in Figure 8.1.

Alderfer (1972) suggested three rather than five need levels in his existence-relatedness-growth theory:

- existence needs, which include both physical and safety needs;
- relatedness needs (Maslow's belongingness or social needs);
- growth needs, which include the needs for self-esteem and self-actualisation.

This theory is similar to Maslow's in that it assumes that the satisfaction of needs on one level activates a need at the next higher level (Figure 8.1). The theory suggests that a staff member who feels secure in their job will strive for a means of feeling related or connected to

Maslow	Alderfer	Herzberg
Self-actualisation	Growth needs	Motivating factors
Esteem needs		
Belongingness (social needs)	Relatedness needs	
Safety needs	Existence needs	Hygiene factors
Physiological needs		

Figure 8.1 A comparison of content theories.

the ward, other staff and the value of the work. Today's employees want to have a voice in how things are done; they want to make a difference and feel that they are valued by the organisation.

Alderfer suggests, however, that frustrated higher-level needs cause a regression to and re-emphasis of the next lower-level need in the hierarchy. In addition, Alderfer's model suggests that more than one need may operate at any time. Although it is somewhat less rigid than Maslow's hierarchy, it presents little that is new or substantially different from Maslow's.

Herzberg's two-factor theory explains motivation as a function of job satisfaction (Herzberg, 1966; Herzberg, Mausner and Snyderman, 1959). Herzberg states that job satisfaction and job dissatisfaction are not opposite ends of the same continuum; rather, they are two different phenomena. The factors that lead to job *satisfaction* are quite different from those that lead to job *dissatisfaction*, and the resulting behaviours from these two states are also quite different.

Based on this concept, Herzberg proposed that hygiene factors and motivating factors, respectively, affect dissatisfaction and satisfaction. Hygiene factors are extrinsic to the nature of the job; they include pay, supervision, organisational policies, relationships with co-workers, working conditions, personal life, status and job security. Unsatisfactory hygiene factors lead to dissatisfaction, which, in turn, leads to increased absences, grievances or resignations. Herzberg likens hygiene factors to the process of treating water to ensure it is safe for drinking. Not treating the water will likely result in illness, but drinking purified water will not necessarily keep one from becoming sick.

Satisfaction and motivation then result from factors intrinsic to the job, such as a sense of achievement for performing a task successfully, recognition and praise, responsibility for one's own or another's work, growth and advancement or changing status through promotion. To the extent that these intrinsic, or motivating, factors are present, an employee is assumed to experience job satisfaction and hence will be highly motivated to perform the job effectively.

Process theories of motivation

Whereas content theories attempt to explain why a person behaves in a particular manner, **process theories of motivation** emphasise how the process works to direct an individual's effort into performance. These theories add another dimension to the understanding of motivation and help to predict employee behaviour in certain circumstances. Examples of process theories are reinforcement theory, expectancy theory, equity theory and goal-setting theory.

Reinforcement theory (behaviour modification) views motivation as a learned response to a given situation (Skinner, 1953). According to this theory, behaviour is learned through a process called operant conditioning, in which a particular behaviour becomes associated with a particular consequence. In **operant conditioning**, the response–consequence connection is strengthened over time, that is, it is learned. Skinner's philosophy depended on an absence of cognition, it was about reflex and immediate pay-off. Pavlov's research on ringing a bell to induce a dog to salivate is a classic example of Skinner's reinforcement theory.

Skinner's work, however, gave rise to the idea that behaviour can be modified by the use of reward or punishment. **Positive reinforcement** is used for the express purpose of increasing a desired behaviour whilst negative reinforcement is used to extinguish or make a particular behaviour less likely.

John, a staff nurse, made a suggestion that would improve patient flow and minimise delays on transfer from his ward to another. His manager supported the idea and helped

John implement the new process. The manager praised John for the extra effort and publicly recognised him for the idea. John was encouraged by the outcome and sought other solutions to work-flow problems.

Negative reinforcement is used to inhibit an undesired behaviour: punishment is a common technique. Rose has a long-standing habit of not attending to the completion of care plans and patient notes. The manager decided that she should be required to come to his office with her patient notes so that he could directly supervise Rose's work and make sure she achieved the expected standard. Rose unsurprisingly found the task laborious and humiliating. Begrudgingly, Rose brought her notes up to standard, so that the manager would let things return to normal.

Because punishment creates compliance at best, often accompanied by emotions such as resentment, anger and defiance, an employee may fail to improve and may also avoid the manager and the job. Research has shown that the effects of punishment are generally temporary. Undesirable behaviour will be suppressed only as long as the manager monitors the situation and the threat of punishment is present. Conversely, research has demonstrated that positive reinforcement is the best way to change behaviour.

Extinction is another technique used to eliminate negative behaviour. By removing reinforcement, undesired behaviour is extinguished. Consider the case of Jane, a chronic complainer. To curb this behaviour, her manager chose to ignore her many complaints and not try to resolve them. Initially Jane complained more, but eventually she realised her behaviour was not getting the desired response and stopped complaining.

There are problems with behaviour modification as a strategy in the workplace. Take the example of Jane above whose complaining behaviour has been ignored, and she has eventually stopped. If, for example, she identifies a significant safety issue that should be brought to the attention of her manager, because her complaints were ignored in the past she may now fail to report the safety issue in the belief that she will again be ignored.

A further problem involves opportunity. For example, a manager may wish to reinforce in Barbara the behaviour of speaking up in multidisciplinary meetings, something she has never done before. In order to use positive reinforcement as a motivating strategy, Barbara has to speak up at least once in the meeting, and this may not happen.

Gauging the impact of a reinforcement action is not always easy; a response intended to be a positive reinforcement may be perceived as negative. Take Mai Lee, for example. As a new employee, Mai Lee conscientiously completed care plans for her patients fully and in good time prior to discharge. When the manager recognised her for her good work, her peers became less friendly, forgetting to invite her for coffee after work or not engaging in small talk in the staff room. Although the manager wanted to motivate Mai Lee to continue with this desired behaviour, the response of Mai Lee's colleagues had a negative effect. Mai Lee stopped completing her care plans, falling into line with her colleagues who were of the opinion that if the care plans were done on time, other work would be asked of them. Mai Lee was more motivated by the acceptance and approval of her colleagues than that of the manager.

Shaping is another technique that falls into the positive reinforcement category. Shaping involves selectively reinforcing behaviours that are successively closer approximations to the desired behaviour. This technique recognises that it is unrealistic to expect a habit or other strong behaviour pattern to be extinguished and replaced by a new behaviour overnight. Making changes is often a gradual approach. A number of personal change programmes such as weight loss or smoking cessation use shaping as a technique, praising people for small successes along the way to the ultimate goal of ideal weight or non-smoking. Each successively closer approximation to the desired behaviour is reinforced and well established before progressive reinforcement is given to closer approximations of the desired behaviour. Shaping

	Interval	Ratio
Fixed	**Fixed interval** Reinforcer given after a given time Weekly or monthly paycheques Regularly scheduled exams	**Fixed ratio** Reinforcer given after a given number of behaviour occurrences Piece rate pay Commissioned salespeople; certain amount is given for each pound of sales
Variable	**Variable interval** Reinforcer given at random times Occasional praise by boss on unscheduled visits Unspecified number of pop quizzes to students	**Variable ratio** Reinforcer given after a random number of behaviour occurrences Random quality checks with praise for zero defects Commissioned salespeople; a varying number of calls is required to obtain a given sale
	Time-based	Behaviour occurrence-based

Figure 8.2 Four types of intermittent reinforcement schedule.

From *Organizational Behavior*, 8th edn, by J. R. Schermerhorn, J. G. Hunt and R. N. Osborn, 2003, Hoboken, NJ: Wiley.

can take time and occasionally an injection of energy along the way. Furthermore, if small improvements receive the same accolades as bigger improvements, the participants in the weight-loss or smoking cessation clinics may slow down their motivation because, as long as they are seen to be losing weight/cutting down on their smoking, they can still be gaining approval.

Behaviour modification works quite well provided rewards can be found that employees value and supervisory personnel can link those rewards to performance. This does not mean that all rewards work equally well or that the same rewards will continue to function effectively over a long time. If a manager praised someone four or five times a day every day, the praise would soon begin to wear thin; it would cease to be a motivating strategy. Care must be taken not to overdo a good thing.

Figure 8.2 illustrates the use of various schedules of reinforcement. Partial schedules of reinforcement (reinforcing behaviour with every second or third occurrence) are usually more effective than other reinforcement schedules in changing behaviour. This fixed-ratio schedule of reinforcement requires very close monitoring to reinforce every nth response and is obviously not very practical. Reinforcing on a fairly regular basis is known as a fixed-interval schedule of reinforcement; an example is the distribution of monthly pay cheques (Ferster and Skinner, 1957).

Some rather interesting research findings have emerged over the years on the subject of continuous and partial schedules of reinforcement. On the one hand, we know that a continuous schedule of reinforcement is the fastest method of establishing or learning a new behaviour, whereas any kind of partial schedule of reinforcement is much slower. On the other hand, behaviours learned under a continuous schedule also extinguish very quickly once reinforcement stops. Behaviour learned on a partial schedule continues for a much longer time without being reinforced. In addition, continuous schedules of reinforcement are probably better when money is used rather than other reinforcements, such as praise (Ferster and Skinner, 1957).

Expectancy theory was developed by Victor Vroom in an attempt to explain why individuals choose to follow certain courses of action in organisations, particularly in decision-making and leadership. Like reinforcement theory, expectancy theory (Vroom, 1995) explores the role of rewards (and consequences) and their relationship to the decisions and actions people make. Expectancy theory says that individuals have different sets of goals and can be motivated if they believe that:

- There is a positive correlation between efforts and performance.
- Favourable performance will result in a desirable reward.
- The reward will satisfy an important need.
- The desire to satisfy the need is strong enough to make the effort worthwhile.

Vroom suggests that three factors interact to create motivation.

- Valence is the perceived value (attractiveness or unattractiveness) of the consequence on offer. Money, status, promotion, time off and satisfaction are all potential consequences for work performance.
- Expectancy is the perception of capability, or confidence in one's ability to do the work.
- Instrumentality is the belief that the consequences will actually materialise. Will the promotion happen? Will the manager actually impose disciplinary action if I am late again for work?

A manager aiming to motivate an individual must first determine an individual's beliefs regarding their ability to carry out the task (expectancy), that their efforts will achieve the expected reward (instrumentality), and that the reward has value (valence). An individual will have greatest motivation when they are capable of accomplishing the task and are confident of receiving a valued reward. Under these circumstances, the person is likely to exert more effort to the task. When any component is drastically reduced, so is motivation (effort).

In an effort to improve the amount of delegation by the nurses on her ward, Andrea approached the situation from an expectancy theory perspective. She identified that the nurses wanted to assign more duties to health care assistants but were reluctant because of concerns about accountability. Once Andrea was able to clarify accountability issues, the nurses were eager to delegate routine tasks in order to be able to devote more time to their professional responsibilities.

Expectancy theory also considers multiple outcomes. Consider the possibility of a promotion to ward manager or team leader. Even though a staff nurse believes such a promotion is positive and is a desirable reward for competent performance in patient care, the nurse also realises that there are some less desirable outcomes of promotion (e.g. working longer hours, losing the close camaraderie enjoyed with other staff members). These multiple outcomes will influence the staff nurse's decision.

Expectancy theory is useful because of its clear implications for managing and leading. Leaders can create motivation by assigning responsibilities to employees that they are capable of performing, or by providing them with the necessary training to achieve competence. By removing obstacles to achievement (inadequate resources, lack of information or cooperation from others), employees' confidence in their success will also increase. Instrumentalities can be maximised by making certain that rewards (and consequences) are made contingent on performance. Rewards must be worth the effort needed to achieve success. Similarly, to act as a deterrent to inappropriate job behaviour, consequences must be regarded as sufficiently undesirable; perhaps even more importantly, the employee must believe that consequences will be applied.

Equity theory suggests that effort and job satisfaction depend on the degree of equity, or perceived fairness, in the work situation (Adams, 1963, 1965). Equity simply means that a person perceives that their own contribution to the job is rewarded in proportion to the contribution of others. Job contributions include such things as capability, education, experience, cooperation and effort, whereas rewards include job satisfaction, pay, prestige and any other outcomes an employee regards as valuable.

Equity does not in any way imply equality; rather, it suggests that employees who bring more to the job will receive greater rewards. Inequity occurs when an employee's effort and rewards are perceived to be disproportional to that of another person, whether a co-worker or a person doing a similar job for a different employer. Inequity, then, motivates a change in behaviour that may either increase or decrease actual effort and job performance.

Agenda for Change, the pay structure introduced in the NHS in 2004, is intended to bring equity across the various job roles within the NHS. Prior to the introduction of Agenda for Change, job evaluation was carried out. Job evaluation is a process of analysing roles against criteria such as levels of responsibility, independence, decision-making, nature of relationships and risk. The results were used to create equity across job roles and disciplines, and to place each job on a pay spine. The idea is that certain roles, perhaps those with the greatest levels of responsibility, should be paid more.

Unfortunately, reducing inequity may or may not change performance. Employees can try to restore what they perceive as equity in a variety of ways. First, they can increase or decrease effort. Nurses can attempt to increase their status by taking on more difficult patient assignments or by volunteering to lead team meetings or other responsibilities reflecting additional effort. Second, they may attempt to persuade the person(s) with whom they are comparing themselves to increase or decrease their inputs – persuading nursing assistants to work less, for instance. Third, they may attempt to persuade the organisation to change either their own rewards or those of the comparison persons. Fourth, they may psychologically distort the perceived importance and value of their own contributions and rewards ('How could they run this ward without me?'). Fifth, they may distort the perceived importance and value of the comparison persons' contributions or rewards ('What can you expect of health care assistants?').

Psychologically distorting the perceptions of a comparison person's outcomes or inputs is probably the easiest way to restore equity without actually changing one's effort. Disrespecting others or minimising their contribution is, sadly, rather common. Alternatively, the staff member may select a different comparison person, someone who is seen as more relevant for the comparison being made, such as the manager. Finally, the individual may actually leave the organisation.

The important point is that perceived fairness of rewards affects the manner in which individuals view their jobs and the organisation, and it can affect the amount of effort they expend in accomplishing tasks. Moreover, evidence indicates that inequitable rewards lead to increased psychological tension, lower job satisfaction and poor job performance. In times of economic constraint, when all salary rises are capped to the rate of inflation for example, employees may perceive the situation as equitable, thus job satisfaction may not be adversely affected. However, simply distributing rewards equitably does not necessarily improve an otherwise poor motivational environment.

Unlike expectancy theory and equity theory, **goal-setting theory** suggests that it is not the rewards or outcomes of task performance per se that cause a person to expend effort, but rather the goal itself.

There are three basic propositions in goal-setting (Locke, 1968):

- Specific goals lead to higher performance than do such general goals such as 'Do your best'.
- Specific, difficult goals lead to higher performance than specific, easy goals, provided that those involved see themselves as capable of reaching the goal.
- Incentives such as money, knowledge of results, praise and criticism, participation, competition and time limits affect behaviour only if they cause individuals to change their goals or to accept goals that have been assigned to them.

Katie, for example, had just taken a post in a hospice. An important skill in care with the terminally ill is communication, in particular when it comes to responding sensitively to family members who are distraught. Katie and her manager recognised that she needed help to improve her skills and confidence. Her manager asked her to write two goals related to communication. Katie's first goal was to attend a workshop offered by the Macmillan cancer charity on communications, and a second goal of using at least one communication strategy she had learned each week. Within a month, Katie's communication skills had already improved. As a result, she was more confident, satisfied with this position, her patients received more compassionate care, and Katie found the work more rewarding.

According to goal-setting theory, the function of rewards is to help ensure that the individual will accept an assigned goal or to set a more specific, difficult personal goal. The specificity and difficulty of the goal mobilise energy and direct behaviour towards goal accomplishment. If the person sees tasks and duties as reasonable and specific, difficult goals are likely to produce higher performance as long as such performance is rewarded and the individual is held accountable for the task.

Obviously there is no single approach to motivating people. Some methods work better than others with different people or in different settings. Each theory of work motivation contributes something to our understanding of, and ultimately our ability to influence, employee motivation.

Figure 8.3 illustrates a simple model of how the various motivational theories are related. First, there is a task to be accomplished. If this task is expressed in terms of a specific, difficult goal that is accepted by the staff member, a relatively high degree of performance may realistically be expected in most situations. How does this happen? Goals, perceived ability and perceived situational constraints all combine to form the imagined likelihood that effort will lead to a given level of performance or goal accomplishment. This expectancy, when combined with the belief that valued rewards will follow from goal attainment (instrumentality), prompts the expenditure of effort (motivation). Thus, goal-setting and expectancy theory suggest not only that staff members should know exactly what they should be doing but also that they should perceive rewards as contingent on performance of their assigned tasks.

Managers who are effective leaders draw from their knowledge of various motivational theories to create the environment in which their staff derive satisfaction from the work itself. No motivation theory provides a complete description of the motivational process; each theory or technique brings a different perspective and contribution to understanding and

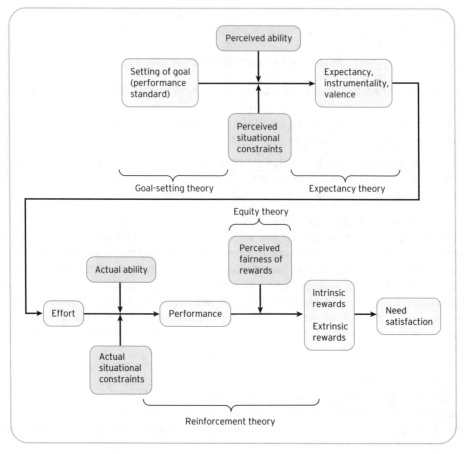

Figure 8.3 An integrated model of the motivational process.

influencing motivation. Effective staff motivation is best accomplished by judiciously combining theories and techniques so that their effects are complementary.

Case Study 8.1 illustrates how one nurse manager used her ingenuity to motivate staff.

Staff development

Job performance is dependent on motivation and ability. Every individual is unique and therefore will have different skills, ability and experience, and will come with a different educational background. There are a few common denominators: all qualified staff will have successfully completed a course of study leading to registration, but even those courses of study may be very different. Some people will not have developed all of the skills and knowledge necessary to perform at the expected level in the job. Even when competence is achieved in one setting, maintaining capability throughout one's career requires continuing education and staff development. One of the ward manager or team leader's important responsibilities is to identify **staff development** needs and enable staff to learn throughout their careers.

Case Study 8.1 — Motivating Staff

Susan's ward had not been a clinical site for student placement in the past. Susan was keen to host students for a number of reasons: they bring fresh ideas and help to keep the existing staff current in practice innovations, mentoring students is a development opportunity for staff nurses and, perhaps most importantly, students that have a good experience on the ward may be attracted to working there, therefore easing the difficulties in recruitment.

Initially staff members were resistant to the idea. They believed that mentoring students would take valuable time away from patient care when they were already short-staffed. There was concern that they wouldn't be able to offer the supervision the students needed, and therefore the incidence of errors would go up. Few staff members had worked with students recently and none had attended mentor support training. Susan listened carefully to these concerns and devised a plan to motivate her staff:

1. She discussed the benefits of student placement on the ward and the potential to attract the best of those students as newly qualified staff; that is, she set up an attractive reward for the staff acting as mentors.

2. Susan set a goal of attracting two students a year to apply to the ward.

3. She set up a project team to discuss staffing patterns, patient assignments and practical considerations of having students on the ward so as to involve others in the planning.

4. Susan asked for staff members to volunteer to mentors students, and increased expectancy by providing training in mentorship for her staff. She also set up a recognition programme for mentors, offering them preferential access to development, and setting aside time from clinical responsibilities for action learning among mentors as a group.

As a result of these actions, the staff were much more motivated to take on the mentoring of students.

Manager's Checklist

The manager is responsible for:

☐ Understanding motivating factors for employees and how motivation affects job performance.

☐ Using motivational techniques to enhance employee performance.

☐ Utilising creative techniques to motivate staff.

☐ Empowering staff to use creativity to enhance job performance.

Life-long learning

There was a time when people believed that the fundamental purpose of education was the transmission of the totality of human knowledge from one generation to the next. This is a workable assumption provided that the quantity of knowledge is small enough to be managed collectively by the educational system and that the rate of change is small enough to allow the increase of knowledge to be packaged and delivered.

Today, however, these conditions do not exist. Instead, we live in a period of knowledge explosion in which cultural and technological change is rapid. For example, by the time a staff nurse has been working for three years, some of what was learned during their training is already out of date. The implications of this are twofold. First, learning must be viewed as **life-long learning,** a continuous process. Second, learning must become a partnership between the learner and others so that learning occurs every day in an unstructured manner.

The process of learning operates constantly during conscious human activity. How people learn, the content of what they need to learn, the processes of learning and how to teach all are important to education. People even need to be taught how to learn so they can do their learning efficiently and are prepared to learn new information as it becomes available.

Most organisations have specialised training and development staff, either assigned directly to the nursing service or more commonly as part of a staff development department. Such departments design and manage induction programmes, mandated training and development programmes targeted at increasing the effectiveness of staff. However, the ward manager or team leader remains important to the staff development process. The manager working with individual staff members identifies development needs and ensures that development and training are provided. It is also important to ensure that training is applied. The team leader has a responsibility to ensure that what is learned is applied, and that standards and practices in work reflect best practice. Effective staff development usually results in higher productivity, fewer accidents or mistakes, better morale, greater pride in work and better, safer patient care.

Training and development needs assessment

The first step in achieving full capability for staff is a comprehensive **training and development needs assessment**. Too often, staff development programmes are offered simply because someone has requested them or they have been done in the past to address a situation that may not still exist. Considering the demands placed on staff already, it is imperative to carefully target staff development where it is most needed. Systematic assessment of development needs based on organisational goals can be used as a basis for developing specific content and appropriate methods.

The ultimate purpose of staff development is to change practices and behaviours in the clinical settings. Practices and behaviours that are appropriate for staff development are ones that:

- can be made more effective and efficient (e.g. a different way of managing transfers between wards, a revised clinical procedure);
- need maintenance usually because they are not done very often on the normal course of work but are essential to be done well when called upon to do so (e.g. cardiopulmonary resuscitation, fire training, hazardous materials and infection control);
- new employees need to learn (e.g. ward-specific practices and standards);
- employees who are new to a role need to learn (e.g. a nurse who transfers to intensive care and needs development on management of the ventilated patient);
- are needed as a result of new knowledge or new technology (e.g. a new chemotherapeutic agent);

- have been identified as a result of information gathered from complaints, near misses, clinical incidents, audit and patient surveys;

Development planning

After needs have been determined, the next step is to plan staff development programmes. **Development planning** entails identifying learner objectives and matching them with educational methods. Learner objectives should be specific, measurable statements about desired behaviours, skills, or knowledge to be acquired within a specific time frame. The strategy used to affect the desired outcome should be based on learning needs, the employee and available resources.

Ward sisters and team leaders have a variety of options for meeting the development needs of their staff. As mentioned above, the staff development department within the organisation will typically offer induction programmes and mandated training and often more. Progressive staff development departments are increasingly using a variety of techniques for staff development such as video tapes, computer-based learning and self-paced learning packages as well as traditional lectures, demonstrations and workshops.

Ward-based learning is also an option. Many wards tap into the expertise within and outside the organisation by inviting staff to present topics for discussion during staff meetings or team meetings. Some clinics have regular educational times where clinic appointments are not scheduled and formal training occurs. Ward-based preceptor and mentoring programmes are also important sources of development.

Three main questions should be considered in assessing learning needs and planning for staff development: Can the learner do what is required? What is the best method to facilitate learning? What can be done to ensure that what is learned will be transferred into practice? As well as underpinning the design of staff development on learning theories, theories of motivation can be applied to build the individual's desire to learn and to apply skills and concepts learned. Three learning theories help guide what we know about staff development: social learning theory, relapse prevention and adult education theory.

Learning theories

Social learning theory

Bandura described **social learning theory** in 1977. It is a behavioural theory based on reinforcement. Bandura believed people learn new skills and behaviours through direct experience or by watching other people. The observer learns that some behaviours are rewarded and therefore should be retained, while other behaviours are punished or go unnoticed or unrewarded and should therefore be abandoned.

According to social learning theory, the anticipation of reward influences what the person does or does not observe. This response suggests that observational learning is more effective when the observer has a good reason to pay attention rather than simply being rewarded for imitating what is seen. For example, a health visitor student may be asked to observe a qualified nurse conducting an interview with a first-time mother. Owing to the student being most interested in developing her capability in the role, she is likely to focus mainly on the

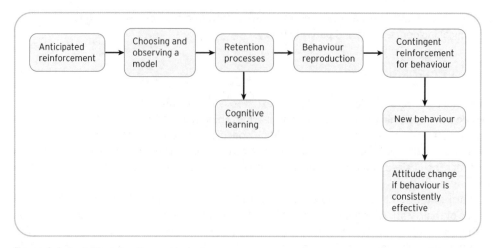

Figure 8.4 Social learning theory.

nurse's actions. The student may not pay as much attention to the mother, therefore missing vital cues as to her confidence in parenting. If the qualified staff member had asked the student to focus on the mother, looking for hesitation and noting the questions the mother asked, she would have learned something very different from the experience.

Figure 8.4 illustrates this theory.

Relapse prevention

Relapse prevention emphasises learning a set of self-control and coping strategies to increase retention of newly learned behaviours. This type of strategy is often used to prevent relapse into harmful personal habits such as overeating, smoking or other addictive behaviour. However, it can also be useful in changing work-related behaviours such as coming to work late or losing your temper with a colleague. The premise behind this model is that learners are:

- taught to anticipate high-risk situations;
- taught coping strategies for avoiding high-risk situations;
- taught that slight slips or relapses are predictable and need not become failures.

As a result, the learner's effectiveness increases because the learner anticipates potential problems and is confident in using coping strategies. In addition, this model minimises the possibility of small relapses turning into absolute failure. Based on this model, learners should be encouraged to identify possible failure situations and ways to cope with them and practise such situations using new skills in the neutral environment of education. Training for response to fire or clinical emergency incorporates this idea. If a fire were to break out in a building, fear would cause most people to react instinctively, putting themselves and others in danger. Fire training is designed to help people to anticipate this high-risk situation (potential for panic) and to respond in a predictable, patterned way that minimises danger.

Adult learning theory

Knowles (1950) proposed the **adult learning theory**, which described differences in the learning styles of adults and children. Prior to Knowles' work, it was assumed that the same teaching principles could be used for both children and adults. Knowles suggests four basic conceptual differences between adult and child education: self-concept, experience, readiness to learn and time perspective. These characteristics are described in Table 8.1.

Table 8.1 Characteristics of adult learners and educational implication

Adult learner characteristics	Implications for adult learning
1. The need to know	Adults need to know why they need to learn something before they will engage with learning. The first task of the teacher or facilitator of learning is to help the learners become aware of the 'need to know'. At the very least, facilitators can make an intellectual case for the value of the learning in improving the effectiveness of the learners' performance or the quality of their lives. Even more potent tools for raising the level of awareness of the need to know are real or simulated experiences in which the learners discover for themselves the gaps between where they are now and where they want to be. Exposure to new or unusual experiences, working with a mentor, undertaking clinical supervision or staff review are all processes that can bring the need for the learning to awareness.
2. The learners' self-concept	Adults see themselves as responsible for their own decisions, for their own lives. Once they have arrived at that self-concept they develop a deep psychological need to be seen by others and treated by others as being capable of self-direction. They resent and resist situations in which they feel others are imposing their wills on them. This presents a serious problem in adult education: the minute some adults walk into an activity labelled 'education', 'training' or anything synonymous, they tend to revert to the conditioning provided by their experience of school, and sit passively waiting for the teacher to teach.
3. The role of the learners' experiences	Adults come into an educational activity with both a vast quantity and varying quality of life and work experiences. The emphasis in adult education is on experiential techniques – techniques that tap into the experience of the learners, such as group discussion, simulation exercises, problem-solving activities, case studies and hands-on practice. Adult learners also benefit from learning from peers and using their experience to benefit others.
4. Readiness to learn	Adults become ready to learn those things they need to know and be able to do in order to cope effectively with their real-life situations. An especially rich source of 'readiness to learn' are the developmental tasks associated with moving from one developmental stage to the next. The critical implication of this assumption is the importance of timing learning experiences to coincide with those developmental tasks.

(continued)

Table 8.1 Characteristics of adult learners and educational implication (*Continued*)

Adult learner characteristics	Implications for adult learning
5. Orientation to learning	There are ways to induce readiness through exposure to models of superior performance, career counselling, simulation exercises and other techniques.
	In contrast to children's and youths' subject-centred orientation to learning (at least in school), adults are life-centred (or task-centred or problem-centred) in their orientation to learning. Adults are motivated to learn to the extent that they perceive that learning will help them perform tasks or deal with problems that they confront in their life situations. Furthermore, they gain new knowledge, understandings, skills, values and attitudes most effectively when they are presented in the context of application to real-life situations.
6. Motivation	Whilst adults are responsive to some external motivators (better jobs, promotions, higher salaries and the like), the most potent motivators are internal (the desire for increased job satisfaction, self-esteem, quality of life and the like). Motivation is often eroded by factors such as not wanting to admit that they have something to learn, lack of opportunity for development, time constraints, competing commitments and experience of poorly designed programmes that fail to consider the unique needs of the adult learner, being afraid that, if they have been out of 'formal' education for a long period, they may have lost that skill and, thereby, show themselves up.

This article was published in *The Adult Learner*, 5th edn, by M. S. Knowles, E. F. Holton III and R. A. Swanson, pp. 64–69, Reed Elsevier (1998).

Staff development programmes

Induction

Ensuring that a new employee has a structured introduction to their role, their colleagues and the systems that guide their work is very important. Among other things, a well-planned **induction** programme reduces the anxiety that new employees feel when beginning the job. Induction supports consistency in practice and standards of care by imparting vital information to the new person about 'the way we do things here'. Induction also provides a vehicle for social integration of the new person into the existing team, therefore promoting effective teamworking, good communication and cooperation.

Induction is a joint responsibility between the staff development department and the team leader or ward manager. In most organisations, the new staff nurse completes the organisational induction programme within the first few days of joining the organisation, whereupon the team leader/manager (or someone appointed to do this) provides induction to the ward or team. The staff development department and ward staff should each have a clear understanding of their respective, specific responsibilities so that nothing is left to chance. The development staff should provide information involving matters that are organisation-wide in nature and relevant to all new employees, such as terms of employment, the structure and governance arrangements, general policies and procedures, safety, infection control and common equipment. The manager/team leader should concentrate on those items unique to the employee's specific job.

The ward manager/team leader needs to outline very specifically what is expected of new employees and assure them that they will be supported in their development and will take on progressively more challenging responsibilities as their confidence and experience increases. Reassuring new staff that others are there to assist and support them is also important. Information and reassurance often have to be given a number of times during induction: with the anxiety people feel when they first come on the job, they simply do not take in all of the information they are given.

Because developing a relationship between the new employee and the ward manager/team leader is a very important part of the induction process, the team leader may find it necessary to set aside time to meet with the new employee on several occasions. The discussions should address everything from standards of performance, attendance, patient care and service standards.

Many wards or teams now use a **preceptor** model for induction of new staff, especially newly qualified staff. Preceptor programmes often benefit the preceptor as well as the newly qualified nurse. Preceptors gain an understanding of new practices that the new nurse may have learned, and an opportunity to use their expertise and experience to teach and support a colleague. Staff nurses who serve as preceptors should be selected based on their clinical competence, organisational skills, ability to work with others, good communication skills and an interest in the success of others. The primary goal is for preceptors to assist newly qualified nurses to acquire the necessary knowledge and skills so that they can function effectively on the job. The preceptor teaches and supervises the new person to gain competence in any unfamiliar procedures and helps the new nurse develop any necessary skills. The preceptor acts as a resource person on matters of ward routine functions as well as policies and procedures. The preceptor also serves as a role model for effective working practices and relationships such as how to set priorities, solve problems and make decisions, manage time, delegate tasks and interact with others.

Professional development

Professional development can be divided into internal (ward- or team-based) and external (off the ward or outside of the clinical area) sources. Internal sources include on-the-job instruction, workshops for staff and ward-specific programmes. External sources are formal workshops offered by staff development department within the hospital and educational activities outside the hospital, including college courses, conferences and continuing education workshops.

For effective adult education, the learner needs, at a minimum:

- information to be presented;
- practice using the new knowledge and/or skill;
- feedback about performance.

There must be opportunity for practice of the desired behaviours and feedback about it. For instance, if an individual is shown how to perform resuscitation, practises it, and is given feedback on his or her success, the person could be expected to be able to perform well in a resuscitation situation. Reading about or listening to a lecture about how to do cardiopulmonary resuscitation provides no assurance that the learner actually could resuscitate an individual in an emergency.

Learning styles

There is a growing body of research to suggest that each individual has a preferred learning style. One of the most popular and well-known learning style systems is Fleming's VARK system. He suggests that there are four basic styles, though a learner could also be multimodal (using more than one style on a regular basis):

- **V**isual learners are those that learn best by watching demonstrations, being shown and having diagrams, maps or models to work from.

- **A**ural (auditory) learners are those that learn through listening, having things described and discussed, and having the chance to ask questions.

- **R**ead/write learners are those that learn best through reading, using lists, notes and books, referring back and rehearsing presentations.

- **K**inaesthetic learners are those that learn best by doing, using real-life examples, visiting exhibits and trying things out.

You can test your personal learning style by visiting the VARK website at http://www.vark-learn.com.

The most widely used and frequently underestimated development method is **on-the-job instruction**. This often involves a structured experience for the learner with an experienced nurse, preceptor, matron or ward manager, a clinical professional such as a doctor, therapist or other specialist, for example from infection control, acting as a learning facilitator. On-the-job instruction has several positive features, one of which is its efficiency. Learners learn at the same time they are providing necessary care. Moreover, this method reduces the need for outside instructional facilities and reliance on professional educators. Transfer of learning is not an issue because the learning occurs on the actual job. However, on-the-job instruction often fails because there is no assurance that accurate and complete information is presented, and the learning facilitator may not know learning principles. As a result, demonstration, practice or feedback may be inadequate or omitted.

On-the-job instruction, though effective and efficient, may not be seen as having equal value to more formal classroom instruction. To implement effective on-the-job instruction, the following are suggested:

- People who function as learning facilitators, preceptors or clinical mentors must be selected for their commitment to the success of others, not simply for their expertise.

- Working as a learning facilitator should be linked to rewards including training and recognition of the importance of the role, and can also be used a part of a portfolio of evidence to support progression.

- Learning facilitators and learners should be carefully matched to minimise the potential for conflict and to enable the establishment of effective and supportive relationships.

- Learning facilitators should be selected based on their ability to teach, not just do.

- Staff nurses chosen as learning facilitators should be offered development in the role.

- Learning facilitators should rotate amongst learners to expose each learner to the specific know-how of various colleagues.

- The manager/team leader must realise that the efficiency of the unit may be reduced when on-the-job instruction occurs.

- The learning facilitator and the manager must supervise the learner closely to prevent them from making any major mistakes and carrying out procedures incorrectly.

Other learning methods

As technology continues to advance rapidly and the number of people requiring instruction increases, teaching is becoming more efficient and the learning process accelerating. Many organisations are using self-learning modules, such as online computer classes, computerised clinical simulations, interactive video instruction, audiotapes and CD packages. These methods allow an instructor to convey information in a uniform manner on several occasions or at several locations at one time; many lessons can be repeated. These methods can enhance the instructor's presentation as well as reduce the need for an instructor to present every detail in person.

Evaluation

Few issues in staff development create as much controversy or discussion as evaluation. **Evaluation of staff development** is an investigative process to determine whether the education was cost-effective, the objective was achieved and learning was applied to the job. Educators and managers usually agree on the need for sound appraisal of educational programmes, but they seldom agree on the best method to do evaluation and rarely do empirical evaluation. Typically, a programme is initially reviewed at the organisational level before its implementation. The same programme is used over and over until someone in authority decides the programme is no longer useful or no longer effective or, more commonly, until attendance decreases.

The purpose of evaluation is to determine whether the educational programme has a positive effect on job performance and to identify elements of the programme that need improvement. Designing sound evaluation tools is difficult and costly, though necessary.

Four evaluation criteria should be used:

1. Learner reaction
2. Learning acquired
3. Behaviour change
4. Organisational impact.

Learner reaction is usually captured on a questionnaire completed at the end of a programme. The questionnaire may ask about the usefulness of the programme's content, the effectiveness of the learning facilitator, the methods used and the venue. There can be a tendency to ask more questions, but long, detailed reaction forms are seldom completed fully, and the irrelevant questions can distract the participant from what is important.

Collecting and analysing learner reactions are important because:

- positive reactions ensure organisational support for a programme;
- reactions can be used to assess the programme;
- reactions indicate whether the learners liked the programme.

Assessing the actual learning is the next level of evaluation. Knowledge is typically measured by paper-and-pencil tests (or computer-based tests) that can include true/false, multiple-choice, fill-in-the-blank, matching and essay questions. Learning skills for the job is usually assessed by return demonstration – can the learner demonstrate proper use of new equipment or accurately follow the steps in a procedure?

However, the acquisition of skills and knowledge is not enough. Was that knowledge converted into different behaviours? One of the biggest problems in staff development is that instruction does not necessarily transfer from the classroom to the job – often because learners are taught the theory and the technique but never learn how to translate these into behaviour. There is a big difference between learning and doing; if behaviour is not measured after the programme (or on the job), it cannot be determined whether the instructional programme has affected behaviour or helped the employee transfer the new behaviour to the job. Transfer from the classroom to the job is critical to the success of the educational programme.

The objective of many staff development programmes can be expressed in terms of organisational impact, such as improved quality of care, a better health and safety record, a reduction in clinical incidents and better patient and staff satisfaction at work. It is often difficult, however, to attribute improvements to staff development alone. In fact, staff development is only one of a number of strategies that are put into place to address deficits in care or service in an organisation. For example, a decrease in infection rates is usually due to a change of work practices (hand washing, gel dispensers, deep cleaning, bare below the elbow) supported by staff development and good management practice. Despite the complexity of evaluating impact of staff development programmes, it is still worth the effort.

What you know now

- Performance is determined by motivation and ability.
- Motivational theories are classified as content theories or process theories. Content theories emphasise individual needs or the rewards that may satisfy those needs. Process theories emphasise how the motivation process itself directs individual performance.
- Staff development is intended to enhance specific job skills and knowledge, through methods such as induction, training, workshops and on-the-job instruction.
- The manager's role in staff development includes assessment of the development needs, planning, implementation based on sound learning principles and evaluation.
- The most important role of staff development is transferring knowledge in order to change work behaviour.
- Staff development programmes should enhance the organisation's effectiveness.

Questions to challenge you

1. What motivational theory appeals to your sense of how you learn? Why?
2. You are a newly appointed ward manager or team leader:
   (a) How would you discover what motivates the individuals on your staff?
   (b) What would you do first to identify your staff's learning needs?
   (c) What are the next steps you would take to meet those needs?
3. What recommendations would you make to a new ward manager/team leader regarding motivating staff? What strategies have you seen work? Explain.

References

Adams, J. S. (1963) Toward an understanding of inequity. *Journal of Abnormal and Social Psychology*, **67**, 422.

Adams, J. S. (1965) Injustice in social exchange. In L. Berkowitz (ed.), *Advances in Experimental Social Psychology*, vol. 2. New York: Academic Press.

Alderfer, C. P. (1972) *Existence, Relatedness, and Growth*. New York: Free Press.

Bandura, A. (1977) *Social Learning Theory*. Englewood Cliffs, NJ: Prentice Hall.

Ferster, C. B. and Skinner, B. F. (1957) *Schedules of Reinforcement*. New York: Appleton-Century-Crofts.

Hersey, P., Blanchard, K. and Johnson, D. E. (2001) *Management of Organizational Behaviour: Utilizing human resources*, 8th edn. Upper Saddle River, NJ: Prentice Hall.

Herzberg, F. (1966) *Work and the Nature of Man*. Cleveland, OH: World.

Herzberg, F., Mausner, B. and Snyderman, B. (1959) *The Motivation to Work*. New York: Wiley.

Knowles, M. S. (1950) *Informal Adult Education*. New York: Association Press.

Locke, E. A. (1968) Toward a theory of task motives and incentives. *Organisational Behaviour and Human Performance*, **3**, 157.

Maslow, A. H. (1943) A theory of human motivation. *Psychological Review*, **50**, 370.

Maslow, A. H. (1954) *Motivation and Personality*. New York: Harper.

Skinner, B. F. (1953) *Science and Human Behaviour*. New York: Free Press.

Thomas, S. and Hume, G. (1998) Delegation competencies: beginning practitioner's reflections. *Nurse Educator*, **23**(1), 38–41.

Vroom, V. H. (1995) *Work and Motivation*, revised edn. San Francisco, CA: Jossey-Bass Classics.

Chapter 9
Working with Conflict and Difference

Introduction

For most people, the word 'conflict' conjures up images of angry exchanges, bad feelings, poor working relationships, tension and distress. Conflict often arises from differences of approach, opinion, intention or interpretation. What turns these differences into conflict is the meaning we attribute to the difference and how we respond. If for example a friend says 'Your football team was rubbish on Saturday', the remark may be interpreted as an invitation to engage in some good-humoured banter, or as a personal insult, causing anger. Differences can escalate into conflict or can be handled in a way that supports good working relationships.

Conflict is one of the most difficult problems managers and leaders face, and learning how to deal with conflict is essential for success in any role. Conflicts occur between staff members, with patients and their families, between nurses and other health care professionals, and with those above you in the organisation. Learning how to prevent conflict, how to respond when you are involved in differences that could lead to conflict, and how to support those in conflict to restore good working relationships are important skills. This chapter shows you how.

Think about a recent conflict at work. What was the nature of the conflict? Was it a difference of opinion about how something should be done, a personality clash, perhaps two people wanting different things, or competing for the same thing? How did people react to the conflict: not only those involved, but those around them? How was it handled: avoidance, arguing, giving in or giving up?

The complexity of conflict

Defining the concept of conflict is a bit like defining art; you know it when you see it, but developing a clear definition is difficult. Conflict arises in every human activity and in every relationship we create. Some theorists such as Sigmund Freud focused on 'intrapsychic conflict where the conscious mind battles with the unconscious mind, whereas others have focused on conflict between individual, within or between families, between nations, religions or cultures' (Strasser and Randolf, 2004). The common element arising from all these different types of conflict is the concept of difference. **Conflict** results from the real or perceived differences in goals, values, ideas, attitudes, beliefs, feelings or actions. Despite the word 'conflict' having a largely negative connotation, writers such as Sacks argues that conflict has a positive side, that of reconciliation (Sacks, 2002). He argues that conflict has a purpose: it can bring people together for the purposes of confronting issues and threats, but more importantly, conflict can lead to understanding and the ground work for reconciliation. In effect, conflict is a powerful force that can generate creativity, focus efforts and deepen understanding, or destroy relationships, waste time and endanger the quality of patient care.

The conflict that consumes our time and energy at work is **disruptive conflict**, that is, differences that disrupt the flow of work. The parties involved are focused on the differences between them and often engaged in activities intended to disadvantage, disrespect, misunderstand, overpower, belittle, embarrass or defeat the others involved. This type of conflict takes place in an environment charged with fear, anger and distress. For example, a mental health team leader that is in conflict with the head of occupational therapy may use disruptive behaviour such as refusing to attend meetings where the other person is expected, not returning phone calls, or withholding information. People often react to disruptive behaviour by being equally disruptive, often using the same techniques as the other person. The head of occupational therapy who is in conflict with the mental health team leader is equally likely to cut off communications, avoid meetings and control information and may also escalate the disruptive behaviour using more subtle means such as starting rumours. Disruptive conflict can, in unusual circumstances, result in irrational, upsetting or even violent behaviour.

Whether a situation becomes disruptive conflict or not very often depends on the responses of those involved. Competition can be a stimulus for disruptive conflict or an opportunity for development. For example, a trust decided to run a competition to find the ward with the best patient experience. One of the criteria that would be assessed by the awarding panel was letters from patients. This factor was immediately seen as unfair by those in A&E

and the medical admissions ward in that they receive relatively few letters compared with the inpatient wards. The trust had set up the competition with the intention of focusing energy on improving patient experience, but unfortunately, because the competition was seen as unfair, the result was conflict between wards and the creators of the competition.

The most common sources of disruptive conflict at work are not competitions; they are differences in values, beliefs, opinions, actions and ideas. Examples of this type of conflict are numerous; two nurses disagree about the level of support a patient needs at home, a nurse and a consultant disagree on the readiness of a patient for discharge, a matron and a ward manager disagree on the cleanliness of the ward. These disagreements can become conflicts when communication breaks down, and the disagreement becomes a power struggle in which there can be only one winner. Being able to discuss differences and come up with a solution that is best for the patient will help to minimise the number of differences that turn into conflict.

Conflict as a power for good

A certain amount of conflict is beneficial to a relationship or to an organisation. It can bring issues into the open, lead to a healthy dialogue, dissipate anger and tension, challenge existing shortcomings of the system and provide a driver for change (Crawley and Graham, 2002). Conflict also can increase creativity by acting as a stimulus for developing new ideas or identifying methods for solving problems. Disagreements can help all parties become more aware of the range of perspectives, experience and solutions that are possible. **Reconciliation**, that is, coming to a friendly resolution following a conflict, can be the start of a powerful, collaborative relationship.

Conflict also helps people recognise legitimate differences within the organisation or profession and serves as a powerful motivator to improve performance and effectiveness, as well as satisfaction. For example, an interdisciplinary group planning a new service may initially be in conflict, but the process of airing differences, enhancing understanding and coming to agreement can set the stage for even more effective working in the future.

Responses to conflict

There are four broad behavioural patterns available to people facing conflict. Most individuals have a preferred strategy to which they are most likely to adhere. Thomas and Kilmann (1974) developed a conflict style inventory called the Thomas–Kilman Conflict Mode Instrument that has been widely used to help individuals to identify their preferred conflict style. Each person develops their preference for conflict response through experience: we learn the consequences of fighting back, giving in and running away at an early age. Whichever strategy we choose in a present conflict situation will be based on our experience, our assessment of the risk, and the type of outcome we want (Crawley and Graham, 2002). A number of conflict styles inventories use the following five styles:

- **Competing** (contending or fighting) is an all-out effort to win, to defend, to be judged right or to prevail in the situation. Competing is characterised by Kilmann as an assertive (pushing) and uncooperative (in it for myself) style often accompanied by anger and aggression. Behaviours such as blaming, insisting, arguing, criticising, forcing and threatening are used to ensure victory.

- **Avoiding** is a failure either to confront the issue or to acknowledge that a conflict exists. Avoidance is low on both assertiveness and cooperation and is often based on fear: a fear of the other person, fear of making things worse, fear of embarrassment or fear of consequences. Behaviours typical of avoidance are worrying, waiting for the situation to get better, absenteeism and doing nothing. Avoidance can also be seen in highly cohesive groups where the group avoids topics that could lead to disagreement and therefore jeopardise the good feelings they have for each other.

- **Accommodating** (giving in, giving up, yielding) is a tactic used when individuals neglect their own concerns in favour of the other person's concerns. There are times when giving in is the best option, especially when it results in gaining an advantage for the future. For example, if by agreeing to trade shifts you gain gratitude and respect from that colleague and willingness to return the favour, then the accommodation is a positive, assertive strategy. If, however, the dominant emotion is fear, then accommodating the other person may be a passive response used simply to end the conflict or to ease the tension of the moment. People are more likely to use accommodating strategies with those that they see as more powerful than themselves, for example people above them in the organisation.

- **Compromising** (making a deal) is a strategy that takes a middle position on assertiveness and cooperation. Both parties get some of what they want, but not all. This strategy is often held up as the best solution in a conflict, but in many ways it can be unsatisfying. Both parties can be left with the impression that they have somehow failed, and often the underlying needs go unaddressed.

- **Collaborating** In this strategy, both parties work to achieve satisfaction for all, by sharing information, insights, concerns and options. The parties hold a high concern for assertiveness and cooperation, being unwilling to agree until understanding is complete and a solution is found that satisfies all concerns.

Studies into the frequency with which nurses use these conflict response strategies consistently suggests that nurses overuse avoidance and compromise and underuse the other three strategies (Valentine, 2001). This suggests that nurses in management and leadership roles may not be getting the optimum results in situations of conflict. Box 9.1 gives you an opportunity to reflect on your conflict response style.

Box 9.1   **Reflective Activity**

Becoming aware of your conflict response habits is an important part of being an effective leader or manager. Self-awareness will help you to plan consciously for managing conflict when it arises. Think through the questions below: they may not all apply to you, but this in itself will be useful. If, for example, you find that you use accommodation almost exclusively in conflict situations, you may lack confidence in dealing with conflict.

Think of a conflict situation you avoided – what were the feelings underlying that situation? What was the result of your avoidance?

Think of a recent situation in which you gave in to the other party. Did you give in for a good reason (showing willingness, gaining respect, building relationships) or did you feel you had no real choice? What was the result of giving in?

Think of a situation in which you were willing to stand up for yourself, to fight for your opinion. What feelings made you want to fight? What behaviours did you use and what was the impact?

Think of a situation where you wanted to leave, to get away as quickly as possible. Why did you want to go? What happened when you did leave? How did the situation get resolved?

Outcomes of conflict situations

Conflict response preferences can affect the outcome of the conflict situation. Covey (2004) identified three potential resolutions to a conflict situation: win-lose, lose-lose and win-win. A win-lose outcome is often arrived at by competing or accommodating strategies that rely on unequal power between the parties wherein one party dominates (often the party with formal power such as a manager or consultant) and wins, and the other party submits and loses (see Figure 9.1).

Voting or majority rule is another example of the **win–lose outcome**, especially within groups. It may be a satisfactory method of resolving conflict, as long as people vote differently on different issues, resulting in each individual winning and losing on occasion. If however people vote in blocks, forming subgroups within the group, there can be a loss of trust and cohesiveness in the group.

Negotiating can also lead to a win-lose outcome. Each party to a negotiation tries to get the best outcome for themselves and has little regard for the other side. Negotiation is a strategy commonly used to make a purchase. Imagine you are going to buy a car. You want to buy at the lowest possible price and the car salesperson wants to sell at the highest potential price. This will lead each party to offer an insincere starting position and to withhold information from the other. If the price agreed is higher than the car salesperson wanted, they will be the winner in that the purchaser has paid more than necessary for the car. Such self-serving tactics can result in a resolution to the situation, but it doesn't necessarily result in building goodwill or long-term positive relationships. Negotiation therefore should not be the first strategy chosen for conflicts within the organisation.

A **lose–lose outcome** means that the settlement reached is unsatisfactory to both sides. Avoiding, withdrawing and compromising may lead to lose-lose outcomes. Avoidance is a very

Outcome win-lose	Outcome win-win
Strategies: Competing Voting Negotiating	Strategies: Open and honest communication Integrative decision-making Consensus building
Outcome lose-lose	Outcome lose-win
Strategies: Avoidance Withdrawal Compromise Formal measures	Strategies: Accommodating Voting Negotiating

Figure 9.1 Outcomes of conflict and strategies leading to the outcomes.

common strategy that leads to a lose-lose outcome. Think of the situation in which a staff member is frequently late for work. The team leader avoids holding a conversation with the staff member because they are afraid that the staff member will go off sick and the staff will be short-handed. The staff member begins to think that being late is not important because the team leader has never said anything and therefore continues to be late. The wider team becomes unhappy that lateness is being overlooked unfairly. The result is that the team loses respect for the leader and the team member who is late. Everyone loses because of the avoidance strategy of the team leader.

Compromise is often offered as a good way of resolving a conflict but caution is needed when using compromise. A common form of compromise is to offer a substitute to encourage cooperation. This can set a dangerous precedent and cause future problems. Take for example the offer of an extra weekend off for a staff member who agrees to cover this weekend coming up. The compromise has addressed the short-term need but actually put the staffing of a future weekend at risk. Expectations have now changed between the ward sister and staff member, in that the staff member may expect something in return for accommodating any shift change. Compromise is best kept for situations that are not likely to occur again between the same two people or groups (such as buying a house) so that the risk of precedent-setting is less likely.

Using rules or a formal process can also lead to a lose-lose outcome. Labour disputes are classic examples of this strategy where neither side ends up with what they really wanted. It can also happen when the formal disciplinary process is invoked. A team leader may want an employee to come to work on time, and the employee may want some flexibility on start time, but once a formal process is undertaken, the employee may end up losing their job, and the team leader loses a valued employee, and all because informal strategies to resolve the conflict have failed.

More often, the use of formal processes results in a win-lose outcome where one person gets what they want and the other does not. There are many examples of this type of outcome. A staff nurse requests the weekend off and the manager says no. The manager has the authority in the role to require the staff nurse to work, and unless the staff member resorts to a passive-aggressive response (such as phoning in sick) then the staff member loses.

The win-lose and lose-lose methods share some common characteristics:

- The conflict is often person-centred (we-they) rather than problem-centred. Parties direct their energy towards victory for themselves and are interested in seeing the other person lose.
- Each party feels misunderstood or wronged in some way and feelings can run high.
- There is a short-term view of the conflict; the goal is to settle the immediate problem rather than to develop greater understanding, respect, common values and stronger relationships.

Win-win outcomes are those where all parties are satisfied. Win-win strategies focus on goals and attempt to meet the needs of both parties. Two specific win-win strategies are consensus and integrative decision-making. Consensus involves attention to the facts and to the position of the other parties and avoidance of trading, voting, or averaging, where everyone loses something. The consensus decision is often superior to even the best individual one. This technique is most useful in a group setting because it is sensitive to the negative characteristics of win-lose and lose-lose outcomes. True **consensus** occurs when the problem is fully explored, the needs and goals of the involved parties are understood, a solution that meets these needs is agreed upon and everyone can sign up to it and give it their full support.

Integrative decision-making focuses on the means of solving a problem rather than the ends. They are most useful when the needs of the parties are polarised. **Integrative decision-making** is a creative thinking process (see Chapter 10) in which the parties jointly identify the problem and their needs. They explore a number of alternative solutions and come to consensus on a solution. The focus of this group activity is to solve the problem, not to force, dominate, suppress or compromise. The group works towards a common goal in an atmosphere that encourages the free exchange of ideas and feelings. Using integrative decision-making methods, the parties jointly identify the value needs of each, conduct an exhaustive search for alternatives that could meet the needs of each and then select the best alternative. Like the consensus methods, integrative decision-making focuses on defeating the problem, not each other.

Conflict conditions

There are a number of conditions that make conflict more or less likely but they are not necessarily the cause. These conditions are present in most workplaces.

Incompatible goals

One of the most important conditions that can lead to conflict is incompatible goals. As discussed in Chapter 3, goals are desired results towards which behaviour is directed. Even though the common goal in health care organisations is to give quality patient care, conflict in achieving this goal is inevitable because individuals have different views on what constitutes quality patient care. The consultant may define quality care as curing a disease or correcting a problem, whereas the nurse may see quality care as assisting someone to regain their confidence to care for themselves at home.

To further complicate matters, individuals and organisations have multiple goals that change over time. NHS organisations are now expected to balance safe, humane and effective care with the need to meet targets and budget constraints, and to genuinely involve staff and the community in shaping the organisation and its services. These goals will frequently conflict with each other, so they will have to be prioritised. Priority setting can be one of the most difficult but important activities a health care manager must face. Goals are important because they become the basis for allocating resources and thus become an important source (antecedent) of conflict in the organisation. Individuals also have multiple goals, and those goals may also conflict. Individuals allocate scarce resources, such as their time, on the basis of priority and therefore might achieve one goal at the expense of others. **Goal conflict**, the inability to attain multiple (and mutually incompatible) goals – whether those goals are personal or organisational – is common.

An example of goal conflict in nursing is the tension between the individual rights of mental health patients and the wish to keep them safe. This type of conflict may find a nurse's personal belief about autonomy and the right to refuse care at odds with professional accountability and legal responsibility. The tension between these goals has no easy solution.

Values and beliefs

Differences in values and beliefs frequently contribute to conflict in health care organisations. An individual's values and beliefs develop from their socialisation and experience. Each health care discipline has different experiences during training and is socialised to certain beliefs. Nurses are often socialised to see themselves as caring, which may lead some nurses to see other disciplines as uncaring.

More often now than in the past nurses are being asked to be conscious of costs when making decisions about care. This has been a reasonably recent expectation, and for some this request is anathema to the values on which the National Health Service was formed. For them the movement away from a purely social model to care to one that has some more commercial elements creates conflict.

Interdependent tasks and role ambiguity

Each member of staff has a number of roles and responsibilities related to their job. Some responsibilities are common to every member of staff (such as health and safety) and some are unique based on profession and experience. Roles become unclear when one or more parties have related responsibilities that are ambiguous or overlapping. The nurse in a team leader or ward sister post experiences conflict between their management, leadership and clinical responsibilities. Team members may see office work as less important than assisting with care and the team leader often experiences stress caused by these differences in role perceptions. This sometimes causes team leaders to take work home with them or to work late to accomplish the management responsibilities.

Role ambiguity is also seen between and within disciplines. The larger the team of staff needed to meet the patient's needs, the greater the interdependence of tasks and the greater the potential for role ambiguity. One situation where this is well illustrated is when a patient with enduring mental illness is admitted to an acute facility for a total hip replacement. A mental health nurse may be with the patient during hospitalisation. The nurse from the surgical ward may see it as the mental health nurse's responsibility to assist the patient to the toilet, whereas the mental health nurse, unfamiliar with postoperative ambulation, may see it as the surgical nurse's role. This lack of clarity sets the stage for conflict.

Structural relationships

The organisational structure creates potential for conflict based on differences in authority or power (such as reporting relationships), group structure (such as departments or directorates) and professional alliances (see Chapter 4). Each of these structural elements affects communication, can lead to differences in priorities and perceptions, and can create competition for resources. A team leader (superior) may risk conflict with a staff member (subordinate) by reprimanding the staff member for some inappropriate act. In this case the ward sister has responsibility for intervening with a staff member when their behaviour is unprofessional. Handled well, the use of position power can enhance relationships and improve care. Used without sensitivity, in an authoritarian leadership style, it can lead the staff member to feel like they are being bullied.

Competition for resources

Competition for scarce resources can be internal (among different teams in the organisation) or external (among different organisations). Internally, competition for resources may involve reducing the establishment in one service (such as inpatient care) and moving those resources to another (such as community care). Cost-improvement programmes within organisations have already resulted in shifts of resource from one area to another.

As commissioning evolves, increasingly organisations will also be involved in external competition with other public and private, volunteer and social enterprise organisations. Competing effectively will involve a variety of means, such as developing new services that are underrepresented in the service area, providing existing services with high levels of patient and public satisfaction, or demonstrating that the organisation can provide the care in such a way as to consistently meet quality and access standards (targets).

Different personality types

Different personality types present the opportunity for conflict. In the 1920s Carl Jung, a Swiss psychiatrist, was one of the first people to identify personality types. This idea has spawned a raft of personality models that help people to understand the differences in the ways that people behave. The Keirsey Temperament Sorter has its own unique model of personality (temperament), which includes four distinct types: the artisan, the guardian, the idealist and the pragmatic (http://www.keirsey.com). Owing to differences in personal qualities, it is not unusual that people have different world views and approaches to a situation. Take for example the following two individuals. Person A is a fun-loving, ideas person, keen to try new things and full of energy. Person B is cautious, reluctant to change things that have worked in the past. Person B may see person A as reckless and frivolous, wanting change for change sake. Person A may see person B as old-fashioned and boring, standing in the way of progress. Working well together and avoiding disruptive conflict will require each person to value and understand the other's point of view.

Conflict starters

Having the conditions for conflict, in other words having differences, does not in itself create conflict. Conflict arises because of what we say or do about our differences (McConnon and McConnon, 2008). Consider this situation. A ward sister and a consultant surgeon have worked together for years. They have mutual respect for each other's ability and skills, and they communicate well together. Unfortunately, the nurses and junior registrars on the ward have clashed over a situation, the nurses going to the ward sister and the registrars going to the consultant. The consultant and the ward sister are left with conflicting accounts of a situation, in which the only agreed-upon fact is that a patient received less-than-appropriate care.

Owing to the ward sister and consultant having a good relationship, there is a shared perception that they can constructively resolve the situation. The ward sister is not concerned that the consultant will 'pull rank' on her and the consultant respects the nurse's judgement ability. With these perceptions and a solid collegial relationship, the consultant and ward sister do not have feelings such as animosity and distrust that could lead to disruptive conflict. They know they can work together while helping their staff to resolve the conflict.

Now consider the same situation, the difference being that the ward sister and consultant have not worked together before. In this version of events, the ward sister and the consultant do not have the benefit of a long-term relationship. Each party is more likely to apply assumptions or generalisations to the situation. The ward sister may assume that the consultant will use position power and influence to get his way. The consultant may assume that the ward manager will avoid the conflict and therefore will accede to his demands. These perceptions will change the feelings that each has about the other. The feelings will then affect the actions each will take.

McConnon and McConnon (2008) identify the following actions as conflict starters:

- Blaming
- Accusing
- Interrupting
- Patronising
- Contradicting
- Exaggerating
- Insulting
- Using hostile languaging
- Bringing up the past
- Making assumptions (such as in the example above)
- Using labels or put downs
- Using absolutes such as 'you always', 'you never' and 'you should'.

Resolution, suppression and the aftermath

The final stages of the conflict process are suppression or resolution and the resulting after-math. **Suppression** occurs when one person or group defeats the other. Suppression could even include the elimination of one of the conflicting parties through going off sick, transfer-ring to a different service or leaving employment. Even if a solution is reached, in suppression only the dominant side is committed to the agreement and the loser may or may not carry out the agreement.

Resolution occurs when a mutually agreed-upon solution is arrived at and both parties commit themselves to carrying out the agreement. The optimal solution is to manage the is-sues in a way that will lead to a solution wherein both parties see themselves as winners and the problem is solved. This leaves a positive aftermath that will affect future relations and in-fluence feelings and attitudes. In the example of conflict between the ward sister and the con-sultant, consider the difference in the aftermath between each scenario: how future issues would be approached if both parties felt positive about the outcome, as compared with future interactions if one or both parties felt they had lost.

Conflict management

Nurses in management and leadership roles often find themselves involved in conflict situa-tions on several different levels. They may be participants in the conflict as individuals, as a result of their role (team leader, modern matron) or as a representative of a ward or service. People in a formal management role may create conflict by confronting staff, individually or collectively, when a problem develops. They may also serve as mediators or facilitators to conflicting parties. There could be a conflict within the unit, between parties from different units, or between internal and external parties (for example, a nursing instructor from the uni-versity may have a conflict with staff on a particular unit).

Anyone who seeks to resolve or manage conflict must be realistic regarding the outcome. When two or more parties hold mutually exclusive ideas, attitudes, feelings or goals, it is extremely difficult, without the commitment and willingness of all concerned, to arrive at an agreeable solution that meets the needs of both.

Conflict management begins with a decision regarding if and when to intervene. Failure to intervene can allow the conflict to get out of hand, whereas early intervention may be detrimental to those involved, causing them to lose confidence in themselves and reduce risk-taking behaviour in the future. Some conflicts are so minor, particularly if they are between only two people, that they do not require intervention and would be better handled by the two people involved. Allowing them to resolve their conflict might provide a developmental experience and improve their abilities to resolve conflict in the future. When the conflict might result in considerable harm, however, the manager must intervene.

Sometimes the manager or leader may postpone intervention purposely to allow the conflict to escalate, because increased intensity can motivate participants to seek resolution. Giving participants a shared task or shared goals not directly related to the conflict may help them understand each other better and increase their chances of resolving their conflicts by themselves. Such a method is useful only if the conflict is not of high intensity, if the participants are not highly anxious about it, and if the manager believes that the conflict will not decrease the efficiency of the department in the meantime.

Conflict management strategies

Several strategies can be used to manage conflict. Some tend to be more successful than others depending on the situation, those involved and the organisation.

Confrontation is considered the most effective means for resolving conflicts. Confrontation is another way of saying that important issues need to be discussed frankly and honestly rather than avoided. In Chapter 7 we looked at a framework for giving feedback and for holding a difficult conversation: these are the basic skill sets of confrontation. Confrontation is a problem-oriented technique in which the conflict is brought out into the open and attempts are made to resolve it through knowledge and reason. The goal of this technique is to achieve win–win solutions.

Mediation is a process by which an impartial third party assists people in a dispute to explore and understand their differences and come to a mutually agreed solution (Crawley and Graham, 2002). Mediation is particularly appropriate for personal conflict where feelings are getting in the way of working relationships.

Many health care organisations now have a workplace mediation service where trained mediators work with staff. The process should always be voluntary, and not part of any disciplinary process. The goal of mediation is for the participants to have the opportunity to express their feelings, identify changes they want in the working relationship and focus on concrete behaviour changes to which they would agree.

It may not be appropriate for a manager to mediate in a conflict between staff members that report to them. The power relationship between manager and staff may make it difficult for staff to be open. However, basic mediation skills can be very useful for a manager to manage disagreements before they become too difficult, and to enable problem-solving at staff level (see Case Study 9.1).

The following are guidelines for mediating a conflict between two or more parties (Strasser and Randolph, 2004):

- Protect each party's self-respect. Deal with a conflict of issues, not personalities. Agreeing ground rules about respect at the beginning of the session is paramount.
- The point of mediation is not to assign blame. Each person will have a different recall of situations from the past, and a different judgement about the intentions of the other party. Whilst it is important to allow parties to discuss their feelings about the situation, long debates about who did what and when are not helpful. Focus on the future.
- Allow open and complete discussion of the problem from each participant.
- Maintain equity in the time allowed to each party. A person of higher status tends to speak more frequently and longer than a person of lower status. If this occurs, the mediator should intervene, inviting responses from the quieter party.
- Encourage full expression of positive and negative feelings in an accepting atmosphere. The novice mediator tends to discourage expressions of disagreement.
- Make sure both parties listen actively to each other's words. One way to do this is to ask one person to summarise the comments of the other prior to stating their own.
- Identify key themes in the discussion, and restate these at frequent intervals.
- Encourage the parties to provide frequent feedback to each other's comments; each must truly understand the other's position.
- The participants are responsible for developing a solution to the problem, *not* the manager. An agreement to disagree is better than an imposed solution. Help the participants develop alternative solutions, select a mutually agreeable one, and develop a plan to carry it out. All parties must agree to the solution for successful resolution to occur.
- At an agreed-upon interval, follow up on the progress of the plan.
- Give positive feedback to participants regarding their cooperation in solving the conflict.

Negotiation involves give-and-take on various issues among the parties. Negotiation is particularly useful when the nature of the conflict is around competing priorities or mutually exclusive goals. It is also good for resolving immediate issues that are non-recurrent such as covering for staff illness, negotiating schedules for tests and procedures for patients with other departments, managing bed capacity and patient transfers, and obtaining assistance from other patient care areas in the event of staff shortages.

Levenstein (1984) lists ten commandments for negotiators:

1. Clarify the common purpose.
2. Keep the discussion relevant.
3. Get agreement on terminology.
4. Avoid abstract principles; concentrate on the facts.
5. Look for potential trade-offs.
6. Listen.
7. Avoid debating tactics; use persuasive tactics.
8. Keep in mind the personal element.
9. Use logic logically.
10. Look for solutions that satisfy the other person's real interests.

Case Study 9.1 Conflict Management

Beverley is the ward sister of a medical ward in a large teaching hospital. The nursing staff are diverse culturally, ethnically and educationally, and there are a number of new graduates and experienced staff in the mix. Beverley believes that nurses should be open to new methods and work processes, with an emphasis on evidenced-based practice.

Ahmed Karim worked for two years on the ward and is enrolled in a master's programme in advanced practice. Ruth Kirk has worked on the same ward for the past 28 years; in fact she trained in the hospital and has worked there ever since. During a recent staff meeting, Ahmed presented some information on new methods for protecting against skin break-down to the staff. Ruth made several comments during the presentation that simply getting patients out of bed and making sure they are eating and drinking well is easier and less time-consuming than the new protocol. 'All these new methods are just fancy degree talk, there is nothing wrong with the way we have been doing this for years,' Ruth says, gathering a chorus of head nods and wry smiles from some of the older nurses on the staff. Ahmed glares at Ruth and responds, 'As nurses become educated we need to reflect and put evidence into practice.' Beverley notices that several staff members are uncomfortable as the meeting ends.

Ahmed and Ruth continue to exchange sarcastic comments and glares over the next two shifts. The tension between them is affecting their co-workers and gossip is distracting people from the work on the ward. Beverley decides to use a mediation approach to the conflict. She schedules individual meetings with Ahmed and Ruth to discuss their personal perspectives. During the one-to-one with Ahmed, he describes how he wants to be respected for bringing new evidence-based practices to the ward, and wants those practices to be considered on their merit by his peers. He says he generally likes and respects Ruth, she has a lot of practical knowledge and experience, but he doesn't like her sarcasm. During Beverley's next private meeting, Ruth makes it clear that she wants her experience to be respected, and as changes are made that the team do not 'throw the baby out with the bathwater' abandoning time-tested effective ways. She also expresses support for Ahmed, enjoying his enthusiasm and respecting the way he shows kindness for the older people. It is clear to Beverley that Ruth and Ahmed have much in common: a desire to be respected, a concern for patient care, and regard for the other. Beverley brings Ahmed and Ruth together for a meeting in her office. Beverley starts out the meeting by saying that she values each of them for the contribution they make to care. She also outlines the impact of their current conflict on the team and care and her confidence in them to come up with a resolution today. She invites each person to tell the other what is upsetting them, and how they want to work together in the future. Ruth tells Ahmed that she feels like he doesn't value traditional ways and Ahmed tells Ruth that he feels like she doesn't value new ideas. Beverley guides the conversation, encouraging both people to describe their feelings and how they would like to work together. After expressing their hurt about the recent comments, both Ahmed and Ruth were able to tell each other about what they value and that they would like to work together more closely. Ahmed and Ruth agree to work together on the skin protection project, leaving the office feeling better about each other and their work.

Beverley was effective in her handling of this situation, choosing to intervene early. Left to fester, this kind of conflict can seriously undermine care and teamworking.

The leader/manager's role in managing conflict: creating a positive conflict environment

Conflict can be a driving force for change and a mechanism for improving understanding and strengthening relationships at work. Therefore it is important that managers and leaders enable differences to be expressed in such a way that it supports improvement without turning into disruptive conflict. The following are some guidelines for creating a work environment that supports constructive challenge:

- Encourage and enable positive working relationships between and among people. Get to know them on a personal and professional basis, their interests, their priorities and their passions.
- Confront (challenge) inappropriate behaviours using a difficult conversations framework early. Make your expectations clear and trust the other person to be able to make the changes necessary.
- Encourage openness and honesty in all communication. Use neutral language when setting expectations. Do not blame, label or belittle another person.
- Develop ground rules for work teams and committees. Get them to take responsibility for setting the standards of behaviour.
- Replace the BCDs (blame, criticism and disrespect) with QRSs (questions, respect and support)
- Understand the antecedent conditions for the conflict and the positions of those involved.
- Enlist others to help solve conflicts.
- Select a conflict management strategy appropriate to the situation.
- Practice the conflict management strategies.

What you know now

- Conflict is a dynamic process, the consequence of real or perceived differences between individuals or groups.
- Conflict can be positive and the first step in initiating change.
- Antecedent conditions are not necessarily the cause of conflict; they are conditions that exist in all organisations that make conflict more likely. Conditions antecedent to conflict include incompatible goals, role ambiguity and overlapping tasks, structural (power) relationships, competition for scarce resources and differences in values and beliefs.
- A number of strategies exist to handle conflict; choosing the best one to use is based on the situation and the people involved.
- Learning to manage conflict is essential for success in management and leadership roles.

Questions to challenge you

1. Think of a colleague that you consider to be a role model, a good leader or manager. How does that person respond to conflict?

2. How do you usually respond to conflict with another person? Which is your least common response?

3. Select a situation in which you have been involved in conflict. How did you handle your part in it? How about the other people involved? Did it turn out well? Explain.

4. What is the most difficult part of handling conflicts between others for you? Understanding others' positions? Devising a successful solution? Enlisting others' help? Encouraging participants to agree to a solution?

References

Covey, S. R. (2004) *The 7 Habits of Highly Effective People*. London: Simon and Schuster.

Crawley, J. and Graham, K. (2002) *Mediation for Managers: Resolving conflict and rebuilding relationships at work*. London: Nicholas Brealey.

Thomas, K. and Kilmann, R. (1974) *The Thomas-Kilmann Conflict Mode Instrument*. Mountain View, CA: Xicom and CPP Inc.

Levenstein, A. (1984) Negotiation vs. confrontation. *Nursing Management*, **15**(1), 52-53.

McConnon, S. and McConnon, M. (2008) *Conflict Management in the Workplace*. Oxford: how-tobooks.

Sacks, J. (2002) *The Dignity of Difference*. London: Continuum.

Strasser, F. and Randolph, P. (2004) *Mediation: A psychological insight into conflict resolution*. London: Continuum.

Valentine, P. (2001) Gender perspective on conflict management strategies of nurses. *Journal of Nursing Scholarship*, **33**(1), 69-74.

Chapter 10

Critical and Creative Thinking, Decision-Making and Problem-Solving

Key terms

Critical thinking
Creative thinking
Decision-making
Routine decisions
Adaptive decisions
Innovative decisions
Problem-solving
Probability:
  Objective
  Subjective
Probability analysis
Rational (normative) decision-
  making model

Descriptive (bounded) rationality model
Satisficing
Optimising
Nominal group technique
Delphi technique
Brainstorming
Appreciative inquiry
Trial-and-error method
Experimentation
Groupthink
Premature concurrence-seeking
Risky shift

Introduction

Problem-solving and decision-making are two of the core skills of good managers and leaders, but they are not easy to learn or to apply. Developing decision-making and problem-solving skills allows individuals and teams to see all sides of an issue, look for creative approaches to problems and make well-thought-out decisions. The effect is a stronger organisation, better patient care and more competent managers and leaders.

Critical and creative thinking underpin problem-solving and decision-making in that critical thinking helps us to analyse the current situation, and creative thinking helps to find new options, solutions and approaches. This chapter explains the nature of critical and creative thinking, decision-making and problem-solving and describes processes and techniques for using each.

> ### Imagine
>
> Think back over the past 24 hours. What decisions did you make? Were they simple, routine decisions such as what to eat for lunch or more complicated ones such as how will I spend my holidays this year? How did you go about making those decisions?
>
> Did you solve any problems yesterday? Perhaps you made child care arrangements of renegotiated your work schedule to enable you to go to a special event? How did you go about solving your problem? What were the options and why did you choose the solution you did?

Critical thinking

Critical thinking is the process of examining underlying assumptions, gathering and interpreting information and evaluating alternatives, for the purpose of reaching a reasoned conclusion that can be justified. Critical thinking is not the same thing as criticism, though it does require enquiring attitudes, knowledge about evidence and analysis and skills to combine them.

Critical-thinking skills can be used to resolve problems rationally. Identifying, analysing and questioning the evidence and implications of each problem stimulate and illuminate critical thought processes. Critical thinking is also an essential component of decision-making. However, compared with problem-solving and decision-making, which involve seeking a single solution, critical thinking is broader and involves considering a range of alternatives and selecting the best one for the situation (Ignatavicius, 2001).

Using critical thinking

Critical thinking underpins a number of important personal, professional and organisational activities. Organisational activities such as purchasing new equipment, changing service configuration, changing policy and practice in response to issues, and near-miss and incident investigation use the critical thinking process. Critical thinking is built into a number of specific quality-improvement tools such as root cause analysis and process mapping.

All nurses are expected to participate in reflective practice and clinical supervision. Critical thinking underpins these activities. Box 10.1 lists the attributes of an expert critical thinker. Reflective practice is a process of reflecting on clinical decisions and actions with a view to understanding the strengths and concerns within those practice choices. Clinical supervision is an opportunity to develop your practice through discussing your actions and reflections with a supervisor.

Critical thinking skills are an important part of being a manager or leader in nursing. One way to develop this skill is to consider a series of questions when examining a specific problem or making a decision. The following questions are suggested:

- What are the assumptions underpinning the problem? Underlying assumptions are unquestioned beliefs that influence an individual's reasoning. They are perceptions that may or may not be grounded in reality. Let's imagine that MRSA rates are rising in your clinical area. If you assume that MRSA is being brought in by visitors, you will probably implement visitor restrictions and install alcohol gel dispensers throughout the ward. If, however, you believe that

MRSA is being passed to vulnerable patients as a result of poor hand hygiene among staff, you will focus your efforts on them. The important first step in critical thinking is identifying the assumptions underlying the issue, and then challenging those assumptions.

- Is there objective evidence to support the arguments? What evidence is available from the literature? What audits or other studies are being done in the organisation? In our example about MRSA it would be important to gather information on whether different strains of MRSA are identified which may mean that they are from different sources. It would also be useful to note how many visitors actually use the alcohol gel and how many staff use alcohol gel or hand washing consistently.

- How is evidence interpreted? What is the context? Interpretation of information also can be value-laden. Is the evidence presented completely and clearly? Are the people present-ing the evidence using emotional or biased information? Are there any errors in reason-ing? For example, someone may come to the infection control committee with evidence that since gel dispensers were introduced, the MRSA rate has dropped. At first this evi-dence appears clear. On deeper examination, you know that other measures such as deep cleaning of the wards and screening of patients for MRSA on admission were also imple-mented at the same time. It is now less clear that the alcohol gel is the reason for the drop in MRSA: other factors may be responsible.

- What are possible alternative perspectives? By considering different assumptions and evidence the critical thinker can develop several different views of an issue. Using our above example, it is possible (though unlikely) that the introduction of alcohol gel on to the wards has been counterproductive because it leads to complacency about other factors that could be the actual cause (such as dirty equipment or poor dressing technique).

Creative thinking

Creative thinking as a process is complementary to critical thinking. **Creative thinking** is the ability to develop and implement new and better solutions or to design new ways of working. It is different from critical thinking in that it relies less on logic and analysis and more on

---

Box 10.1 **Characteristics of an Expert Critical Thinker**

Outcome-directed	Persistent
Open to new ideas	Caring
Flexible	Energetic
Willing to change	Risk-taker
Innovative	Knowledgeable
Creative	Resourceful
Analytical	Observant
Communicator	Intuitive
Assertive	'Out of the box' thinker

From Six critical thinking skills for at-the-bedside success, by D. D. Ignatavicius, 2001, *Nursing Management*, **32**(1), 37-39.

---

imagination and innovation. Creative thinking is important to organisations, especially those organisations that are in rapidly changing situations, in that it is sometimes necessary to start with a blank page, putting aside the assumptions and practices that are currently in place and imagining a different future.

Creative thinking works differently from critical thinking. Whereas critical thinking starts with a detailed analysis of what is known about the current situation, creative thinking starts with imagining the desired future. Once the desired future is clear, creative thinking works back to the present to identify the steps needed to make the desired future a reality.

One particularly useful tool for stimulating creative thinking is the use of appreciative questions. Appreciative questions help people to move away from the present where they may feel mired down in the situation and unable to find a way out. **Appreciative questions** focus on the future, and what is going well, to help people develop more options. See Box 10.2 for some examples of appreciative questions.

Box 10.2   Appreciative Questions

The following questions are useful in inspiring creative thinking and to help people to clarify the desired future:

- What do you want?
- How will you know when you have achieved it? What will it be like to work in this way? What will have improved?
- What is going well now that can help us achieve this future?
- What will we need to change?
- What are the first steps?

Here is an example of how appreciative questions can work:

Question: What do you want the admitting process for the patients to be like?

Answer: We want the admitting process to be thorough, quick and friendly. The patient will feel welcome, and the staff will have all the important information they need to care for the patient.

Question: How will you know when you have achieved it? What will it be like to work in this way? What will have improved?

Answer: Every patient will be greeted and shown to their bed by the nurse who will take care of them. The patients will be settled in their beds within the first hour of arrival and the admitting process will be complete. Patients will be less anxious, and feel confident in the staff. The staff will feel good because they have had a chance to settle the patient in, and now know enough about them to take care of their needs.

Question: What is going well now and can help us achieve this?

Answer: When patients come in between 10 a.m. and 2 p.m. we can usually manage to achieve this. At other times, especially on the late shift, we aren't as successful. What helps on early shift is that there is a ward clerk to help with the paperwork and the charge nurse is able to cover our other patients whilst we are admitting.

Question: What needs to change on late shift and other times that would move us in the right direction?

Answer: There are many answers to this question, and they will vary with each situation. At this point in the process, people are ready to generate ideas that can achieve the desired future. They are not likely to get bogged down in the current situation; they are ready to move ahead.

Decision-making

Considering all the practice individuals get in making decisions, it would seem they might become very good at it. However, the number of decisions a person makes does not correspond to the person's skill at making them. The assumption is that decision-making comes naturally, like breathing. That is because most individuals are not aware of how they make decisions, they just seem to happen. Anyone can gain a greater awareness of their decision-making process, and through developing their skills in decision-making gain confidence in the decisions they make.

The term 'decision-making' is often used interchangeably with 'problem-solving'. Although the two processes appear similar and may in some instances depend on one another, they are not synonymous. The main distinctions between the two are that decision-making may or may not involve a problem; **decision-making** always involves evaluating and selecting one of several alternatives, each of which may be appropriate under certain circumstances. Problem-solving involves data gathering, analysis, generation of potential solutions and the choice of a solution. Decision-making is part of that process: decisions on what data to collect, how to analyse the data and which solution is best are all decision steps within problem-solving (Figure 10.1).

Many decisions are not of a problem-solving nature, such as decisions about duty rosters, equipment, staff development, or other matters that do not involve problem-solving as a deliberate process. Research has discredited the early belief that all decisions are choices people make after extensive evaluation of all options in order to find an optimal solution. Simon (1955) and others recognised that evaluation is seldom extensive and virtually never exhaustive. In the 1970s it was recognised that decision-makers have a variety of strategies for making choices and a variety of aims and that people usually people rely on past experiences in making decisions. Making a well-considered choice is relatively rare and usually is done by screening out the unacceptable options and choosing the best option from the remainders.

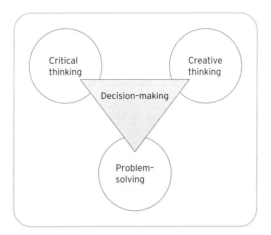

Figure 10.1 An integrated model of critical and creative thinking, decision-making and problem-solving.

Matching decision technique to decision type

The types of decision people make vary widely and determine the decision-making methods they choose. **Routine decisions** are those that are relatively common and well defined, and satisfactory results can usually be achieved by applying policies, rules and experience. For instance, staffing decisions are usually taken based on the historical staffing pattern. Also, when a nurse makes a medication error, the manager's actions are guided by policy.

Increasingly, technology can support routine decision-making. Cardiac monitors for example now have the capacity to analyse the rhythm and give a preliminary diagnosis. There are also software programs that can create work schedules using the rules you programme in.

For more complex **adaptive decisions** involving moderately ambiguous problems and modification of known and well-defined alternative solutions, there are a variety of techniques. For example, if you are choosing between having open visiting or defined visiting hours you may decide to do a SWOT analysis. SWOT is a process of identifying the **s**trengths, **w**eaknesses, **o**pportunities and **t**hreats for each alternative, and then deciding based on the information gained. There are many such tools that help organisations make adaptive decisions such as cause-and-effect diagrams, flow charts, Pareto charts, run charts, histograms, control charts and scatter diagrams. These tools help people to organise and analyse information and develop confidence in decisions taken.

Making **innovative decisions** requires both discovering and investigating unfamiliar and ambiguous situations and developing unique and creative solutions (Figure 10.2). These decisions involve considerable uncertainty and, often, risk. Deciding to offer a home birth service is a good example. Even though the women in the community have been asking for the service, it is difficult to predict actual use. There is an element of clinical risk in offering the service, and midwives and doctors may have different views about how it should function. There is a careful balance to be struck between safety, professional practice and patient choice in making this decision.

Decision-making conditions

Decision-making is situational, that is, decisions are made in light of a particular set of circumstances. For example, decisions about what to eat are dependent on how hungry you are, what food you like and what food is available. Managers make decisions both as individuals and in groups from within the context of the organisation. The conditions surrounding decision-making can vary and change dramatically. It is essential for the manager to consider the total system, realising that whatever decisions are made they will succeed only if they are compatible with other parts of the system. Within the organisation, decisions are made under conditions of certainty risk, or uncertainty.

Decision-making under certainty

When an individual knows the alternatives and the conditions surrounding each alternative, a state of certainty is said to exist. Suppose a community mental health team leader wants to set up a support group for families of drug users in the community. Three alternatives exist. The team leader could:

- set up the group himself;
- support family members of drug users to set the group up themselves;
- bring in a group facilitator with experience in this type of work to set up and run the group.

These alternatives are relatively clear cut, and the costs, benefits and drawbacks of each solution are relatively easy to identify. A condition of certainty is said to exist and the decision can be made with confidence in the likely outcome choosing each alternative.

Decision-making under uncertainty and risk

Seldom do decision-makers have perfect information, defined by McConnell (2000) as knowing everything there is to know about a subject or situation. If everything was known, the decision would be obvious for all to see. Most important decision-making in organisations is done, therefore, under conditions of uncertainty and risk (Figure 10.3). The individual or group making the decision does not know all the alternatives, attendant risks or likely consequences of each option. Uncertainty and risk are inevitable because of the complex and dynamic nature of health care organisations. Successful decisions, McConnell (2000) asserts, are dependent on human judgement.

Here is an example. If there is an important football match scheduled to be played at the team's home ground, the ward manager of A&E knows that it is likely to be busier that day than on a day when the team is playing away. He knows from experience that if the home team loses, especially against traditional rival teams, there could be trouble and even more patients coming to casualty. Whilst the nurse manager can apply guidelines from past experience, he cannot know which team will win and therefore accurately anticipate how busy they will be.

In a risk situation, each alternative and potential outcome can be associated with probability estimates. Most health care organisations now have to keep a risk register which identifies events and the probability that they will occur. **Probability** can be **objective** (based on statistical analysis, facts or verified, reliable information) or **subjective** (based on judgement and experience). Probability is the likelihood, expressed as a percentage, or sometimes in a relative scale (high, medium or low), that an event will or will not occur. If something is certain to happen, its probability is 100 per cent. If it is certain not to happen, its probability is 0 per cent. If there is a 50-50 chance, its probability is 50 per cent (or medium). In the example given above, the A&E charge nurse can conduct a **probability analysis** and therefore estimate the chances of the home team winning. Imagine that the home team is expected to win, but not by a large margin,

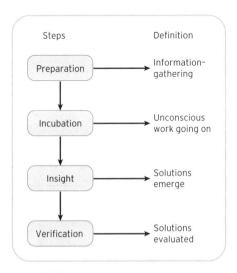

Figure 10.2 The creative process.

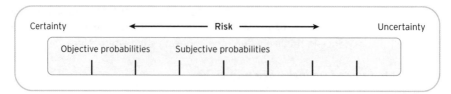

Figure 10.3 Conditions under which decisions are made.
From Hellriegel, Jackson and Slocum (2002)

so the charge nurse puts the probability at 60–40. Based on this probability, he will schedule the same number of staff as the last winning home game. Because the probability is not strong, he will also ask a colleague to be on call to cover should there be the need.

The decision-making process

The management literature often describes decisions as discrete events made by an individual manager or a group using an orderly, rational process. This process, the **rational, or normative, decision-making model**, is a series of steps that managers take in an effort to make logical, well-grounded rational choices that maximise the achievement of objectives (see Figure 10.4). The rationality of the decision made depends on the manager's ability to use information and analysis and on their values, beliefs and objectives. The decision-making process is a sequence of the basic steps; however, not every step is used in every decision.

The rational or normative decision-making model is thought of as the ideal and suits some sorts of decisions better than others. The cost–benefit analysis or business plan is one form of rational decision-making. Often used to look at alternatives for purchasing supplies and equipment, it offers a useful framework for comparing alternatives about which reasonable certainty exists.

In reality, individuals seldom make major decisions at a single point in time and often are unable to recall when a decision was finally reached. Some major decisions are the result of

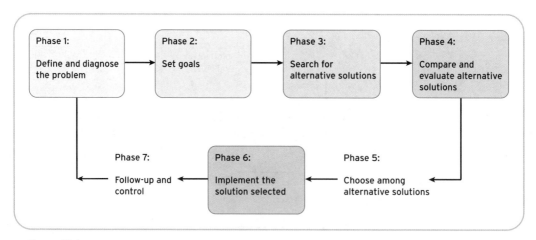

Figure 10.4 A rational decision-making model.
From Hellriegel, Jackson and Slocum (2002)

many small actions or incremental choices the person makes without regarding larger strategic issues. In addition, decision processes are likely to be characterised more by confusion, disorder and emotionality than by rationality. For these reasons, it is essential that the nurse manager develop appropriate technical skills and the capacity to find a good balance between lengthy processes and quick, decisive action.

The **descriptive, or bounded, rationality model**, developed by Simon in 1955 and supported by research in the 1990s (Simon, 1993), finds that there are limits to rationality in decision-making. It recognises three ways in which decision makers depart from the rational decision-making model:

- The decision-maker's search for possible objectives or alternative solutions is limited because of time, energy and money.

- Managers frequently lack adequate information about problems and cannot control the conditions under which they operate.

- Managers often use a satisficing strategy. **Satisficing** is not a misspelled word; it is a decision-making strategy whereby the individual chooses an alternative that is not ideal but either is good enough (suffices) under existing circumstances to meet minimum standards of acceptance or is the first acceptable alternative.

Managers who solve problems using satisficing will often make decisions with relatively simple rules of thumb or from force of habit. Decisions made from force of habit (we always staff three nurses on the late shift, for example) has its limits. As patient care needs change, rule of thumb decisions can become out of line with the needs of the patient or staff. Management situations present a multitude of problems that are solved ineffectively with satisficing strategies. Elena, a nurse manager in charge of a busy medical admissions ward with high activity and sick patients, uses a satisficing alternative when looking at weekend scheduling of staff. She doesn't want to create dissatisfaction with her staff by giving them undesirable shifts, so she uses bank staff on the weekends. This has led to problems with patient care, and when regular staff do work on the weekends, they are unhappy about working with so many different people. A better approach would be for Elena to involve her staff in deciding the pattern of weekend staffing that provides reasonable cover by core staff and minimises bank staff use. Elena should also look at her staffing complement and way of working to ensure that it matches more closely the patient admissions and needs.

It is difficult to argue with the statement that decisions should be made using **optimising** strategies, meaning that the best of all possible alternatives is chosen. In reality, the process of making optimal decisions can be time-consuming and it takes considerable skill to use the process effectively. Both satisficing and optimising have a role to play. Where rule-of-thumb decisions continue to deliver the desired result in most situations, there is no need to change. When the tipping point is reached where the rule of thumb is no longer reliable, undertaking the process of optimising becomes worth while.

The decision-making process begins when the individual perceives a gap between what is actually happening and what should be happening; and it ends with action that will narrow or close this gap. The simplest way to learn decision-making skills is to integrate a model into one's thinking by breaking the components down into individual steps. The seven steps of the decision-making process (Box 10.3) are as applicable to personal problems as they are to nursing management problems. Each step is elaborated by pertinent questions clarifying the statements, and they should be followed in the order in which they are presented.

Box 10.3   **Steps in Decision-Making**

1. *Identify the purpose of the decision.* Why is a decision necessary? What needs to be determined? State the issue in the broadest possible terms.

2. *Set the criteria.* What needs to be achieved, preserved and avoided by whatever decision is made? The answers to these questions are the standards by which solutions will be evaluated.

3. *Weight the criteria.* Rank each criterion on a scale of values from 1 (totally unimportant) to 10 (extremely important).

4. *Seek alternatives.* List all possible courses of action. Is one alternative more significant than another? Does one alternative have weaknesses in some areas? Can these be overcome? Can two alternatives or features of many alternatives be combined?

5. *Test alternatives.* First, using the same methodology as in step 3, rank each alternative on a scale of 1 to 10. Second, multiply the weight of each criterion by the rating of each alternative. Third, add the scores and compare the results.

6. *Troubleshoot.* What could go wrong? How can you plan? Can the choice be improved?

7. *Evaluate the action.* Is the solution being implemented? Is it effective? What has it cost in terms of time, resources and people?

Group decision-making

The widespread use of partnerships, multiprofessional and multi-agency groups, committees and teams requires every manager or leader to determine when group, rather than individual, decisions are desirable and how to use groups effectively. Group decision-making about important issues casts the manager in the role of facilitator. Compared with individual decision-making, groups can provide more input, often produce better decisions and generate more commitment. Several group decision-making techniques can be used.

Nominal group technique

The **nominal group technique** (NGT) developed by Delbecq, VandeVen and Gustafson (1975) is a structured and precise method of eliciting written questions, ideas and reactions from group members. NGT is a group process in name only because no direct exchange occurs among members. NGT consists of:

- silently generating ideas in writing;
- round-robin presentation by group members of their individual ideas in a terse phrase on a flip chart;
- discussion of each recorded idea for clarification and evaluation;
- voting individually on priority ideas, with the group solution being derived mathematically through rank ordering or rating using the group's decision rule.

Delphi technique

In the **Delphi technique**, judgements on a particular topic are systematically gathered from participants who do not meet face-to-face. Ideas are collected through a carefully designed sequence of questionnaires interspersed with summaries of information and opinions derived from previous questionnaires. The process may involve many rounds but normally does not exceed three. This technique can rely on the input of experts who are widely dispersed geographically. It can be used to evaluate the quality of research proposals or to make predictions about the future based on current scientific knowledge. This technique is useful when expert opinions are needed and expense would prohibit bringing them together.

For fact-finding problems with no known solution, the NGT and the Delphi technique are superior to other group techniques. Both minimise the chances of more vocal members dominating discussion and allow independent consideration of ideas.

Brainstorming

In **brainstorming**, group members meet together and generate many diverse ideas about the nature, cause, definition or solution to a problem without consideration of their relative value. A premium is placed on generating lots of ideas as quickly as possible and on coming up with unusual ideas. The wilder the idea, the better! Most importantly, members do not critique ideas as they are proposed. Evaluation takes place after all the ideas have been generated. Members are encouraged to improve on each other's ideas. These sessions are very enjoyable but are often unsuccessful because members inevitably begin to critique ideas and, as a result, meetings shift to the ordinary interacting group format. Criticisms of this approach are the high cost factor, the time consumed and the superficiality of many solutions. Figure 10.5 shows the results of a brainstorming exercise, presented as a cause-and-effect, or fishbone, diagram.

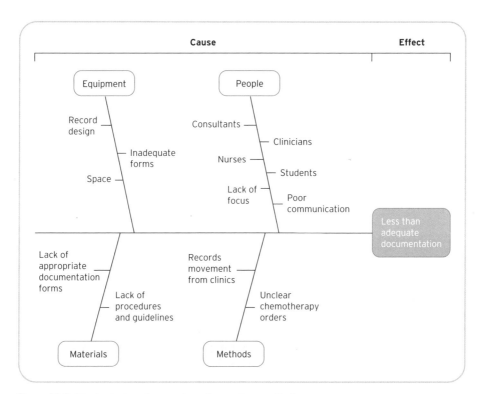

Figure 10.5 The brainstorming session of a nursing quality team.

> ### Box 10.4   The Four Phases of the Model
>
> 1. *Discover*. People talk to one another to discover the times when the organisation is at its best. Storytelling is encouraged and people feel good about what is working well.
>
> 2. *Dream*. People are brought together to envision the organisation as if the peak moments from the discovery phase were the norm rather than the exception.
>
> 3. *Design*. In this phase, people sign up to design particular elements of the future. For example, ward clerks may agree to design the admitting paperwork whereas nurses may sign up to design the care pathway.
>
> 4. *Deliver*. In this phase, experimentation and improvisation occur and the designs are tested and improved.
>
> The four phases of the model, Seel, R. 2008, Introduction to Appreciative Inquiry, http://www.new-paradigm.co.uk/introduction_to_ai.htm

---

Appreciative inquiry

Appreciative inquiry is one method of group decision-making or problem-solving that is particularly good at getting teams to think about possibilities and to move forward. It was developed by David Cooperrider and Suresh Srivastva in the 1980s. The approach is based on the idea that 'organisations change in the direction in which they inquire'. So an organisation which enquires into problems will keep finding problems but an organisation which attempts to appreciate what is best in itself will discover more and more that is good. It can then use these discoveries to build a new future in which the best becomes more common (Seel, 2008) (see Box 10.4).

Problem-solving

People use problem-solving when they perceive a gap between an existing state (what is going on) and a desired state (what should be going on). Critical and creative thinking are both necessary for problem-solving. The use of analytical questions (what is happening now? what evidence is there?) and appreciative questions (what do we want in the future? what is working? what needs to change?) both have a role to play.

Problem-solving methods

A variety of methods can be used to solve problems. People with little management experience tend to use the **trial-and-error method**, applying one solution after another until the problem is solved or appears to be improving. These managers often cite lack of experience and of time and resources to search for alternative solutions.

In an elderly ward there have been an increasing number of falls. Michael, the charge nurse, decides that every patient should be taken to the toilet every two hours during the day and once at night. Whilst this approach decreases the falls, it doesn't eliminate them. Some of the patients are complaining that they do not get enough rest, and it is annoying to be taken to the toilet when they don't need it. The staff are complaining that the toileting is time-consuming and unnecessary for some patients. Clearly Michael had the best of intentions, and while this approach has helped in some cases, it has been a poor choice in others.

As the above example shows, a trial-and-error process can be time-consuming and may even be detrimental. Although some learning can occur during the process, the manager risks being perceived as a poor problem-solver who has wasted time and money on ineffective solutions.

Experimentation, another type of problem-solving, is more rigorous than trial and error. Pilot projects or limited trials are examples of experimentation. Experimentation involves testing a theory (hypothesis) or hunch to enhance knowledge, understanding or prediction. A project or study is carried out in either a controlled (e.g. a laboratory) or uncontrolled setting (e.g. a ward or community team). Data are collected and analysed and results interpreted to determine whether the solution tried has been effective.

Helen, the ward sister on an elderly care ward, has received many complaints from family members that they rarely see the nurses whilst visiting their relatives in the evening. This makes them worried that their family member will not get the care they need. Helen knows there are enough staff on the shift but suspects that when families are visiting, the nurses are taking time to do other duties rather than being with the patients. She can test her theory by setting up a small study. Working with the late shift staff, she asks that they make an effort to speak to each set of visitors and to make sure someone from the staff goes into each patient room at least every hour during visiting hours. She can try this new approach for two weeks and see how it affects complaints.

Experimentation may be creative and effective or uninspired and ineffective, depending on how it is used. As a major method of problem-solving, experimentation may be inefficient because of the amount of time and control involved. However, a well-designed experiment can be persuasive in situations in which an idea or activity, such as a new staffing system or care procedure, can be tried in one of two similar groups and results compared objectively.

Still other problem-solving techniques rely on past experience and intuition. Everyone has various and countless experiences. Individuals build a repertoire of these experiences and base future actions on what they considered successful solutions in the past. If a particular course of action consistently resulted in positive outcomes, the person will try it again when similar circumstances occur. In some instances, an individual's past experience can determine how much risk they will take in present circumstances. The nature and frequency of the experience also contribute significantly to the effectiveness of this problem-solving method. How much the person has learned from these experiences, positive or negative, can affect the current viewpoint and can result in either subjective and narrow judgements or very wise ones.

This is especially true in relationship problems. A charge nurse who has had a difficult time with a staff member who has a poor sickness record may, in the future, judge negatively the performance of all nurses with poor sickness records. Intuition relies heavily on past experience and trial and error. The extent to which past experience is related to intuition is difficult to determine, but nurses' wisdom, sensitivity and intuition are known to be valuable in solving problems.

Some problems are self-solving: if permitted to run a natural course, they are solved by those personally involved. This is not to say that a uniform laissez-faire management style solves all problems. The manager must not ignore managerial responsibilities, but often difficult situations become more manageable when participants are given time, resources and support to discover their own solutions. This typically happens, for example, when a newly qualified nurse joins a unit where most of the staff are experienced and resent the time they have to spend helping the new person. If the charge nurse intervenes, a problem that the staff might have worked out on their own becomes an ongoing source of conflict. The important skill required here is knowing when to do nothing.

The scientific problem-solving process

Most problems encountered in day-to-day situations can be solved using a step-by-step problem-solving process. Problem-solving uses critical thinking to gather and analyse information, creative thinking to come up with solutions and decision-making at key steps on the process. There are many different approaches to problem-solving, most of which follow the same basic steps of problem identification, analysis, creating options and taking action. One method of problem-solving, which uses a seven-step process, is outlined in Box 10.5.

Box 10.5   **Steps in Problem-Solving**

1. *Define the problem.* The most important part of problem-solving is defining the problem. How problems are perceived determines the solutions or identifies needed changes. This step relies heavily on critical thinking. It is important to ask yourself 'What is actually happening? What assumptions am I making about the cause of the problem? Are there other reasons why this could be happening?'

   Suppose a ward manager reluctantly implements a self-rostering system and finds that each time the roster is posted, some weekend shifts are not adequately covered. The ward manager might identify the problem as the staff being unwilling to take responsibility for staffing and that therefore the ward sister needs to take back control of the roster. In fact there could be a number of other reasons why the system is not working. Perhaps there is a lack of understanding about the system or poor relationships among some staff that is causing a lack of fairness in the distribution of shifts. Perhaps the timing of the posting or the location is the problem. Each of these problems would have different solutions so it is very important to get the right problem identified before taking the problem-solving process forward.

2. *Gather information.* Problem-solving begins with collecting information from as wide a range of sources as possible, in order to find clues as to the scope and nature of the problem. Information gathered will probably be a combination of facts, feelings and experience. The manager or team may choose to have everyone involved provide information. Although this may not always provide objective information, it reduces misinformation and allows everyone an opportunity to say what they think is wrong with a situation.

3. *Analyse the information.* The information is ready to be analysed once it has been sorted into an orderly arrangement. We suggest:

   - Categorise information in order of reliability.

   - List information from most important to least important.

   - Set information into a time sequence. What happened first? Next? What came before what? What were the concurrent circumstances?

   - Set up information in terms of cause and effect. Is A causing B, or vice versa?

   - Classify information into categories: human factors, such as personality, maturity, education, age, relationships among people; external factors: staff availability, national policy priorities, commissioning; and organisational factors: services offered, size and structure of the organisation, history and policy.

   - Consider how long the situation has been going on.

Because no amount of information is ever complete or comprehensive enough, critical thinking skills are important. Some data will be useless, some inaccurate, but some will be useful to develop innovative ideas worth pursuing. There is a risk of 'analysis paralysis' where you get stuck in the information-gathering stage and don't solve the problem.

4. *Develop solutions.* As the manager or group analyses information, numerous possible solutions will suggest themselves. Don't limit yourself to these: this is a good time to use creative thinking. Brainstorming works well with a group to stimulate ideas that are not just 'the same old thing'. Developing alternative solutions makes it possible to combine the best parts of several solutions into a superior one. Also, alternatives are valuable in case the first choice of alternatives proves impossible to implement.

When exploring a variety of solutions, it is important to maintain an uncritical attitude towards the way the problem has been handled in the past. Some problems have had a long-standing history, and attempts may have been made to resolve them over a long period of time. 'We tried this before and it didn't work' is often said and may apply – or more likely, may not apply – in a changed situation.

Past experience may not always supply an answer, but it can aid the critical thinking process and help prepare for future problem-solving. Sometimes others have solved similar problems and those methods can be applied to a comparable problem.

5. *Make a decision.* After reviewing the list of potential solutions, the manager or group should select the one that is most feasible and satisfactory and has the fewest undesirable consequences. If the problem is a technical one and its solution brings about a change in the method of doing work (or using new equipment), there may be resistance. All people become disturbed by changes that reorder their habit patterns and threaten personal security or status. Many solutions fail because the manager does not recognise the change process that must be initiated before solutions can be implemented. If the solution involves change, the manager should fully involve those who will be affected by it, if possible, or at least inform them of the process. (See Chapter 11 for discussion of the change process.)

6. *Implement the decision.* If unforeseen new problems emerge after implementation, it is important to evaluate these impediments as carefully as any other problem. One must be careful, however, not to abandon a workable solution just because a few people object; a minority always will. If the previous steps in the problem-solving process have been followed, the solution has been carefully thought out and potential problems have been addressed, implementation should move forward. No solution is perfect and, regardless of the benefits, all change is stressful.

7. *Evaluate the solution.* After the solution has been implemented, the plan should be reviewed to see if it has been fully implemented and has actually achieved the expected results. People tend to fall back into old patterns of habit, and it is therefore important to build in a structured evaluation as a mechanism to remind staff that the change is important. A periodic check-up gives the manager valuable insight and experience to use in other situations and keeps the problem-solving process on course.

The manager should study outcomes of the solution somewhat as a sport coach studies videotapes of an athletic performance. Where were mistakes made? How can they be avoided in the future? What decisions were successes? Why? Many ineffective solutions are never challenged once they are implemented. If the nurse manager evaluates the outcome to ensure that the problem has indeed been solved and builds on that experience, problem-solving becomes an expert skill that the nurse can use throughout a management career.

Group problem-solving

The complexity of problems encountered in health care today, and the staff's desire and expectation for meaningful involvement at work, has given rise to greater use of group problem-solving. Groups collectively possess greater knowledge and information than any single member and may access more strategies to solve a problem. Under the right circumstances and with appropriate leadership, groups can deal with more complex problems than a single individual, especially if there is no one right or wrong solution to the problem (Surowiecki, 2004).

Group members will often have diverse backgrounds and experiences and will approach problems from different points of view. Groups may deal more effectively with problems that cross organisational boundaries or involve change that requires support from all departments affected. Participative problem-solving has additional advantages: it increases the likelihood of acceptance and understanding of the decision, and it enhances cooperation in implementation.

Disadvantages of group problem-solving

Group problem-solving also has disadvantages: it takes time and resources and may involve conflict. Members who are less informed or less confident may allow stronger members to control group discussion and problem-solving. A disparity in participation may contribute to a power struggle between the members of the group.

Group problem-solving also can be affected by **groupthink.** Groupthink can occur in highly cohesive groups that become isolated. Through prolonged close association, group members come to think alike and have similar prejudices and blind spots, such as stereotypical views of outsiders. They exhibit a strong tendency to seek concurrence, which interferes with critical thinking about important decisions. The leader of the group may contribute to groupthink by suppressing open, freewheeling discussion and controlling what ideas will be discussed and how much dissent will be tolerated. Groupthink seriously impairs problem-solving and can result in erroneous and damaging decisions.

Two phenomena are associated with groupthink (Forsyth, 1983): **premature concurrence-seeking** and illusions and misperceptions. In a group where premature concurrence-seeking (the push to come up with a decision before the process has run its course) is happening, it is likely that you will see:

- pressure to conform;
- taboos against expressing dissent or criticising ideas presented by the majority, a leader or some other powerful member;
- self-censorship of dissenting opinions, in which members with questions or concerns remain silent;
- mindguards, who use 'gatekeeping' to protect the group from controversial information and discourage dissent by diverting doubts about the group's decisions or beliefs;
- apparent unanimity, reflected in the illusion that everyone is in agreement despite objections or concerns.

Misperceptions and illusions are also characteristic of groupthink. They may include:

- apparent unanimity, reflected in the illusion that the group is in concurrence despite objections and concerns;

- a belief that the group is morally correct, which encourages members to ignore the ethical and moral consequences of their decisions;
- rationalisation of warnings and other forms of negative feedback;
- biased perceptions of the out-group;
- collective rationalisation of contradictory information (Janis, 1982).

Leaders and group members may use the following tactics to prevent groupthink in cohesive groups (Janis, 1982):

- Promote open enquiry by asking every member of the group to be an evaluator. Encourage the group to give high priority to airing objections and doubts. Reinforce by accepting criticism.
- The leader initially should delay stating their preferences and expectations until others' views have been fully disclosed.
- The leader may set up several independent work groups to tackle the same issue. The groups then reconvene to explore a variety of approaches to problem-solving and to hammer out differences.
- Each member of the decision-making group should discuss the group's deliberations periodically with trusted associates in their own work team and report back non-members' views and reactions.
- One or more people who are not core members of the problem-solving group should be invited to each meeting on a rotating basis to challenge the views of the core members.
- At every problem-solving meeting, at least one group member should be assigned the role of devil's advocate by attempting to find fault with any argument that might be considered valid.
- After reaching a preliminary consensus (agreement that everyone can support, arrived at without formal voting) about the best alternative, the problem-solving group should hold a second-chance meeting at which every member is expected to express as vividly as possible all residual doubts and to rethink the entire issue before making a final choice.

Managers must recognise that although managing dissent may be complicated, time-consuming and at times unpleasant, conflict is not always dysfunctional and it is often necessary for quality decision-making.

Groups tend to make riskier decisions than individuals. Groups are more likely to support unusual or unpopular positions (e.g. public demonstrations). Groups tend to be less conservative than individual decision-makers and frequently display more courage and support for unusual or creative solutions to problems. This phenomenon is referred to as **risky shift** (Napier and Gershenfeld, 1981). Several factors contribute to this phenomenon. Individuals who lack information about alternatives may make a safe choice, but after group discussion they acquire additional information and become more comfortable with a less secure alternative. The group setting also allows for the diffusion of responsibility. If something goes wrong, others also can be assigned the blame or risk. In addition, leaders may be greater risk-takers than individuals, and group members may attach a social value to risk-taking because they identify it with leadership. Risky shift may be less of a problem in health care organisations because society discourages risk about health matters. However, nurse managers should be aware of this phenomenon, especially in relation to organisational decisions (e.g. starting or terminating a service).

What you know now

- Critical thinking requires examining underlying assumptions about current evidence, interpreting information and evaluating the arguments presented to reach a new and exciting conclusion.
- Creative thinking involves the use of imagination and innovation to identify a desired future, and release the energy to achieve that future.
- Problem-solving and decision-making processes use critical and creative thinking skills.
- The decision-making process may employ several models: rational or normative, descriptive or bounded rationality, satisficing and political.
- Decision-making techniques vary according to the problem and the degree of risk and uncertainty in the situation.
- Methods of problem-solving include trial and error, intuition, experimentation, past experience, tradition and recognising problems that are self-solving.
- The problem-solving process involves defining the problem, gathering information, analysing information, developing solutions, making a decision, implementing the decision and evaluating the solution.

Questions to challenge you

1. Identify someone you believe has critical thinking skills. What are they?
2. Describe a situation when you made an important decision. What content in this chapter applied to that situation? What was the outcome?
3. Have you been involved in group decision-making at school or work? What techniques were used? Were they effective?
4. From the models discussed in this chapter, describe fictional or real situations using these models.
5. A number of ways that problem-solving might fail were discussed in this chapter. Name three more.

References

Delbecq, A. L., VandeVen, A. H. and Gustafson, D. H. (1975) *Group Techniques for Program Planning*. Glenview, IL: Foresman.

Forsyth, D. R. (1983) *An Introduction to Group Dynamics*. Monterey, CA: Brooks/Cole.

Ignatavicius, D. D. (2001) Six critical thinking skills for at-the-bedside success. *Nursing Management*, **32**(1), 37-39.

Janis, I. L. (1982) *Groupthink: Psychological studies of policy decisions and fiascoes*, 2nd edn. Boston, MA: Houghton Mifflin.

McConnell, C. R. (2000) The anatomy of a decision. *Health Care Manager*, **18**(4), 63–74.

Napier, R. W. and Gershenfeld, M. K. (1981) *Groups: Theory and experience*. Boston, MA: Houghton Mifflin.

Seel, R. (2008) *Introduction to Appreciative Inquiry*. Available at http://www.new-paradigm.co.uk.

Simon, H. A. (1955) A behavioral model of rational choice. *Quarterly Journal of Economics*, **69**, 99–118.

Simon, H. A. (1993) Decision-making: rational, nonrational, and irrational. *Education Administration Quarterly*, **29**(3), 392–411.

Surowiecki, J. (2004) *The Wisdom of Crowds: Why the many are smarter than the few*. London: Little Brown.

Chapter 11
Leading and Managing Change and Transition

Key terms

Change
Transition
Driving forces
Restraining forces

Change agent
Power-coercive strategy
Empirical-rational strategy
Normative-re-educative strategies

Introduction

How do you view change? Does it bring up feelings of anxiety and distrust, or do you see it as a challenge? Today's health care environment is changing rapidly; and as we've shown in the opening chapters, it pervades every aspect of our work. Managing change is one of the most important skills for a manager and leader in health care today. This chapter looks at some theories of change and how planned change can be handled effectively.

Imagine

Being able to introduce change in such as way as to strengthen the team, minimising conflict and stress, and bring about improvements in care. By paying attention to the process of change, and the feelings change engenders, an effective leader can do just that.

Types of change

Change is simply the process of making something different from what it was. Change is situational: the development of a new service, taking a new job, restructuring of a team or merging services. **Transition** is psychological: the process people go through to come to terms with change (Bridges, 2003). An effective manager must learn to manage both the situation and the people it affects. Without proper attention to the psychology of change, the effectiveness of the individuals and the team will suffer, which has the potential to create conflict, lower productivity and possibly deficits in care.

Changes are either planned or unplanned, and welcome (an opportunity, advancement, fulfilment of a goal) or unwelcome (a change that is anticipated to cause distress or inconvenience) (Table 11.1).

Table 11.1 Types of change

Unplanned and welcome	Planned and welcome
A happy surprise such as receiving an award or personal acknowledgement	Achievement of a goal, advancement, successful bid for additional funds
Unplanned and unwelcome	**Planned and unwelcome**
A change for which the individual is unprepared, and that causes anger, pain, concern, anxiety, a loss of control or distrust	A change that is anticipated, for which there is time to plan, but is perceived as less favourable than the current situation, or one in which a significant loss is anticipated

Unplanned and welcome changes can create an emotional boost, and can build trust and optimism. Being allocated a pot of money to use for improvements in care or being in receipt of an award for service innovation after a particularly difficult stretch of staff shortages can do wonders for staff morale.

Unplanned and unwelcome changes are often labelled 'disasters' in that they engender a sense distress and loss of control. Because nurses and other health care providers are trained to manage emergency situations, the immediate response is often to rally together and get through the situation, only experiencing the impact of the change later on. For example, having to relocate services because a clinical area has been damaged by flood or fire, or having to replace a key member of staff taken suddenly and seriously ill, start out as unplanned and unwelcome changes handled at the time. Once the immediate situation is over, owing to the change being long term, planning for the continuing situation is important.

Planned change is almost always what change theorists mean when they talk about change. In complex organisations such as health care, there will always be those who see the change as welcome, and those who see it as unwelcome. Those who see the benefits of the change will push for its accomplishment, becoming a driving force, whilst those who see the change more in terms of loss will resist, becoming a restraining force. For example, a manager in the community may want to combine the health visiting team with school nursing in order to create a more comprehensive and integrated service that is responsive to the development of children's health services. Some members of the respective teams will see the change as an opportunity to take on new roles, learn new skills and improve services to clients. Other team members may be resistant; they are concerned about the loss of their unique identities, the need to take on new and unfamiliar responsibilities and the necessity to work differently, therefore disrupting long-term working relationships. Accomplishing this change will take skilled planning for the practical aspects - office space, training, budgeting - and working with the emotional responses and concerns of staff involved.

Change theories

Lewin's force-field model

Lewin (1951) provided a social-psychological view of the change process. He saw behaviour as a dynamic balance of forces working in opposing directions within a field (such as an organisation). **Driving forces** facilitate change because they push participants in the desired direction. **Restraining forces** impede change because they push participants in the opposite direction. To plan change, one must analyse these forces and shift the balance in the direction of change through a three-step process: unfreezing, moving and refreezing. Change occurs by adding a new force, changing the direction of a force or changing the magnitude of any one force. Basically, strategies for change are aimed at increasing driving forces, decreasing restraining forces, or both.

Lewin's force-field model and an example of how it works are illustrated in Figure 11.1. This scheme shows how a system's driving and restraining forces oppose each other. These forces, which are part of the system's maintenance and adaptive mechanisms, are balanced at the

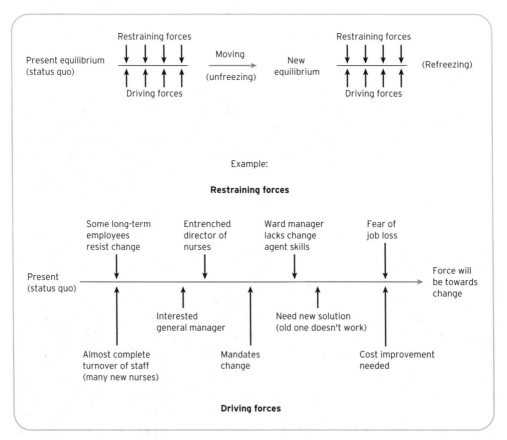

Figure 11.1 Lewin's force-field model of change.

Adapted from *Field Theory in Social Science*, by K. Lewin, 1997, New York: Harper and Row.

present, or status quo, level. To achieve change, first an imbalance must occur between the driving and restraining forces, which unfreezes the present patterned behaviour. Behaviour moves to a new level, at which the opposing forces are brought into a new state of equilibrium. Once participants integrate new patterns of behaviour into their personalities and relationships with others, a refreezing takes place. The new level becomes institutionalised into formal and informal behavioural patterns.

Lewin's change strategies fall within this three-step process:

1. Unfreeze the existing equilibrium. Motivate participants by getting them ready for change. Build trust and recognition for the need to change. To thaw attitudes, participate actively in identifying problems and generate alternative solutions.

2. Move the target system to a new level of equilibrium. Get participants to identify the drawbacks to the present situation (the status quo) for themselves and the patients. Encourage participants to view the problem from a new perspective, one that involves the possibility for benefit from change. Encourage others to bring information that provides a clear picture of the deficiencies of the current situation, such as audit data, waiting times, clinical incidents and satisfaction, so that a clear picture emerges.

3. Refreeze the system at the new level of equilibrium. Reinforce the new patterns of behaviour. Institutionalise them through formal and informal mechanisms (e.g. policies, systems, relationships, monitoring).

Lewin's change model is instrumental to the thinking of later theorists. The image of people's attitudes thawing and then refreezing is conceptually useful because this symbolism helps to keep theory and reality in mind simultaneously.

Lippitt's phases of change

Lippitt, Watson and Westley (1958) extended Lewin's theory to a seven-step process and focused more on what the change agent, that is, the person who initiates and manages the change process, must do rather than on the evolution of change itself. (See Table 11.2 for a comparison of four change theories.) They emphasised participation of key members of the target system

Table 11.2 Comparison of change models

Lewin	Lippitt	Rogers	Bridges
1. Unfreezing	1. Diagnose problem	1. Knowledge	1. Endings
2. Moving	2. Assess motivation	2. Persuasion	2. Neutral zone
3. Refreezing	3. Assess change agent's motivations	3. Decision	3. New beginnings
	4. Select progressive change objects	4. Implementation	
	5. Choose change agent role	5. Confirmation	
	6. Maintain change		
	7. Terminate helping relationships		

throughout the change process, particularly during planning. Communication skills, rapport building and problem-solving strategies underlie their phases.

The seven steps are:

1. *Diagnose the problem.* Involve key people in data collection and problem-solving.

2. *Assess the motivation and capacity for change.* What are the financial and human resources constraints? Are the structure and function of the organisation conducive to change? What are the possible solutions, and which are preferred?

3. *Assess the change agent's motivation and resources.* This assessment is important. Consider the change agent's own commitment to change, energy level, future ambitions and power bases. Starting a change and dropping it midstream can waste valuable personal energy and undermine the confidence of colleagues and subordinates.

4. *Select progressive change objects (milestones).* Develop the action plan, evaluation criteria and specify strategies.

5. *Choose a change agent role.* The change agent can act as cheerleader, expert, consultant or group facilitator. Whichever role is selected, all participants should recognise it so that expectations are clear.

6. *Maintain the change.* Communication, feedback, revision and coordination are essential components of this phase.

7. *Terminate the helping relationship.* The change agent withdraws from the selected role gradually as the change becomes stabilised.

Rogers' diffusion of innovations

Rogers (1983) takes a different approach than Lewin or Lippitt, (see Table 11.1). Unlike the earlier theories that focus on situational change, in particular unwelcome change, Rogers focuses on the uptake of innovative practices. His five-step innovation–decision process details how an individual or decision-making unit passes from first knowledge of an innovation to confirmation of the decision to adopt or reject a new idea. His framework emphasises the reversible nature of change: participants may initially adopt a proposal but later discontinue it or the reverse – they may initially reject it but adopt it at a later time. This is a useful distinction. If the change agent is unsuccessful in achieving full implementation of a proposal, it should not be assumed that the issue is dead. It can be resurrected, perhaps in an altered form or at a more opportune time. However, if it is accepted, one also cannot assume permanence. This model could be particularly useful when helping people adapt to new technology (hand-held electronic diaries) or ways of working (telephone advice, telemedicine).

Rogers' five steps to the diffusion of innovation are:

1. *Knowledge.* The decision-making unit is introduced to the innovation and begins to understand it.

2. *Persuasion.* A favourable (or unfavourable) attitude toward the innovation forms.

3. *Decision.* Activities lead to a decision to adopt or reject the innovation.

4. *Implementation.* The innovation is put to use, and reinvention or alterations may occur.

5. *Confirmation.* The individual or decision-making unit seeks reinforcement that the decision was correct. If there are conflicting messages or experiences, the original decision may be reversed.

Finally, Rogers stresses two important aspects of successful planned change: key people and policy-makers must be interested in the innovation and committed to making it happen.

Bridges' model of managing transitions

William Bridges (2003) added an important focus on psychological responses to the earlier work on change. Originally published in 1991, Bridges' belief is that changing is easy; it is the human response to change that, if poorly managed, gets in the way. He describes the process of managing transitions as helping people through three phases:

1. *Managing endings*. Help people let go of old ways and old identities. This phase is an ending, and a time to help people deal with their losses. Emotions commonly associated with this phase are also the signs of grieving – anger, bargaining, anxiety, sadness, disorientation or depression.

2. *Leading people through the neutral zone*. After people have let go of the old ways they enter a phase where the situation is neither what it was before nor what it will become. The neutral zone is a bridge stretching between two shores, neither here nor there. During this phase people can become unsettled, anxiety rises and motivation declines. Staff members can become distracted and less productive, and problems re-emerge. People feel that things are ambiguous, uncertain and unclear.

3. *Launching a new beginning*. The final phase of transition is the new beginning, the release of energy in a new direction and the expression of a new identity. Successful management of this phase results in people feeling comfortable with the new way, having established new relationships and a feeling that they have moved on. It is more than coming to terms with the change; it is embracing the new way as the desired state.

Bridges' model, like Lippit's, focuses on the change agent and provides the manager with an 'emotional barometer' for the change process which helps them to assess the progress along the transition path for each person affected, and to apply targeted interventions.

The change process

The change process is very similar to the problem-solving process and involves four steps: identifying the problem (opportunity) including data collection and analysis, planning, implementation and evaluation.

Identifying the problem or the opportunity

Change is often planned to close a gap between the current and desired state of affairs. Gaps may arise from failure to achieve an existing standard (a problem) or because new standards have been created (an opportunity or aspiration). Opportunities demand change as much as (or more than) problems do, but they are often overlooked. Be it a problem or an opportunity, it must be identified clearly. If the issue is perceived differently by key individuals, the search for solutions becomes confused. Start by asking the right questions:

- What are we doing now?
- What are the requirements imposed on our organisation that are different from those of the past?
- What services are being commissioned and should we be looking to develop more strongly in that direction?
- What factors will influence our final decisions?
- What prevents us from moving in the direction we wish to go?
- What kind of change is required?

This last question generates creative thinking about the potential effect of change on the system. Organisational change involves modifications in the system's interacting components: services, structure and people.

The introduction of new services necessitates changes in the structure of the organisation. Relationships among the people who work in the system change when the structure is changed. New units open; others close. New rules and regulations, new roles and new resource allocations may emerge. They, in turn, change staffing needs, requiring people with different skills, knowledge bases, attitudes and motivations.

Data collection

Once the problem or opportunity has been identified, the change agent and others collect data external and internal to the system. This step is crucial to the eventual success of the planned change process. The aim is to get a clear picture of the current situation and the impact of the proposed change through as many different data sources as possible. Data can include facts and figures (hard data) such as waiting times, admission rates, length of stay and readmission rates. The manager also needs to assess resources – especially those the manager can control.

Whilst useful, facts and figures will not provide the entire picture. Audit, patient experience surveys, clinical events and staff satisfaction are often called soft data because they are less analytical than facts and figures. Soft data are an equally important source of information because they describe the impact the situation has on the people involved. For example, the hard data may say that waiting times for knee replacement surgery are within the targeted 18-week time frame, yet the patients may report that during that time they were virtually immobile from the pain and the inactivity resulted in muscular weakness that delayed recovery.

The data collection phase should also yield insight into the driving and restraining forces at work. Often the driving forces are external to the organisation, for example a national policy initiative. This can be translated into an internal driver for change if the organisation is seeking to become a foundation trust or to win contracts from the primary care trust. Teams within the organisation may see the opportunity in the external driver, or, more commonly, can perceive the driver as just another thing that has to be done.

It is also important to consider the emotional and psychological impact of the change on those affected. Bridges (2003) recommends that during the data collection phase the following questions are asked: Who will gain from this change? Who will lose? Who has more power and why? Can those power bases be altered? How?

Analysis

The kinds, amounts and sources of data collected are useless unless they are looked at in relation to each other, and interpreted to give them meaning. The process of bringing the data together and creating meaning is called analysis. Data analysis needs to focus on identifying relationships between the hard and soft data, driving and restraining forces and psychological responses to gain an insight into which solutions are most likely to have the desired outcomes.

Planning

Planning the who, how and when of the change is a key step. Those affected by the change should be active participants in the planning stage. The more involved they are at this point, the less resistance there will be later. Lewin's unfreezing imagery is relevant here, as is Bridges' idea of managing endings. Present attitudes, habits and ways of thinking have to soften, and people have to let go of existing ways so that they are ready for new ways of thinking and behaving. Boundaries must melt before the system can shift and restructure.

This is the time to make people uncomfortable with the status quo. Plant the seeds of discontent by introducing information that may make people feel dissatisfied with the present and interested in something new. This information comes from the data collected and analysed effectively to paint a clear picture of the desired future as well as the deficits of the current situation. Couch the proposed change in comfortable terms as far as possible, and minimise anxiety about the new change.

Managers need to plan the resources required to make the change and establish feedback mechanisms to evaluate its progress and success. Establish milestones with people who will provide the feedback and work with these people to set specific goals with time frames. Develop operational indicators that signal success or failure in terms of performance and satisfaction.

Implementation

The plans are put into motion (Lewin's moving stage). It is here that not only the practical steps for change are enacted but also the strategies for managing the psychological transitions are set in motion. Bridges (2003) recommends the following strategies for managing people in transition:

- *Managing endings.* Helping people let go of old ways and identities is not easy. It requires accurate assessment of the feelings of the staff member and a willingness to respond to the emotions with empathy and compassion. It is important to:
  - identify who is losing what so as to anticipate and plan for behaviours that may emerge;
  - give people information, and do it again, and again;
  - accept the other person's experience of loss as genuine;
  - acknowledge losses openly and sympathetically;
  - accept and expect signs of grieving;
  - compensate for losses – this does not always mean money: it can be saving face in a change of role, more flexible working hours, or other actions that help people let go;
  - treat the past with respect: allow people to take a piece of the past with them into the future;
  - clarify what is *not* changing, the stable and important things that will go forwards.

- *Managing in the neutral zone.* The most important part of helping people cross the bridge between the old way and the new is to recognise just how difficult and disruptive this time can be. There is a natural tendency to want to get the change over with and therefore impatience can erupt. Bridges recommends the following management strategies:
  - Redefine the neutral zone as a normal part of any change, and as a time to be creative, released from some of the constraints of the past.
  - Design temporary systems to contain some of the confusion. It is important not to impose a 'final system' too soon. Whatever is put into place should be temporary, and reviewed every few months, with a view to refining the system towards the new way.
  - Strengthen relationships. This is a time to focus on common goals and values, and to build effective teams.
- *Managing new beginnings – stabilise the change.* Lewin describes this stage of the change process as refreezing the target system whilst Bridges calls this phase new beginnings. The change agent takes on a very different role, no longer driving change and managing emotions; the change agent is transferring responsibility back to the team members, and helping them to celebrate their effort and achievement.
  - It may seem that the job is done once people begin to actually behave differently, but the change is complete only when people are committed to the new way of working. Compliance is not enough to sustain change. Bridges recommends the following actions to reinforce the new beginning and prevent slippage into the old way.
  - Be consistent. In this phase it is important that every policy, procedure, priority and practice sends a consistent message. For example, when implementing a new computer system, it is important to ensure all members of staff are using the system and no exceptions are made.
  - Ensure quick successes. Owing to the neutral zone's impact on confidence and productivity, it is important to find a quick win to boost morale.
  - Symbolise the new identity. Ensure that identification badges, new uniforms, name plates and telephone listings reflect new titles and roles.
  - Celebrate success. Marking the attainment of the new way of working is important. It should be part of the change management plan from the beginning.

Evaluation

At each milestone, the situation is assessed to see if the plan is on track. The change agent determines whether the goals are being achieved within the time frames and resources allocated. Identifying whether unintended consequences and undesirable outcomes may have occurred is also important so that the next phase of the change plan can be adjusted to prevent further problems.

Change agent strategies

The role of change agent, that is, the driving force for change, involves a number of decisions about the best way to proceed. Chin and Benne (1969) proposed three different strategies for effecting change. Each strategy has a different power base and all achieve change through different methods.

The **power-coercive strategy** is based on the application of power by legitimate authority, economic sanctions or political clout. This strategy is intended to achieve compliance through compulsions and authority over individuals or organisations. Changes are made through law, policy or financial constraints. Regulatory bodies such as the Health and Safety Commission have the right under law to require safety measures to be implemented. The Care Quality Commission has the authority to set standards for care quality and to conduct inspections, announced or unannounced. Failure to meet the standards set by either organisation could result in fines, penalties or legal judgments against the organisation and its executives.

Within organisations, the restricting of budgets or the introduction of policy can be a power-coercive strategy. This approach is sometimes useful within organisations when a consensus is unlikely despite efforts to stimulate participation by those involved. When much resistance is anticipated, time is short, and the change is critical for organisational success, power-coercive strategies may be necessary. For example, an organisation under sanction from the Health and Safety Executive for dangerous practices is likely to use power-coercion through policy and diktat to bring the situation back into line. It is important to recognise that power-coercive strategies should always be the choice of last resort because the application of power over an individual or team will breed resentment and lower cooperation in the future.

The **empirical-rational strategy** is based in knowledge, not authority. The assumption is that people are rational and will follow their rational self-interest if that self-interest is made clear to them. It is also assumed that the change agent who has knowledge has the expert power to persuade people to accept a rationally justified change that will benefit them. The flow of influence moves from those who know to those who do not know. New ideas are invented and communicated or diffused to all participants. This strategy relies on the idea that once enlightened, rational people will either accept or reject the idea based on its merits and consequences.

Empirical rational strategies underpin evidence-based practice. For example, research and audit into pain management in cancer has caused a shift from under-prescribing of analgesics out of fear of overdosing the patient that prevailed 30 years ago to extremely effective pain management practices that have a profoundly positive impact on the quality of life of cancer patients.

Empirical-rational strategies are often effective when little resistance to the proposed change is expected and the change is perceived as reasonable. Introduction of new technology that is easy to use, saves time and improves quality of care would meet little resistance as long as the implementation plan included training and support from the information technology department. In this case there is little need for staff participation in the early steps of the change process, although input is useful for the evaluation and stabilisation stages. The benefits of change for the staff and perhaps research findings regarding patient outcomes are the major driving forces. Well-researched, cost-effective technology can be implemented using these strategies.

Unfortunately, not everyone is persuaded by a rational argument. In practice, people like to do things the familiar way and will often resist change even when supported by evidence. People with a more pessimistic mindset will tend to see the drawbacks in the change whereas the optimistic people will see the benefits. This may call for consideration of the last of Chin and Benne's change strategies.

Normative-re-educative strategies are based on the assumption that people act in accordance with social norms and values. Information and rational arguments are insufficient to change people's patterns of actions; the change agent must focus on the psychology of change as well. People's roles and relationships, values, beliefs and feelings will influence their acceptance of change. Bridges' idea of managing transition is closely aligned to this change strategy.

In this strategy, the power basis is not authority or knowledge, but skill in interpersonal relationships. The change agent uses personal engagement, recognition, common values and principles to achieve collaboration. Members of the target system are involved throughout the change process. Value conflicts from all parts of the system are brought into the open and worked through so change can progress.

Normative-re-educative strategies are well suited to the creative problem-solving needed in health care today. With their firm grasp of the behavioural sciences and communication skills, people are comfortable with this model. Changing from a traditional hierarchical way of working to self-directed teams or developing a new integrated service for asthma sufferers are the types of change suited to this sort of strategy. In most cases, the normative-re-educative approach to change will be effective in reducing resistance and stimulating personal and organisational creativity. The obvious drawback is the time required for consultation, negotiation and integration of ideas throughout the change process. When there is adequate time or when group consensus is fundamental to successful adoption of the change, the manager is well advised to adopt this framework.

Resistance to change

Response to change varies from ready acceptance to full-blown resistance. Rogers (1983) identified six typical ways in which people respond to change:

- Innovators love change and thrive on it.
- Early adopters are receptive to change but need a little more persuading at the beginning.
- The early majority prefers the status quo but eventually accepts the change.
- The late majority is resistive, accepting change after most others have.
- Laggards dislike change and are openly antagonistic.
- Rejecters actively oppose and may even sabotage change.

Resistance to change is to be expected for a number of reasons: lack of trust, vested interest in the status quo, fear of failure, loss of status or income, misunderstanding and belief that change is unnecessary or that it will not improve the situation (Yukl, 2002; Hellriegel, Jackson and Slocum, 2002). Employees may resist change because they dislike or disapprove of the person responsible for implementing the change or they may distrust the change process. Regardless, managers deal continually with change – both the change that they themselves initiate and change initiated by the larger organisation.

The change agent should anticipate and look for resistance to change. It will be lurking somewhere, perhaps where least expected. It can be recognised in such statements as:

- We tried that before.
- It won't work.
- No one else does it like that.
- We've always done it this way.
- We can't afford it.

- We don't have the time.
- It will cause too much commotion.
- You'll never get it past the board.
- Let's wait a while.
- Every new boss wants to do something different.
- Let's start a task force to look at it; put it on the agenda.

Expect resistance and listen carefully to who says what, when and in what circumstances. Open resisters are easier to deal with than closet resisters. Look for non-verbal signs of resistance, such as poor work habits and lack of interest in the change.

Resistance has positive and negative aspects. On the one hand, resistance forces the change agent to be clear about why the change is needed. The manager must know the change inside and out because they must defend it against challengers. The positive part of resistance is the sharper focus and problem-solving it encourages. It prevents the unexpected. It forces the manager to clarify information, keep interest levels high and establish why change is necessary. Resistance is a stimulant as much as it is a force to be overcome. It may even motivate the group to do better what it is doing now, so that it does not have to change.

On the other hand, resistance is not always beneficial, especially if it persists beyond the planning stage and well into the implementation phase. It can wear down supporters and redirect energy from implementing the change to dealing with resisters. Morale can suffer.

When handling resistance, the manager must first decide if the resistance is getting in the way, or a natural part of the process such as occurs in the managing ending phase of Bridges' model. Resistance can be used to sharpen decision, for example, and eventually gain consensus. If the resistance is lasting too long or getting in the way, it is important to separate the behaviour from the person. Remain calm and supportive of the individual whilst sticking to the problem-solving change process. Consider the following guidelines:

- Speak in person and privately with those who oppose the change. Get to the root of their reasons for opposition.
- Clarify information, and provide accurate feedback.
- Be open to suggestions but clear about the overall purpose and goals. Do not compromise on the intended outcome.
- Discuss the consequences of resistance (e.g. threats to organisational success, compromised patient care).
- Emphasise the goals of the change and how the individual or group will benefit. However, do not spend too much energy on rational analysis of why the change is good and why the arguments against it do not hold up. People's resistance frequently flows from feelings that are not rational.
- Keep resisters involved in face-to-face contact with supporters. Encourage proponents to empathise with opponents, recognise valid objections and relieve unnecessary fears.
- Maintain a climate of trust, support and confidence.
- Divert attention by creating a different focus. Energy can shift to a more important problem inside the system, thereby redirecting resistance. When members perceive a greater threat (such as closure of a service altogether or the organisation being placed on special measure), they tend to unify internally.

A manager of a district nursing service used change management strategies to overcome resistance as shown in Case Study 11.1.

Case Study 11.1   **Change Management**

Peter Beasley is the manager of a district nursing team covering a rural community comprising a relatively higher percentage of older people. Last year the decision was taken to implement electronic patient records. Each visit was to be recorded on hand-held devices and a copy kept on disk at the patient's home.

Sarah Ramsey has been a district nurse for 18 years, working for Peter's team for the past 5 years. Although she was part of the pilot, Sarah is very much opposed to using the new hand-held devices. She has rarely used a computer and complains she can't see the small display well enough to use the device. At a recent staff meeting, Sarah said she would rather quit than learn to use the new hand-held devices.

Peter empathises with Sarah's reluctance to use the new hand-held computers. He also recognises how much Sarah contributes in expertise and leadership to the department. However, he knows that the new performance standards require all employees to use the hand-held computers. After Sarah fails to attend the training sessions, she tells co-workers 'We've tried things like this before, it never works. We'll be back on paper within six months, so why waste my time learning this stuff?'

Peter meets privately with Sarah to discuss her concerns about the new technology. Sarah again states that she sees no need for the hand-held devices, claiming they will take more time away from care and offer no benefits over the existing paper system. Peter reviews the new standards with Sarah, emphasising the benefit that computerised records will have in collecting and analysing important data about treatment effectiveness and service productivity. He asks Sarah about her personal experience of using the device and asks her what her concerns are. She admits she has trouble reading the display and that it takes her far longer to complete her notes using the device. Peter refers Sarah to the occupational health service who arrange for an eye examination and prescription for special spectacles suited to small-screen display devices. Peter also talks to the IT people to see if text shortcuts can be added to Sarah's device so that entries can be made more quickly. Once Sarah's specific needs were addressed, she was much more willing to try the devices.

Manager's Checklist

The manager is responsible for:

☐ Communicating openly and honestly with employees who oppose change.

☐ Understanding the resistance to change.

☐ Maintaining support and confidence in staff even if they are resistive to change.

☐ Emphasising the positive outcomes from initiating change.

☐ Finding solutions to problems that are obstacles to change.

The manager's role in implementing change

Leading change is not easy, but it is a necessary skill for managers. Successful change agents demonstrate certain characteristics that can be cultivated and mastered with practice. Among these are:

- the ability to combine ideas from unconnected sources;

- the ability to energise others by keeping the interest level up and demonstrating a high personal energy level;
- skill in human relations: well-developed interpersonal communication, group management and problem-solving skills. Knox and Irving (1997) noted that communication was the most important factor in promoting change;
- integrative thinking: the ability to see the big picture and keep the end in mind whilst dealing with the small steps needed to achieve success;
- sufficient flexibility to modify ideas when modifications will improve the change, but enough persistence to resist non-productive tampering with the planned change;
- confidence and the tendency not to be easily discouraged;
- realistic thinking;
- trustworthiness: a track record of integrity and success with other changes;
- the ability to articulate a vision through insights and versatile thinking;
- the ability to handle resistance.

Contrary to popular opinion, change is often not initiated by top-level management (Yukl, 2002), but rather emerges as new initiatives or problems are identified. Thus, all managers must be able to initiate change and to participate in implementing change.

Energy is needed to change a system. Power is the main source of that energy. Informational power, expertise and possibly positional power can be used to persuade others. To access optimum power, use the following strategies:

- Analyse the organisational chart. Know the formal lines of authority. Identify informal lines as well.
- Identify key people who will be affected by the change. Pay attention to those immediately above and below the point of change.
- Find out as much as possible about these key people. What are their special interests, what excites them, and what turns them off? What is on their personal and organisational agendas? Who typically aligns with whom on important decisions?
- Begin to build a coalition of support before you start the change process. Identify the key people who will most likely support your idea and those who are most likely to be persuaded easily. Talk informally with them to flush out possible objections to your idea and potential opponents. What will be the costs and benefits to them – especially in political terms? Can your idea be modified in ways that retain your objectives but appeal to more key people?

This information helps the manager develop the most sellable idea or at least pinpoint probable resistance. It is a broad beginning to the data-collection step of the change process and has to be fine-tuned once the idea is better defined. The astute manager keeps alert at all times to monitor power struggles.

Although a cardinal rule of change is don't try to change too much too fast, the savvy manager develops a sense of exquisite timing by pacing the change process according to the political pulse. For example, the manager unfreezes the system during a period of coalition-building and high interest, while resistance is low or at least unorganised.

The manager may stall the project beyond a pilot stage if resistance solidifies or gains a powerful ally. In this case, the manager exercises mechanisms to reduce resistance. If resistance continues, two options should be considered:

1. The change is not workable and should be modified to meet the strongest objections (compromise).
2. The change is fine-tuned sufficiently, but change must proceed now and resistance must be overcome.

If the latter option is selected, energy is focused on overcoming resistance. Supporters are mobilised, and constant, consistent pressure is exerted to move ahead.

How the manager participates in the change process depends on whether they are an insider or outsider. Someone who is part of the system being changed knows that system, has a stake in the outcome and is familiar with the people, language and politics. However, being an insider can restrict one's ability to move freely throughout the system. The manager may be locked into certain roles, authority structures and expectations. Perspective may be limited. However, blinders to insight can be removed. An outsider offers a fresh perspective and is independent of internal policies but is unfamiliar with the system, people's values and personal agendas. Either insiders or outsiders can accomplish change, but change must be assessed and used differently.

What you know now

- In today's health care system, change is rapid, constant, persuasive and persistent.
- Evaluation of planned change theories and selection of a theory suited to the situation at hand is useful in managing change.
- The change process is similar to the problem-solving process: identification of the problem, data collection and analysis, planning, implementation and evaluation.
- The manager will use change agent skills in initiating change and in implementing organisational change.
- Resistance to change is to be expected, and it can be a stimulant as well as a force to be overcome.
- The manager must understand resistance and develop skills to handle it.
- The manager needs to understand the politics of change and use power strategies successfully.

Questions to challenge you

1. Identify a needed change in the organisation where you work. Using the change process, outline the steps you would take to initiate change.

2. Consider your school or college. What change do you think is needed? Explain how you would change it to become a better place for learning.

3. Have you had an experience with change occurring in your organisation? What was your initial reaction? Did that change? How well did the change process work? Was the change successful?

4. Do you have a behaviour you would like to change? Using the steps in the change process, describe how you might effect that change.

5. How do you normally react to change? Choose from the following:
   (a) I love new ideas, and I'm ready to try new things.
   (b) I like to know that something will work out before I try it.
   (c) I try to avoid change as much as possible.

   Did your response to the above question alter how you would like to view change? Think about this the next time change is presented to you.

References

Bridges, W. (2003) *Managing Transitions: Making the most of change*. London: Nicholas Brealey.

Chin, R and Benne, K. D. (1969) General strategies for effecting changes in human systems. In Bennis, W. G., Benne, K. D. and Chin, R. (eds) *The Planning of Change*, 2nd edn. New York: Holt, Rinehart and Winston.

Hellriegel, D., Jackson, S. E. and Slocum, J. W. Jr (2002) *Management: A competency-based approach*, 9th edn. Egan, MN: South Western.

Knox, S. and Irving, J. A. (1997) Nurse manager perceptions of heathcare executive behaviours during organisational change. *Journal of Nursing Administration*, **27**(11), 33-39.

Lewin, K. (1951) *Field Theory in Social Science*. New York: Harper and Row.

Lippitt, R., Watson, J. and Westley, B. (1958) *The Dynamics of Planned Change*. New York: Harcourt, Brace.

Rogers, E. (1983) *Diffusion of Innovations*, 3rd edn. New York: Free Press.

Yukl, G. (2002) *Leadership in Organisations*, 5th edn. Upper Saddle River, NJ: Prentice Hall.

Chapter 12
Self-Care: Managing Stress and Time

Introduction

Learning to cope with stress and manage time wisely is important to becoming an effective leader and manager. Consider the scenario in Case Study 12.1.

Imagine

Feeling calm and in control every day. You are focused, relaxed and even feeling energised by the challenges of work. You have time to think things through, and plan for important developments coming to your team.

Case Study 12.1

Suzanne is a ward sister with 10 years' experience leading and managing a large acute medical ward in a teaching hospital. She is married and has two children under the age of six who attend preschool while Suzanne is at work. She often receives calls from the ward during the evenings and nights, and approximately once a week she has to return to the ward to cover for staff absence or to manage a non-clinical situation. Suzanne is responsible for staffing on the ward. The trust is struggling to make cost improvements and so has imposed a freeze on hiring and on the use of bank and agency staff. Suzanne's ward has one nurse on maternity leave, another on long-term sick, and two whole-time-equivalent vacancies. Suzanne sits on two directorate committees and the trust-wide committee on patient involvement. Every night she takes work home, including the rota, appraisals, reports to read and write and reading. Although provided with an office, Suzanne has little opportunity to use it because of constant interruptions from nurses, consultants, matrons, ward clerks and even patients' families. Recently, Suzanne saw her GP, complaining of persistent headaches, weight loss and a feeling of constant fatigue. Suzanne was found to have high blood pressure, with a resting pulse rate of 100. Her GP referred her to the practice nurse for advice on diet, exercise, relaxation and stress reduction. She was advised to lighten her workload, take some time off and reduce her stress level, or she may find her health problems increasing.

Sound familiar?

The nature of stress

The Health and Safety Executive (2008) defines **stress** as 'the adverse reaction people have to excessive pressures or other types of demands placed on them'. In Case Study 12.1 Suzanne was experiencing a high level of demand at work and home and felt pressure to make sure both roles were done well. She was suffering from a number of the adverse reactions to stress, including physical changes and a sense of not being able to cope.

Hans Selye (1990), the pioneer of stress research, suggests that the body's wear and tear results from its response to stressors. The rate and intensity of damage increase when a person experiences greater stress than they are capable of accommodating. Selye maintains that the physiological response to stress is the same whether the stressor is positive (**eustress**) or negative (**distress**). It is easy to see how negative events, such as job loss, illness and financial problems can cause stress, but happy events, such as marriage, a new baby, a new job or promotion, bring new demands and can therefore be a cause of stress as well. In Case Study 12.2 Anthony was experiencing stress resulting from welcome and demanding circumstances, and a strong personal commitment to high standards.

The experience of stress is subjective and individual. One person's stressful event is another's ordinary daily responsibility. One individual may cope comfortably with an event, positive or negative, that would prove overwhelming for someone else. Even a minor change in organisational policy may cause some individuals to experience stress, whereas others welcome it. Some people seem to thrive on the demands of work, family, school and community involvement, whereas others find that even one set of responsibilities is enough.

> ## Case Study 12.2
>
> Anthony had 15 years' experience in the community working with diabetic patients. He was offered a modern matron role developing an integrated diabetic service for the primary care trust. He wanted to be successful, and held a high personal standard for his own work performance. His colleagues sometimes saw him as a perfectionist, never resting until he felt things were just right. Anthony was very committed to developing the best service possible, and began putting in long hours and working weekends. As the project progressed, Anthony became unable to sleep, and for much of the night his active mind was worrying whether what he did was up to the highest standard. He often ate at his desk rather than fixing nutritious meals and gained 10 pounds. After the diabetic service was fully functioning, Anthony's sleep pattern and weight returned to normal.

Causes of stress in the workplace

The Health and Safety Executive (2008) has identified six primary sources of stress at work. These are:

- *Demands* – workload, work patterns (shift work, split shifts and unsocial hours) and work environment (noise, working outdoors in all weather, pace of work).
- *Control* - how much say the person has in the work they do and how it is done.
- *Support* - encouragement, sponsorship (someone in the organisation that values and promotes your work), resources, access to information and other people such as the manager or colleagues.
- *Relationships* – respectful working relationships that minimise conflict and address unacceptable behaviours such as bullying.
- *Role* – lack of clarity in roles, overlap in roles and responsibilities that conflict with each other or the individual's values and beliefs.
- *Change* - how change is managed and communicated.

Demands

Management and leadership are demanding roles with accountability for not only one's own work but also the work of others. Many nurses in management and leadership roles continue to have clinical responsibilities and therefore clinical accountability adds an additional layer of demand. Patients in acute settings are sicker than in the past, and their needs for highly skilled care are growing. Pressures on beds and on community service capacity continue, as do the need to meet targets for access to service and ever-increasing patient expectations. Nurses in the community are also working with sicker patients, and they may be working alone, driving long distances and having to focus on complex social issues as well as health problems.

Shift working, unsocial hours and weekend work required in health care can be a source of stress. People who work on evening or night shifts may have an increasingly complex family life if their spouse and children are on different schedules, especially if the person rotates shifts. It takes several weeks to adjust physiologically to a change in shifts; however, most rotation patterns require nurses to change shifts several times a month.

The physical environment in which one works may also create stress. In Case Study 12.1 Suzanne had to cope with constant interruptions in her office and therefore ended up taking work home. Working in the community can also be stressful, though the environment of work is very different. Community staff members have to cope with driving around crowded city streets fighting traffic or trying to find a parking place, or perhaps making visits in areas with high levels of crime or in remote villages.

Control

There are a number of factors that can affect the sense of control experienced by managers and leaders at work. Statutory regulation, policy and budgets have an effect as well as individual circumstances. In Case Study 12.1 Suzanne had limited control over staffing shortages even though she was responsible for staffing the ward. Commonly, managers have 24 hours a day, 7 days a week responsibility for their area even though they are not physically present in the work setting for most of those hours. Developing a greater sense of control for managers is dependent on good working relationships with others on the team who manage and lead when the team leader is not there.

Support

Support in this context is about feeling equipped to do the job well. Resources are one form of support, such as equipment, supplies and the right type and number of staff to meet the demands. Access to education, training and development for the manager and their staff are also a form of support. Someone to turn to for advice, direction and information helps a manager feel supported and able to achieve the expected results. A substantial deficit in any of these forms of support can lead to an organisational environment that by its very nature is stressful.

Relationships

Borrill et al.'s (2001) important research into team effectiveness found that teams that work well together have much lower levels of stress than those working in looser groupings or working alone. Working well together involves a number of factors: clear objectives, high levels of participation, emphasis on quality and support for innovation. The nature of leadership was also found to be important. Teams without clear leadership were associated with a high level of stress amongst team members. Clear leadership involves creating alignment amongst members around shared objectives, enthusiasm and excitement, optimism and confidence, helping others to appreciate others' contributions, helping team members to confront and resolve differences constructively, coordinating activities and developing capabilities and flexibility.

Roles

Role conflicts can occur when an individual has two competing roles, such as when a manager has both clinical and managerial responsibility. Stress can result from incongruence between one's expectations for performance and one's perception of the resulting performance (**intra-role conflict**). For example, a manager in A&E may be very focused on ensuring the two-hour trolley wait targets are met and yet feel that meeting the target does not always represent good care. In this case, successfully meeting targets may feel like a hollow accomplishment because it challenges the manager's professional judgement about best care standards.

Similarly, **inter-role conflict** is the tension that results from having a number of roles for which you are responsible. Doing a job such as taking care of patients and directing others to do the job are different. Nurses may undervalue the management role and believe that the manager should be helping on the ward rather than attending a meeting. Managers such as Suzanne in Case Study 12.1 may find themselves effectively doing two jobs if they fail to clarify roles and responsibilities, delegate and manage time well.

Interdisciplinary difficulties may cause stress. For example, a consultant may wish to do ward rounds in the late morning whereas the ward may have a protected meal time programme in operation which would be compromised by meeting the consultant's request. Similarly, there may be stress arising from the need to coordinate diagnostic and therapeutic activities that meet the constraints of other departments. Conflicts arising from these complex activities can result in stress.

Change

Change is one of the leading causes of stress at work, especially if the change is imposed, which is increasingly common these days (see Chapter 11). The fact that a change is imposed is in itself stressful in that the people involved feel a loss of control. Changes are often seen as positive or negative, though no change is entirely one or the other. For example, a restructuring of a community team may have negative aspects (loss of close working relationships) and positive aspects (opportunity to work with a new client group and to develop skills in new areas). One of the roles of the manager faced with changes that will affect the team is to present a realistic assessment of the impact of the change, highlighting the benefits as well as the losses.

Personal causes of stress

Work is not the only source of stress for individuals at work. What is happening outside work, the person's level of optimism, how they benchmark themselves against others, past experience of stress and self-esteem can all affect stress levels.

Life events

Psychiatrists Holmes and Rahe (1967) examined the medical records of over 5,000 patients in 1967 to see whether stressful events might cause illness. The results were published as the Social Readjustment Rating Scale. In this scale, life events are associated with 'life change units' (Table 12.1). The higher the life change units experienced recently by an individual, the more likely the person was to experience illness (Rahe, Mahan and Arthur, 1970). Having an awareness of the life events experienced by staff members can be a useful management tool. Decreasing the work demands during times of life change may be useful in managing both stress and staff illness.

Outlook on life

Martin Seligman (2006) found that **optimism**, a sense of confidence about the future and an expectation that outcomes are likely to be positive, is not only associated with achieving more

Table 12.1 The Holmes and Rahe stress scale

Life event	Life change units
Death of a spouse	100
Divorce	73
Marital separation	65
Imprisonment	63
Death of a close family member	63
Personal injury or illness	53
Marriage	50
Dismissal from work	47
Marital reconciliation	45
Change in health of family member	44
Pregnancy	40
Sexual difficulties	39
Gaining a new family member	39
Business readjustment	39
Change in financial situation	38
Change in frequency of arguments	35
Taking on a mortgage	32
Foreclosure of a mortgage or loan	30
Change in responsibilities at work	29
Child leaving home	29
Trouble with in-laws	29
Outstanding personal achievement	28
Spouse starting or stopping work	26
Beginning or ending school	26
Change in living conditions	25
Change to personal habits	24
Trouble with a boss or manager	23
Change in working hours or conditions	20
Change of residence	20
Change in schools	20
Change in recreation	19
Change in church activities	19
Change in social activities	18
Small mortgage or loan	17
Change in sleeping habits	16
Change in number of family reunions	15
Change in eating habits	15
Taking a holiday	13
Christmas	12
Minor violation of the law	11

Source: Homes and Rahe (1967)

at work but also has better physical health and may even cause one to live longer. **Pessimism** is the opposite of optimism; it is a lack of confidence in the future and an anticipation of negative outcomes. Seligman (2006) found that an optimist faced with a difficult situation sees the situation as temporary (this too shall pass), external (caused by factors largely outside themselves) and specific (a unique occurrence that does not relate to other experiences). A pessimist sees a bad event as permanent (things will never change), internal (I am to blame) and universal (I am a bad manager). Let's look how the same situation could be interpreted by an optimist and a pessimist.

According to Seligman (2006) optimism can be learned. As the example in Case Study 12.3 illustrates, what we tell ourselves about the situation can cause us to feel more resilient, hopeful and in control, or, conversely, hopeless and depressed. Using an optimistic explanation style when things go wrong in the team can decrease stress. Box 12.1 gives some examples of optimistic statements that could be useful when adversity arises and decrease stress in a team.

Case Study 12.3 Optimism versus Pessimism

Karen and Liz have completed an assessment of their staffing allocation and both have decided to submit a request for the addition of one whole-time-equivalent staff member. Both requests have been turned down.

Karen takes a pessimistic view of the situation whilst Liz remains optimistic. Here is what each has to say about the staffing request being turned down:

Karen	Perception	Liz	Perception
This organisation will never approve staffing increases for medical wards; medical wards are always low priority.	Permanent	The request was turned down this time.	Temporary
I'm not good at writing staffing requests. It's no wonder it was turned down.	Permanent and internal	This wasn't the right time to make a staffing request with all the cost improvement targets to meet. I will try again in a few months.	Temporary and external
I'm not a good ward manager.	Universal	The feedback from the committee was very useful. I didn't include enough hard data in the request this time, but I will next time.	Specific

> ### Box 12.1   **An Optimistic Explanatory Style**
>
> An optimistic explanatory style seeks to give individuals greater hope and control over adverse situations by giving them a specific, temporary and external explanation. Here are some statements to consider:
>
> 'Staffing is tight now, and will remain tight until the cost containment targets are met. The demands on the team have gone up and we can be proud of keeping standards high. I will pursue the staffing allocation again in three months.'
>
> 'That situation didn't go as expected; the outcomes didn't match our usual high standard. What can we do to improve for next time?'
>
> 'Our team is going to be restructured in a way that will make support consistent achievement of care standards and promote efficiency. You have been very successful at building this team, and those skills will serve you well in this restructure.'

Benchmarking

Stress can result from comparing yourself, your service or your team with others. Newly qualified staff members, for example, often compare themselves with more experienced members of the team, and therefore see themselves as inadequate in the role. Moving from a staff nurse position to a management position also creates tension. New managers often experience a sense of isolation from the peer group of staff nurses who previously provided support. In each of these cases, the individual often questions their abilities to make the transition to the new role. Therefore, low skill recognition is not to be overlooked as a key element in developing stress resiliency.

Past experience

Past experience in coping with stress provides insight into an individual's ability for successful coping in current experiences. People tend to repeat coping behaviours in similar situations, regardless of whether the initial behaviour reduced stress.

Self-esteem

One's **self-esteem**, that is, a person's overall evaluation of their worth, also affects coping. Individuals with low self-esteem often have difficulty coping with role conflict and role ambiguity. Role ambiguity results from unclear expectations for one's performance. Individuals with high tolerances for ambiguity can deal better with the strains that come from uncertainties and, therefore, are likely to be able to cope with role ambiguity.

Symptoms and consequences of stress

What happens to a person when their ability to cope with stress is overwhelmed? The physical and psychological symptoms of stress are:

- Anger or irritability
- Anxiety

- Depression
- Changes in behaviour
- Food cravings or lack of appetite
- Crying
- Difficulty sleeping
- Feeling tired
- Difficulty concentrating
- Chest pains
- Diarrhoea or constipation
- Cramps, aching muscles or muscle spasm
- Dizziness or fainting
- Feeling restless
- Pins and needles
- A tendency to sweat
- Sexual difficulties
- Breathlessness.

  Source: NHS Direct, 2008

Job performance suffers during times of high stress; so much energy and attention are needed to manage the stress that little energy is available for performance. Such a situation is financially costly but even more costly in human health and well-being.

Stress can also result in absenteeism and turnover. Although there are various causes of absenteeism and turnover, both may result when the individual attempts to withdraw from a stressful situation.

Burnout is thought by some to be a result of stress over a prolonged period. **Burnout** is the perception that an individual has used up all available energy to perform the job and feels that they don't have enough energy to complete the task. Burnout is a combination of physical fatigue, emotional exhaustion and cognitive weariness (Cordes and Dougherty, 1993).

Managing stress

We will always have factors in our lives that create stress. To manage those factors effectively and keep stress at levels that enhance one's performance rather than deplete energy, the key is to develop some resiliency. To accomplish this requires a comprehensive approach to managing stress, which involves planning, time and energy.

Personal methods

One of the first steps in managing stress is to recognise stressors in the environment and control them. Nurses tend to think they can be 'all things to all people'. Therefore, it is important to improve one's self-awareness regarding stressors.

Caring for yourself physically (e.g. eating a well-balanced diet, exercising regularly, getting adequate sleep) and developing effective mental habits are also important for coping with stress. These effective habits include role review, improved time-management techniques and relaxation. Development of interpersonal skills and identifying and nurturing social supports can also facilitate stress management.

Role review involves analysing and clarifying roles, and attempting to tie together the various roles individuals play. If there is role conflict or ambiguity, it is important to confront others by pointing out conflicting messages. Role review may also involve renegotiation of roles in an attempt to lessen overload.

Much of the stress managers experience results from the perception that staff, patient and workgroup needs must be met immediately and simultaneously. A common feeling is the need to slow down or 'get off the treadmill'. A method of coping with and reducing the stress is through time management; we take control of how, where and when our time is used. Time is the essence of living, and it is the scarcest resource. Because the manager has a limited amount of time, it is essential that time is used expeditiously. One lost hour a day every day for a year results in 260 hours of waste, or 6.5 weeks of missed opportunity, annually. (Time management is discussed later in this chapter.)

It also is important to practise an optimistic explanation style and to learn how to relax. This is not easy, especially for an individual with a high-stress job. Some relaxation methods are listening to music, reading and socialising with friends. Developing outside interests, such as hobbies and recreational activities, can provide diversion and enjoyment and can also be a source of relaxation. Taking regular time away from work, regardless of job pressures, is important for renewal and revitalisation.

Organisational methods of stress management

Managers have a both a legal and moral responsibility to create a working environment that reduces stress and takes action to help people who are experiencing stress. Each organisation will have its own policy on stress, and if you are in a formal management role, you will have specific responsibilities under that policy. The Health and Safety Executive (2008) suggests that managers should be responsible for the following actions in respect of creating a healthy work environment:

- Implement recommendations arising from any risk assessment activities.
- Ensure good communication between management and staff, particularly when there are organisational and procedural changes.
- Ensure staff are fully trained.
- Ensure staff are provided with meaningful developmental opportunities.
- Monitor workloads to ensure staff are not overloaded.
- Monitor working hours and overtime to ensure staff are not overworking.
- Monitor holidays to ensure staff are taking the full allocation.
- Attend training in good management practice.
- Ensure that bullying and harassment are not tolerated.
- Be vigilant and offer support to staff who are experiencing stress outside work.

Health and Safety Executive (2008)

This list illustrates that good management practices – communication, change management, monitoring workload and offering support – are essential to the effective management of work-related stress. However, sometimes the most important thing a manager can do is to notice the symptoms of stress and intervene early in supporting the staff member. It may be that the staff member needs time off, an adjustment of workload or a change in working hours to enable them to manage their stress level.

Most organisations have an occupational health service that will assist the manager to support the staff member. Employee assistance programmes are also a resource to managers as they offer counselling and increasingly other supportive services such as debt management.

Time management

Time management is a misnomer. No one manages time; what is managed is how time is used. Covey, Merrill and Merrill (1994) conceived a time management approach intended to help a person achieve personal effectiveness aligned with personal principles. They use the analogy of 'clock and compass', the clock representing time, and the compass representing priorities. They suggest that time should be allocated to activities that will bring about the desired results, not simply because they are urgent. Table 12.2 illustrates a simple clock and compass time management strategy called the Importance/Urgency grid.

Box 12.2 shows some of the behaviours that get in the way of clock and compass time management. These patterns of behaviour must be understood and dealt with to achieve effective time management.

In addition to these patterns of behaviour, certain time wasters prevent the individual from effectively managing time. A **time waster** is something that prevents a person from accomplishing the job or achieving the goal. Common time wasters include:

- interruptions, such as telephone calls and drop-in visitors;
- meetings, both scheduled and unscheduled;
- lack of clear-cut goals, objectives and priorities;
- lack of daily and/or weekly plans;
- lack of personal organisation and self-discipline;
- lack of knowledge about how one spends one's time;

Table 12.2 Importance-urgency grid

Category of time use	Example
Important and urgent	Ensuring sufficient staffing for the upcoming shift
Important, not urgent	Reviewing audit data
Urgent, not important (or not the best use of your time as a manager)	Helping out on the ward, answering the phone
Busy work	Tidying ward areas, filing
Wasted time	Untargeted web or email reading

Box 12.2 — **Behaviours that Impede Effective Time Management**

- We do what we like to do before we do what we don't like to do.
- We do things we know how to do faster than things we do not know how to do.
- We do things that are easiest before things that are difficult.
- We do things that require a little time before things that require a lot of time.
- We do things for which resources are available.
- We do things that are scheduled (for example, meetings) before non-scheduled things.
- We sometimes do things that are planned before things that are unplanned.
- We respond to demands from others before demands from ourselves.
- We do things that are urgent before things that are important.
- We readily respond to crises and emergencies.
- We do interesting things before uninteresting things.
- We do things that advance our personal objectives or that are politically expedient.
- We wait until a deadline approaches before we really get moving.
- We do things that provide the most immediate closure.
- We respond on the basis of who wants it.
- We respond on the basis of the consequences to us of doing or not doing something.
- We tackle small jobs before large jobs.
- We work on things in the order of their arrival.
- We work on the basis of the squeaky-wheel principle (the squeaky wheel gets the grease).
- We work on the basis of consequences to the group.

- failure to delegate and working on routine tasks;
- ineffective communication;
- waiting for others and not using transition time effectively;
- inability to say no.

Enabling effective time management

A significant difficulty in moving from a staff nurse position to a leadership position is the need to develop different time management and organisational skills. In a staff nurse role, the individual has little, if any, free or uncommitted time. Almost every minute of the shift is assigned to a task. No planning is required, because every minute is taken. In contrast, when the nurse moves to a leadership position, they are responsible for defining how time will be spent.

Effective time management involves a number of strategies designed to help the manager take control of how time is spent. These strategies draw on the skills of critical and creative thinking, and take planning and commitment. It is not uncommon that busy people will say they don't have time to be organised or to plan. The time and effort expended in creating a personal time-management approach is seldom wasted and the reward is a better sense of control and reduction of stress.

Goal-setting

A critical component of time management for managers and leaders is establishing goals and time frames for themselves, their teams and the service. Goals provide direction and vision for actions as well as a timeline in which activities will be accomplished. Defining goals and time frames helps reduce stress by preventing the panic people often feel when confronted with multiple demands. Although time frames may not be as fast as the manager would like (the tendency is to expect change yesterday), necessary actions have been identified.

Individual or organisational goals encourage thinking about the future and what might happen. Goal-setting helps to relate current behaviour, activities or operations to the organisation's or individual's long-range goals. Without this future orientation, activities may not lead to the outcomes that will help achieve the goals and meet the ideals of the individual or organisation. The focus should be to develop measurable, realistic and achievable goals.

It is useful to think of individual or personal goals in categories, such as:

- Ward or team
- Interpersonal (at work)
- Professional
- Financial
- Family and friends (outside of work)
- Holiday and travel
- Physical
- Lifestyle
- Community
- Spiritual.

This list is a guide to stimulate thinking about goals. In considering individual goals, individuals should think about long-term, lifetime and short-term goals. These should be divided into job-related goals and personal goals. Job-related goals may revolve around ward or departmental changes, whereas personal goals may include personal life and community involvement.

Short-term goals should be set for the next 6 to 12 months but need to be related to long-term goals. To manage time effectively, the manager must answer five major questions about these goals:

1. What specific objectives are to be achieved?
2. What specific activities are necessary to achieve these objectives?
3. How much time is required for each activity?
4. Which activities can be planned and scheduled for concurrent action, and which must be planned and scheduled sequentially?
5. Which activities can be delegated to staff?

Delegation

Delegating tasks to others can be an efficient time-management tool. Delegation involves assigning tasks, determining expected results and granting authority to the individual expected to accomplish these tasks. Delegation is perhaps the most difficult leadership skill for individuals to acquire. Chapter 7 discusses delegation in detail.

Time analysis

The first step in time analysis is to identify how time is being used. The second is to determine whether time use is appropriate to the manager's role. Managers find much of their time is taken up doing things that seem to be 'busy work' rather than activities that contribute to a particular outcome. Job redesign places emphasis on ensuring that time is spent wisely and that the right individual is correctly assigned the responsibility for tasks. Time logs, typically kept in intervals of 30 to 60 minutes, are useful in analysing the actual time spent on various activities. These logs can be reviewed to determine which activities are essential to the manager's job and which activities can be delegated to others or eliminated. Instead of a separate log, the manager's diary also may be used to review patterns of time use.

You should repeat your time analysis at least twice a year to see how well you are managing your time, whether the job or the environment has changed and which requires changes in planning activities. This can help prevent reverting to poor time-management habits.

Setting priorities

Managers and leaders should establish priorities, taking into consideration both short- and long-term goals as well as the importance and urgency of each activity. Table 12.2 illustrates examples of five types of activities. Activities can be identified as

- urgent and important;
- important but not urgent;
- urgent but not important;
- busy work, or wasted time.

Activities that are both urgent and important, such as the example described in Table 12.2, must be completed. They are top priority and need attention first. Activities that are important but not urgent need planning. It is easy to overlook these activities until they do become urgent, but this is both a stressful and ineffective strategy. For example, a team leader may be asked to make a contribution to the departmental service plan. The contribution includes specific activity data as well as analysis and predictions for the next year. If the manager leaves this activity until the last minute, it is likely that the work will be stressful and that the analysis and forecasting will not be as well considered as possible and could therefore put the future of the service at risk.

Urgent but not important activities can take up a great deal of time. A common example from this category is telephone calls or email. Most people can't resist a ringing phone or the 'you have mail' message on their computer screen. The problem with these is that unless you check the message or answer the phone, you are unable to determine the importance. We worry that an important and urgent activity will be missed. The truth is that few phone calls or emails are both important and urgent. Your personal time management plan should make provision for ensuring that messages that are both urgent and important reach you immediately, but other messages, especially emails, are best treated as important and not urgent. This will allow you to manage messages more efficiently.

Daily planning and scheduling

Once goals and priorities have been established, the manager can concentrate on scheduling activities. A to-do list should be prepared each day, either after work hours the previous day or early before work on the same day. To-do lists should also include the due date and priority for the activity to use as a visual reminder. The list is typically planned by workday or work-week. Because managers combine many responsibilities, a weekly to-do list may be more effective. Flexibility must be a major consideration in this plan; some time should remain uncommitted to allow the manager to use deal with emergencies and crises that are sure to happen. The focus is not on activities and events, but rather on the outcomes that can be achieved in the time available.

There are now a number of computer software programs that combine email, diary, to-do lists, meeting planning, and address and phone lists. These systems can keep track of regularly scheduled meetings (staff meetings), regular events (annual or quarterly report due dates), tasks and appointments, and can coordinate diaries for a number of people. Many managers still prefer to have a paper-based to-do list as this is able to be carried around easily and can be amended at any point. The advent of hand-held, web-linked, wireless organisers may eventually make the paper to-do list redundant. There is a satisfaction, however, in drawing a line through a task on a list, symbolising the accomplishment of something important.

Grouping activities and minimising routine work

Work items that are similar in nature and require similar surroundings and resources for their accomplishment should be grouped together in time. Set aside blocks of uninterrupted time for the really important tasks, such as preparing the service plan. Routine tasks, especially those that are not important or urgent and contribute little to overall objectives, should be minimised. If you insist on doing them, group them together and do them in your least productive time. For example, deciding that you will devote 15 minutes twice a day to checking your email is a better use of time than reading and responding to each message as it arrives.

For many of us, a lot of time is spent waiting. We all have to wait sometimes; waiting for a meeting to start or waiting to talk to someone are just two examples. Bring along materials to read or work on in case you are kept waiting. View waiting time as an opportunity.

If you are having difficulty completing important tasks and are feeling stressed, doing routine tasks for a while often helps to reduce stress. Pick a task that can be successfully completed and save it for the end of the day. Accomplishing even a routine task at the end of the day can reduce the sense of overload and stress.

Personal organisation and self-discipline

Though not everyone is at risk, significant time can be wasted because of a lack of personal organisation and self-discipline, including the inability to say no. Effective personal organisation results from clearly defined priorities based on well-defined, measurable and achievable objectives. Because the manager does not work alone, priorities and objectives are often related to those of many professionals, as well as to objectives of patients and their families.

How time is used is often a matter of resolving conflicts among competing priorities. It is easy, and common, for the manager to become overloaded with responsibilities and with more to do than should be expected in the time available. There is never sufficient time for all the activities, situations and events in which one might like to become involved. Being realistic about the amount of work to which you commit is an indication of effective time management. If a superior is overloading you, make sure the person understands the consequences of additional assignments. Be assertive in communicating your own needs to others.

A cluttered desk, working on too many tasks at one time and failing to set aside blocks of uninterrupted time to do important tasks also indicate a lack of personal self-discipline. Clean your desk, get out the materials you need to complete your highest-priority task, and start working on it immediately. Focus on one task at a time, making sure to start with a high-priority task.

Controlling interruptions

An interruption occurs any time a person is stopped in the middle of one activity to give attention to something else. Not all interruptions are time wasters. An interruption that is more important and urgent than the activity in which the person is involved is an appropriate re-prioritisation; it deserves immediate attention. Certain events such as fire, fire drills, power failures, clinical emergencies and security threats should command the immediate attention of everyone.

Some interruptions interfere with achieving the priorities of the job and are less important and urgent than current activities. As the manager's role changes, more decision-making is undertaken by clinical staff. When a manager is interrupted to solve clinical problems within the staff nurse's scope of accountability, the manager should coach the individual to solve the problem themself, thereby beginning to break old patterns of behaviour and help develop individual responsibility. Although this type of coaching can be time-consuming in the beginning, this practice eventually reduces the number of interruptions.

Keeping an interruption log on an occasional basis may help. The log should show who interrupted, the nature of the interruption, when it occurred, how long it lasted, what topics were discussed, the importance of the topics and time-saving actions to be taken. Analysis of these data may identify patterns that the manager can use to plan ways to reduce the frequency and duration of interruptions. These patterns may indicate that certain staff members are the most frequent interrupters and require individual attention to develop problem-solving skills.

Telephone calls

Telephone calls are a major source of interruption, and the interruption log will provide considerable insight for the nurse manager regarding the nature of telephone calls received. Although it is not possible to function today without a telephone, some people do not use the telephone effectively. A ringing telephone is highly compelling; few people can allow it to go unanswered. Handling telephone calls effectively is a must:

- Minimise socialising and small talk. If you answer the phone with 'Hello, what can I do for you?' rather than 'Hello, how are you?' the caller is encouraged to get to business first.

Be warm, friendly and courteous, but do not allow others to waste time with inappropriate or extensive small talk. Calls placed and returned just prior to lunchtime, at the end of the day and on Friday afternoons tend to result in more business and less socialising.

- Plan calls. The manager who plans telephone calls does not waste anyone's time, including that of the person called. Write down topics to be discussed before making the call. This prevents the need for additional calls to inform the other party of an important point or to ask a forgotten question.

- Set a time for calls. The nurse manager may have a number of calls to return as well as calls to initiate. It is best to set aside a time to handle routine phone calls, especially during 'downtime'. Try not to interrupt what is being done at the moment. If an answer is necessary before a project can be continued, phone immediately; if not, phone for the information at a later time.

- State and ask for preferred call times and the purpose of the call. If a party is not available, state the purpose of the call, and provide several time frames when you will be available for a return call. Have those accepting messages ask for the same information. This makes it easier for the responder to be prepared for the call and helps to prevent 'telephone tag'.

- Voice mail is an excellent way to send and receive messages when a real-time interaction is not essential, especially if computer access is limited. For example, one person or a large group of people can be informed about an upcoming meeting in one voice mail message. They can phone their responses at their convenience, thus obviating the need for continuing to try to reach each other directly. Like other forms of communication, voice mail must be used appropriately. Long messages or sensitive information are better conveyed one-on-one. Also, another person such as an assistant or ward clerk may be responsible for taking voice mail messages off the system, so it is important to state the message in a professional manner, omitting personal or confidential information.

- Email is another tool that enhances time management. Email minimises time wasted trying to contact individuals and provides a means whereby the urgency of the message can be coded. Tone, however, is difficult to convey by email. Therefore it is advisable to use more personal forms of communication, such as the telephone or in-person contact, for potentially sensitive or troublesome issues.

- Deal with drop-in visitors. Although often friendly and seemingly harmless, the typical 'Got-a-minute?' drop-in visit can last several minutes. Rather than eliminate drop-in visits, the manager should skilfully direct the visit by identifying the issue or question, arranging an alternative meeting, referring the visitor to someone else, or redirecting the visitor's problem-solving efforts. An additional strategy is to stand up to greet the visitor and remain standing. The gesture appears gracious yet is obvious enough to encourage a short visit.

The manager who is fortunate enough to have an office will find that open doors are open invitations for interruption. Although it is essential that managers are available and accessible, concentration time also is necessary. The manager can obtain concentration time by informing the staff that a specific block of time (such as between the hours of 1:00 p.m. and 2:00 p.m. each day) will be available to address issues. This arrangement is best done in consultation with the staff so that an agreement about what types of issue can be brought outside that time is made. This will encourage staff to problem-solve for themselves but also to bring urgent and important issues to the manager's attention.

Interruptions also can be controlled by the arrangement of furniture. The manager whose desk is arranged so that immediate eye contact is made with passers-by or drop-in visitors is asking for interruptions. A desk turned 90 or even 180 degrees from the door minimises potential eye contact.

Encouraging appointments to deal with routine matters also reduces interruptions. Regularly scheduled meetings with those who need to see the manager allow them to hold routine matters for those appointments. Holding such meetings in the other person's office places the nurse manager in charge of keeping the time. It is easier to leave someone's office than to remove an individual from yours.

Paperwork

Health care organisations cannot function effectively without good information systems. In addition to telephone calls and face-to-face conversations, managers spend considerable time writing and reading communications. Some basic principles can help the manager process information while reducing the risk of time wasting.

- Plan and schedule paperwork. Writing and reading reports, forms, email and letters are essential elements of the manager's job and cannot be ignored. They will, however, become a major source of frustration if their processing is not planned and scheduled as an integral part of daily activities.

- Sort paperwork for effective processing. A system of file folders either for paper mail or for email can be very helpful. Here is one way to handle it:
  - Place all paperwork (or email) requiring personal action in a red file or in an 'action' folder on your computer's hard drive. It can then be handled according to its relative importance and urgency.
  - Place work that can be delegated in a separate pile, and distribute it appropriately.
  - Place all work that is informational in nature and related to present work in a yellow file folder or in an 'information' folder on the hard drive.
  - Place other reading material, such as professional journals, technical reports and other items that do not relate directly to the immediate work, in a blue file folder or a file labelled 'R'.

  The 'information' file contains materials that must be read immediately, whereas the 'reading' file materials are not as urgent and can be read later. Do not be afraid to throw away or delete messages. When they no longer have value, do not let them become clutter.

- Use the computer for all letters, memos, reports and messages. The computer revolutionised communications; take advantage of it.

- Analyse paperwork frequently. Review record retention and file storage policies and rules regularly, and purge or archive (according to your record retention policy) files at least once each year. All standard forms, reports and memos should be reviewed annually. Each should justify its continued existence and its present format. Do not be afraid to recommend changes and, when possible, initiate those changes.

- Do not be a paper shuffler. 'Handle a piece of paper only once' is a common adage but impossible to follow if taken literally. It really means that each time a piece of paper or email message is handled, some action should be taken to further process it. Paper shufflers are those who continually move things around on their desks or accumulate unread emails. They delay action unreasonably, and the problem mounts. A desktop is a working surface; it is not for files and piles.

Respecting time

The key to using time-management techniques is to respect one's own time as well as that of others. People who respect their own time are likely to find others respecting it also. The same values and attitudes indicate respect for one's own time and for that of others. Using the above suggestions regarding time management communicates to those you interact with that respect for time is expected.

The manager, however, must reciprocate by respecting the time needs of others. If you need to talk to someone, it is appropriate to arrange an appointment, particularly for routine matters. One should continually ask 'What is the best use of my time right now?' and should answer in three ways:

- For myself and my goals.
- For my staff and their goals.
- For the organisation and its goals.

One manager who felt stressed by all of her responsibilities used the strategies shown in Case Study 12.4 to help her solve her problems.

Case Study 12.4   Time Management

For the past six years, Jane Schumann has been manager of a health visiting team. Consistent with the primary care trust's new commissioning framework for child health, the trust has combined health visiting with school nursing and community midwifery as well as a number of specialist children's services. Jane was asked to take on this new child health team.

Jane has been overwhelmed with her new responsibilities. Wanting to establish trust and learn more about her staff, Jane has adopted an 'open-door policy' resulting in many drop-in visits each day. She has been working much longer hours and most weekends. Her desk is stacked with paperwork and her inbox for her email is full of messages to be read, sorted and responded to. Although Jane is pleased she was chosen for the additional responsibilities, she has difficulty sleeping and is concerned about the effect of career responsibilities on her family life.

Jane decides to take two days away from the office and asks the team not to contact her unless it is an emergency. She makes a list of priorities for each of her teams and a time frame for completing each project. She makes daily plans for the next two weeks and a three-month plan for the upcoming quarter. Jane also determines who among her new staff members can assume additional responsibilities and notes tasks that can be delegated. She sorts through paperwork and establishes a filing system for each department. Jane's assistant will be trained to file routine paperwork and route other paperwork to Jane or delegated personnel. Jane also decides that at each departmental meeting she will establish specific times when she will be available for drop-in visitors. Jane schedules a meeting with the director of nursing and community matrons to discuss the implications for staff development and service reconfiguration. Finally, she takes a day's leave combined with her weekend to catch up on some well-deserved rest and time with family and friends.

Manager's Checklist

The manager is responsible for:

☐ Recognising the impact of stress on professional and personal effectiveness, health and well-being.

☐ Prioritising workload and determining the best use of resources.

☐ Delegating tasks and projects to staff effectively.

☐ Identifying staff who are experiencing stress and taking action before problems or delays arise.

☐ Respecting their own time and the time of others.

☐ Knowing how best to request assistance when appropriate.

What you know now

- Stress is the adverse reaction people have to excessive pressures or other types of demand placed on them.
- Stress can result from work demands and personal situations.
- Stress can cause physical and psychological symptoms in the individual that can lead to burnout, poor job performance, low job satisfaction and high absenteeism.
- Strategies to help individuals, as well as organisations, manage stress include clarifying goals and roles; providing support, including training and education on stress management; using participative management techniques; and practising personal stress management techniques.
- Managers and leaders must use time wisely to accomplish everything that is expected of them: this takes planning.
- Nurse managers who respect their own time are likely to find others respecting it also.

Questions to challenge you

1. Have you experienced any of the symptoms or consequences of stress described in the chapter? How did you handle it? What could you do next time you are feeling stressed to manage the situation better?

2. Have you experienced role ambiguity or role conflict? Describe the situation. How did you handle it?

3. Choose a personal goal that you wish to accomplish in the next six months. Develop a plan to achieve that goal using effective time management.

4. Identify three time wasters that are problems for you. Explain how you can minimise them.

References

Borrill, C. S., Carletta, J., Carter, A. J., Dawson, J. F., Garrod, S., Rees, A., Richards, A., Shapiro, D. and West, M. A. (2001) *The Effectiveness of Healthcare Teams in the National Health Service*. Birmingham: Aston Centre for Health Service Organisation Research, Aston University.

Cordes, C. and Dougherty, T. (1993) A review and integration of research on job burnout. *Academy of Management Review*, **18**, 621–656.

Covey, S, Merrill, R. and Merrill, R (1994) *First Things First: To live, to love, to learn, to leave a legacy*. New York: Simon and Schuster

Health and Safety Executive (2008) *Tackling Stress: The management standards approach*. London: Health and Safety Executive. Available at http://www.hse.gov.uk/pubns/indg406.pdf.

Holmes, T. H. and Rahe, R. H. (1967) The Social Readjustment Rating scale. *Journal of Psychosomatic Research*, **11**(2), 213–218

NHS Direct (2008) *Stress*. Available at http://www.nhsdirect.nhs.uk/articles/article.aspx?articleid=350.

Rahe, R. H., Mahan, J. L. and Arthur, R. J. (1970) Predictions of near-future health change from subjects' preceding life changes. *Journal of Psychosomatic Research*, **14**(4), 401–406.

Seligman, M. (2006) *Learned Optimism: How to change your mind and your life*. New York: Vintage.

Selye, H. (1978) *The Stress of Life*, 2nd edn. New York: McGraw-Hill.

Part 3
Practical First-Level Management

Chapter 13
Budgeting, Staffing and Managing Resources

Key terms

Budget
Budgeting
Controlling
Incremental (line-item) budget
Fixed budget
Variable budget
Operating budget
Financial year
Revenue budget
Block contract
Payment by results
Health care resource groups
Expense budget

Cost centre
Profit
Fixed costs
Variable costs
Direct costs
Indirect costs
Salary (personnel) budget
Capital budget
Variance
Efficiency variance
Rate variance
Non-salary expenditure
Establishment control

Introduction

This chapter examines one of the most important factors contributing to the success of modern health care organisations and effectiveness in the role of the ward manager or team leader: the economic climate in which health care is provided. It is crucial that managers understand fully how budgets are made, and how their spending decisions affect not only the work of their team but also the organisation as a whole. In addition to managing their existing budget well, ward managers are being asked to make cost improvements that call for careful assessment of current ways of working. Changes to services and improvements in care that give greater weight to the experience of the patient are also expected. The challenge is to be able to juggle these responsibilities competently in an increasingly cost-conscious climate.

With the advent of foundation trusts, and a general move to greater financial autonomy and accountability for each provider organisation, greater attention is being given to cost containment and operational efficiency. The nursing budget accounts for as much as half of an organisation's total expenditure, and managers at all levels are facing significant pressure to become proficient in the budgeting process, to allocate resources and to control and monitor expenditures. This level of financial accountability is new to many managers.

This chapter explains the budgeting process, defines budget terms and presents guidelines for developing a budget, including how to determine salary costs and operating and capital equipment budgets. It also explains how to monitor and control financial performance and how to project costs based on current and anticipated needs.

Budgets and budgeting

A **budget** is a quantitative statement, usually in monetary terms, of the plans and expectations of a defined team, ward or service over a specified period of time (usually a year). Budgets provide a foundation for managing and evaluating financial performance. Budgets detail how resources – money, time, people, supplies, equipment – will be acquired and used to support planned services within the defined time period. The budget's purpose is to allow managers to project action plans and their economic impact on the future so that objectives of the organisation are coordinated and met.

The budget process also helps ensure that the resources necessary to achieve these objectives are available at the appropriate time and that operations are carried out within the resources available. The budgeting process increases the awareness of costs and also helps employees understand the relationships between goals, expenses and income. As a result, employees are committed to the goals and objectives of the organisation, and various departments are able to coordinate activities and collaborate to achieve the organisation's objectives. Budgets also help management to control the resources expended through an organisational awareness of costs. Finally, budget performance provides management with feedback about resources management and the impact on the budget.

Budgeting is a process of planning and controlling future operations by comparing actual results with planned expectations. Planning first involves reviewing established goals and objectives of the organisation. Goals and objectives help identify the organisation's priorities and direct the organisation's efforts. To plan, the organisation must anticipate the future by gathering information about the following:

- Demographics of the population served (age, deprivation, ethnic origin)
- Previous pattern of service use
- Statistical data, including the number of admissions or patient visits, patient days, average length of stay and projected occupancy or visits
- Projected salary increases and price increases, including inflation rate, for supplies and other costs
- Anticipated changes to the organisation's funding through contract allocation
- Information about changes to regulation or policy outside the organisation such as changes to targets for waiting times
- Organisational changes (combining services, changes to hours of service) that may result in changes to staffing or supply use.

The organisation may use sophisticated and complex forecasting methods, including statistical techniques, to assist in making projections related to the budget period. Normally, the past is the starting point for projecting the future, but in today's world, the past may be a poor predictor of the future. This is one of the major drawbacks of the budgeting process. In a rapidly changing situation, basing budgets on historical data often necessitates readjustment during the actual budget period.

Controlling is the process of comparing actual results with those projected in the budget. Two techniques for controlling budget performance are variance analysis and position control. By measuring the differences between the projected and the actual results, management is better able to make modifications and corrections: therefore controlling depends on planning.

Approaches to budgeting

Budgets may be developed in various formats depending on how the department fits into the overall financial framework of the organisation (Contino, 2001). Departments may be considered as follows:

- *Cost centres*. Managers are responsible for predicting, documenting and managing the costs (staffing, supplies) of the department.
- *Revenue centres*. Managers are responsible for generating revenues.
- *Profit centres*. Managers are responsible for generating revenues and managing costs so that the department shows a profit (revenues exceed costs).
- *Investment centres*. Managers are responsible for generating revenues and managing costs and capital equipment (assets).

Nursing teams and wards are typically considered cost centres, that is, the manager is responsible for managing costs only. Some managers are responsible for a multidisciplinary service, and their teams are from several different disciplines and departments. Other managers are responsible for a single ward, such as an accident and emergency ward, or a diabetic clinic.

Most budgets in NHS organisations are **incremental** or **line-item budgets** in which each expense is listed on a separate line on the budget sheet and has a specific allocation against the item. The expense line is usually divided into salary and non-salary items. A budget worksheet is often used for calculations to be submitted for the next year. It may include several columns for the amount budgeted for the current year, the amount actually spent year-to-date, the projected total for the year based on the actual amount spent, increases and decreases in the expense amount for the new budget and the request for the next year with an explanation attached.

The base or starting point for calculating next year's budget request may be either the previous year's actual results or projected expenditures for the current year. The finance department usually provides an estimate of the average increase in salaries based on agreed rises during the period of a collective agreement, or an estimate of salary rises based on the rate of inflation if a contract is being renegotiated. For supplies, a standard measure of cost increases, perhaps the consumer or price index projected for the next year, is used.

For managers to complete budget worksheets accurately, they must be familiar with expense account categories and should understand what types of expense, such as instruments and minor equipment, are included under each line item. In addition, the manager has to keep abreast of different factors that have affected the expenditure level for each expense line during the current year. The projected impact of next year's activities will be translated into increases or decreases in expense levels of the ward or service expenditures for the coming year.

The advantage of the line budget method is its simplicity. The disadvantage of this method is that it discourages cost efficiency. To avoid budget cuts for the next year, an astute manager learns to spend the entire budget amount established for the current year, because this amount becomes the base for the next year.

Fixed or variable budgets

Budgets also can be categorised as fixed or variable. Budgets are considered **fixed budget**s when the budgeted amounts are set without regard to changes that may occur during the year, such as patient volume or service activities that have an impact on the cost assumptions originally used for the coming year. In contrast, **variable budget**s are developed with the understanding that adjustments to the budget may be made during the year based on changes in allocated funds, patient activity, use of supplies and other expenses.

The operating budget

The **operating budget** is the organisation's statement of expected revenues and expenses for the coming year. It coincides with the **financial year** of the organisation, a specified 12-month period during which the operational and financial performance of the organisation is measured. The financial year in the NHS is 1 April to 31 March to correspond with the government funding cycle for public services, though private organisations may choose a different 12-month period. The operating budget may be further broken down into smaller periods of six months or four quarters; each quarter may be further separated into three one-month periods. The revenues (income) and expenses are organised separately, with a bottom-line net profit or loss calculated.

The revenue (income) budget

The **revenue budget** represents the income expected for the budget period. Projections are developed from historical volume data, impact of new or modified clinical programmes, shifts from inpatient to outpatient procedures and other influences. Most NHS organisations do not include a revenue line on the budget statements for individual teams or wards that are deemed cost centres. Whether or not it is included on the budget sheet, there is income set aside to meet the expenses on the budget. Income comes into the organisation as an allocation from the primary care trust based on contracts for the provision of services. These include:

- block cost and volume contracts;
- payment by results (PbR).

Block contracts

Until 2002 and the publication of the NHS Plan in England, NHS services were funded by block contracts; this remains the main payment method in Scotland, Northern Ireland and Wales. Services not covered by PbR include primary care services, community services, mental health services and ambulance services. In addition, a number of specific health resource groups (HRGs) and outpatient specialties fall outside the scope of PbR because they have low volumes, have volatile costs and/or are of a specialised nature.

Block contracts are usually issued based on historical budgets for the provision of services. Typically, commissioners such as primary care trusts or health authorities look at the volume of services in the previous year and make adjustments to the contract based on anticipated costs for the following year. Block contracts are therefore negotiated between the commissioner and the provider organisation based on a business case for the future. Commissioners are increasingly making funding or block contracts contingent on assurances around quality or increases in the volume or nature of services offered.

Payment by results

Payment by results was first introduced in 2003 and signalled a fundamental change in the funding of care commissioned by the NHS. For services under PbR, funding is now linked directly to activity. This necessitated a substantial cultural shift, not only in finance departments but for all professionals in the health service, with the aim of improving care for patients through improved utilisation of resources. PbR has grown over its four years of operation, and currently around 35 per cent of PCT revenue allocations are subject to PbR (DoH, 2008).

One of the problems with block contracts is that there is little incentive to improve care or services. Payment by results is an attempt to align the patient choice policy to funding. If, for example, three local hospitals each receive an equal share of funding for hip replacement surgery, but 80 per cent of patients needing the surgery choose one hospital, then the chosen hospital will be underfunded for its service whilst the other two will have received funds and not had to do the work. Payment by results aims to have 'funds follow patients' and therefore fairly reimburse hospitals for the services they provide, and also to create incentives for hospitals to attract patients based on the quality and care provided (Royal College of Nursing, 2007).

Payment by results involves a process of coding of treatment so that the proper reimbursement can be obtained. So far, 14,000 diagnostic codes and 8,500 intervention codes have been developed, and these have been grouped together into just over 600 healthcare resource groups (HRGs). **Health care resource groups** are standard groupings of clinically similar treatments which use common levels of health care resource. HRGs offer organisations the ability to understand their activity in terms of the types of patients they care for and the treatments they undertake. They enable the comparison of activity within and between different organisations and provide an opportunity to benchmark treatments and services to support trend analysis over time. HRGs are currently used as a means of determining fair and equitable reimbursement for care services delivered by providers. Their use as consistent 'units of currency' supports standardised health care commissioning across the service (Information Centre for Health and Social Care, 2008).

There are different codes for the same treatment based on variables such as age or complication that is known to result in more care. It is very important therefore that nurses document care accurately, and help those people who are doing the coding to get it right. There can be a difference of a thousand pounds or more based on things that nurses would notice and record. Things such as diarrhoea, constipation, dementia, diabetes and obesity are all important and should be recorded so that accurate coding can occur (Royal College of Nursing, 2007).

The expense budget

The **expense budget** consists of salary and non-salary items. It should be comprehensive and thorough; it should also take into consideration all available information regarding the next year's expectations. Described below are several concepts and definitions related to the budget process in a health care setting.

Cost centres

In health care organisations, wards and teams are typically considered cost centres. A **cost centre** is described as the smallest area of activity within an organisation for which costs are accumulated. Nursing managers are commonly given the responsibility for costs incurred by their department, but they have no revenue responsibilities.

Classification of costs

Costs are commonly classified as fixed or variable. **Fixed costs** are those that will remain the same for the budget period regardless of the activity level of the organisation, such as staff costs. **Variable costs** depend on and change in direct proportion to patient volume such as patient care supply expenses. If more patients are admitted to a ward more supplies are used, causing higher supply expenses.

Expenditures also may be direct or indirect. **Direct costs** are expenses that directly affect patient care. For example, salaries for nurses who provide hands-on patient care are considered direct costs. **Indirect costs** are expenditures that are necessary but don't affect patient care directly. Salaries for support staff such as ward clerks, for example, are classified as indirect costs.

Determining the salary budget

The **salary (personnel) budget** projects the salary costs that will be paid and charged to the cost centre in the budget period (see Table 13.1). Managing the salary budget is directly related to the manager's ability to supervise and lead the staff. Better managers tend to have more stable staff with less money spent on bank or agency staff, turnover, or absenteeism.

In addition to anticipated salary expenses, factors such as unsocial hours, overtime and on-call expenses may also affect the salary budget. Replacement for long-term sick leave or maternity leave also puts a strain on the salary budget.

Table 13.1 Monthly salary budget and year-to-date budget comparison report

Position	March Actual	March Budgeted	March Variance	Year to date Actual salary	Year to date Budgeted salary	Year to date Variance
Ward manager	6,250	6,250	0	68,750	75,000	6,250
Staff nurses	95,722	93,825	(1,897)	1,048,813	1,125,878	77,065
Nursing assistants	14,886	13,200	(1,686)	159,500	158,400	(1,100)
Ward clerks	5,483	5,495	12	60,391	65,273	4,882
Total salary:	**122,341**	**118,770**	**3,571**	**1,337,454**	**1,424,551**	**87,097**

Calculating available staff hours

The working week for all NHS staff covered by Agenda for Change is 37.5 hours in accordance with the European Working Time Directive. On appointment, all staff members are entitled to 27 days' annual leave plus 8 public holidays. As length of service increases, so does annual leave entitlement, though public holiday entitlement is constant. These figures have an impact on the hours available for care.

Annual hours

37.5 hours per week $\times$ 52 weeks per year = 1950 hours
(Whole time equivalent [WTE] annual full time paid hours)
Less: Annual leave 7.5 $\times$ hours per day $\times$ 35 days (27 annual leave + 8 public holiday days)
= 262.5
Available hours   1687.5 = (WTE available staff hours)

The available hours calculation is very useful for budget planning, in that it provides a way of estimating how many staff are needed to cover the work. Based on available hours, any one staff member is available for 225 shifts of 7.5 hours per year. This figure then needs to be adjusted to take into consideration mandated training and other responsibilities other than direct care, for example, five shifts per year. Then average sickness can be factored in at, for example, another five shifts per year. When estimating for budget purposes, it would be realistic to consider direct care shifts per year at 215.

Unsocial hours

Unsocial hours are those hours on Saturday and Sunday and any week day after 8:00 p.m. and before 6:00 a.m. These hours attract a percentage premium of 30 per cent for Saturday and weekday hours, and 60 per cent for Sunday hours.

Overtime

All staff in pay bands 1 to 7 of Agenda for Change are eligible for overtime payments. There is a single harmonised rate for overtime of time-and-a-half, with the exception of work on public holidays, where the rate is double time. Fluctuations in workload, patient volume, variability in admission patterns and temporary replacement of staff due to illness or time off all create overtime. Clearly, overtime can have a substantial impact on the budget as a whole. The ward manager/team leader should explore alternatives to overtime, such as skill mix and part-time work, in order to keep the costs in line with budget. A competent manager certainly would also evaluate unit productivity to decrease overtime.

On-call hours

If the ward or team uses an on-call system, the approximate number of hours that employees are on call for the year should be estimated and that cost added to the budget. Typically under the on-call system, staff members are requested to be available to be called back to work if patient need arises. If they are actually called in to work, they may incur overtime pay.

Salary rises

Salary rises also need to be factored into budget projections. These increases are usually calculated on base pay. For example, if a 3 per cent cost-of-living raise is projected and the base salary for a nurse is £21,000, then the new base becomes £21,630.

Additional considerations

Other important factors to consider when developing the salary budget are changes in technology, care delivery systems, clinical procedures and quality initiatives such as ward cleaning. Changes in patient care technology or introduction of new equipment may influence the number, skill or time that people need to gain competence within the new situation. If significant, the projected number of additional labour hours for the new budget period should be incorporated into the annual budget plan.

Support services such as estates services, catering and clinical services such as laboratory or radiography affect the way in which care is delivered. Any change in the services they provide, and the effect of such change on the ward's staffing levels, should be quantified for the next year's budget request.

Changes in the method of delivering care (team nursing or primary nursing) or staff mix (qualified and unqualified staff, support staff) will also affect staffing patterns for the next year. Any changes in staffing can place new demands on the team, and therefore induction, training and additional workload needs also should be considered.

Managing the supply and non-salary expense budget

The supply and non-salary expense budget identifies patient-related supplies needed to operate the ward or team. In addition to supplies, other operating expenses, such as office supplies, travel, uniforms and equipment service contracts, may also be paid out of the ward or team non-salary budget.

An analysis of the current expense pattern and a determination of its applicability for the next budget period should be performed first. Any projected changes in patient volume, acuity and patient mix also should be considered because they will affect next year's supply use and other non-salary expenses. As an example, if patient days for a particular type of patient are projected to multiply and cause a 5 per cent increase in the use of dressing supplies, this increase should be addressed in the budget request by requesting an additional 5 per cent for dressing supplies for the next year.

Increases estimated by the finance or purchasing department are included as part of the budget request. A simple way of calculating the effect of a price increase is to take the estimated total ending expense for the year and multiply it by the inflationary factor.

To determine projected price increases:

Multiply the current total line item expense £12,758 by the inflation factor 1.05 = £13,396

Increases in expenses, such as maintenance agreements and rental fees, should also be incorporated as part of the budget request. The introduction of new technology and changes in programmes and regulatory requirements may require additional resources for supplies as well as increased salaries.

The capital budget

The **capital budget** is an important component of the plan to meet the organisation's long-term goals. This budget identifies physical renovations, new construction and new or replacement equipment planned within the budget period. Organisations define capital items based on certain conditions or criteria. Usually, capital items must have an expected performance of 1 year or more and exceed a certain value, such as £500 or £1,000. Capital budgets also may be designed with a time horizon longer than 1 year, such as 3, 5, 10 or more years.

Today few ward managers or team leaders are asked to prepare a capital budget because most organisations are buying through consortiums or negotiated agreements with the suppliers. Many health care organisations have departments that coordinate bringing in selected vendors and items and limit equipment choices to those. The ward manager would then be responsible for assisting in selecting and determining the amount of equipment needed. The capital pool is expensed out across all units that use the equipment.

The impact of the new equipment on the ward's expenses, such as the number of staff needed to run the equipment, use of supplies and maintenance costs, needs to be considered as part of the operating budget, however. For example, if monitoring equipment is being requested, the cost of electrocardiogram paper and electrodes should be determined, documented and included in the supply budget. Likewise, the need for additional nursing and non-nursing personnel to operate the new equipment, additional workload and training of personnel should be quantified for the next year's budget.

Timetable for the budgeting process

Depending on the size and complexity of the organisation, the budgeting process takes 3 to 6 months. The process begins with the ward manager or team leader helping to identifying resources based on experience and expertise linked to anticipating needs and trends for the upcoming budget period. The manager seeks information from staff about areas of needed improvement or change, reviews unit productivity and the need for updated technology or supplies and then uses this information to prepare the first draft of the budget proposal.

Depending on the levels of organisational management, this proposal ascends through the managerial hierarchy. Each subsequent manager evaluates the budget proposal, making adjustments as needed. By the time the budget is approved by the executive team, significant changes to the original proposal have usually been made.

The final step in the budget planning process is approval by the board of directors. Typically, the budget process timetable is structured so that the budget is approved a few months before the beginning of the new financial year.

Managers must recognise the importance of articulating their budget needs clearly. Senior management must balance budget requests for the entire organisation, and they base those decisions on strong supporting documentation. Managers should not expect to receive all of their budget requests, but they need to be prepared to defend their priorities.

Monitoring budget performance during the year

In many organisations, managers receive a monthly report prepared by the accounting department summarising the expenses for the department (see Table 13.1). This report shows expense line items with the budgeted amount, actual expenditure, variance from budget and the percentage from the budgeted amount that such variance represents. Usually these monthly reports also show the comparison between actual year-to-date results and the year-to-date budget.

The difference between the amounts budgeted for a specific revenue or cost and the actual revenue or cost that resulted is known as the **variance**. In the case of wards or teams, variance might occur in the actual cost of delivering patient care for a certain expense line item in a specified period of time. Ward managers/team leaders are commonly asked to explain any variance, and to identify how the variance can be corrected or avoided in the future. For example, if a number of agency shifts were used to cover patient care, it is important that the ward manager identifies the reason and the likely impact. For example, if a staff member was away for a short-term illness, the variance is not likely to continue. However, if the agency shifts were needed because there is a recruitment freeze, the situation is likely to continue for the duration of the freeze and may need a specific action plan to be put into place.

Variance analysis

In the daily course of events, it is unlikely that projected budget items will be completely on target in all situations. One of the manager's most important jobs is to manage the financial resources for the department and to be able to respond to variances in a timely fashion (Kirkby, 2003).

When expenses occur that differ from the budgeted amounts, organisations usually have an established level at which a variance needs to be investigated and explained or justified by the manager of the department. This level may be a certain amount, such as £500, or it may be a percentage, such as a 5 or 10 per cent increase above the budget.

In determining causes for variance, the manager must review the activity level of the ward or team for the same period. There may have been increases in census or patient acuity that generated additional expense in salary and supplies. Also, in many situations, variances might not be independent of one another. Variances may result from expenses that follow a seasonal pattern, occurring only at determined times in the year. Expenses may also follow a tendency or trend to either increase or decrease during the year. Even if the situation is outside the manager's usual responsibility or control, the manager needs to understand and be able to identify the cause or reason for the variance.

To determine when a variance is favourable or unfavourable, it is important to relate the variance to its impact on the organisation in terms of revenues and expenses. If more earnings came in than expected, the variance is favourable; if less, the variance is negative. Likewise, if less was spent than expected, the variance is favourable; if more was spent, the variance is negative.

For instance, the ward manager might receive the following expense report:

Medical/surgical supplies

Budgeted expenditures	Actual expenditures	Variance (in £)	Percentage (in %)
£34,560	£36,958	(2,398)	(6.9)

This expense variance is considered unfavourable because the actual expense was greater than the budget. In this example, more money was spent on medical/surgical supplies than was projected in the budget. If the variance percentage of the actual budget amount is not presented in the reports, it can be calculated as follows:

Divide the variance by the budget amount, then multiply by 100:

$$£2,398$$
$$£34,560 \times 0.069$$
$$0.069 \times 100 \times 6.9 \text{ per cent over budget}$$

Salary variances

With salary expenditures, variances may occur in volume, efficiency or rate. Typically these factors are related and have an impact on each other. Volume variances result when there is a difference in the budgeted and actual workload requirements, which would occur with increases in patient days. An increase in the actual number of patient days will increase the salary expense, resulting in an unfavourable volume variance. Although the variance is unfavourable, under payment by results this variance may be matched with a corresponding increase in revenue. Thus the impact to the organisation is positive even though it generated higher salary costs at the nursing level.

Efficiency variance, also called quantity or use variance, reflects the difference between budgeted and actual nursing care hours provided. Patient acuity, nursing skill, unit management, technology and productivity all affect the number of patient care hours actually provided versus the original number planned or required. At the same time, if the census had been higher than expected, it would be understandable if more hours of nursing care were provided and paid. A favourable efficiency, or fewer nursing care hours paid, could suggest that patient acuity was lower than projected, that staff was more efficient, or that higher-skilled employees were used. An unfavourable efficiency may be due to greater patient acuity than allowed for in the budget, overstaffing of the unit, or the use of less experienced or less efficient employees.

Rate variances, also known as price or spending variance, reflect the difference in budgeted and actual hourly rates paid. A favourable rate variance may reflect the use of new employees who were paid lower salaries. Unfavourable rate variance may reflect unanticipated salary increases or increased use of personnel paid at higher wages, such as agency personnel.

Non-salary expenditure variances may be due to changes in patient volume, patient mix, supply quantities or prices paid. New, additional or more expensive supplies used at the nursing unit because of technology changes or new regulations could also influence expenditure totals.

Establishment control

Another monitoring tool used by managers is the establishment control. The establishment control is used to compare actual numbers of employees to the number of budgeted working time equivalent (WTE) for the team. The **establishment control** is a list of approved, budgeted WTE posts for the cost centre. The posts are displayed by category or job classification, such as the ward manager, staff nurses, nursing assistants and others. The manager updates the establishment control with employee names and WTE factors for each individual with respect to changes, new hires and resignations that take place during the year.

Though managers usually need permission to make changes to their establishment, this strategy should be considered when circumstances change. If, for example, recruiting to a post may be difficult, it could be worth converting a staff nurse post into a health care assistant post if the care delivery system permits. Similarly, instead of recruiting a full-time nurse, two part-time nurses may be a better option in that it allows greater flexibility in rostering.

Staff impact on budget performance

Money spent on staff can affect the organisation's finances acutely. Misuse of sick time, excessive overtime or turnover and wasteful use of resources can result in negative variance. The manager plays a key role in explaining the unit's goals, the organisation's financial goals and how each individual is responsible for helping the organisation meet those goals.

Future trends

In an effort to be a successful provider of health care, organisations are strongly motivated to be cost-effective. This trend has serious implications for nursing. Nursing has always been considered a cost, not a source of revenue. It is nursing's challenge to be consistently cost-conscious and to measure, manage and document nursing's cost-effectiveness in this financial environment.

What you know now

- A budget is a quantitative statement, usually written in monetary terms, of plans and expectations over a specified period of time.
- The operating or annual budget is the organisation's statement of expected revenues and expenses for the coming year.
- The revenue budget represents the patient care revenues expected for the budget period based on volume and mix of patients, rates and discounts that will prevail during the same period of time.
- Wards and teams are typically considered cost centres, but may be considered revenue centres, profit centres or investment centres.
- Managers may be responsible for service lines and staff from multiple disciplines and departments.
- Managers have input into capital expenses and are responsible for salary and operating costs related to new equipment.
- A working time equivalent (WTE) post is a full-time position that can be equated to 37.5 hours of work per week for 52 weeks, or 1950 hours per year.
- The establishment control is a list of approved, budgeted WTEs that compares the budgeted number of WTEs by classification with the actual available employees of the unit.
- Variance is the difference between the amount that was budgeted for a specific revenue or cost and the actual revenue or cost that resulted during the course of activities.

Questions to challenge you

1. Do you have a budget for your personal and professional income and expenses? If so, how well do you manage it? If not, begin next month to track your income and expenses for one month. See whether you are surprised at the results.

2. How well does your organisation manage its resources? Can you make suggestions for improvement?

3. Are there tasks or functions in your work that you believe are redundant, unnecessary or repetitive or that could be done by a lesser-paid employee? Explain.

4. Does your organisation waste salary or non-salary resources? If not, think of ways that organisations could waste resources. Describe them.

References

Contino, D. S. (2001) Budget training: it's overdue. *Nursing Management*, **32**(8), 16–17.

Department of Health (DoH) (2008) *Payment by Results: Background and history.* Available at http://www.dh.gov.uk/en/Managingyourorganisation/Financeandplanning/NHSFinancialReforms/DH_077259.

Information Centre for Health and Social Care (2008) *Case Mix.* Available at http://www.ic.nhs.uk/casemix.

Kirkby, M. P. (2003) Number crunching with variable budgets. *Nursing Management*, **34**(2), 28–33.

Royal College of Nursing (2007) *Nurses' Business: An introduction to costing and coding health care.* London: Royal College of Nursing.

Chapter 14
Recruiting and Selecting Staff

Key terms

Role review
Business case for recruitment
Job description or role profile
Interview guide

Work sample questions
Intra-rater reliability
Inter-rater reliability
Validity

Introduction

Recruitment and selection is the process of finding quality people who are suitable for a particular job and engaging their services. This task consists of numerous components, from creating a business case for hiring, reviewing the role, developing a recruitment strategy and conducting interviews to comparing candidates and arriving at a consensual decision.

In health care organisations, the quality of people hired and retained determines whether an organisation successfully accomplishes its objectives. The cost of improper selection can be high. The visible cost is in recruiting, selecting and training an employee; but the hidden costs may be even more expensive and include the low quality of work performed by the unmotivated employee, disruption of harmonious working relationships, poor patient care and dissatisfaction. The planning and skilful conducting of recruitment and selection is an important role for front line managers.

The recruitment and selection process

The purpose of the selection process is to match people to jobs. It includes the following elements:

- Role review
- Business case
- Advertising and recruiting
- Skilful interview

- Selection
- Communicating the job offer.

Responsibility for selecting nursing staff in health care organisations is usually shared by the human resources (HR) department and the first-line manager. First-line managers are the most knowledgeable about job requirements and can best describe the job to applicants. HR usually collects in the applications, performs the pre-employment checks and monitors hiring practices to be sure they adhere to employment standards.

The purpose of recruitment activities is to generate a pool of qualified applicants, whereas the purpose of the selection process is to assess an applicant's ability, skills and motivation relative to the requirements and rewards of the job so that a matching process can be carried out. To the extent that these matches are made effectively, positive outcomes such as high job satisfaction, low turnover and high-quality performance can result.

Figure 14.1 shows a flowchart of the recruitment and selection process and suggested responsibilities. As indicated in the chart, this process is a joint effort among the first-line manager and the HR department. The recruitment and selection process begins with role review, which is a careful determination of job duties and requirements. Based on the role review and role profile (see Figure 14.2 on page 240) selected, recruiting plans and selection systems are developed and implemented.

Once an applicant makes contact with the organisation, HR or the first-line manager reviews the application. If the applicant does not meet the basic requirements of the post, they should be so informed. Rejected applicants may be qualified for other posts or may refer friends to the organisation and thus should be treated with utmost courtesy.

The next stage includes interviews and pre-employment checks. In most cases, the interview is conducted before employment checks are done, but practices may vary. The first-line manager should participate in the interview process because they (a) are generally in the best position to assess applicants' technical competence, potential and overall suitability, and (b) are able to answer applicants' technical, work-related questions more realistically. In some organisations, the candidate's future co-workers also participate in the interview process to assess compatibility.

After the interview, employment checks by the HR department are conducted. These include the following:

- *Verification of identity.* This check is carried out to determine that the identity provided is genuine and relates to a real person, and to establish that the individual owns and is rightfully using that identity. This is accomplished by requesting original identity documents with photograph such as a passport, identity card and a document verifying address.

- *Right to work.* This check is to satisfy the requirements under the Immigration, Asylum and Nationality Act (2006) that makes it a criminal offence to employ illegal workers. Satisfying this requirement can be accomplished by the person supplying a passport, birth certificate, adoption certificate, work visa or residence card.

- *Registration and qualification.* This check ensures that the nurse or other registered professional is recognised by the appropriate regulatory body, and that they have the right qualifications to do the job. This is done through contact with the registering authority, in the case of nurses with the Nursing and Midwifery Council.

- *Employment history and references.* Previous employment history, including training completed, is an important part of verifying the individual's capability and suitability for the role.

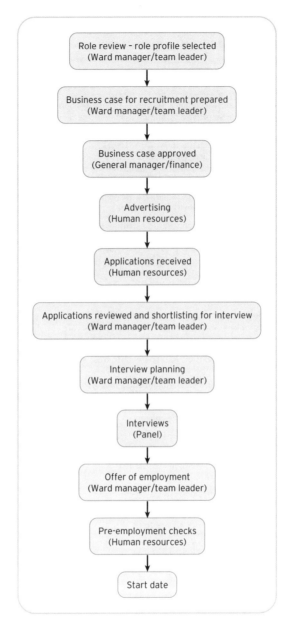

Figure 14.1 A flowchart for recruitment and selection.

- *Criminal records check.* The Criminal Records Bureau provides access across the UK about criminal convictions and other police records. Two levels of clearance are needed to work with patients, standard and enhanced. Standard clearance reveals any current and past convictions whilst an enhanced clearance also shows police force information considered relevant. Whilst having a criminal record does not preclude employment, the offer of employment can be withdrawn if the applicant has been shown to provide false or misleading information.

Profile Label: Nurse
Current Job Titles: Staff Nurse, Registered Nurse, Registered Practitioner
Job Statement: 1. Assesses patients, plans, implements care, provides advice: maintains associated records
2. Carries out nursing procedures
3. Provides clinical supervision to other staff, students

Factor	Relevant Job Information	JE Level
1. Communication and Relationship Skills	Provide and receive complex, sensitive information; barriers to understanding Communicates sensitive information concerning patient's medical condition, requires persuasive, reassurance skills: some patients have special needs, learning disabilities	4(a)
2. Knowledge, Training and Experience	Expertise within a discipline, underpinned by theory Professional/clinical knowledge acquired through training to degree/diploma level	5
3. Analytical and Judgemental Skills	Range of facts, situations requiring analysis, comparison of range of options Judgements on problems requiring investigation, analysis e.g. assessment of patient condition, suitability for discharge	3
4. Planning and Organisational Skills	Plan and organise straightforward activities, some ongoing Organises own time and that of junior staff and learners	2
5. Physical Skills	Highly developed physical skills, accuracy important, manipulation of fine tools, materials Dexterity and accuracy required for e.g. intravenous injections, syringe pumps and infusions, insertion of catheters, removal of sutures.	3(b)
6. Responsibility for Patient/Client Care	Develop programmes of care/care packages Assesses, plans, implements and evaluates clinical care of patients	5(a)
7. Responsibility for Policy/Service Development	Follow policies in own role, may be required to comment Professionally responsible for adherence to trust policies and procedures	1
8. Responsibility for Financial and Physical Resources	Personal duty of care in relation to equipment, resources/handle cash, valuables; maintain stock control; authorised signatory, small payments Personal duty of care/handles patient valuables: orders supplies when necessary; signs agency time sheets	1/2(a) (c) (d)
9. Responsibility for Human Resources	Day-to-day supervision; professional/clinical supervision Allocates, checks work of staff on ward; clinical supervision of junior staff	2(a) (b)
10. Responsibility for Information Resources	Record personally generated information Maintains patient records	1
11. Responsibility for Research and Development	Undertake surveys or audits, as necessary to own role/regularly undertakes R&D activity; clinical trials Undertakes R&D activity, clinical trials	1/2 (a) (b)
12. Freedom to Act	Clearly defined occupational policies, work is managed rather than supervised Works within codes of practice and professional guidelines	3
13. Physical Effort	Frequent sitting of standing in a restricted position; frequent light effort for several short periods/occasional/frequent, moderate effort for several short periods Walks, stands most of shift/pushes and pulls trolleys and commodes; kneels and crouches to dress wounds/manoeuvres patients	2(a)(b)/ 3(c)-4(b)
14. Mental Effort	Frequent concentration, work pattern predictable Concentration checking documents; calculating drug dosages for infusions	2(a)
15. Emotional Effort	Occasional/frequent distressing/highly distressing circumstances Deals with distressed relatives, care of terminally ill/deals with consequences of terminal illness	2(a)/ 3(a) (b)- 4(b)
16. Working Conditions	Frequent unpleasant; occasional/frequent highly unpleasant conditions Smell, noise, dust/body fluids, faeces, vomit, emptying bed pans and urinals, catheter bags	3(a), (b) 4(b)
JE Score/Band	JE Score 340–385	Band 5

Figure 14.2 A sample role profile.

Source: http://www.nhsemployers.org.

- *Occupational health check.* All staff must have a pre-employment health check to ensure that they are physically and psychologically capable of doing the work, to identify their risk of developing work-related disease and to ensure where possible that the employee does not pose a health risk to the patients.

  Source: http://www.nhsemployers.org.

Role review

Before recruiting or selecting new staff, those responsible for hiring must conduct a **role review,** which consists of reviewing the job description, person specification and role requirements to ensure that those documents reflect the job to be recruited to. Roles change over time, and job descriptions should be reviewed regularly.

Since the introduction of Agenda for Change, all roles in the NHS have gone through a process of job evaluation which matched jobs to national profiles, and evaluating jobs locally, to determine in which pay band a post should sit. National profiles are now available for most jobs and include a job statement as well as the relevant job information. Best practice suggests that local job descriptions should be carefully reviewed and matched to a national profile.

It is important, however, not to just replace like for like in terms of staff without careful thought. For example, the employee that has left may have been a very experienced staff member working as a team leader. It would be important to offer the team leader role to existing staff before advertising externally. The external recruitment may therefore be for a staff nurse rather than a team leader, assuming a suitable internal candidate can be appointed.

Creating a business case for recruitment

It should not be assumed that when a post becomes vacant there will be permission to recruit. Organisations will sometimes have staff in need of redeployment due to restructuring, or may wish to hold a post open, using bank or agency staff as an interim measure. Whilst financial savings are sometimes the reason for such a decision, there may be other service development or service reconfigurations that come into play.

Many organisations have a pro forma that will need to be completed, and therefore guides you through the process of developing a **business case for recruitment**. The business case usually includes the following information:

- The nature of the post – for example, staff nurse or team leader
- The salary band
- The working time equivalent (WTE) full time or part time
- Whether it is a temporary (maternity cover, for example) or permanent post
- The name of the previous post holder
- Alternatives to recruitment – this section asks you if you have looked at alternatives. If the post is a maternity cover, are there existing part-time staff for example that may wish to pick up extra hours to cover? Are there staff elsewhere that are coming to the end of a temporary contract that may be able to fill in?
- Statement of need – this part of the business case is where you provide evidence that the post is needed. In this section, it is important to put some workload data (bed occupancy,

clinic visits) to demonstrate that current staff are up to capacity. You will also want to include the extent of bank and agency staff use and describe the anticipated reduction in this costly resource if the post was filled.

The business case for recruitment will need to follow an approval process within the organisation. Typically, the business case will need to be signed off by the general manager responsible for your area, and may also need approval by the finance office.

Recruitment

The purpose of recruitment is to locate and attract enough qualified applicants to provide a pool from which the required number of individuals can be selected. Even though recruiting is primarily carried out by HR staff, the front-line manager plays an important role in the process.

Box 14.1 lists questions for consideration in assessing the attractiveness of your organisation to potential employees and the often overlooked messages it might be sending.

To a very large extent, the 'feel' of the workplace, its culture, can serve as the best recruiting tool. A positive work environment through leadership style and clinical expertise will have a positive impact on recruitment because potential staff members will hear about and be attracted to that area. In contrast, an area in which the staff are unhappy and managed in an unsupportive and overbearing way is more likely to have a higher turnover rate and is less likely to attract sufficient numbers of high-quality nurses.

Any recruiting strategy includes four essential elements:

- Where to look
- How to look
- When to look
- How to sell the organisation to potential recruits.

Each of these elements may be affected by the availability of staff for recruitment, the reputation of the organisation and the clinical area, visibility and location.

Box 14.1   What Messages Does Your Organisation Send?

- Are all people involved in recruiting courteous and friendly, welcoming and assisting potential candidates?
- Is it easy for people to find information on employment opportunities?
- Do your website and printed materials about your organisation convey the message that you are serious about providing flexibility in employment, staff development and career potential?
- Are the work spaces, reception areas, buildings and grounds tidy and organised?
- Are there bulletin boards or leaflets clearly visible that display continuing education and staff development offerings?
- Will the candidate have support during induction and the early months in the new job?

Where to look

For most health care organisations, the best place to look for nurses is in the local area. During times of severe shortages, or when attracting staff locally is difficult (especially staff with specialist skills), many organisations conduct national searches. Owing to the fact that most nurses look for jobs in their local area, national searches should be the last resort. If the organisation is in a major metropolitan area, a search may be relatively easy; if it is located in a rural area, however, recruitment may need to be conducted in the nearest city. Organisations tend to recruit where past efforts have been the most successful. Most organisations adopt an incremental strategy whereby they recruit locally first and then expand to larger and larger markets until a sufficient applicant pool is obtained.

Because proximity to home is a key factor in choosing a job, recruitment efforts should focus on nurses living nearby. Students in local schools of nursing are obviously an excellent potential source of employees. One way to recruit them is to serve as a clinical training site and treat students well. Nurses who work with students play a key role in recruitment. Students feel welcomed and valued when their care and contributions are acknowledged. In doing so, the staff conveys a positive impression of the work group.

Employing nursing students as part-time support workers may provide another recruitment tool because it allows students to learn first-hand about the organisation and what it has to offer. In turn, the organisation can evaluate the student as a potential employee when they qualify.

Another potential source of staff is to recruit from bank and agency staff that have worked in the organisation. Whilst many people work on bank and agency for the flexibility and variety that is offered, sometimes the positive experience of working with a welcoming and supportive team with an effective and compassionate ward sister/team leader may be enough to entice them on to the staff.

How to look

Recommendations by existing staff, advertising in newspapers, professional journals and on the Internet, and attendance at professional conventions, job fairs and career days are all recruiting sources. Direct applications and recommendations by existing staff are quick and relatively inexpensive ways of recruiting people. Nurses referred to the organisation by friends or relatives that either work there or have had a good experience of the organisation are more likely to be happy employees. The reason is that nurses coming from these informal sources of referral are likely to have more realistic information about the job and the organisation and, therefore, their expectations more closely fit reality. Those who come to the job with unrealistic expectations may experience dissatisfaction as a result. In an open labour market, these individuals may leave the organisation, creating high turnover. When nursing jobs are less plentiful, dissatisfied staff members tend to stay in the organisation because they need the job, but they are not likely to perform as well as other employees. Consequently, where applicants are sought may have significant consequences later on.

Most applicants, however, are drawn to the organisation by some form of advertising. Your organisation will have a preference about where advertising is done. All organisations provide a space on their websites for job advertisements, and this can be a relatively inexpensive option, though the ad will not be seen unless a potential staff member actually initiates the search themselves. Advertisements may be placed in the classified sections of local newspapers or professional journals where they may be seen more widely, but this is more expensive. Nevertheless, if the organisation intends to add staff, placing display ads in local newspapers reassures currently employed nurses that the organisation is serious about its commitment to do so.

Another advertising medium is the Internet. Because the Internet is readily accessible, it is an attractive way to explore job opportunities anywhere in the world. There are numerous websites that target nurses. Ads can be purchased on some sites; others are directly available for recruiting. In recruiting, both the medium and the message must be considered. The medium is the agent of contact between the organisation and the potential applicant. Obviously, it is desirable to find a medium that gives the widest exposure. Unfortunately, these media tend to be inefficient and low in credibility. The more influential media tend to be the more personal ones: present employees and recruiters. Acquaintances or friends of the recruit have prior credibility and the ability to communicate more subtle aspects of the organisation and the job.

When to look

The time lag in recruiting is a concern to nursing, especially during times of shortage. Ideally, the recruitment process should be undertaken as soon as an existing staff member gives their notice. In practice, the process of recruitment can take several months owing in part to the time needed to complete pre-employment checks. Even when there is an adequate supply of nurses, certain locations (e.g. rural areas) and specialties (e.g. critical care) may experience shortages. Careful planning is necessary to ensure that recruitment begins well in advance of anticipated needs.

How to sell the organisation

A critical component of any recruiting effort is marketing the organisation and available positions to potential employees. The nursing divisions working with HR should develop a comprehensive marketing plan. Generally, four strategies are included in marketing plans and are called the 3 Ps of marketing:

Product

Place

Promotion

The potential recruit is the key figure around which the three concepts are oriented and designing the recruitment strategy should be done from the point of view of the potential employee.

Product is the available post within the organisation. Consider several aspects of the post and organisation, such as:

- specialty;
- flexibility of scheduling;

- opportunity for career development;
- education, reward and progression;
- the reputation and culture of the team in which the post holder will work.

Place refers to the physical characteristics and location of the organisation, its buildings and community, such as:

- accessibility;
- public transport and parking;
- community reputation;
- organisational culture.

Promotion includes

- advertising;
- public relations;
- direct word of mouth.

Personal selling (e.g. job fairs, professional meetings)

Developing an effective marketing message is important. Sometimes the tendency is to use a 'scatter-gun' approach, soften the message or make it very slick. A more balanced message, which includes honest communication and personal contact, is preferable. Overselling the organisation creates unrealistic expectations that may lead to later dissatisfaction and turnover. Presenting the job requirements and rewards realistically improves job satisfaction, in that the new recruit learns what the job is actually like.

Promising a nurse a particular shift schedule and then being unable to consistently meet that expectation due to staff shortages is an example of unrealistic job information. It is important to represent the situation honestly and describe the steps that are being taken to improve situations that the applicant might find undesirable. The candidate can then make an informed decision about the job offer.

The application process

In almost every selection situation, an applicant fills out an application form that requests information regarding previous experience, education and references. As application forms are reviewed, the critical question to be asked is whether the applicant has distorted responses, either intentionally or unintentionally. Studies indicate that there is usually little distortion, at least not on the easily verifiable information. Applicants may stretch the truth a bit, but rarely are there complete falsehoods. Relative to other predictors, the application form may be one of the more valid predictors in a selection process.

Most job postings have a date by which applications are to be received. HR usually receives the applications and forwards them to the first-line manager following the application closing date. The first-line manager then screens the applications to ensure that the necessary job requisites are met. For example, it may be that a nurse is interested in working in the community on graduation, but the role requires at least one year's acute care experience. The initial screening of applications should ensure that all applicants have the required experience, and those who do not are set aside.

The first-line manager will create a list of applicants suitable for interview. Ideally, three or four applicants should be selected for interview so that there is a real opportunity to select from a range of suitable candidates. In times of shortage, it is possible that very few applications are received, and it may be that there are posts available for all applicants that meet the job requirements. In this case, it is still important to interview each applicant. There are times when the applicant displays unsuitable behaviour, or a lack of judgement during the interview process, and that person is identified as unsuitable for employment even though shortages exist.

Interviewing

The most common selection method, the interview, is an information-seeking mechanism between an individual applying for a post and people within the organisation that are responsible for hiring. In the NHS, most applicants are interviewed by a panel consisting of a variety of people from the organisation. The first-line manager responsible for the area will be on the interview panel, as will a nursing manager from elsewhere in the organisation and potentially members of the team where the nurse will be working.

The interview is used to clarify information gathered from the application form, evaluate the applicant's responses to questions and determine the fit of the applicant to the post and the organisation. In addition, the interviewers should provide information about the job and the organisation. Finally, the interview should create goodwill towards the employing organisation through courteous and professional treatment of all candidates.

An effective interviewer must learn to solicit information efficiently and to gather relevant data. Interviews typically last for 30 minutes to an hour, and include an opening, an information-gathering and information-giving phase and a closing. The opening is important because it is an attempt to establish rapport with the applicant so that they will provide relevant information.

Gathering information, however, is the core of the interview. Giving information is also important because it allows the interviewer to create realistic expectations in the applicant and sell the organisation if that is needed. However, this portion of the interview should take place after the information has been gathered so that the applicant's answers will be as candid as possible. The interviewer should answer any direct questions the candidate poses. Box 14.2 is an example of realistic information to present to applicants. Finally, the closing is intended to provide information to the candidate on the mechanics of possible employment.

Principles for effective interviewing

Structured interview guides

Unstructured interviews present problems; if interviewers fail to ask the same questions of every candidate, it is often difficult to compare them, which can lead to accusations of discrimination. With any human skill or trait, no absolute standard exists that can serve as a basis on which to compare applicants. People can only be compared to other people. Consequently, the interview is most effective when the information on the pool of interviewees is as comparable as possible.

Box 14.2 **Staff Nurse Post, Burn Ward: Realistic Preview Information**

- Patients are usually on the burn ward for a month or more, which allows for development of close supportive relationships with patients and families.
- The ward is a teaching ward, and has a good reputation as a learning environment.
- There will be an opportunity to assist with research.
- The ward is small and has a dedicated, close-knit, multidisciplinary staff team.
- Children as well as adults are treated there.
- Patients can be challenging: some have history of drug or alcohol misuse and mental health problems.
- The ward can be emotionally demanding: deaths do occur, as well as poor outcomes.
- The work is sometimes physically demanding.

Comparability is maximised via a structured interview supported by an **interview guide**. An interview guide is a written document containing questions, interviewer directions and other pertinent information so that the same process is followed and the same basic information is gathered from each applicant. The guide should be specific to the job, or job category, as shown in Boxes 14.3 and 14.4.

Box 14.3 lists questions you could ask in an interview, but do not copy the questions verbatim; develop your own questions based on the specific job. For example, you may want to add questions on teamwork and collaboration as they relate to the post. Box 14.4 is an example of job-related questions that could be asked for an oncology ward position.

Interview guides reduce interviewer bias, provide relevant and effective questions, minimise leading questions, and facilitate comparison among applicants. Space left between the questions on the guide provides room for note taking, and the guide also provides a written record of the interview.

Preparing for the interview

Most first-line managers do not prepare adequately for the interview, which should be planned just like any important undertaking. All needed materials should be on hand, and the interview site should be quiet and pleasant. Water should be provided as a courtesy to the interviewee. Someone should be on hand to meet the interviewees and find a comfortable place for them to wait. Lack of advance preparation may lead to insufficient interviewing time, interruptions or failure to gather important information. Other problems include losing focus in the interview because of a desire to be courteous or because a particularly dominant interviewee is encountered. This typically keeps the interviewer from obtaining the needed information.

The shortlisting of applicants should have screened out any applicant that does not meet the specification for the post. However, there are times where the application and curriculum vitae (CV) are not detailed enough to give a clear picture of their previous experience. Before the interview, the interview panel members should review job requirements and the application and make a note specific information to be clarified or explored. Remember that the CV

Box 14.3 **Questions to Ask in an Interview**

1. Tell me about yourself.
2. What do you know about our organisation?
3. What are you looking for in this post?
4. Why are you looking for a new post?
5. What do you like best about being a nurse? The least?
6. How would your colleagues describe you?
7. How would your ward manager describe you?
8. How would you describe yourself?
9. What are the most significant accomplishments you have made in your career so far?
10. Why do you want to work for us?
11. What other positions are you considering?
12. What continuing education have you completed recently?
13. What are your career goals?
14. How does this position fit into your long-term career goals?
15. What would you like to be doing in five years?
16. What are your strong points?
17. What are your weaknesses?
18. What would you like to know about the position and the area?
19. Do you have any other questions for me?

Box 14.4 **Job-Related Questions for an Oncology Ward**

Describe how you would intervene in the following situations:

- A patient that you admitted with a diagnosis of lymphoma is going to begin chemotherapy, and you are preparing to hang the first dose. When you enter the room she says, 'You know, I just can't believe that I have cancer. I know it is what the doctor says, but it just doesn't seem possible to me.'

- A young man is diagnosed with acute leukaemia and expresses anger and frustration in the presence of his wife. You witness the frequent outbursts and become increasingly aware of the sense of hopelessness on the part of both him and his wife.

- You are working nights and caring for an extremely seriously ill man receiving platelets and antibiotic therapy. The patient's blood pressure is continuing to drop. You have talked to the junior doctor on call twice by telephone, and he tells you to continue the present orders. The man's condition continues to decline. What would you do?

---

is prepared by the applicant and is intended to market the applicant's assets to the organisation. It does not give a balanced view of strengths and weaknesses. So, examine the CV critically and make notes about areas where you need more information.

To provide a relaxed, informal atmosphere, the setting is important. Both the panel and the applicant should be in comfortable chairs, as close as comfortably possible. There should be complete freedom from distracting phone calls and other interruptions. If the view is distracting, do not seat the applicant so that they can look out a window.

Opening the interview

The interview should start on time. Give a warm, friendly greeting, introduce yourself and the panel members, and ask the applicant their preferred name. The objective is to establish an open atmosphere so applicants reveal as much as possible about themselves. Start the interview by outlining what will be discussed and setting the time limits for the interview.

It is important that at no time in the interview you show bias based on age, religion, gender, sexual orientation, disability or race/ethnicity (see Table 14.1). This means that a candidate needs to be selected based on their ability to do the job and nothing else. You may be meeting the candidate for the first time at interview, and it is important that you are not influenced by such features as cultural or religious dress, accents or other observations that link to origin or ethnicity. Interviewers tend to be influenced by first impressions of a candidate, and such judgements often lead to poor decisions. First impressions may degrade the quality of the interview by colouring the search for information to justify their first impressions, good or bad. An observer from HR will usually be in attendance to ensure that the interview process is free of discrimination and that the interviewers use good practice in the role.

The structured interview schedule should be adhered to in each interview with the same panel member asking the same questions of each candidate. Where possible open-ended questions should be used, such as, 'Please tell me about your most rewarding experience as a nurse.' Open-ended questions cannot be answered with a single yes, no or one-word answer and usually elicit more information about the applicant. Closed questions (e.g. what, where, why, when, how many) should be used only to elicit specific information.

Work sample questions are used to determine an applicant's knowledge about work tasks and ability to perform the job. It is easy to ask a nurse whether they know how to care for a patient who has a central intravenous line in place. An answer of yes does not necessarily prove the ability, so you might ask some very specific questions about central lines. Avoid leading questions, in which the answer is implied by the question (e.g. 'We have lots of overtime. Do you mind overtime?'). You may also want to summarise what has been said, use silence to elicit more information, reflect back the applicant's feelings to clarify the issue, or indicate acceptance by urging the applicant to continue.

Giving information

In planning for the interview, it is important to agree what information about the work area will be provided, and by whom. Details about salary, pension, holidays and such are usually answered by HR. Questions about schedules, clinical care and the team are usually best answered by the first-line manager. If a candidate's questions cannot be answered, arrange for someone to contact the candidate later with the desired information.

Closing the interview

In closing the interview, ask the applicant whether they have anything to add or questions to ask related to the job and the organisation. It is important to tell the candidate when you will

Table 14.1 Pre-employment questions

	Appropriate to ask	Inappropriate to ask
Name	Applicant's name. Whether applicant has school or work records under a different name.	Questions about any name or title that indicate race, colour, religion, sex, national origin or ancestry.
		Questions about father's surname or mother's maiden name.
Address	Questions concerning place and length of current and previous addresses.	Any specific probes into foreign addresses that would indicate national origin.
Age		Any question about age directly or indirectly.
Birthplace or national origin		Any question about place of birth of applicant or place of birth of parents, grandparents or spouse.
		Any other question (direct or indirect) about applicant's national origin.
Race or colour		Any enquiry that would indicate race or colour.
Sex		Any question on an application blank that would indicate sex.
Religion		Any questions to indicate applicant's religious denomination or beliefs.
		A recommendation or reference from the applicant's religious denomination.
Citizenship	Do you have the right to work in the UK?	Questions of whether the applicant, parents or spouse are native born or naturalised.
Photographs	Photographic identification required for pre-employment checks.	
Education	Questions concerning any academic, professional or vocational schools attended.	Questions asking specifically the nationality, racial or religious affiliation of any school attended.
	Enquiry into language skills, such as reading and writing of foreign languages.	Enquiries as to the applicant's mother tongue or how any foreign language ability was acquired (unless it is necessary for the job).
Relatives	Name, relationship and address of a person to be notified in case of an emergency.	Any unlawful enquiry about a relative or partner.
Children		Questions about the number and ages of the applicant's children or information on child-care arrangements.

(Continued)

Table 14.1 Pre-employment questions (Continued)

	Appropriate to ask	Inappropriate to ask
Transportation		Enquiries about transportation to or from work (unless a car is necessary for the job).
Organisation		Questions about any organisation an applicant belongs to that may indicate the race, age, disabilities, colour, religion, sex, national origin or ancestry of its members.
Physical condition/ disabilities	Questions about being able to meet the job requirements, with or without some accommodation.	Questions about general medical condition, state of health, specific diseases, or nature/severity of disability.
Work schedule	Questions about the applicant's willingness to work the required work schedule.	Questions about applicant's willingness to work any particular religious holiday.
References	General and work references not relating to race, colour, religion, sex, national origin or ancestry, age or disability.	References specifically from clergy (as specified above) or any other people who might reflect race, age, disability, colour, sex, national origin or ancestry of applicant.
Financial		Questions about banking, credit rating, outstanding loans or bankruptcy.
Other qualifications	Any question that has direct reflection on the job to be applied for.	Any non-job-related enquiry that may present information permitting unlawful discrimination. Questions about arrests or convictions (unless necessary for job, such as security clearance).

be contacting them with a decision and get their contact details for that time period. Thanking the applicant and completing any notes made during the interview concludes the interview process.

Interview reliability and validity

Numerous research studies have been performed on the reliability and validity of employment interviews. In general, agreement between two interviews of the same measure by the same interviewer (**intra-rater reliability**) is fairly high, agreement between two interviews of the same measure by several interviewers (**inter-rater reliability**) is rather low, and the ability to predict job performance (**validity**) of the typical interview is very low. Research has also shown that:

- structured interviews are more reliable and valid;
- interviewers who are under pressure to hire in a short time or meet a recruitment quota are less accurate than other interviewers;

- interviewers who have detailed information about the job for which they are interviewing exhibit higher inter-rater reliability and validity;
- the interviewer's experience does not seem to be related to reliability and validity;
- there is a decided tendency for interviewers to make quick decisions and therefore be less accurate;
- interviewers develop stereotypes of ideal applicants against which interviewees are evaluated, and individual interviewers may hold different stereotypes, thus decreasing inter-rater reliability and validity;
- race and gender may influence interviewers' perceptions.

Possibly the greatest weakness in the selection interview is the tendency for the interviewer to try to assess an applicant's personality characteristics. Although it is difficult to eliminate such subjectivity, evaluations of applicants are often more subjective than they need to be, particularly when interviewers try to assess personality characteristics.

Information collected during an interview should answer three fundamental questions:

1. Can the applicant perform the job?
2. Will the applicant perform the job?
3. Will the candidate fit into the culture of the unit and the organisation?

The best predictor of the applicant's future behaviour in these respects is past performance. Previous work and other experience, previous education and training and current job performance all should be considered, not personality characteristics, which even psychologists cannot measure very accurately.

Integrating the information

When comparing candidates, first weigh the qualities required for the job in order of importance, placing more emphasis on the most important elements. Second, weigh the qualities desired on the basis of the reliability of the data. The more consistent the observation of behaviour from different elements in the selection system, the more weight that dimension should be given. Third, weigh job dimensions by trainability – consider the amount of education, experience and additional training the applicant can reasonably be expected to receive, and consider the likelihood that the behaviour in that dimension can be improved with training. Dimensions most likely to be learned in training (e.g. using new equipment) should be given the least weight so that more weight is placed on dimensions less likely to be learned in training (e.g. being able to care for terminally ill children).

Attempt to compare data across individuals in making a decision. It is more accurate to make decisions based on a comparison of several persons than to make a decision for each individual after each interview. Analysis of the entire applicant pool requires good interview records but lessens the impact of early impressions on the hiring decision because the interviewer must consider each job element across the entire pool.

Communicating the outcome of the hiring decision

Once the panel has met to agree the outcome of the interviews, it is important that each candidate that was interviewed receives a personal call from the organisation. Though practices vary, it is best if the first-line manager or member from HR communicates the decision at the agreed time.

The successful candidate is often contacted first and an offer of employment made. Once that offer has been accepted, the unsuccessful candidates are contacted. Calling the preferred candidate first is important. If they turn down the offer of employment, then the second preferred candidate can be offered the post instead. Though rare, it is sometimes the case that none of the candidates is suitable for the post and the position is unfilled.

Unsuccessful candidates should be offered the opportunity for feedback on their interview. They should be told the strengths that they offered, the areas in which they fell short (for example, the successful candidate may have had more experience or a specialist qualification). The person offering the feedback should be a skilled communicator able to convey the information in a sensitive and clear way.

Manager's checklist

The first-level manager is responsible for:

- understanding the organisation's human resource policies and procedures related to selecting staff;
- working closely with the human resources department to facilitate the selection and hiring of qualified staff;
- preparing for the interview process;
- organising and serving as part of the interview panel;
- following up with applicants in a timely manner.

The eight strands of equality

In recruitment and selection as well as every other aspect of employment, there are legal duties that an employer must follow in order to ensure equality and promote diversity within the workforce. The UK is increasingly diverse (see Chapter 1) and large employers such as the NHS are careful to implement protection for workers in respect of that diversity. Recent legislations has identified eight areas that are the focus of equality and diversity attentions; age, disability, gender, sexual orientation, race or ethnicity, religion or belief, human rights and carers.

Age

The Employment Equality (Age) Regulations 2006 make it illegal to discriminate against workers, employees, job seekers or trainees based on their age. The regulations cover recruitment, promotion, training, terms and conditions, transfers and terminations.

Disability

There are three pieces of legislation that set out the requirements for compliance: the Equality Act 2006, and the Disability Discrimination Acts of 1995 and 2005. These make it unlawful to discriminate against anyone with a disability. Each organisation is now required to actively promote disability equality and to publish a disability equality scheme which is reviewed every three years. This requirement makes it necessary for employers to make 'reasonable adaptations' to enable people to work. This could include the provision of a personal attendant to assist the individual.

Gender

The Equality Act 2006 (Gender Equality Duty) prohibits discrimination based on gender but also introduces a responsibility to actively promote gender equality. This duty includes the need to publish a gender equality scheme including equal pay policies, and to actively promote gender equality. Gender equality protection is also extended to transgender individuals.

Sexual orientation

The Equality in Employment Regulations (Sexual Orientation 2003) make it unlawful to discriminate on the basis of sexuality, directly or indirectly, or to harass or victimise somebody because they have made, or intend to make a complaint.

Race and ethnicity

The Race Relations (Amendment) Act 2000 requires all employers to eliminate unlawful discrimination, promote equality of opportunity and promote good relations between different racial groups. This particular law requires employers to publish a race equality scheme that is reviewed every three years and includes a requirement to conduct training on the racial equality duty.

Religion or belief

The Equality in Employment Regulations (Religion or Belief) 2003 makes it unlawful to discriminate on the basis of religion or belief, directly or indirectly, or to harass or victimise somebody because they have made, or intend to make, a complaint.

Carers

The Work and Families Act (2006) gives the right to parents of children under six (or 18 if disabled) to request flexible working arrangements. This right to request flexible working was extended in 2007 to include carers of adults living at the same residence as them.

Human rights

The Human Rights Act of 1998 gives each individual the right to life, liberty and security, respect for private and family life, freedom of expression and freedom of thought, conscience and religion.

What you know now

- Recruitment of applicants and selection of staff are important processes to ensure the best fit between employees and the needs of the organisation.
- The selection of staff is a critical function that requires matching people to jobs, and responsibility for hiring is often shared by HR and nurse managers.
- Role review is fundamental to selection efforts because it defines the job.
- Recruitment is the process of locating and attracting enough qualified applicants to provide a pool from which the required number of new staff members can be chosen.
- Selection processes should be job-related and most often include receipt and screening of application forms and CVs, interviews, pre-employment checks and offers of employment.
- Interviewing is a complex skill that is intended to obtain information about the applicant and give the applicant information about the organisation.
- Successful interviews require planning, implementation and follow-up in order to make the best decisions.
- Developing a structured interview guide is a critical element in interviewing.
- Selection decisions are subject to provisions within legislation in respect of equality and diversity.

Questions to challenge you

1. What approach does your organisation use to recruit employees? Is it effective? How could they improve?

2. Imagine that a potential candidate asks you to describe your present workplace. What would you say?

3. Consider the last interview you had for a job or school. Did the interviewer follow the principles discussed in this chapter? Explain.

Chapter 15
Clinical Supervision, Capability and Development Review

Key terms

Clinical supervision
Knowledge and Skills Framework
Role profile
Personal development review

Leniency error
Overemphasis on recent events error
Halo effect
Event register

Introduction

Ward managers and team leaders are instrumental in supporting life-long learning for staff in their areas, to ensure safe and competent clinical care continues. Clinical supervision has been recognised by the Nursing and Midwifery Council as a supportive way to facilitate learning from experience. This learning feeds into the personal development review process that identifies areas for development annually, and supports career progression through the Knowledge and Skills Framework. Clinical supervision and personal development review are important for determining the strengths and areas for development of individuals and help to plan for service development.

This chapter explains the importance of these complementary processes of clinical supervision and personal development review and provides guidance for team leaders and ward managers. The desired result of these processes is that each person is effective in the performance of their job and works with motivated and capable staff.

Clinical supervision

Clinical supervision is an activity that brings skilled supervisors and practitioners together in order to reflect on practice. 'Supervision aims to identify solutions to problems, improve practice and increase understanding of professional issues' (Nursing and Midwifery Council, 2008). Six principles have been identified:

1. Clinical supervision supports practice, enabling practitioners to maintain and promote standards of care.

2. Clinical supervision is a practice-focused professional relationship involving practitioner reflection on practice guided by a skilled advisor.

3. The process of clinical supervision should be developed by practitioners and managers according to local circumstances. Ground rules should be agreed so that practitioners and supervisors approach clinical supervision openly and confidently and are aware of what is involved.

4. Every practitioner should have access to clinical supervision. Each supervisor should supervise a realistic number of practitioners.

5. Preparation for supervisors can be effected using 'in house' or external education programmes. The principles and relevance of clinical supervision should be included in pre- and post-registration education programmes.

6. Evaluation of clinical supervision is needed to assess how it influences care, practice standards and the services. Evaluation systems should be determined locally.

Although nurses are not required to undertake clinical supervision, it is a requirement for midwives.

Clinical supervision is most commonly undertaken as a one-to-one session, but it can be structured as a group session particularly if a team is seeking supervision about the care of a particular client or client group. The role of the supervisor is to assist the participants to reflect on their practice, through listening, asking clarifying questions, and offering guidance and advice. What is discussed in clinical supervision is confidential and does not form part of the personal development review.

Whilst in many organisations the staff member's manager does not act as their clinical supervisor, the manager has an important role to play in enabling supervision to happen:

- The manager should participate in clinical supervision as a supervisee, therefore demonstrating support for supervision and confidence in the process.

- The manager should encourage all members of staff to participate in clinical supervision, describing its value to the individual and to patient care.

- The manager will need to facilitate time away from clinical care to allow individuals to prepare for and participate in clinical supervision.

Knowledge and Skills Framework

The **Knowledge and Skills Framework** (KSF) (Table 15.1) defines and describes the knowledge and skills which NHS staff need to apply in their work in order to deliver quality services. It provides a single, consistent, comprehensive and explicit framework on which to base review and development for all staff.

Dimensions	Level descriptors			
CORE	1	2	3	4
1 Communication	Communicate with a limited range of people on day-to-day matters	Communicate with a range of people on a range of matters	Develop and maintain communication with people about difficult matters and/or in difficult situations	Develop and maintain communication with people on complex matters, issues and ideas and/or in complex situations
2 Personal and people development	Contribute to own personal development	Develop own skills and knowledge and provide information to others to help their development	Develop oneself and contribute to the development of others	Develop oneself and others in areas of practice
3 Health, safety and security	Assist in maintaining own and others' health, safety and security	Monitor and maintain health, safety and security of self and others	Promote, monitor and maintain best practice in health, safety and security	Maintain and develop an environment and culture that improves health, safety and security
4 Service improvement	Make changes in own practice and offer suggestions for improving services	Contribute to the improvement of services	Appraise, interpret and apply suggestions, recommendations and directives to improve services	Work in partnership with others to develop, take forward and evaluate direction, policies and strategies
5 Quality	Maintain the quality of own work	Maintain quality in own work and encourage others to do so	Contribute to improving quality	Develop a culture that improves quality
6 Equality and diversity	Act in ways that support equality and value diversity	Support equality and value diversity	Promote equality and value diversity	Develop a culture that promotes equality and values diversity

Table 15.1 An overview of the NHS Knowledge and Skills Framework
Source: © Crown copyright

Each post in the NHS has a **role profile** which sets out the actual requirements for the post in terms of knowledge and skills needed. The role profile does not seek to define the personal qualities of an individual (integrity, honesty, sense of humour); it sets out the knowledge and skills needed to carry out the post. All roles in the NHS have the same six core elements within the Knowledge and Skills Framework:

- Communication
- Personal and people development

- Health safety and security
- Service improvement
- Quality
- Equality and diversity.

These core elements are defined in each post outline as a level on a scale from 1 to 4 depending on the complexity of the skills needed. Additional skills are added to the core skills within the post outline depending on the nature of the work. Most nursing posts also include health and well-being dimensions such as 'HWB2 – Assessment and care planning to meet health and wellbeing needs' or HWB5 – Provision of care to meet health and wellbeing needs' (NHS Employers, 2006). Each post outline is uniquely created and therefore will differ between organisations.

Personal development review

The personal development review process is an integral part of the career and pay progression strand of Agenda for Change. **Personal development review** is an ongoing cycle of review, planning, development and evaluation for all staff which links organisational and personal development needs (see Figure 15.1). The review is a partnership process undertaken between a staff member and a reviewer, usually but not always the person's line manager. Support and development for reviewers is usually offered within each organisation.

The development review process consists of:

- reviewing how individuals are applying their skills and knowledge to meet the demands of their current post and identifying whether they have development needs;
- creating a personal development plan for each individual detailing the learning and development to take place in the coming months and identifying the date of the next review;

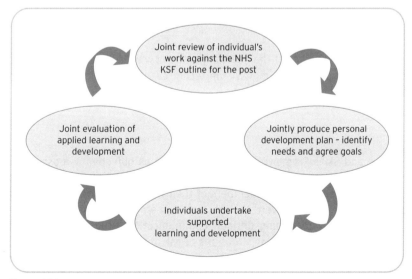

Figure 15.1 The development review process.
Source: © Crown copyright

- learning and development for the individual supported by the reviewer;
- evaluating the learning and development and how it was applied to work.

Personal development review guidelines

Development review is conducted for a number of reasons. The primary reason is to give feedback that ensures that staff know what they are to do and how well they are doing it.

- The personal development review meeting should be carried out at least once a year.

- Since the review process is a partnership, all information used in the review meeting should be shared with the employee.

- The staff member being reviewed should have the opportunity to present their evidence and have it recorded at the review meeting.

- The organisational policy will have a process for the development review to be appealed.

- Notes on the employee's performance should be kept during the entire evaluation period review period. Any incidents of inadequate care or poor performance must be shared with the employee at the time they occurred. There should be no surprises at the review meeting.

- All reviewers should be trained as reviewers.

- The development review must focus on application of skills and knowledge, not on personal traits.

Performance review must accurately and completely reflect the actual performance in the role over the review period. For development review to successful, the needs of the staff and requirements of the organisation must be bridged (Wilson and Smith-Bodden, 1999).

Common development review errors

Errors that lessen the accuracy of the development review process can arise. The most common errors include leniency, overemphasis on recent events, the halo effect and inaccuracy or bias in the written comments.

Leniency error

The Knowledge and Skills Framework is designed to be as objective as possible, yet some managers tend to overrate their staff's performance. This is called **leniency error**. For example, a manager may believe that all members of their staff are performing the communication standard at a level 3 even though some members of staff are stronger in communication, willingly managing difficult communication situations with good results whilst some other nurses avoid those situations or ask others to handle them. This error occurs for a variety of reasons. Sometimes the manager wants to be liked and will therefore be reluctant to tell a colleague that they are not up to the expected standard. More commonly, the manager involved will want to avoid any potential for conflict (see Chapter 9) and therefore rate some individuals higher than the level at which they actually perform. Some managers have not developed their communication skills, particularly when it comes to giving feedback (see Chapter 6).

A pattern of the manager being lenient with staff members who do not perform as expected can be demoralising to the best staff nurses, because they would have received high ratings without the leniency error. Thus, leniency error tends to be welcomed by poorer performers and disliked by better ones.

Overemphasis on recent events

Another difficulty with development review systems is the length of time over which the application of knowledge and skills is observed. In most organisations, employees are formally reviewed every 12 months. Evaluating employee performance over such an extended period of time, particularly if one supervises more than a few individuals, is a difficult task. Typically, as the review appointment approaches, the reviewer begins to pay greater attention to the individual's work, and therefore recent events may feature more fully in the review with distant events being forgotten. Thus, the review reflects what the employee has contributed lately rather than over the entire evaluation period.

If a disgruntled employee can demonstrate that a review that supposedly reflects 12 months actually reflects performance over the past 2 or 3 months, particularly if the latest performance is less favourable, there is potential for the employee to challenge the review. In terms of motivation, overemphasising the recent events at the expense of less recent performance can send a message that individuals only need to demonstrate the desired skills and knowledge for the short period around the time of the review. In such situations, an employee is highly motivated just prior to the review but considerably less motivated as soon as it is completed.

As with leniency error, **overemphasis on recent events** benefits the poorly performing individual. Nurses who perform well year round may receive ratings similar to those nurses who change their behaviour as their annual review appointment time approaches. Fortunately, a manager who records events and examples of application of skills and knowledge throughout the year can greatly lessen the impact of this type of error.

Halo effect

Sometimes a reviewer fails to differentiate among the various performance dimensions (the six core skills and other dimensions within the role profile) and conducts the review on the basis of an overall impression, positive or negative, of the employee. Thus, some employees are rated above average across dimensions, others are rated average and a few are rated below average on all dimensions. This is referred to as the **halo effect**.

If a nurse is excellent, average or poor on all dimensions of the role, they deserve to be rated accordingly, but in most instances, employees have uneven strengths and weaknesses. Thus, it should be relatively uncommon for an employee to receive the same rating on all knowledge and skills dimensions. Although the halo effect is less common and troublesome than leniency and overemphasis on recent events, it is still not an accurate assessment and can overlook the need to focus on specific skills or knowledge within the personal development plan.

The reviewer

In most organisations, an employee's manager conducts the review of their staff members. In many situations, this makes sense. The manager is familiar with the employee's work and thus is best able to evaluate it. If the immediate supervisor does not have enough information to evaluate an employee's performance accurately, alternatives are necessary. The manager can informally seek out performance-related information from other sources, such as the employee's co-workers, patients, or other managers who are familiar with the person being reviewed. The manager weighs this additional information, integrates it with their own judgement and completes the review.

Documenting performance

Reviewing an employee's performance can be a difficult job. A reviewer is required to reflect on a staff member's performance over an extended period of time (usually 12 months) and then describe it accurately. Given that many reviewers have several people to review, it is not surprising that they forget what an individual did several months ago or that they may actually confuse what one employee did with what another worker did.

A useful mechanism for fighting such memory problems is the use of **event register**s, which capture unusual or illustrative events, in either a positive or a negative direction. These events are recorded on a form or an index card with space for four items: name of employee, date and time of incident, a brief description of what occurred, and the nurse manager's comments on what transpired (Figure 15.2). Index cards are usually preferred to a page-size form because cards are more easily carried and are less likely to get torn.

1. Name of employee: ___Cindy Siegler_____

2. Date and time of incident: ___22 March, 8:22 a.m._____

3. Description: ___Ms Siegler came to work late. This was the third time in the_____
   _____past 2 weeks._____

4. Comments: ___Ms Siegler has only worked for the clinic for 4 months and her_____
   _____repeatedly late attendance is having an effect on the other clinic staff. I_____
   _____spoke with her privately and conveyed the above concerns on 22 March_____
   _____at 10:35 a.m. She acknowledged the problem she has had with baby_____
   _____sitters but reassured me that she has enrolled her child in preschool_____
   _____and that she should be on time from now on. We agreed to meet again_____
   _____in 2 weeks to evaluate her attendance._____

Figure 15.2 An example of an event register.

Event recording at the time the event occurs is bound to increase the accuracy of the year-end performance review. Events should be shared with employees as they occur, particularly events of concern, so that there is an opportunity to develop as the time progresses. The event record should focus specifically on what took place, not on an interpretation of what happened. For example, instead of writing 'Ms Hudson was rude,' write 'Ms Hudson referred to the patient as a slob.' The nature of what is recorded should be consistent for all employees and shared with the people to be reviewed.

Based on the experience of organisations that have introduced the use of event records, reviewers tend to make three types of mistake in using notes:

- Some reviewers fail to make them specific and behaviour-oriented; rather, they record that a nurse was 'careless' or 'difficult to supervise'.
- Some reviewers record only undesirable behaviour.
- Some reviewers fail to give feedback to the employee at the time that a note was written.

Each of these errors can undermine the effectiveness of the note-taking process. If the notes are vague, the employee may not know specifically what was done wrong and therefore does not know how to improve. If only poor performance is documented, employees will resent the system and the reviewer. If the reviewer does not share notes as they are written, the employee will often react defensively when confronted with them at the end of the evaluation period. In sum, any reviewer who is considering using this event record system needs to take the process seriously and to use it as it is designed.

One final issue needs to be addressed. Different employees react differently to the use of notes. Good employees react positively. Although the reviewer records both what is done well and what is done poorly, good employees will have many more positive than negative notes and therefore will benefit from notes being taken. In contrast, poorer employees do not react well to notes being taken.

Diagnosing performance problems

If the manager notes poor or inconsistent performance during the review process, the reviewer has a responsibility for addressing the performance and creating a plan with the employee to give them every opportunity to meet the expected standard.

The first step is to begin with accepted standards of performance and an accurate assessment of the current performance of the staff member. This means that role profiles must be current and accurately reflect any substantial changes to the role. If major changes have occurred, a role evaluation may be necessary. Each organisation will have a process for completing a role evaluation.

Next decide whether the problem demands immediate attention and whether it is a skill-related or motivation-related problem. Skill-related problems can be solved through formal or informal training,

If the performance problem is due to motivation rather than ability, the reviewer must address a different set of questions. Specifically, the manager must determine whether the employee believes that there are obstacles to the expected behaviour or that the behaviour leads to punishment, reward or inaction. For example, if the reward for conscientiously coming to work on holidays (rather than calling in sick) leads to always being scheduled for

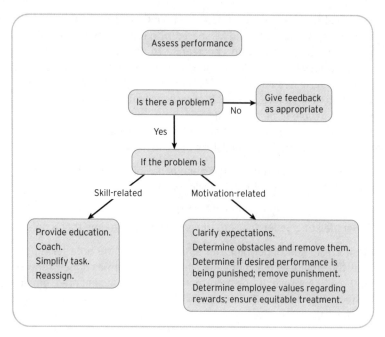

Figure 15.3 A decision tree for evaluating performance.

holiday work, then good performance is associated with punishment. Only when the employee sees a strong link between valued outcomes and meeting performance expectations will motivation strategies succeed. The manager plays a role in tailoring motivational efforts to meet the individual needs of the employee. Unfortunately, creating a performance-reward climate does not eliminate all problem behaviours (see Chapter 8).

To differentiate between lack of ability and lack of motivation, the reviewer can examine past performance. If past performance has been acceptable and little change in standards of performance has taken place, then the problem results from a lack of motivation. In contrast, if the nurse has never performed at an acceptable level, then the problem may be primarily skill related.

Different intervention strategies should be used, depending on the source of the problem. The objective should be to enhance performance rather than to punish the employee. Figure 15.3 summarises the steps to take.

Preparation for the personal development review meeting

Personal development review is a partnership process between reviewer and individual; therefore each person has a responsibility for preparing for the review meeting. The individual is usually responsible for:

- reviewing the record of the previous review meeting to identify personal development goals;
- gathering evidence of learning and development and the application of those skills;

- identifying any new development issues that have arisen since the previous meeting.

The reviewer also has specific preparation to do in advance of the review meeting:

- Review the record of the previous review meeting to identify personal goals.
- Gather records of development programmes attended, annual updates and participation in any continuing education.
- Informal feedback from peers and mentors that will assist in identifying learning needs.

A key step for making the development review process go well is proper planning. The reviewer should set up the personal development review meeting in advance, preferably giving at least two days' notice. The reviewer should schedule enough time: most review meetings take an hour, although the time needed will vary considerably depending on the degree to which the reviewer and staff member have talked regularly during the year.

In preparing for the review, the reviewer should have specific examples of behaviour. Such documentation is particularly important for performance areas in which an employee needs development. In addition, the reviewer should try to anticipate how the staff member will react to the review.

The setting also should be considered in planning the meeting. It is critical that the interview takes place in a setting that is private and relatively free from interruptions. This allows a frank, in-depth conversation with the employee. Although it is difficult to limit interruptions in a health care setting, choosing the meeting time carefully will help. A reviewer may be able to schedule the meeting when additional cover can be obtained or at a time when interruptions are least likely to occur. The most important point to remember is that a poor setting limits the usefulness of the interview.

The review meeting

The review meeting is most likely to go well if the reviewer has written and shared events throughout the evaluation period. If such feedback has occurred, staff members go into the interview with a good idea of what will be discussed. If the reviewer has not kept notes throughout the year, it is very important to recall numerous, specific examples of behaviour, both positive and negative, to support the review.

The primary focus of the review meeting should be on how the reviewer and the staff member can work together to improve performance in the coming year. However, establishing such an improvement-oriented climate is easier said than done. In giving feedback, a reviewer needs to use the skill of effective feedback and difficult conversations described in Chapter 6. Criticism has no place in a personal development review in that the intention is to give an accurate picture of how the individual is meeting standard, and what can be done to help those who are not meeting standard. Criticism causes defensiveness and can demotivate staff.

The following is a list of recommendations for conducting a review meeting:

- Put the employee at ease. Many people are nervous at the start of the review meeting, especially new employees who are facing their first review or those who have not received much feedback over the course of the evaluation period. To facilitate two-way communication during the meeting, some reviewers start by chatting about personal interests; others begin the review by giving an overview of the type of information that was used to prepare for the meeting, such as 'In preparing for this review, I relied heavily on the notes I have taken and shared with you throughout the year.' Rather than trying to reduce the tension an employee may have at the start of the review, it is better for a reviewer to ignore it. In many cases, if the reviewer has given the employee feedback throughout the evaluation period, the employee will not be unduly nervous at the start of the session.

- Clearly state the purpose of the review meeting as an opportunity to reflect on progress, set goals and value their work. This improvement-oriented theme should be conveyed at the beginning of the interview and will help the employee do the best possible job in the coming year.

- Go through the dimensions of the role one by one. Provide a number of specific examples of behaviour that illustrate the level of performance of that element. In reviewing the ratings, the reviewer should be careful not to rush. By systematically going through the dimensions and providing behavioural examples, the reviewer projects an image of being prepared and of being a professional.

- Draw out the employee's reactions. More specifically, the reviewer needs to ask for the employee's reaction to each dimension and then listen, accept and respond to them. Sometimes the reviewer's judgement is questioned. After having listened to the employee's reactions, the reviewer should accept and respond to them in a manner that conveys the reviewer has heard what the employee said (e.g. paraphrase some of the comments) and accepts the individual's opinion ('I understand your view'). In addition, the reviewer may want to clarify what has been said ('Could you cite specific examples that I may have missed?'). The reviewer strives for a candid, two-way conversation and wants to know exactly how the employee feels.

- Decide on specific ways in which performance areas can be strengthened. The focus of the review should now shift to the future. If a thorough review of an employee's performance reveals deficiencies, the reviewer and employee may jointly develop personal development plans to help the individual improve. A personal development plan describes mutually agreed-on activities for improving performance. Such developmental activities may include formal training, academic course work, or mentoring with experienced people. Together, the reviewer and the staff nurse should write down the resulting plans.

  Because of the possibility of defensiveness, only one or two performance areas needing improvement should be addressed. Together with the individual, the reviewer should choose the area(s) that is (are) most important and focus attention on this (these). In arriving at plans for improving performance, the reviewer should begin by asking the staff member for ideas on how to enhance personal performance. After the individual has offered suggestions, the reviewer can offer additional suggestions.

- Set a follow-up date. After having agreed on specific ways to strengthen performance in problem areas, the reviewer should schedule a subsequent meeting, usually four to six weeks after the review meeting. At this later meeting, the reviewer provides specific feedback on the nurse's recent performance. This meeting also gives the reviewer and the nurse an opportunity to discuss any problems they have encountered in attempting to carry out their agreed-on personal development plans. In most cases, this follow-up session is quite positive. With only one or two areas to work on and a specific date on which feedback will be given, the nurse's performance usually improves dramatically. Thus, the follow-up meeting is one in which the reviewer has the opportunity to praise the employee.

- Express confidence in the employee. This final key behaviour is simple but often overlooked. It is nevertheless important that the reviewer indicates confidence that improvement will be forthcoming.

Reviewer motivation

Although it is often assumed that reviewers are motivated to appraise their employees accurately, such an assumption is sometimes optimistic. Owing to the volume of work and the demands of everyday care, it is tempting for the reviewer to view the personal development review process as something that can be done later. Furthermore, many managers do not see doing reviews as a particularly important task, and some question the need for doing them at all. It is important that the review process is supported throughout the organisation and that the people who review the managers clearly expect reviews do be done, on time and well.

Manager's Checklist

When acting as a reviewer the manager is responsible for:

☐ Understanding the personal development review process.

☐ Providing honest and timely feedback to all employees.

☐ Communicating as needed with the human resources department when performance issues arise.

☐ Accurately and thoroughly documenting all performance-related issues.

☐ Identifying the impact of poor performers on the morale and productivity of staff.

☐ Acting on performance issues in a timely manner.

☐ Following up on reviews.

Rules of thumb

For approximately 5 per cent of employees, the prescriptions given in this chapter will not work, for reasons yet unknown. Additional suggestions or 'rules of thumb' derived from practical experience include the following.

Postpone the review meeting if necessary. Once the review meeting begins, there is no need to complete it on the day. If the review is not going well, a reviewer should discontinue it until a later time. Such a postponement allows both the reviewer and the employee some time to reflect on what has transpired as well as some time to calm down. In postponing the meeting, the reviewer should not assign blame, but should adopt a more positive approach ('This meeting isn't going as I hoped it would; I'd like to postpone it to give us some time to collect our thoughts'). Most reviewers who have used this technique find that the second session, which generally takes place one or two days later, goes much better.

Don't be afraid to be influenced by the employee and to change a proposed rating. The review process is a partnership and reasonable evidence should be considered. New reviewers often ask whether they should change a rating if an employee challenges it. They fear that by changing a rating, they will be admitting an error. They also fear that changing a rating will lead to other ratings being challenged. A practical rule of thumb for this situation is: if the rating is inaccurate, change it. The logic behind this is: if a reviewer does a careful job of evaluating performance, few inaccurate ratings will be made. But no one is perfect, and on occasion reviewers will err. When such an error occurs, the reviewer should correct it.

What you know now

- Clinical supervision is a way for nurses and midwives to reflect on their practice with a respected colleague.
- Doing personal development reviews is one of the most difficult and most important management activities.
- Accurate reviews provide a sound basis for employee development.
- To enhance the accuracy of personal development reviews, the reviewer should record events throughout the evaluation period.
- Problems with development reviews include leniency error, recency error and halo effect.
- To improve the value of the personal development review meeting, the reviewer should follow the key behaviours for conducting an appraisal interview.

Questions to challenge you

1. What components of your job (or clinical placement) are reviewed? Are they the appropriate ones?

2. What has been your experience with being reviewed as an employee? What did you learn from the experience?

3. Have you ever reviewed someone else's performance at work? How closely did your actions follow the suggestions in the chapter?

References

NHS Employers (2006) *The Knowledge and Skills Framework: A short guide to KSF dimensions*. London: Department of Health.

Nursing and Midwifery Council (2008) *Clinical Supervision for Registered Nurses*. London: Nursing and Midwifery Council.

Wilson, P. and Smith-Bodden, J. (1999) Does your appraisal system measure up? *Nursing Management*, **6**(1), 27-30.

Chapter 16
Quality Improvement and Risk Management

Key terms

Quality standards
Clinical governance
Structure standards
Process standards
Outcome standards
Indicator
Benchmarking
Clinical audit

Retrospective audit
Concurrent audit
Systematic process improvement
Risk management
National Patient Safety Agency
Incident
Perfection myth
Punishment myth

Introduction

Defining quality in health care has never been simple. Clinical professionals tend to define quality in terms of clinical outcomes, that is, what is achieved as a result of a treatment process. Patients define quality differently and include elements of both care and service. Whilst they want effective treatments and good outcomes, they also want to be sure that they are safe in the hands of clinical professionals, and that they are treated with respect, dignity and compassion. They want some say over the services they receive, specifically where and when they receive care and what treatment options are available to them. They also want help to stay healthy and prevent health problems in the future (DoH, 2008a).

Enabling and requiring health care organisations and professionals to provide high-quality care and service in an efficient and effective way is the primary focus of the next stage of reforms in the NHS (DoH, 2008a). Health care organisations have implemented quality management programmes to coordinate the various activities that measure and enhance the quality of care and service. Each member of the health care organisation has a role to play in the quality of health care. This chapter will explore a number of ways in which quality is measured, and look at the role of the ward manager/team leader in achieving quality standards.

Risk management is a process whereby activities that pose a risk to patient care are assessed, identified, monitored and controlled. Many of the activities of patient care involve risk, such as the administering of medication, observation levels for mental health patients and dangers involved in treatments. This chapter will also examine risk management and the role of the manager in this process.

Quality standards

The Health and Social Care Act 2008 called for the formation of the Care Quality Commission to regulate health and social care in the UK. The Care Quality Commission replaced the Commission for Healthcare Audit and Inspection (also known as the Healthcare Commission), the Commission for Social Care Inspection and the Mental Health Act Commission. The purpose of the Care Quality Commission is to encourage the improvement of health and social care services, in such a way as to focus on the needs and experiences of people who use the services, and to encourage the efficient and effective use of resources (DoH, 2008b).

The Care Quality Commission is developing an integrated regulatory framework to assure safety and quality, to measure the performance of organisations and to coordinate and manage inspection and regulation. It is anticipated that the new system will be similar to the system used by the Healthcare Commission, though the quality indicators will evolve. Main features of the inspection and regulatory system under the Healthcare Commission include:

- the annual publication of *The operating framework* (DoH, 2008c) that sets out the national priorities for quality improvement for the year ahead. The priorities are derived from surveys of the patients and professionals, and information gathered to determine the areas of focus. For the year 2008–09 the national priorities included:
  - improving cleanliness and reducing health care-acquired infections;
  - improving access through achievement of the 18-week referral to treatment pledge and improving access (including at evenings and weekends) to GP services;
  - keeping adults and children well, improving their health and reducing health inequalities;
  - improving patient experience, staff satisfaction and engagement, and preparing to respond to a state of emergency such as an outbreak of pandemic flu;
- working with commissioners of services to ensure that they are incorporating the priority areas into their commissioning of services for their community;
- conducting inspections of organisations to ensure they meet standards and priorities.

The Care Quality Commission has the power to require organisations to meet the standards set out and to apply sanctions for failure. In extreme situations, the Care Quality Commission can require the closure of a ward or service, or withdraw registration of an organisation.

The Healthcare Commission conducted annual inspection visits of all organisations, but the Care Quality Commission plans to use a different method. The frequency and focus of inspection for each organisation will depend on the performance at the previous inspection. Those organisations that are meeting **quality standards** may be inspected less often than weaker organisations. The Care Quality Commission can also go into an organisation if there is a concern over quality, such as an outbreak of infection or patient safety concern.

In addition to the national priorities set out by the care quality commission, each local commissioning organisation will set out local standards that pertain to their area. For example an area served by a particular primary care trust (PCT) may have a large number of immigrants and a particularly low childhood immunisation rate. The PCT may choose to commission a special immigrant outreach service where health visitors go to local community centres and places of worship with a translator to talk about immunisation. That same PCT could put a target on GP services to achieve a certain percentage improvement in order to focus attention on the problem.

Each organisation, ward, team or service will also have unique issues with quality and will set their own quality standards in addition to the organisational priorities set out in the quality strategy. For example, a district nursing team may have a standard that they see 90% of newly discharged patients within 24 hours of discharge. Due to staffing shortages and increasing workload, the team now sees less than 50% of patients within 24 hours, and 15% are still waiting more than 48 hours for their first visit. The team could choose to focus on this quality standard and put a plan together to meet the standard consistently once again.

Quality management programmes

Quality management programmes encompass a number of different strategies intended to prevent problems and to improve care. Quality management is based on an integrated system of information and accountability. Information is gathered from a number of sources such as performance data (waiting time, length of stay, admissions, discharges and financial information), clinical audit, incident and accident reports, near-miss reporting and patient and staff surveys. Increasingly, the information used for quality monitoring and improvement is available electronically, and increasingly sophisticated forms of information and communication technology (ICT) mean that the data can tell a much more complex story.

Accountability in quality management programmes means that individuals or committees (such as the clinical governance committee) are responsible for ensuring that problems are detected and appropriate steps taken to remedy the situation. The chief executive in any organisation has the ultimate accountability for quality, in that the expectation is that every organisation will have comprehensive systems in place to monitor and intervene in issues of quality. The executive and non-executive directors of organisations share in this accountability. Often the nurse director and medical director share the accountability for quality of care; if poor care results in patient injury or death, the chief executive, and potentially the nurse director or medical director, are called to account.

Clinical governance is a concept introduced to health care organisations which means that clinical professionals have a substantial role in the governance of organisations; in particular they are actively involved in setting quality standards for patient care. Clinical governance is intended to balance the corporate accountability (the responsibility for financial performance) with clinical quality. Each organisation is required to have a structure within the organisation where nurses, doctors and other professionals sit on committees or in some other way make decisions about care.

The quality improvement programme

A comprehensive quality improvement programme includes:

- a quality improvement plan;
- standards and indicators;
- data collection;
- data analysis and benchmarking;
- action planning.

Quality improvement plan

A quality improvement plan is a comprehensive, systematic approach to assessing and monitoring quality, determining priorities for quality improvement, identifying strategies for improvement and allocating the resources needed to achieve the plan. Quality improvement plans may be written to address a single issue or, more commonly, a whole systems organisational approach. Quality improvement plans should be regularly reviewed and updated to include challenges that arise and to refocus the plan on the priorities that arise.

Standards and indicators

Standards are written statements that define a level of performance or a set of conditions determined to be acceptable. Standards relate to three major dimensions of quality care:

- Structure
- Process
- Outcome.

Structure standards relate to the physical environment, organisation and management of an organisation. A budget is a form of structure standard as it identifies the resources available to a ward or team. An organisational chart is also a form of structure standard in that it identifies the reporting relationships and responsibilities of people in the organisation. Foundation trusts have standards they must meet for the structure of the board of governors for example, in order to become a foundation trust.

Process standards are standards for the systems in the organisation and often relate to time frames along a pathway; for example, waiting times are a process standard. Steps in a process can also be process standards. There may be a process standard in a care pathway which says that a mammogram must be carried out on any woman presenting with a breast lump before she is referred to a specialist.

Outcome standards involve the end results of care that has been given. Infection rates are one type of outcome standard that not only measures the number of patients that acquire infections but also indirectly measures the effectiveness of infection control techniques. Table 16.1 illustrates the relationship between the three types of standard.

An **indicator** is a tool used to measure the performance of structure, process and outcome standards. Indicators should be measurable, objective and based on current knowledge or best practice. For example, one of the indicators published by the Healthcare Commission for mental health trusts for 2008-09 was that there was a follow-up within seven days for all mental health service users who are on an enhanced care programme approach who were discharged following a spell in hospital. This indicator is specific, measurable and objective, and

Table 16.1 The relationship between the three types of standard

	Structure standards	Process standards	Outcome standards
Infection control	There are alcohol gel dispensers in all entrances to wards	Visitors use the alcohol gel on entering and leaving the ward	MRSA and *C. difficile* rates are reduced
Falls	Handrails are available in all toilet and bath areas	All patients have a falls risk assessment done within 24 hours of admission	Falls are reduced

is related to research indicating that mental health service users are at greater risk of suicide following an acute admission.

Indicators from the Care Quality Commission are under development and do not as yet contain enough specific and measurable criteria to be considered a true indicator. For example, the *Operating framework* document published by the Healthcare Commission in 2008-09 (DoH, 2008c) contained several indicators related to patient experience. The indicator simply said that all trusts were expected to obtain feedback from patients about their experience of care. As it stands this indicator could potentially be met by asking a very few patients one question: 'Was your experience of care good or bad?' Clearly the Commission wishes to encourage all trusts to have a comprehensive and meaningful patient experience survey process, but because it is a new standard, the indicator needs to be further defined.

Data collection

A quality improvement programme needs a system for collecting data about the standards and indicators it is striving to meet. The data collection should be carefully linked to the standard or indicator. For example, data about patient experience are best collected by interviewing patients or carers or by giving patients a questionnaire to complete. However, if the organisation wishes to track infection rates, it is not appropriate to use a survey method: it is much better to get the data straight from the microbiology lab where infections are recorded. Potential sources of data that can influence quality management are:

- surveys of patients, carers and staff;
- laboratory data such as infection rates;
- incident reports (see below);
- complaints;
- admission, discharge, length of stay and other service usage data;
- clinical audit.

Data analysis and benchmarking

Once indicators are identified and data collected, the data are analysed. Data analysis is the process of making sense of the data within the context. For example, a trust may fail to meet a waiting time target for a period of one month. During data analysis it is important to consider the circumstances in which the failure occurred. Situational factors such as higher than normal occupancy due to a flu epidemic can explain a short-term failure to admit and treat surgical patients. However, if there are no unusual situations that explain the failure, it may be important to look at the system for bed management or waiting list management. **Benchmarking**, or comparing data with other reliable sources internally and externally, is a very useful process in determining best practice. Benchmarking against previous data from within the organisation can reveal whether improvements are progressing as planned. Benchmarking against national standards such as those within National Service Frameworks can also help teams and organisations to decide where resources need to be channelled and where improvement activities in the future need to be undertaken.

Action planning

The final component of an effective quality management programme is action planning. This step is where decisions are made about changes to processes and procedures that will correct deficits in quality.

Clinical audit is a process for systematically investigating an aspect of clinical care or a course of care. It can be used to evaluate a process standard such as whether or not care plans are completed in the time frame outlined in the policy, or to assess clinical outcomes such as wound healing or weight loss in elderly people in hospital. Audit can be retrospective or concurrent. A **retrospective audit** is conducted after a patient's discharge and involves examining records of a large number of cases. Often the patient's entire course of care is evaluated and comparisons made across cases. The use of care pathways provides a process standard by which care across a large group of patients with similar diagnoses can be compared and improved. Recommendations for change can be based on the experiences of many patients with similar care problems as well as on the spectrum of care considered.

A **concurrent audit** is conducted during the patient's course of care; it examines the care being given to achieve a desired outcome in the patient's health and evaluates the care activities being provided. Changes can be made if patient outcomes so indicate.

Systematic process improvement

Systematic process improvement is a term used for a collection of methods for measuring performance and designing the most efficient and effective set of steps to achieve a result. Most methods have been developed in industries such as manufacturing and later adopted to health care. Process improvement methods such as Total Quality Management (TQM), Continuous Quality Improvement (CQI) and Six Sigma/Lean Thinking all intend to eliminate waste, delay and unnecessary steps that fail to add value to the customer so that quality improves and resources are saved.

Systematic process improvement systems share many of the same principles:

- Eliminate steps in the process that do not add value to the final result. In other words, everything we do should have a clear and positive impact on the final outcome, in terms of either clinical effectiveness or patient experience.
- Define quality from the patient's perspective. The process is not for the convenience of the professional, but for the benefit of the patient.
- Set standards and measure against those standards.
- Use data, not opinion, to inform the process improvement.

Systematic process improvement methods use a four-step model illustrated in Figure 16.1 called the PDCA model. The original idea dates back to early work by Deming in the early

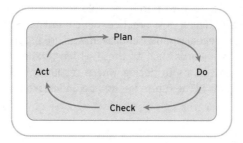

Figure 16.1 The PDCA cycle.
From *Improving Quality Performance*, by P. Schroeder, 1994, St Louis: Mosby.

1950s. He advocated the plan, do, check, act steps so that at every stage of process improvement there is a clear series of actions that lead forward.

There are many practical applications in nursing for systematic process improvement. Take, for example, health visiting. Traditionally in many areas, the health visitor would visit new mothers at home without an appointment. The reasoning for this was sound: it was envisioned that health visitors would get a better insight into the family with unannounced visits. Whilst the reasoning may be sound, practically speaking, many new mothers are now extremely mobile, taking their newborn babies with them in the car and on the bus to do their daily activities. Showing up at a family home unannounced carries the risk of a wasted visit. Most health visitors now make appointments for home visits or contact the mother on the day so as to ensure the visit is productive. The health visitor can still conduct unannounced visits if she has concern about the family.

One of the important roles for a ward manager/team leader is to be looking for opportunities to improve the way things are done. Much of what is done in health care is done because it has always been done that way. When patients are in hospital, we tend to serve all three meals within eight hours, not because this is best nutritionally but because it is most convenient for the catering staff. There are a number of appreciative questions (see Chapter 10) that a ward manager can use when improving the process of care:

- 'If you were the patient, what would you want?'
- 'If we were to start from scratch without any of the existing constraints, what would we design?'
- 'How can we do this better, meaning better in the patient's eyes?'

Fostering innovation

Systematic process improvement methods all involve a commitment to measure performance against set standards. If the organisation embraces these systems to such an extent that all variance is discouraged, then innovation is also suppressed (Harris and Zeisler, 2002). Improvement in the quality of care may have been sacrificed at the expense of innovative ideas and processes. Ultimately, then, organisations fail to allow input, become stagnant and cease to be effective. This is the danger of all living systems that depend on outside input for survival. This is not to say that quality systems are not essential. They are. Organisations must find ways to foster creativity and innovation without compromising quality management.

Risk management

Risk management is a system of actions intended to identify evaluate and take corrective action against potential risks that could lead to the injury of patients, staff or visitors, or harm to the organisation. Risk management is problem-focused, whereas quality management is a prevention-focused approach. Risk management is a planned programme of loss prevention and liability control and it is an essential component of a quality management programme. Risk management is an ongoing daily programme of detection education and intervention.

A risk management programme

A risk management programme involves all people that work in the organisation. It is an organisation-wide programme, with the board of directors' approval and input from all departments. The programme must have high-level commitment, including that of the chief executive officer and the board of directors.

A risk management programme:

- identifies potential risks for accident, injury, or financial loss. A risk assessment is undertaken to identify potential risks, their likelihood of occurrence and the potential consequences. Formal and informal communication with all organisational departments and inspection of facilities are essential to identify problem areas;
- reviews current organisation-wide monitoring systems (incident reports, audits, committee minutes, complaints, patient surveys), evaluates completeness and determines additional systems needed to provide the factual data essential for risk management;
- analyses the frequency, severity and causes of general categories and specific types of event causing injury or adverse outcomes to patients, staff or visitors. To plan risk intervention strategies, it is necessary to estimate the possible loss associated with the various types of incidents;
- reviews and appraises safety and risk aspects of patient care procedures and new programme;
- monitors laws and regulations related to patient safety, consent and care;
- eliminates or reduces risks as much as possible;
- identifies needs for patient, family and staff education suggested by all of the foregoing and implementing the appropriate educational programmes;
- evaluates the results of a risk management programme;
- provides periodic reports.

Most organisations have a risk manager or risk management department. The structure supporting the function or risk management may vary, but somewhere there will be a group or individual whose job it is to take responsibility for the overall planning and decision-making that are involved in risk management. A risk manager should be appointed to manage the day-to-day operation of the programme.

The National Patient Safety Agency

The **National Patient Safety Agency** (NPSA) is a special health authority set up in 2001 following the recommendations in the report into patient safety by the Chief Medical Officer called *An organisation with a memory* (DoH, 2000) and the follow-on report *Building a safer NHS for patients* (2001). The NPSA's role is to improve the safety of patients by promoting a culture of reporting and learning from patient safety incidents. An **incident** is defined as 'times when things go wrong in the NHS that did or could have harmed a patient'.

One of the key findings of the Chief Medical Officer's reports is that most incidents occur due to problems with the system, not the individual. Studies have shown that the best way to reduce error rates is to target the underlying system failures, rather than take action against individual members of staff. It is vital that we dispel two myths that still persist in health care and were identified by Lucian Leape at the Harvard School of Public Health:

- The **perfection myth**: if people try hard enough, they will not make errors.
- The **punishment myth**: if we punish people when they make errors, they will make fewer of them.

Research is clear: the error itself is almost never the problem. The system is the problem, and focusing on improving that, through approaches such as process improvement, is much more productive than focusing on the individual.

The NPSA has established the National Reporting and Learning System which collects data on incidents and near misses that is intended to help NHS organisations to:

- identify trends and patterns of avoidable incidents and underlying causes;
- develop models of good practice and solutions at a national level;
- improve working practices in the NHS organisations locally through feedback and training;
- support ongoing education and learning (National Patient Safety Agency, 2004).

The NPSA (2004) identifies seven steps to patient safety:

1. Build a safety culture – create a culture that is open and fair, and promotes accountability without blame.
2. Lead and support your staff – create a clear and strong focus on safety throughout the organisation.
3. Integrate your risk management activities – develop systems and processes to manage your risks and identify and assess things that go wrong.
4. Promote reporting – make sure that staff can easily report incidents.
5. Involve and communicate with patients and the public – develop ways to communicate openly and listen to patients.
6. Learn and share safety lessons – encourage staff to use root cause analysis to learn how and why incidents occur.
7. Implement solutions – embed lessons through changes to practice, processes and systems.

In 2008, the NPSA held a seminar for organisations with a consistently high level of incident reporting where representatives came together to share their experiences. These organisations have a better safety record than others, contrary to what you might associate with a high reporting rate. Strong messages came out of the seminar and included the following:

- Give feedback to staff – acknowledge and praise reporting, share experiences in newsletters and bulletins, share stories and ensure reports are cascaded through the organisation.
- Focus on learning – all reports should focus on what was learned and how systems have changed as a result.
- Engage front-line staff through training, safety champions and highly visible safety messages.
- Make it easy to report.
- Make reporting matter – implement strong and visible safety leadership, bring incident reporting together with other data and make changes visible.

It is important to remember that it is the staff, with their daily patient contact, who actually implement a risk management programme.

Incident Reporting Form

Complete in black ink using BLOCK CAPITALS
Use a separate form for each person and each incident
Please note that the information you give could form the basis of legal action
Completing and signing this form does not constitute an admission of liability of any
kind, either by the person making the report or any other person.
Please record facts only

IR1 Number:

Datix Reference
Number:

1 Where and when
- Where did the incident happen

CMT
Speciality
Directorate
Location - e.g. Bedside/Toilet
Ward/Dept/Other

- When did the incident happen
Date   /   /   Time   24 hour clock

2 Person involved/affected (see notes)
- Type of person involved/affected
EITHER ☐ Member of staff
Occupation
OR ☐ In-patient   ☐ A&E patient
☐ Out-patient
Patient Number
Patient Ethnic Code (see notes)
OR ☐ Visitor
OR ☐ Contractor
OR ☐ Other please specify below

- Details of person involved/affected
Name
☐ Male   ☐ Female
Date of birth   /   /
Address

Postcode
Phone (home)
Phone (work)

3 The incident (see notes)
- Type of incident (see notes)
Select type from front cover
(e.g. clinical, security, staff)
- Stage of care (see notes)
Select type from front cover
Other (please specify):

- Description of what happened (facts only)

If necessary, continue on separate sheet
located at back of IR1 book
- Has patient/relative been informed of incident?
☐ Yes   ☐ No
- Was any equipment involved?
☐ Yes   ☐ No
Details of equipment involved:
Type (e.g. infusion pump)
Make
Model
Equipment number
Lot/Batch number
Has equipment been sent for repair?
☐ Yes   ☐ No
All parts must be retained until instructions are received
authorising disposal.

3 Medication Related Incident
- Drug Name
- Correct Drug
☐ Yes   ☐ No   ☐ Not applicable
- Correct form administered?
☐ Yes   ☐ No   ☐ Not applicable
- Correct Route?
☐ Yes   ☐ No   ☐ Not applicable
- Dose Administered
- Correct Dose
☐ Yes   ☐ No

4 Impact on individual (if any)
- Severity of injury (use Table 1)
☐ None ☐ Low ☐ Moderate ☐ Severe
☐ Death
If severe or death inform line manager immediately
Part of body injured:
☐ Left ☐ Right ☐ N/A
Injury sustained (e.g. bruise/laceration)

RIDDOR reportable   ☐ No
☐ Yes
5 Treatment (if any)
☐ None required   ☐ A&E/Minor injuries
☐ First Aid   ☐ Occupational Health
☐ Seen by Doctor   ☐ Admitted to Hospital
☐ Advised to see GP ☐ Observations
6 Staff absence
☐ None   ☐ 3 – 10 days
☐ Less than 3 days ☐ More than 10 days
7 Witnesses (see notes)
*Name
Address

Phone
Name
Address

Phone
*state designation of staff
8 Action taken to reduce recurrence

9 Risk Evaluation Score (refer to tables 1 & 2 opposite)

10 Signature
- Person completing the form
Signed   Date   /   /

Print Name
Job Title
Phone
- Forward both copies of completed form to
Line Manager
11 Management action

Refer to Table 3 on inside cover

Further action planned

12 Lessons learned
Leave blank if IR2 to be completed

13 Signature - Manager
                    Date   /   /

Print Name
Job Title
Phone
Final risk evaluation score:
- What to do with this form:

Stage of care	
AAT	Access, Appointment, Admission, Transfer, Discharge Related Issues
ABUSE	Abuse, Violent, Disruptive or Self-harming behaviour
ACCID	Accident that may result in personal injury
ANAES	Anaesthesia related incidents
ASSESS	Clinical assessment (investigations, images and lab tests)
CCCP	Consent, Confidentiality, Communication Issues
DIAG	Diagnosis, failed or delayed
INFO	Patient information (records, documents, test results, scans)
LABOUR	Labour or Delivery
MEEDEV	Medical device/equipment
MEDIC	Medication
MONIT	Implementation of care or ongoing monitoring/review
OTHER	Please specify in description
TMTPRO	Treatment, Procedure

Patient related	
	Not Patient Related
ABUSE	Abusive, Violent, Disruptive
ACCID	Accident that may result in personal injury
FINANC	Financial Loss
INFRA	Infrastructure or Resources
SECRTY	Security

Figure 16.2 A sample incident report form.
Adapted from *Incident Reporting and Investigating Policy*, p. 17, Leeds Teaching Hospitals NHS Trust, Leeds

Incident reports

Accurate and comprehensive reporting in the incident report is essential to inform the organisation so that learning can take place, and problems that may be the subject of legal issues can be identified in advance. Incident reporting is often the nurse's responsibility. Reluctance to report incidents is usually due to fear of the consequences. This fear can be alleviated by:

- holding staff education programmes that emphasise objective reporting;
- omitting inflammatory words and judgemental statements;
- having a clear understanding that the purposes of the incident reporting process are documentation and follow-up;
- never using the report, under any circumstances, for disciplinary action.

A reportable incident should include any unexpected or unplanned occurrence that affects or could potentially affect a patient, family member or staff. The report is only as effective as the form on which it is reported (Figure 16.2), so attention should be paid to the adequacy of the form as well as to the data required.

The NPSA identifies six steps in managing incidents that they call the circle of safety (Figure 16.3):

1. *Reporting.* Managing safety and risk starts with the report. These are usually reviewed by the ward manager before being sent to the risk management department.
2. *Analysis.* Incidents are analysed using root cause analysis where possible and comparisons with other incidents undertaken to identify trends and commonalities.
3. *Solution development.* Solutions that address the root cause of the incident are developed.
4. Implementation of the solution.
5. Audit and monitoring.
6. Feedback to the department that reported the incident and more widely to the organisation of the lessons learned.

Figure 16.3 The circle of safety.
From National Patient Safety Agency, 2004

Risk assessment

Risk management first involves a risk assessment which has three parts: the type of risk, the likelihood of the risk actually occurring and the potential consequences if the event actually happens. Most organisations will then make a risk register that records the potential risks they have identified. This work is usually done by a risk management professional, but the ward manager/team leader may be asked to identify risks for the register. Figure 16.4 shows an example of a risk register.

Role of the ward manager/team leader in risk management

The ward manager/team leader plays a key role in the success of any risk management programme. Managers can reduce risk by helping their staff view health and illness from the patient's perspective. Usually, the staff's understanding of quality differs from the patient's expectations and perceptions. By understanding the meaning of the course of illness to the patient and the family, the nurse will manage risk better because that understanding can enable the nurse to individualise patient care. This individualised attention produces respect and, in turn, reduces risk.

A patient incident or a patient's or family's expression of dissatisfaction regarding care indicates not only some slippage in quality of care but also potential liability. A distraught, dissatisfied, complaining patient is a high risk; a satisfied patient or family is a low risk. A risk management programme should therefore emphasise a personal approach. Many claims are filed because of a breakdown in communication between the health care provider and the patient. In many instances, after an incident or bad outcome, a quick visit or call from an organisation's representative to the patient or family can soothe tempers and clarify misinformation.

Prompt attention and care by the ward manager protects the patients involved and supports staff members involved. Once an incident has occurred, the important factors in successful risk management are:

- recognition of the incident;
- quick follow-up and action;
- personal contact and compassionate attention.

It is estimated that 90 per cent of patients' concerns can and should be handled at the ward or team level. When that first line of communication breaks down, however, the ward manager team leader needs a resource – usually the risk manager.

Handling complaints

Handling a patient's or family member's complaints stemming from an incident can be very difficult. These confrontations are often highly emotional; the patient or family member must

	Consequence score (severity level) and examples of descriptors				
	1	2	3	4	5
Domains	Negligible	Minor	Moderate	Major	Catastrophic
Impact on the safety of patients, staff or public (physical or psychological harm)	Minimal injury requiring no/minimal intervention or treatment	Minor injury or illness requiring minor intervention	Moderate injury requiring professional intervention	Major injury leading to long-term incapacity or disability	Incident leading to death, multiple permanent injuries or irreversible health effects

Likelihood score	1	2	3	4	5
	Rare	Unlikely	Possible	Likely	Almost certain
Descriptor	This will probably never happen/recur	Do not expect it to happen or recur but it is possible that it may do so	Might happen or occur occasionally	Will probably happen/recur but it is not a persisting issue	Will undoubtedly happen/recur possibly often

Risk scoring = consequence × likelihood

	Likelihood				
Consequence	1	2	3	4	5
	Rare	Unlikely	Possible	Likely	Almost certain
5. Catastrophic	5	10	15	20	25
4. Major	4	8	12	16	20
3. Moderate	3	6	9	12	15
2. Minor	2	4	6	8	10
1. Negligible	1	2	3	4	5

Figure 16.4 Consequence, likelihood and risk scoring.

Source: Risk Matrix for Managers, National Patient Safety Agency, 2008.

be calmed down and yet have their concerns satisfied. Sometimes just an opportunity to re-lease the anger or emotion is all that is needed.

The first step is to listen to the person, to hear concerns and to help defuse the situation. Often the person making the complaint simply wants an opportunity to express their concern and to feel listened to. They also want to ensure that what happened to them will not happen to others. Arguing or interrupting only increases the person's anger or emotion. After the pa-tient or family member has had their say, the manager can then attempt to solve the problem

Manager's Checklist for Risk Management and Complaint Handling

The ward manager/team leader is responsible for:

☐ Encouraging reporting and a culture of safety.

☐ The initial investigation of any complaint or incident to determine the nature and circumstances in which the complaint happened.

☐ Completing and forwarding the report on the complaint investigation in the time frames specified in your organisation's policy.

☐ Completing audits and gathering and analysing data to determine whether an incident is part of a pattern or an isolated incident.

☐ Providing the results of any audits or discussions with staff to appropriate people.

☐ Educating staff as appropriate.

☐ Giving feedback to and supporting staff involved in any incident or complaint.

☐ Communicating and cooperating with any other person or department involved.

by asking what is expected in the form of a solution. The manager or other organisational representative should then explain what can and cannot be done and try to agree a solution. It is important to be specific. Offering vague solutions (e.g. 'Everything will be taken care of') may only lead to more problems later on if expectations as to solution and timing differ.

Handling a complaint without punishing a staff member is a delicate situation. The manager must determine what happened in order to prevent another occurrence, but using an incident report for discipline might result in fewer or erroneous incident reports in the future. Talking to a staff member about a complaint is best handled sensitively using the guidelines for handling a challenging conversation in Chapter 6.

A caring attitude

The ward manager/team leader is instrumental in building a culture of safety and quality that contributes to a low-risk, high-quality environment. One of the most important ways to reduce risk is to instil a sense of confidence in both patients and families by paying attention to the elements that instil confidence in care. The Office of the Chief Nursing Officer published a report on an initiative to determine the elements that create confidence in care. This confidence is created environmentally and interpersonally.

Examples of environmental factors include cleanliness, attention to patients' privacy, an orderly-looking unit and minimal social conversations in front of patients. Interpersonal confidence factors include the nature of the interaction between staff, good teamwork, personalised care and efficiency. Importantly, the study showed that the quality of leadership and management on the ward was important. Patients wanted to know that someone was in charge and that they would act on the patient's behalf when needed. The person in charge should be visible and approachable, taking pride in their ward and 'running a tight ship'. When in charge, a brief visit to each patient can be reassuring (DoH, 2008a).

The nurse manager needs to foster the attitude that any mistake that does occur is perceived as an opportunity to learn, to improve a system or a process rather than to punish an individual. If the nurse manager has developed a patient-focused atmosphere in which patients believe their best interests are a priority, the potential for risk will be reduced.

What you know now

- Quality management is the method by which performance of care is evaluated and improved.
- The principles of quality management in health care include a focus on the patient, empowerment of employees and the collective work of the team.
- A quality improvement programme is a prevention-focused approach that provides the basis for managing risk.
- Successful quality management improves patient care, reduces liability and is cost-effective.
- The key ingredients in a successful risk management programme are an organised programme of incident reporting, review and follow-up and, most importantly, an environment that the patient and family perceive as friendly and caring.
- The ward manager/team leader's support of the risk management programme is essential to its success.
- Risk management programmes help to reduce costs and demonstrate the organisation's concern for its patients, visitors and employees.

Questions to challenge you

1. Do you know what standards and outcome measures are used in the organisation where you work or have your clinical experiences? How are the data handled? Are they shared with employees?

2. What comparable groups, both internal and external, are used for benchmarking performance in your organisation?

3. Universities also use benchmarking. What institutions does your college or university use to benchmark its performance? Find out.

4. Imagine that an organisation is debating between several quality management programmes. What would you recommend? Why?

5. Have you, a family member or a friend ever had a serious problem in a health care organisation that resulted in injury? What was the outcome? Is this how you would have handled it? What will you do in the future in a similar situation?

References

Department of Health (DoH) (2000) *An Organisation with a Memory: Report of an expert group on learning from adverse events in the NHS.* London: Department of Health.

Department of Health (DoH) (2001) *Building a Safer NHS for Patients: Implementing an organisation with a memory.* London: Department of Health.

Department of Health (DoH) (2008a) *High Quality Care for All: NHS next stage review final report.* London: Department of Health.

Department of Health (DoH) (2008b) *Care Quality Commission.* Available at http://www.dh.gov.uk.

Department of Health (DoH) (2008c) *The Operating Framework for the NHS in England.* London: Department of Health.

Harris, S. D. and Zeisler, S. (2002) Weak signals: detecting the next big thing. *The Futurist,* **36**(6), 21-28.

National Patient Safety Agency (2004) *Seven Steps to Patient Safety: A guide for NHS staff.* Available at http://www.npsa.nhs.uk/sevensteps.

National Patient Safety Agency (2008) Act on reporting. *Briefing,* June, Issue 161.

Chapter 17
Information Management

Key terms

Information systems
Information technology
Information management
Electronic staff records

Data Protection Act
Freedom of Information Act
Point-of-care devices

Introduction

Information management is an increasing part of any ward manager/team leader's role. Our society has moved into an age of technology and health care is no exception. Rapid advances in technology and communication management have altered approaches to health care. Computers can store vast amounts of information to facilitate communication about patients across the health system, support teaching and research, and connect people from around the world. This chapter introduces the various health care technology systems that are in use or in development in the UK, and the role of the manager in the safe and ethical use of information.

Information systems

Information systems are complex automated systems that are integrated through networked computers to process data in order to answer questions, solve problems or make decisions. **Information technology**, the machines and applications that provide the infrastructure for information systems, can link separate entities into a seamless system of information available to all users, with the potential to eliminate paper records in the future. **Information management** is the collection, storage and analysis of information needed for a specific purpose such as patient care. Nurses have become information managers as part of their everyday work by creating records of the care they deliver and by communicating with others.

Information technology in the NHS

The first modern strategy for information technology, *Information for health* (DoH, 1998), committed the NHS to developing life-long electronic health records for patients, around-the-clock online access to patient records for clinicians and information about clinical practice for all. When this visionary document was published, the NHS was far behind the rest of business and industry in its use of technology. The technology that was in use was often outdated and, because there was no consistency in hardware or software applications, there was no hope of an integrated systems approach to delivering the vision (NHS Connecting for Health, 2008).

In 2001 Derek Wanless, a commissioner with the Statistics Commission, was asked to examine future trends affecting the UK health service in the following two decades. The report *Securing our future health: taking a long-term view* (Wanless Report: DoH, 2002a) made several key recommendations:

- A doubling of the spending on IT and protecting those funds from being used for anything else
- Stringent, centrally managed national standards for data and IT
- A national programme for IT implementation in the NHS.

The Department of Health published its new strategy for developing IT in the NHS, *Delivering 21st century IT support for the NHS: a national strategic programme* in June 2002 (DoH, 2002b). This strategy laid the foundations for the National Programme for IT (NPfIT). In 2004, the creation of a new organisation was announced combining responsibility for the delivery of the national programme for IT with the management of IT-related functions in the NHS Information Authority, resulting in the creation of NHS Connecting for Health. In 2006 the NPfIT Local Ownership Programme was commissioned which gave strategic health authorities and primary care trusts the opportunity to define local priorities for IT supported by NHS Connecting for Health.

NHS Connecting for Health

Since 2008 NHS Connecting for Health has been responsible and accountable for all nationally coordinated major IT programmes across the NHS. NHS Connecting for Health is connecting 8,500 general practices and their respective community services with 300 hospitals. It will enable patients to have easier access to their own personal health and care information. It is envisioned that NHS Connecting for Health will continue to evolve responsibility for national IT projects and the list of programmes it currently oversees will continue to expand. Here are the current projects within the national programme as of 2008 (NHS Connecting for Health, 2008):

1. *Choose and Book* is an electronic booking service that enables primary care team members to make an initial outpatient appointment at a date, time and place of a patient's choosing. This supports achievement of the goals to reduce the time lag between referral and appointment and gives patients choice over where they are seen.

2. *Data Accreditation and PRIMIS+* –in 2006 data standards for primary care were published to allow general practices to demonstrate that data held on GP systems were fit for sharing. Data accreditation to this standard is required before the patient's data can be sent from the practices to the Spine. The Spine is a central database that stores summary care records which contain important health information such as allergies, medications and chronic conditions. PRIMIS+ is a national contract available to GPs to get help in improving data quality and therefore achieving accreditation.

3. *Direct enhanced services* are special services or activities to support GP practices to take up information management and to be properly equipped with the skills and knowledge to take advantage of new services such as Choose and Book, electronic prescriptions and the care records service.

4. *The Electronic Prescription Service* will enable electronic prescriptions, including repeat prescriptions, to be generated, received and, once dispensed, sent to the reimbursement agency for payment. Initially it will use barcodes to activate payment when the prescription is filled, and eventually it will use electronic signatures. This means that repeat prescriptions no longer need to be individually signed; they can be done in batches, and the patient can simply go directly to the pharmacy rather than the GP practice. This system should eliminate a number of prescribing errors and improve patient safety and convenience.

5. *GP2GP Electronic Records Transfer* enables patient's electronic health records to be transferred directly from one practice to another when the patient moves or changes doctors. This is already well under way.

6. *GP Systems of Choice* (GPSoC) allows GPs to choose between clinical systems offered by their local system provider or to remain with their current system and to undergo upgrading as they become available.

7. *National Network for the NHS* (N3) replaced NHS net for email communication. This new system is faster, is more reliable, has better service provisions than the older system, and is less costly. The new system is also developing a method to merge voice and image transmission thereby allowing multimedia conferencing and virtual presence (where the clinician and the patient are connected by computer and can see and hear each other in real time).

8. *NHS Care Records Service* (NHS CRS) will allow a patient's detailed health records to be securely shared between different parts of the local NHS, such as GP practice to hospital, and will also enable a summary care record to be available to authorised NHS staff treating them anywhere in England.

9. *NHS Classifications Service* is the definitive source of coding guidance to NHS coding professionals, and is meant to assist commissioners of services in interpreting the data they receive from suppliers.

10. *NHS Number* is fundamental to the NPfIT in that in order for the system to work properly, each patient must have a unique identifier.

11. *NHSmail* is a secure email and directory service linking the whole of the NHS. This will allow staff to keep the same email address throughout their NHS career, send and receive emails and safely exchange patient information, send faxes, share diaries, and create and use distribution lists.

12. *Personal Demographics Service* (PDS) is the national electronic database of demographic details. It allows health care professionals to readily identify a patient and their latest personal details.

13. *Picture Archiving and Communications System* (PACS) allows X-rays and scans to be managed digitally and allows hospitals to capture, view and store these images electronically. This should result in faster, better-quality images.

14. *Quality Management and Analysis System* (QMAS) supports the Quality Outcome Framework and captures and analyses the data against quality indicators.

15. *Smartcards* regulate the access an individual staff member can have to the NHS Care Records Service and other systems and services. Each staff member must be registered and the smartcards used with a password. This provides additional record security and an audit trail of record access.

16. *SNOMED* (Systematised NOmenclature MEDicine Clinical Terms) will replace the current coding system to allow more complex information to be gathered.

17. *Spine Directory Service* (SDS) is the main information source about NHS registered users and services. It provides security and information support.

© Crown copyright

Electronic staff records

The NHS recently completed a transition to **electronic staff records** (ESR), a single national system that enables a consistent approach to all aspects of staff administration, human resources, payroll, recruitment, work structures, absence management and training and development records. The system will link to other NHS systems such as pensions. When it is fully functional in all areas, staff will be able to review and update their own records, request training courses and design an online personal development programme. The organisation benefits from the information the system can generate which helps in recruitment decisions, setting budgets, staffing establishment control, changes in posts and tracking staff expenditure.

Ward managers and team leaders have access to sensitive staff records as part of their role. They will have personal data on staff such as addresses, home phone numbers, salary information, grading and personal circumstances such as family information. They also have access to employment history, staff review information, disciplinary actions and performance improvement plans. Whether kept on paper or electronically, these records must be kept strictly confidential to the staff member involved unless the staff member agrees to those records being shared.

Your organisation will have policies on providing references for staff seeking a change of role or moving to a new organisation. It is important that these policies are followed. Whilst it is tempting to share your experience of working with a staff member informally with another manager, this can put you or the staff member in a difficult position. If the member of staff is disadvantaged in obtaining employment because of something you said, there can be serious repercussions. Always take advice from human resources before you share any staff information.

The Data Protection Act

The **Data Protection Act** came into force in 1998. Its main purpose was to protect the fundamental rights of individuals against unwarranted use of personal information. Data protection does not just relate to electronic records: it relates to all records, including patients, staff and organisational functions such as meetings and committees.

Eight specific principles apply under the Data Protection Act and these will have been translated into the practical policies for data protection in your organisation (DoH, 2009a):

1. Personal data must be processed fairly and lawfully.

2. Personal data shall be obtained only for the specified purpose and no one else.

3. Personal data shall be adequate, relevant and not excessive for the purposes.

4. Personal data shall be accurate and kept up to date.

5. Personal data shall not be kept for longer than necessary for the purpose specified.

6. Personal data shall be processed in accordance with the rights of the individual.

7. Appropriate technical and organisational measures shall be taken to prevent unauthorised or unlawful access to personal data and to protect against accidental loss or destruction.

8. Personal data shall not be transferred abroad unless the country receiving the data has protection comparable to this Act.

In practical terms this means that ward managers and team leaders have to be particularly aware of the protection and use of personal information to which they and their staff have access. When patient records are fully automated, and smartcards are in use across the NHS, limiting access to patient records and tracking who is accessing the records will be greatly improved. Until then the following practices are suggested:

- Only staff members who are currently caring for a patient have the right to access their health records. This means that even if a patient has been in your service previously, but is now being seen elsewhere, you have no right to access their records.

- Similarly, only people who have managerial or supervisory responsibility for staff, or who are authorised as a part of human resource management, should have access to staff records.

- Follow your organisation's policies about record protection. This may include locking away patient records when an office is unmanned or closed.

- Any records on staff such as personal data, phone numbers, staff reviews and letters should be kept locked up.

- Do not take information on patients or staff away from the workplace unless absolutely necessary, and if you do, follow the organisational policy on encryption or other security carefully.

Freedom of Information Act

Patients now have the right to see their health records on request under the **Freedom of Information Act**. There will be a policy in your organisation that usually requires the request to be in writing and approved by someone whose responsibility it is to manage those requests. The patients do not have the right simply to pick up their records and look at them without going through this process. It is important that records are stored securely.

Staff also can request access to all information kept on them. This makes it important that staff records are accurate and non-judgemental. The policies on staff access to their records varies between organisations, but the rule of thumb is that staff should be given copies of all reviews and letters pertaining to them at the time, and that there should be no surprises in their human resource file or the staff review files kept in the manager's possession (DoH, 2009b).

Obstacles to using information technology

Although information technology offers many benefits, there are also a number of obstacles. One is user resistance, including 'technophobia', a dislike or distrust of computers, a lack of keyboard or web skills, a belief that computers take too much time, lack of equipment, previous negative experiences and resistance to change. As hardware and software continue to improve and become more user-friendly, user resistance diminishes somewhat. Widespread use of computers and the Internet outside of work also improves user ability and comfort in using the technology.

Point-of-care devices such as hand-held terminals and laptop computers allow nurses and others to access information and record care electronically. Pilots of wireless and remote devices have taken place in the UK, and plans are evolving to make the technology more widespread. As the programmes that support electronic record-keeping, such as the electronic patient record and the National Network for the NHS, progress, making access to the system from patients' homes and clinics will follow suit. These devices make it even more important that data protection through encryption, password protection and secure wireless systems is reliable and convenient (NHS Connection for Health, 2008). For examples of projects that have won awards in the NHS, see the NHS Leadership for Health Informatics Accolade Scheme (NHS Connecting for Health, 2007).

Patient care technologies

Biomedical technologies continue to expand, specifically offering less invasive examinations (e.g. imaging) and interventions (e.g. lasers). In addition, nanotechnology, genetics, replacement organs and tissues, targeted medications and vaccines are just a few of the many patient care technologies in development or in use today. Sensors that monitor bodily functions as well as the effects of treatments can also monitor room conditions.

Minimally invasive surgery in the operating room has proved to be an advantage to nurses (Perry, 2003). The integration of technology with surgical procedures has resulted in a more egalitarian setting because nurses have their hands on the technology as much as surgeons do. The environment is now more peer-to-peer, according to Perry.

Telehealth is the use of telecommunications technology to provide health care at a distance. Medical and nursing care can be delivered using various video, audio and communications technologies. Radiological, visual and audio examinations and even tele-surgery are now possible (Johnson, 2002). Information can be exchanged between providers and patients in real time or they can communicate by voice mail or email.

Technology in education and research

Educational applications

Distance learning

The earliest use of technology in distance learning occurred through the use of video and/or audio connections. Today distance education is online, using web-based technology that may include video and audio applications. Most web-based learning is asynchronous, that is, exchanges do not occur in real time. This is a tremendous advantage to both instructors and students, allowing them to access and respond at their convenience.

With online instruction, instructors provide lectures, case studies and sometimes clinical slides, graphics or video; monitor discussion; and answer questions. Students can register for classes, order textbooks and supplementary material, use the library, submit assignments and take tests, all from a location far from campus.

In addition, other forms of computer-assisted technology can be used to teach nurses, students, patients or carers essential information about their conditions, treatments and care. This technology uses CD-ROMs or the Internet and typically involves tutorials or simulations, allowing individuals to interact with the system at their own pace. Other applications useful in education are graphics packages that allow the use of clip, live or graphic art to develop figures and presentation packages, such as PowerPoint, to develop slides and overheads.

Simulation

The increasing sophistication of simulators to mimic human conditions and responses is revolutionising clinical education. Simulators allow students to practise on computerised models, repeating techniques as often as necessary without jeopardising live patients.

Technology in research

Computerised literature searches have radically changed the time involved in searching the literature for research studies. Whatever is not available online is often available for purchase as a download or a document that can be mailed or faxed. Databases make subject selection accurate and rapid, and contact with subjects can sometimes be accomplished by email. Statistical packages speed analysis of data.

Consumer health information

With the expansion of the Internet and the accompanying growth of computer hardware and software and communications technology, consumers can easily access unprecedented amounts of information about any subject of interest, including health information. The accuracy of the information is, however, unknown, and consumers may be unable to interpret information correctly. Nevertheless it is common today to have an informed consumer who is able, at the least, to pose pointed questions.

The paternalistic system of the past is fast disappearing as consumers become partners in their care. All health care professionals are challenged to be as current regarding the latest information as their patients are likely to be cognisant of research results. Providers must be prepared to collaborate with their patients in care decisions.

The nurse informatics specialist

Nursing informatics is a growing specialty, combining clinical knowledge and skills with informatics expertise. Nursing informatics supports the work of nurses by integrating science with technology and also supports the work of nurse educators, researchers and administrators. Several universities offer advanced degrees in nursing informatics.

The manager/team leader's role in information management

The nurse manager's responsibilities for information management may include participation in consultation about the local needs for information technology, implementing an information system, preparing and training staff for information technology or patient care technology, and monitoring performance and effectiveness of the technology and systems in use.

The leader's belief in the value of the new technology can help the staff accept the difficult, and sometimes frustrating, process of learning how to use it. Remind staff that the technologies that make their work easier today were once awkward to learn and that learning requires persistence and patience to yield results they desire, such as rapid access to accurate information.

Future trends in health care technology

Technology advances will continue into the future, offering new solutions as well as problems. Voice-input interfaces, virtual reality, robotics, barcodes and augmented technology (computers embedded in a variety of products) are a few examples of future expectations (Turley, 2000).

Just as the Volkswagen Beetle began the automobile age in Europe, so computers have initiated the technology age. Although we may not be able to envision everything that lies ahead, what we do know is that technology will continue to be essential in our lives and in health care.

What you know now

- Information technology helps nurses to care for patients, manage information and records, teach, perform research and communicate.
- Technology supports the collection, sharing and storage of information about patients and staff, facilitates communication and supports clinical care through biotechnology. It is a valuable resource for educating and informing health professionals and the public.
- Knowledgeable consumers are becoming partners with their health care providers.

- Confidentiality and security are major concerns associated with electronic patient records, and policies and practices must conform to the Data Protection Act and be managed within the security arrangements in place.
- The ward manager/team leader may be involved in consultation about local needs, preparing staff for IT implementation and monitoring the effectiveness of the technology.
- Advances in technology and information systems can be anticipated well into the future.

Questions to challenge you

1. What experiences have you had using information technology? What were the problems? Benefits?

2. What biomedical technologies are in use where you work? Are they reliable, easy to use, helpful? Explain. Hint: patient monitors.

3. What obstacles have you seen in using technology? Describe how those could be overcome.

4. How have data protection regulations affected how you or your organisation does its work? Are you/they successful in adhering to the law?

References

Department of Health (DoH) (1998) *Information for Health*. London: Department of Health. Available at http://www.dh.gov.uk/en/Publicationsandstatistics/Lettersandcirculars/Health servicecirculars/DH_4005016.

Department of Health (DoH) (2002a) *Securing Our Future Health: Taking a long-term view*. London: Department of Health.

Department of Health (DoH) (2002b) *Delivering 21st Century IT Support for the NHS: A national strategic programme*. London: Department of Health. Available at http://www.dh.gov.uk/en/Publicationsandstatistics/Publications/PublicationsPolicyAndGuidance/DH_4008227.

Department of Health (DoH) (2009a) *Data Protection Act 1998*. London: Department of Health. Available at http://www.dh.gov.uk/en/Managingyourorganisation/Informationpolicy/Recordsmanagement/DH_4000489.

Department of Health (DoH) (2009b) *Freedom of Information (FOI)*. London: Department of Health. Available at http://www.dh.gov.uk/en/FreedomOfInformation/index.htm.

Johnson, D. (2002) Technology: the telesurgery revolution. *The Futurist*, **36**(1), 6-7.

NHS Connecting for Health (2007) *NHS Leadership for Health Informatics Accolade Scheme 2007*. Available at http://www.connectingforhealth.nhs.uk/newsroom/news-stories/accoladesbrochu.pdf?searchterm=accolade+scheme.

NHS Connecting for Health (2008) *Supporting Transformation: A practical Guide to NHS Connecting for Health.* Available at http://information.connectingforhealth.nhs.uk/prod_images/pdfs/31556.pdf.

Perry, G. (2003) Nurses in the new OR. *Excellence in Clinical Practice,* **4**(3). Available at http://www.nursingsociety.org/publications.

Turley, J. P. (2000) Nursing future: ubiquitous computing, virtual reality and augmented reality. In M. J. Ball, K. J. Hannah, S. K. Newbold and J. V. Douglas (eds), *Nursing Informatics: Where caring and technology meet*, 3rd edn. New York: Springer.

Glossary

A

Accommodating a response to conflict characterised as giving in or giving up: a tactic used when individuals neglect their own concerns in favour of the other person's concerns.

Accountability accepting ownership for results.

Adaptive decisions decisions involving moderately ambiguous problems requiring modification of known and well-defined alternative solutions.

Adjourning the final stage of group development in which a group dissolves after achieving its objectives.

Adult learning theory a theory, described by Knowles, that children and adults learn differently.

Appreciative inquiry a group decision-making technique based on enhancing what is working well and using those strengths to move towards the desired future.

Appreciative questions questions that focus attention on the future, and what is going well, to help people develop more options.

Authority the right to act.

Autocratic leadership a leadership style in which the leader assumes that individuals are motivated by external forces, such as power, authority and need for approval; the leader makes all the decisions and uses coercion, punishment and direction to change followers' behaviour and achieve results.

Avoiding a response to conflict characterised by a failure to either confront the issue or acknowledge that a conflict exists.

B

Benchmarking the process of comparing data with reliable internal and external sources.

Block contract a set amount of money to fund all services, typically based on previous spending.

Brainstorming a decision-making method in which group members meet and generate diverse ideas about the nature, cause, definition or solution to a problem.

Budget a quantitative statement, usually in monetary terms, of the expectations of a defined area of the organisation over a specified period of time in order to manage financial performance.

Budgeting the process of planning and controlling future operations by comparing actual results with planned expectations.

Bureaucracy a term proposed by Max Weber to define the ideal organisation which he believed to be a logically structured, rational and efficient form of organisation.

Bureaucratic leadership a leadership style in which the leader assumes that employees are motivated by external forces. This leader trusts neither followers nor self to make decisions and therefore relies on organisational policies and rules to identify goals and direct work processes.

Burnout the perception that an individual has used up all available energy to perform the job and feels that they don't have enough energy to complete the task.

Business case for recruitment a critical analysis and justification of the need to recruit to a post.

C

Capital budget a component of the budget plan that includes equipment and renovations needed by an organisation in order to meet long-term goals.

Care Quality Commission the inspection and assessment body for health and social care.

Centralised authority decisions are taken by those in executive roles in the organisation and then passed back down the line.

Chain of command the hierarchy of authority and responsibility within the organisation.

Change the process of making something different from what it was.

Change agent one who initiates and manages the change process.

Chaos theory a scientific theory based on quantum mechanics that suggests that the natural world is a self-organising adaptive system.

Charismatic leadership leadership based on valued personal characteristics and beliefs.

Clinical audit a process for systematically investigating an aspect of clinical care.

Clinical governance a governance model wherein clinical professionals have a substantial role in the governance of organisations; in particular they are actively involved in setting quality standards for patient care.

Clinical supervision an activity that brings skilled supervisors and practitioners together in order to reflect on practice.

Cohesiveness the degree to which the members are attracted to the group and wish to retain membership in it.

Collaborating a response to conflict characterised by all parties working together to achieve satisfaction for all.

Committees groups that deal with specific issues involving several service areas.

Communication a complex, ongoing, dynamic process in which the participants simultaneously create shared meaning in an interaction.

Commissioning purchasing services on behalf of the service user.

Commissioning organisation an organisation that purchases services on behalf of the public.

Competing a response to conflict characterised by contending or fighting which is an all out effort to win, to defend, to be judged right or to prevail in the situation.

Competing groups groups in which members compete for resources or recognition.

Complex open system a term within organisational systems theory to describe a system that takes inputs from the environment, processes those inputs through a process called throughput and creates outputs in the form of products or services.

Complexity theory a scientific model that suggests that complex tasks are impacted by random events and therefore less likely to have predictable results.

Compromising a response to conflict characterised by an agreement wherein both parties get some but not all of what they want.

Concurrent audit an audit conducted during the patient's course of care.

Conflict real or perceived differences in goals, values, ideas, attitudes, beliefs, feelings or actions.

Confrontation a conflict management strategy in which the conflict is brought out in the open and attempts are made to resolve it through open and honest communication.

Consensus an agreement or understanding that all parties involved can fully support.

Content theories motivational theories that emphasise individual needs or the rewards that may satisfy those needs.

Contingency planning planning for problems that arise, or may arise.

Controlling establishing standards of performance, determining the means to be used in measuring performance, evaluating performance and providing feedback.

Cost centre the smallest area of activity within an organisation for which costs are accumulated.

Creative thinking a process of designing the desired future through imagination and innovation with the purpose of creating a new way of working suited to a new situation or set of conditions.

Critical thinking a process of examining underlying assumptions, interpreting and evaluating arguments, and developing alternatives for the purpose of reaching a reasoned, justifiable conclusion. Reflective practice and clinical supervision incorporate critical thinking.

D

Data Protection Act legislation protecting the access to and use of personal information.

Decentralised authority the right to make decisions is spread throughout the organisation.

Decision-making the process of evaluating and selecting from a range of options.

Delegation the process by which responsibility and authority for performing a task (function, activity or decision) is transferred to another individual who accepts that authority and responsibility.

Delphi technique a decision-making technique in which judgements on a particular topic are systematically gathered from participants who do not meet face-to-face.

Democratic leadership an English leadership style in which the leader assumes that individuals are motivated by internal drives and impulses, want active participation in decisions and want to get the task done. The leader uses participation and the group get the chance to inform the leader's decisions about setting goals and how the work is accomplished.

Department of Health (DoH) an English department of state responsible for improving standards in public health and for leading and driving forward changes in the NHS and social care; accountable to the public and the government through the Secretary of State for Health.

Descriptive (bounded) rationality model a decision-making process that emphasises the limitations of the rationality of the decision-maker and the situation.

Development planning the preparation for learning including obtaining materials and matching learner needs with educational methods.

Diagonal communication communication involving individuals who are at different organisational levels (outside a reporting relationship such as staff to manager) or outside the organisation.

Difficult conversations conversations that involve risk to one or more of the participants.

Direct costs expenses that directly affect patient care.

Directing guiding the process of getting the organisation's work done.

Disruptive conflict differences that disrupt the flow of work.

Distress stress caused by a negative event or circumstance.

Division and specialisation of labour a model of working wherein the work is divided into component tasks, thereby reducing the number and range of tasks for each employee. It results in employees becoming specialists in their assigned tasks.

Downward communication communication, generally directive, given from an authority figure or manager to staff.

Driving forces behaviours that facilitate change by pushing participants in the desired direction.

E

Efficiency variance The difference between budgeted and actual nursing care hours provided.

Electronic staff records (ESR) a single national electronic system that enables a consistent approach to all aspects of staff administration, human resources, payroll, recruitment, work structures, absence management and training and development records.

Empirical-rational strategies a change agent strategy based on the assumption that people are rational and follow self-interest if that self-interest is made clear.

Equity theory a motivational theory that suggests effort and job satisfaction depend on the degree of equity or perceived fairness in the work situation.

Establishment control a list of approved, budgeted working time equivalent posts within a cost centre.

Eustress stress resulting from a positive life event or circumstance.

Evaluation of staff development an investigative process to determine whether the education was cost-effective, the objective was achieved and learning was applied to the job.

Event register a record of events that are unusual or particularly illustrative for the purposes of accurately reviewing an individual.

Expectancy theory a motivational theory that emphasises the role of rewards and their relationship to the performance of desired behaviours.

Expense budget a comprehensive budget that lists salary and non-salary items that reflect patient care objectives and activity parameters for the nursing unit.

Experimentation a type of problem solving in which a theory is tested to enhance knowledge, understanding or prediction.

Extinction a technique used to eliminate negative behaviour in which a positive reinforcement is removed and the undesired behaviour is extinguished.

F

Failed delegation a delegate is unable to fulfil the expectations of the delegation, or unable to achieve the outcome, resulting in the delegated responsibility being withdrawn.

Feedback information offered to another person, in the form of evidence and impact.

Financial year a specified 12-month period during which operational and financial performance is measured.

First-level management also known as front-line management, the responsibility for the work of front-line staff and coordinating the day-to-day activities of a ward or team.

Fixed budget a budget in which amounts are set regardless of changes that occur during the year.

Fixed costs expenses that remain the same for the budget period regardless of the activity level of the organisation.

Formal committees committees with authority and a specific role.

Formal groups clusters of individuals designated by an organisation to perform specified organisational tasks.

Formal leadership a position or role with responsibilities for leadership described in a job description.

Forming the initial stage of group development, in which individuals assemble into a well-defined cluster.

Foundation trust (FT) a type of NHS trust which is a legally independent organisation classified as a public benefit corporation and no longer subject to the direction of the Secretary of State for Health.

Freedom of Information Act legislation allowing patients access to their own records.

G

Goal conflict the inability to attain mutually incompatible goals.

Goals specific statements of what is to be achieved.

Goal-setting the relating of current behaviour, activities, or operations to the organisation's or individual's long-range goals.

Goal-setting theory a theory of motivation that suggests that an individual is motivated by the goal to be achieved.

Gross domestic product (GDP) a measure of the total value of goods and services produced by a nation.

Group an aggregate of individuals who interact and mutually influence each other.

Groupthink a negative phenomenon occurring in highly cohesive, isolated groups in which group members come to think alike, which interferes with critical thinking.

H

Halo effect the failure to differentiate among the various performance dimensions when conducting a review.

Hawthorne effect the tendency of people to perform as expected due to the attention paid to their performance.

Health service reform a series of structural and functional changes to the NHS intended to bring the service in line with the current and future expectations of the people who work in and who are served by the NHS.

Healthcare resource groups (HRG) a classification system that creates standard groupings of clinically similar treatments which use common levels of health care resource.

Hidden agendas a group member's individual, unspoken objectives that interfere with the commitment or enthusiasm of others, or with attaining the spoken objectives of the group.

I

Incident times when things go wrong that did or could have harmed a patient.

Incremental (line-item) budget a style of budget in which each expense is listed on a separate line on the budget sheet and has a specific allocation against the item.

Indicator a tool used to measure the performance of structure, process and outcome standards.

Indirect costs necessary expenditures that do not affect patient care directly.

Induction the process by which a new employee is introduced to and assisted in learning the unique features and practices of the workplace.

Informal committees committees with no delegated authority that are organised for discussion.

Informal groups groups which evolve from social interactions that are not defined by an organisational structure.

Informal leadership influence exercised by someone who does not have a specified leadership or management role.

Information management the collection, storage and analysis of information needed for a specific purpose such as patient care.

Information systems complex automated systems that are integrated through networked computers to process data in order to answer questions, solve problems or make decisions.

Information technology the machines and applications that provide the infrastructure for information systems.

Innovative decisions decisions that require both discovering and investigating unfamiliar and ambiguous situations and developing unique and creative solutions.

Integrative decision-making a creative thinking process in which the parties jointly identify the problem and their needs, explore a number of alternative solutions and come to consensus on a solution.

Interrater reliability agreement between two measures by several interviewers.

Inter-role conflict conflict resulting from incongruence between the different roles an individual might play, such as doing a job and directing others to do the job.

Interview guide a written document containing questions, interviewer directions and other pertinent information so that the same process is followed and the same basic information is gathered from each applicant.

Intra-rater reliability agreement between two measures by the same interviewer.

Intra-role conflict conflict resulting from incongruence between one's expectations for performance and one's perception of the resulting performance.

J

Job description or role profile details the knowledge, skills and abilities needed, the tasks to be performed and the behavioural standards to be met.

K

Knowledge and Skills Framework (KSF) a framework that defines and describes the knowledge and skills which NHS staff need to apply in their work in order to deliver quality services.

L

Laissez-faire leadership a leadership style in which the leader assumes that individuals are motivated by internal drives and impulses and that they need to be left alone to make decisions about how to complete the work; the leader provides little direction or facilitation.

Lateral communication communication that occurs between individuals at the same organisational level.

Leader anyone who uses interpersonal skills to influence others to accomplish a specific goal.

Leadership a system of action intended to influence others, to cope with change and to achieve outcomes.

Leniency error a reviewer's tendency to overrate the performance of a person being reviewed.

Life-long learning the process of continually updating knowledge and skills throughout life.

Long-term condition a health condition that cannot be cured, and therefore must be managed to prevent the condition from worsening or causing further complications.

Lose–lose outcome an outcome of conflict or negotiation in which the solution agreed, or settlement reached, is unsatisfactory to both parties.

M

Management a system of action intended to cope with complexity, to provide order and consistency to quality of care and work roles.

Manager an individual employed by an organisation who is responsible and accountable for efficiently accomplishing the goals of the organisation.

Mediation a conflict management strategy wherein an impartial third party assists those in conflict to come to a mutually agreeable resolution.

Middle-level management management of the activities and outcomes of a number of services within their defined area, and typically supervise a number of first-level managers.

Mission a broad, general statement of the organisation's remit.

Motivation the factors that initiate and direct behaviour.

N

National Health Service (NHS) the organisation established by the British government to provide health services to the general public; funded by central taxation.

National Patient Safety Agency (NPSA) a special health authority charged with the role of improving the safety of patients by promoting a culture of reporting and learning from patient safety incidents.

Negative reinforcement punishing a behaviour in order to decrease the frequency of that behaviour.

Negotiation a conflict management technique in which the conflicting parties give and take on various issues.

NHS Direct a telephone- and Internet-based patient and public advice service.

NHS trust a public sector corporation run by a board of executive and non-executive directors, funded by the Department of Health and responsible for providing health services to their community.

Nominal group technique (NGT) a decision-making technique that elicits written questions, ideas and reactions from group members.

Non-salary expenditure variance deviation from the budget as a result of changes in patient volume, supply quantities or prices paid.

Non-verbal communication a method of sending a message without using words. Non-verbal communications can take the form of gestures, facial expressions, body positioning and actions.

Normative-re-educative strategy a change agent strategy based on the assumption that people act in accordance with social norms and values.

Norming the third stage of group development, in which group members define goals and rules of behaviour.

Norms informal rules of behaviour shared by group members.

O

Objectives statements of outcome.

Objective probability the likelihood that an event will or will not occur based on facts and reliable information.

Online instruction a method of instruction that uses the Internet for teaching and learning. It is the fastest-growing method of distance education.

On-the-job instruction an educational method using observation and practice that involves employees learning new skills after being employed.

Operant conditioning the process by which a behaviour becomes associated with a particular consequence.

Operating budget an organisation's statement of expected revenues and expenses for the upcoming year.

Optimising a decision-making strategy where the best of all possible alternatives is chosen, even if the decision is controversial.

Optimism a sense of confidence about the future and an expectation that outcomes are likely to be positive.

Ordinary interacting groups the most common type of group which generally has no formal leader and is run according to an informal structure with the purpose of solving a problem or making a decision.

Organisation a collection of people working together under a defined structure to achieve predetermined outcomes using financial, human and material resources.

Organisational culture the norms and traditions of an organisation.

Organisational environment the conditions (the people, objects and ideas) outside the organisation that influence the organisation.

Organisational structure the division of labour and the relationship between and among work groups.

Organising the process of coordinating the work to be done in an organisation.

Outcome standards standards that reflect the desired result or outcome of care.

Over-emphasis on recent events error the tendency of a manager to rate an employee based on recent events, rather than over the entire evaluation period.

P

Passive approach to communication the sender approaches the receiver in a subservient way and communicates through body language, tone of voice and choice of words that there is respect for the receiver but not for self.

Patient choice a commitment embedded in national health policy to giving patients a choice of when and where they are treated.

Patient involvement a process of seeking the views and opinions of patients and the public.

Payment by results (PBR) funding for services is linked to the choice patients make and only paid when services are chosen.

Perfection myth the belief that if people try hard enough, they will not make errors.

Performing the fourth stage of group development, in which group members agree on basic purposes and activities and carry out the work.

Personal development review an ongoing cycle of review, planning, development and evaluation for all staff which links organisational and personal development needs.

Pessimism the opposite of optimism; a lack of confidence in the future and an anticipation of negative outcomes.

Planning a four-stage process that includes establishing objectives, evaluating the present situation, formulating a planning statement (means) and converting the plan into an action statement.

Point-of-care-devices hand-held or portable devices that can be used to access information and keep records.

Position control a monitoring tool used to compare actual numbers of employees with the number of budgeted time equivalents (WTEs) for the nursing unit.

Positive reinforcement rewarding behaviour in order to increase the frequency of that behaviour.

Power-coercive strategies change agent strategies based on the application of power by legitimate authority, economic sanctions or political clout.

Preceptor an experienced individual who assists a new person in acquiring the necessary knowledge and skills to function effectively in a new environment.

Premature concurrence-seeking a result of groupthink caused by pressure to conform, self-censorship and apparent unanimity.

Primary care trust (PCT) an organisation that is both a provider and a commissioning organisation tasked with ensuring services locally.

Probability the likelihood that an event will or will not occur.

Probability analysis a calculation of the expected risk made to determine the probabilities of each alternative accurately.

Problem-solving a process whereby a situation is analysed and changes made with the intention of creating different results.

Process standards standards connected with the system of care delivery care.

Process theories   motivational theories that emphasise how the motivation process works to direct an individual's effort into performance.

Productivity   a measure of how well the work group or team uses the resources available to achieve its goals and produce its services.

Profit   the difference between revenues and expenses.

Provider organisation   an organisation that provides health services to patients.

Punishment myth   the belief that if we punish people when they make errors, they will make fewer of them.

Q

Quality care   safe and effective care, available locally and encompassing a satisfying and pleasant experience.

Quality standards   written statements that define a level of performance or a set of conditions determined to be acceptable as determined by an external policy or agency.

Quantum leadership   a leadership model based on the concepts of chaos theory.

R

Rate variance   the difference between budgeted and actual hourly rates paid.

Rational (normative) decision-making model   a decision-making process based on logical, well-grounded rational choices that maximise the achievement of objectives.

Real (command) groups   groups that accomplish tasks in an organisation and are recognised as legitimate organisational entities.

Reconciliation   coming to a friendly resolution following a conflict.

Re-forming   a stage of group development in which the group reassembles after a major change in the environment or in the goals of the group that requires the group to refocus its activities.

Reinforcement theory   the motivational theory that views motivation as learning and proposes that behaviour is learned through a process called operant conditioning.

Relapse prevention   a model that emphasises learning a set of self-control and coping strategies to increase the retention of newly learned behaviour.

Resolution   the stage of conflict that occurs when a mutually agreed-upon solution is arrived at and both parties commit to carrying out the agreement.

Responsibility   an obligation to accomplish a task.

Restraining forces   behaviours that impede change by discouraging participants from making specified changes.

Retrospective audit   an audit conducted after a patient's discharge that involves examining records of a large number of cases.

Revenue budget   a projection of expected income for a budget period.

Reverse delegation   a delegation that is given back to the delegator short of completion.

Risk management   a programme directed at identifying, evaluating and taking corrective action against potential risks that could lead to injury.

Risky shift   a phenomenon seen in groups in which riskier, more controversial decisions are made.

Role   a set of expectations about behaviour ascribed to a specific position in society or at work.

Role ambiguity   the frustrations that result from unclear expectations for one's performance.

Role review   the clarification of roles and an attempt to integrate or tie together the various roles individuals play.

Routine decisions   decisions that are relatively common and well defined, where satisfactory results can usually be achieved by applying policies, rules and experience.

S

Salary (personnel) budget   a budget that projects salary costs to be paid and charged to the cost centre during the budget period.

Satisficing   a decision-making strategy whereby the individual chooses a less than ideal alternative that meets minimum standards of acceptance.

Scientific management a theory of management based on the belief that standard methods should be used for each job, and that variation should be eliminated.

Self-esteem a person's overall evaluation of their own worth.

Servant leadership a leadership model based on the premise that leadership emerges from the desire to serve.

Service planning the operational plan for the delivery of a service.

Shaping the selective reinforcement of behaviours that are successively closer approximations to the desired behaviour.

Shared leadership an organisational structure in which several people share the responsibility for achieving the goals of the organisation.

Situational leadership a contingency theory of leadership developed by Hersey, Blanchard and Johnson that suggests that the leadership style should be matched to the developmental level of the follower.

Social enterprise a small business that is not for profit and is based on social benefit.

Social learning theory a behavioural theory based on reinforcement theory that proposes new behaviours are learned through direct experience or observation.

Span of control the number of employees a manager can effectively supervise.

Status the social ranking of individuals relative to others in a group based on the position they occupy.

Status incongruence the disruptive impact that occurs when factors associated with group status are not congruent.

Structure standards standards that relate to the physical environment, organisation and management of an organisation.

Staff development the process of enhancing staff performance with specific learning activities.

Storming the second stage of group development, in which group members develop roles and relationships; competition and conflict generally occur.

Strategic Health Authority (SHA) organisation that functions as an extension of the Department of Health to ensure the delivery of Department of Health priorities throughout the country.

Strategic organisation an organisation that provides guidance, oversight and advice to provider organisations and professionals.

Strategic planning a process of planning the future direction and goals of the organisation, and the methods for attaining those goals.

Strategies specific actions to be taken.

Stress the adverse reaction people have to excessive pressures or other types of demand placed on them.

Subjective probability the likelihood that an event will or will not occur based on personal judgement and experience.

Suppression the stage of conflict that occurs when one person or group defeats the other and only the dominant side is committed to the agreement; the loser may or may not carry out the agreement.

Systematic process improvement a collection of methods for measuring performance and designing the most efficient and effective set of steps to achieve a result.

T

Task groups ad hoc committees appointed for a specific purpose and a limited time.

Teams real groups in which people work interdependently to deliver services for which they are mutually accountable.

Telehealth the use of network technology to provide medical, nursing and other health care through electronic linkages.

Time logs journals of activities that are useful in analysing actual time spent on specific activities.

Time waster something that prevents a person from accomplishing a job or achieving a goal.

To-do list a list of responsibilities to be accomplished within a specific time frame.

Training and development needs assessment an evaluation of learning needs in a select population.

Transactional leadership a leadership model concerned with 'transacting', that is, performing work according to policy and procedures and stabilising both the process and outcome of care.

Transformational leadership a leadership model concerned with transforming or bringing about change through generating the commitment of others to the vision of the organisation.

Transition the psychological process people go through to come to terms with change.

Trial-and-error method a method whereby one solution after another is tried until the problem is solved or appears to be improving.

U

Upper-level management a group of managers that are responsible for establishing the goals and direction for the organisation.

Upward communication communication from a position of lesser authority in the organisation to someone of greater authority.

V

Validity the ability to predict outcomes with some accuracy.

Values the beliefs or attitudes one has about people, ideas, objects or actions that form a basis for behaviour.

Variable budget a budget developed with the understanding that adjustments to the budget may be made during the year.

Variable costs expenses that depend on and change in direct proportion to patient volume and acuity.

Variance the difference between the amount that was budgeted for a specific cost and the actual cost.

Vision statement a statement of the overarching goal to which the organisation aspires.

Volume variances differences in the budget as a result of increases or decreases in patient volume.

W

Whole time equivalent (WTE) The annual paid hours for a full-time member of staff

Win–lose outcome an outcome of conflict or negotiation wherein one person gets what they want and the other does not.

Win–win outcome an outcome of a conflict or negotiation where all parties are satisfied.

Work allocation the assignment of tasks that reflect job descriptions and requirements.

Work sample questions questions used to determine an applicant's knowledge about work tasks and ability to perform the job.

Index